Pastoral Care, Clerical Education
and Canon Law, 1200-1400

Autograph of Amaury de Montfort, 1276. (See VII)
Oxford, Bodleian Library, MS. Auct.D.4.13, fol.218.
(*Scale 19:20*)

Leonard E. Boyle

Pastoral Care, Clerical Education and Canon Law, 1200-1400

VARIORUM REPRINTS

London 1981

British Library CIP data

Boyle, Leonard E.
Pastoral care, clerical education and canon
law, 1200-1400. — (Collected studies series;
CS135).
1. Canon law — History
2. Church history — Middle Ages, 600-1500
I. Title   II. Series
262.9′094   BV760.2

ISBN 0-86078-081-3

Published in Great Britain by   Variorum Reprints
20 Pembridge Mews London W11 3EQ

Printed in Great Britain by   Galliard (Printers) Ltd
Great Yarmouth Norfolk

VARIORUM REPRINT CS135

CONTENTS

This volume contains a total of 362 pages.

PREFACE

The fifteen essays in this volume may seem a mixed bag, but in fact they owe their existence directly or indirectly to a doctoral subject which the late W. A. Pantin suggested to me exactly thirty years ago — the *Oculus sacerdotis* of William Poul of Pagula (or, simply, William of Pagula).

The first fruit of that suggestion is now item IV in this collection. When preparing that, I was fortunate enough to identify and locate manuscripts of four other works of this retiring Berkshire vicar of the 1320s, with results to be seen in items V and XV.

The fact that William was a parish priest, yet took a doctorate in canon law at Oxford during a leave of absence from his parish of Winkfield in Windsor Forest, prompted an investigation of the phenomenon of licences to study and of the place of the constitution *Cum ex eo* of Pope Boniface VIII in the history of clerical education and of the pastoral care in general (items VIII, IX). Likewise, problems connected with the length of time spent by William at Oxford gave rise to item XIV on the curriculum of the Faculty of Canon Law there.

While working on *Cum ex eo* and the whole business of clerical literacy, I had of necessity to look at the constitution *Super specula* of Pope Honorius III in 1219, which first set up a form of university 'scholarships' for promising young clerics, and stumbled upon the relationship between the *Compilatio quinta*, where the constitution was divided into three parts by the compiler Tancred, and the registers of letters of Honorius III in the Vatican Archives, where it occurs as one continuous piece (item XI). At much the same time I chanced on the probable influence of William Duranti the Elder on Boniface VIII and *Cum ex eo* through remarks of his on clerical education in his commentary on the constitutions of the Second Council of Lyons in 1274 (see item XII).

The article (item XIII) on the *De regno* of Thomas Aquinas (taking up, incidentally, a much-respected Dominican colleague at Toronto, the late I. T. Eschmann) was another, if devious, product of *Cum ex eo*, and sprang from a desire to understand just why Boniface VIII has had such a bad press, and what were the roots of the position of John of Paris, to me a clear disciple of Aquinas, in his famous *De potestate regia et papali*, during Boniface's pontificate.

The remaining articles in the collection were occasioned by research into the background of the *Oculus* and into its place in the education of a pastoral clergy.

To my surprise, the *Oculus* and other works of William of Pagula showed a familiarity with the moral teaching of Aquinas in his *Secunda secundae* and, curiously, his Quodlibets, and this finally led to John of Freiburg and his *Summa confessorum* (item III), to the relationship of the Quodlibets of Aquinas to the pastoral care (II), to the place of 'moral' education within the Dominican Order to which both Aquinas and John of Freiburg belonged (VI), and to the dependence on John's *Summa confessorum*, where moral teaching is concerned, of manuals such as the *Oculus* itself and the famous *Summa praedicantium* of John Bromyard, the date of the latter of which became important at one point (item X).

Again, while looking into the manual tradition to which the *Summa* and the *Oculus* belonged, I came across the *Templum domini* of Robert Grosseteste, and a study of that, and then of his extant letters relative to the pastoral care, provided the basis for the present first item.

Another manual which came my way in those days, and one which appears more than once in these pages, was the *Summa 'Qui bene praesunt'* of Richard Wethersett (c. 1230). If I mention it now, however, this is not for its own excellent qualities but because it was the occasion of the discovery of the autograph writings of Amaury de Montfort. The works of Wethersett and de Montfort were side by side in a composite volume I was examining, and out of curiosity I began to read what the luckless Amaury had written from prison, and finally to follow the fortunes (item VII) of this very literate layman and his sister Eleanor.

In one way or another, then, clerical education and the manualist tradition form the backbone of the collection. It is not an area that appears at all in histories of medieval thought or of medieval theology, not to speak of general histories of the church or the middle ages. Yet it has a place. It was, for example, through manuals like the *Summa confessorum* of John of Freiburg and the *Oculus sacerdotis* of William of Pagula that the teaching of the schools was communicated, with more or less success, to the generality of the clergy in the pastoral care and to the literate public at large.

It is hoped that these essays scattered over the past twenty-five years will suggest at least that the field is neither forbidding nor arid.

LEONARD E. BOYLE, OP

Pontifical Institute of Mediaeval Studies,
Toronto

September 1980

PASTORAL CARE

I

Robert Grosseteste and the Pastoral Care

Robert Grosseteste of Stowe, philosopher, theologian, and scientist, quondam chancellor of Oxford University, was elected to the see of Lincoln on 27 March 1235. He was then aged about sixty-seven and had a long and distinguished university career behind him.[1]

We know very little of Grosseteste's thoughts on the pastoral care during his pre-episcopal years. As it is, even his career in general is known with any certainty only from his presence at Oxford after 1215. Possibly he had lectured in the infant university of Oxford between 1200 and 1209, and had, like so many other scholars of that period, departed England to return to Oxford only when King John and Archbishop Langton had composed their differences.[2]

From at least 1215 until 1235 Grosseteste taught at Oxford, and, after the arrival of the Dominicans and Franciscans about 1224, he helped the latter to organize their schools. These twenty years or more at Oxford probably afforded him no great experience of the pastoral care, although it is not unlikely that in the ten or eleven years preceding his provision to Lincoln as bishop he caught some of the apostolic spirit of the friars with whom he was daily in contact at Oxford.[3]

Possibly it was this contact that impelled him in 1225 to take up the *cura animarum* for the very first time. He was about fifty-seven and still a deacon when he was appointed rector of Abbotsley, Huntingdonshire, in April, 1225. When he became a priest is not certain, but presumably it was not long afterwards. The Third Lateran Council (1179) had ordered that those admitted to the *cura animarum* should become priests "within the time

appointed by the canons."[4] The Council of Oxford in 1222 was
equally vague, specifying only that perpetual vicars should be
ordained "within a short time" of institution.[5] However, since
Grosseteste was appointed to Abbotsley on 25 April 1225, in the
third week after Easter, it may be suggested that he was ordained
a month later on 24 May 1225, that is, on the Whitsun Ember
Saturday, the nearest regular day for ordination to the priesthood after his institution as rector.

Some four years later he was made archdeacon of Leicester,
and possibly he became a canon of Lincoln and prebend of St.
Margaret in Leicester at the same time. Shortly afterwards, on
the completion of the Franciscan schools at Oxford about 1229–
30, he was persuaded to lecture formally to the Franciscans
there.[6]

How much time Grosseteste was able to spare from his Oxford teaching to look after his archdeaconry and his two parochial
churches (Abbotsley and Leicester St. Margaret) is not at all clear.
There is some record of his activity as an archdeacon, and there
is at least one act relating to St. Margaret in Leicester.[7] At all
events he soon found that the work was too much for him, and
that the whole situation was distasteful.

In November or December, 1231, after an illness of which he
wrote to his sister Juetta, a nun, and to the Franciscan Adam
Marsh, Grosseteste decided to divest himself of two of his three
preferments.[8] As he related to the papal legate Otto of Tonengo
some ten years later, he had had doubts about the propriety of
his position as a pluralist with two *curae animarum* (Abbotsley
and St. Margaret), and, indeed, had consulted the Pope on the
question through the good offices of "a wise friend." He had
been informed by the Pope that it was utterly illicit to hold down
two *curae animarum* simultaneously, in this case a regular parish
church (Abbotsley) and a prebend to which a cure of souls was
attached (St. Margaret).[9]

Grosseteste's subsequent action, however, was not due to his
illness, nor, as one might have expected, was it taken out of a desire to give undivided attention to a solitary *cura animarum*. For
instead of doing the obvious thing and resigning one or the

Robert Grosseteste and the Pastoral Care

other of the incompatible *curae animarum*, Grosseteste, it seems, immediately withdrew from both and also from the office of archdeacon, retaining only the sinecure portion of the Lincoln prebend of St. Margaret in Leicester: "You must know also," he wrote in that letter of November or December, 1231, to his sister Juetta, "that I have resigned all my sources of income, excepting my prebend in the church of Lincoln."[10]

Now it is generally held that because Grosseteste retained the prebend of Leicester St. Margaret in the cathedral church of Lincoln, he also continued as rector of St. Margaret, and thus in the *cura animarum*. In the light of the events which followed his renunciation of all but one of his benefices, it is difficult to allow this, for if some of his relatives were aghast at what appeared to be financial suicide, there were others who felt outraged at what seemed to them a callous rejection of the cure of souls. Indeed it is precisely of charges that he had fled the pastoral care that Grosseteste complained to the Franciscan Adam Marsh in late 1231, when he wrote to thank him for his letter of "sweet consolation" at a moment when he was enduring "bitter reproaches as well as the contempt of those close to me."

Some critics, in fact, thought that in this charge of desertion they had their surest shaft, but, as Grosseteste explained in that letter, he had, as Marsh well knew, an ample and ready defense. In the plainest terms, his decision was not due to any distaste for the pastoral care, but rather to an ever-pressing awareness of his inability to carry a burden he should never have dared to shoulder in the first place: "urgebat me impotentia agendi curam . . . quam minus circumspecte nimisque audacter susceperam."[11] He would be poorer of pocket, he wrote Juetta, but richer in virtue; his reduced circumstances should not, in any case, distress her, since she was a nun and poor by profession. In a way it was a comedown, he admitted to Marsh, but he was not at all downcast. One more occasion of sin, and a prolific one at that, was now behind him. He had come to understand what he should have admitted much earlier, that he was no fit instrument for the *cura animarum*. As he said to Marsh, his resolve had been "born of the fear of the Lord" and of an obedience which impelled him to observe the constitutions of the Church. Of course, he admitted, he knew full well that these constitutions ordered that the pastoral care, once undertaken, should not lightly be abandoned. But, as Marsh was well aware, there were circumstances which could allow one to bypass the constitutions, and surely one of these was the sincere conviction of inability, by which inability Grosseteste now sought to explain, although not to justify, his recent renunciation.

In fine, Grosseteste shed the *cura animarum* more because of an acute awareness of the responsibilities of the pastoral care than out of a desire to shirk them. For some six years since his ordination as a priest he had been a fitful rector of the parish of Abbotsley, his first cure of souls; for the past two years, while shouldering the burdens of the archdeacon's office and teaching the Franciscans at Oxford, he had become an absentee rector not just of one but of two parishes. Knowing that his position was legally unsound, he dropped the living at Abbotsley. Realizing that it was impossible to teach at Oxford and act as archdeacon at one and the same time, he resigned his archdeaconry. Convinced, too, that at his advanced age the unaccustomed *cura animarum* was altogether beyond him, he relinquished the pastoral side (Leicester St. Margaret) of the Lincoln prebend. All that he retained was the canonry in the cathedral at Lincoln.[12]

Grosseteste was not destitute as a result. His Lincoln prebend had other holdings in Leicester besides St. Margaret. But without the rectory and church of St. Margaret, the prebend probably did not yield much of an income. Nor, seemingly, did it provide Grosseteste with a home in which to live out his retirement, nor even with the land and capital to put one up. A year after the above events, on 12 November 1232, a certain Walter quitclaimed to Grosseteste for fifteen marks four virgates of land in Leicester which the chapter of Lincoln warranted as belonging to Grosseteste's prebend.[13] Some five months later (1 April 1233) the Bishop of Lincoln, Hugh Wells, drew up a will in which there was a legacy of forty marks to the canon (unnamed, but Grosseteste) of the prebend of Leicester St. Margaret, "towards

Robert Grosseteste and the Pastoral Care

the construction of a dwelling-place for himself in his prebend, unless I shall have made him the grant he requested." [14]

All of this hardly prepares us for what happened later. Within four years of fleeing the duties of a pastor so conscientiously in 1231, Robert Grosseteste was called at the age of sixty-seven to a much more exacting *cura animarum* as Bishop of Lincoln.

Was there again a shrinking from responsibility when faced with this heavier burden? Logically there should have been, if only to protect the sincerity of his previous action from suspicion. Certainly it must have been a wrench to have to leave Oxford at a respected old age, and to abandon the Franciscans before they were fledged academically. The late Sir Maurice Powicke, who did not advert to Grosseteste's earlier crisis of conscience, felt that the decision of this "elderly scholar" to exchange his life at Oxford for the duties of a diocesan had something to do with his friendship for and admiration of the new mendicant orders.[15] Powicke, indeed, suggests that Grosseteste "must have heard" and possibly taken to heart a striking address by Jordan of Saxony, the successor of St. Dominic, when he preached at Oxford on St. Martin's Day, 1229. Jordan had issued a "challenge to the prelates assembled there to save the souls of the people throughout England." And when he had gone on to wonder if "the salvation of all the parishes of England" would come from "their prelates residing at Oxford," all that he could answer to his own question was, "God only knows, for I do not."

Grosseteste and Jordan certainly met at Oxford. Indeed, Grosseteste reminds Jordan in a letter of 1237 how close they had become in those days.[16] All the same it is curious that Jordan's challenge to the masters of Oxford on behalf of the *cura animarum* had to wait for some six years before it had an effect on Grosseteste, and that in 1231, two years after Jordan's address, a more immediate opportunity for a splendid gesture renouncing Oxford was allowed to pass when Grosseteste chose to withdraw himself entirely from the pastoral care. For my part, all that I can venture at present is that Grosseteste's urgent and dramatic consciousness of ineptitude in 1231 seems effectively to have disappeared by the time that he was offered the bishopric of Lincoln in 1235.

I am not for a moment doubting Grosseteste's sincerity. In 1231, late in life, after some years of dallying with parochial responsibilities and an illegal tenure of two *curae animarum*, he had drastically purged his way of life. Now as bishop he would have an opportunity of spreading his own hard-won convictions and of making some compensation for any of his own neglect of the pastoral care during six years of avoidable absenteeism.

Much has been written about Robert Grosseteste as bishop. Indeed, in the wake of excellent essays in recent times by Srawley and Pantin[17] and of many sensitive pages by Sir Maurice Powicke, it may seem superfluous to go over some of the ground again. Most of the incidents related here are well known and in any case may be found in detail in Stevenson's old biography of 1899. But some aspects of the episcopal career of Grosseteste bear repetition, just as there are others that may be looked at afresh.

From the very beginning of his long episcopate of eighteen years, Robert Grosseteste worked conscientiously and unflaggingly in his large and scattered diocese. In 1236, for example, a short year after his consecration, he instructed his archdeacons to oversee and care for the souls in his diocese "and to nourish them on knowledge and doctrine."[18] Two years later he began a series of addresses to his clergy, urging them to preach by word and instruct by example. Since it was impossible for him to gather all his priests together into one place, he traveled from deanery to deanery, addressing the clergy of each deanery as a whole.[19]

Grosseteste, of course, was impelled by more than a great personal regard for the spiritual well-being of his people and clergy. Twenty years before his election to Lincoln the Fourth Lateran Council of 1215 had legislated widely for a renewal of the *cura animarum*. Within those twenty years strenuous efforts had been made in the Church at large to enforce or to forward these reforms. In England Richard Poore of Salisbury, Stephen Langton of Canterbury (at the Council of Oxford in 1222), and many other English bishops had legislated in the spirit of the Lateran

Robert Grosseteste and the Pastoral Care

Council,[20] while the pastoral manuals of Robert Flamborough, Thomas Chabham, and Richard Wethersett had done much to popularize some of its principles. On the Continent there was local legislation of a similar nature, and there were the influential manuals of confession of the Dominicans Paul of Hungary, Conrad Höxter, and Raymund of Peñafort.[21]

Robert Grosseteste has no mean place in this tradition of synodal statutes and pastoral manuals. There are sermons, diocesan constitutions, homiletic tracts, and other pastoralia from his pen during his eighteen years as bishop; in all, they occupy some twenty-six pages of Harrison Thomson's catalogue of Grosseteste's writings.[22]

Some of the sermons, indeed, are sufficiently long and well-knit to form tracts on their own. Thus Sermon 32 in Thomson's list occurs as a "Sermo magistralis de virtutibus et vitiis" in a manuscript in the Bodleian Library (Rawl. A 446, not noted by Thomson). Similarly the short work which Thomson lists as "De Confessione III," remarking that "this work seems to be a sermon or an extract from a longer work," is in fact called "Speculum confessionis" by Grosseteste himself in his prologue and is so designated in the colophon of MS Harley 5441, fol. 147ᵛ, in the British Library (another manuscript not recorded by Thomson).[23]

On the other hand Sermon 31 (the famous "Scriptum est de Levitis" which the Lollard Purvey used at the end of the fourteenth century)[24] really is a sermon, though it could well serve as a useful pastoral manual and, in fact, is called "De cura pastorali" in MS Digby 91 in the Bodleian Library. Preached to a clerical audience (possibly at one of the deanery gatherings) at a time when Grosseteste was "old and infirm," it deals with the three principal things in which the pastoral care consists: "In doctrina secundum affectionem mentis; in ostensione simplicis conversationis et in administratione debita et devota sacramentorum." Among the many points in this sermon, Grosseteste proposes a model clerical day which includes a rather long period of study and spiritual reading. After Mass each day, he says, books are to be read until midday, adding that if a priest does not have books at hand he can always fall back on the missal and the breviary. The Gospel for the following Sunday should be studied during the week. If any priest feels uneasy about his Latin he could, perhaps, persuade a neighboring parish priest to put him through the Gospel passage and prepare him for the Sunday Mass and his sermon at it.[25]

Apart from his episcopal constitutions (a brief series of instructions of a pastoral nature for priests),[26] Grosseteste's most influential pastoral work is his *Templum Domini*. Written between 1239 (the probable date of the constitutions) and 1246, and possibly as a supplement to those constitutions,[27] the *Templum* survives in some eighty-five manuscripts.[28] Beginning from a description of the priest as the temple of God (1 Cor. 3:16), Grosseteste goes on to show that the temple of God which is in the soul of man has two parts, a corporeal part (of which the four cardinal virtues are the integral parts) and a spiritual part (of which faith is the foundation, hope the walls, charity the roof). The whole life of man consists in building up and preserving this temple ("In hoc ergo duplici templo aedificando et custodiendo consistit tota vita hominis"), the whole pastoral care in helping man to maintain it in its integrity. Since this is the function of a priest in caring for souls, then he, the physician of souls, must know intimately not only the foundations of the Christian edifice but also all those influences that can threaten or undermine it and that he must counteract in the confessional. Because of this, Grosseteste presents a table of sevens which lays out the various vices and the virtues that offset them. In his opinion, "the whole of the pastoral care is in this schema."[29]

In this manner, moving gradually over the structure of the temple of the soul, feeling its strengths, baring its weaknesses, Grosseteste covers the articles of faith, the ten commandments, the principal vices and virtues, simony, usury, and excommunication. The whole *Templum* is thus primarily a statement of what a priest needs to know if he is to interrogate understandingly and counsel effectively those penitents who come to him. There is no list of penances, nor is there much about the imposition of penances. Indeed, since Grosseteste does not deal in any explicit way with these matters, or with interrogation as such, it

Robert Grosseteste and the Pastoral Care

is conceivable that the *Templum* is only a part of a trilogy *De poenitentia*, the second and third parts of which are Sermon 32 (the confessional interrogatory mentioned above)[30] and the tract "Canones poenitentiales," which is a list of the traditional penances for certain types of sin.[31] Hence the *Templum Domini* is less than a full-blown *Summa confessorum* and much more than an interrogatory. With its lists of definitions, its elaborate but well-defined schemata, it is in essence a mnemonic of the knowledge that is required of a priest who has to hear confessions. Its mnemonic quality, together with the fact that the *Templum* covers synoptically almost as much ground as Robert Flamborough's *Liber poenitentialis* and Richard Wethersett's "Qui bene praesunt," assured its popularity. In fact it may be suggested that, broadly speaking, the *Templum* is a schematization of these two treatises, both of which had been in circulation in England for some twenty years. Some of the mnemonic verses which appear in some manuscripts of the *Templum* come from the "Qui bene praesunt," while some of the canonical matter has definitely been adopted from Robert Flamborough.[32]

One *Summa* of consequence, however, that of Raymund of Peñafort, does not appear to have had any influence on the *Templum*, although by the time the *Templum* was written Raymund's famous *Summa* was known in England and, indeed, had been used extensively by writers as far apart professionally as the moralist Odo of Cheriton and the theologian Richard Fishacre.[33] Ten or eleven years earlier, when writing to Raymund shortly after becoming Bishop of Lincoln, Grosseteste had to confess that he knew of Raymund and his writings only from hearsay.[34] Perhaps he had still to make the acquaintance of the *Summa de casibus* when he wrote the *Templum Domini*.[35]

With all this pastoral activity and writing, Grosseteste's life was very full indeed. Yet he found time for the translation of various works from the Greek, a notable example of which is the version, the first ever in Latin, of Aristotle's *Nichomachean Ethics* in 1245.[36] And if he invited some competent scholars from abroad to help him in this work of translation, he was always on the lookout also for scholarly men for the *cura animarum* itself.

As he wrote to his archdeacons in 1244, his diocese was not in the happiest shape. Some priests had concubines; others were not saying the divine office properly; still others would not hold the divine services at hours convenient for the people or, stupidly, would not allow the Dominicans and Franciscans to preach in their parishes.[37]

To offset the spotted quality of his clergy, Grosseteste began shortly after his consecration to borrow Dominicans and Franciscans, those free lances of the pastoral care,[38] and to entice well-educated priests back to or into his diocese. There is, for example, a notable appeal in 1235 to a young man in Paris to return to the diocese: "Christ descended from the bosom of the Father into the womb of the Virgin and went to His death on the Cross for the sins of mankind, yet you, young man, are aghast at the thought of coming down from your master's chair to save those same souls by word, example, and prayer." This will not do, he says. At best he can allow the young man (Cerda) another year at his books. In the meantime the parish will be held for him, and suitable preachers provided to look after the cure of souls.[39]

Two years later Grosseteste offered the archdeaconry of Lincoln to a Master Thomas Walleys. Suspecting that Walleys would find it hard to leave his university, he wrote to encourage him:

But if it is better to teach than to preach, could not the Son of God, the highest wisdom, have been content to teach wisdom rather than to go about healing the sick and humbly preaching to the people? With the help of Christ you will not be deserting wisdom if you take on this office. Rather will you find it more abundantly in the *cura animarum* and teach it in practice.[40]

The same ideas are found in a letter of 1237/8 offering a prebend at Lincoln to Master Richard of Cornwall, an Englishman resident in or teaching at Rome: "Do not be filled with distaste at the thought of coming down from the high places of Rome to look after English sheep. It was precisely to redeem these same sheep that the Son of God descended from the seat of majesty to undergo the ignominy of the Cross."[41]

The pressing problem, however, that Grosseteste had to face

Robert Grosseteste and the Pastoral Care

was not so much that of attracting good and learned priests to his diocese as that of keeping indifferent or illiterate ones out. From the very beginning of his episcopate he dealt firmly and on occasion ruthlessly with clerics presented to a benefice in his diocese by some patron or other. Presentation to the *cura animarum* was, in Grosseteste's opinion, a serious business without room for any form of favoritism or foolhardiness. Ability and obedience had been the measures of Grosseteste's resolve that in his own case the best way to advance the *cura animarum* was to quit it altogether. These were now to be the yardsticks by which all persons presented to him, and all things in any way connected with the *cura animarum*, would be measured implacably. In fact the very first letter we possess for the period after his election (April–June, 1235) exhibits a force and resolution which, hardening with adversity and the passage of time, in the end would not spare the papacy itself.

Shortly after Grosseteste's election, it seems, a certain Master Michael Beleth had written to criticize his rejection of a presentee to a parish living. Grosseteste answered Beleth with savage courtesy.[42] The cleric in question, he said, was an untonsured deacon who, upon inspection, had proved to be well-nigh illiterate and, with his ring and red getup, was for all the world a layman or a soldier. In short, he was a living example of the sort of thing that the recent council at Oxford in 1222 had condemned. As for the monk who had presented this deacon, Grosseteste told Beleth that he had rebuked him with some severity. He was a monk who was obliged by profession to court death for the sake of souls, yet he had brazenly sponsored one for a *cura animarum* who manifestly would bring death to those for whom Christ had shed His blood. If this was all that the monk cared about the blood of Christ, then surely he would wind up in hell.

This summary treatment of the monk apparently had given widespread offense. Grosseteste, however, was at no pains to excuse himself to Beleth. Master Beleth, he wrote, could see for himself from the facts that no injustice had been done, no lie had been told, no truth had been suppressed. The monk-sponsor was in truth exposing souls to death, souls for which Grosseteste,

I

their bishop, was responsible before God: "ego . . . teneor pro qualibet animarum illarum." This was not an occasion for half-measures, he reminded Beleth. It was not enough to reject the presentee; his mentor, too, had to be castigated. A wise doctor, he added, will thrust gentleness to one side where a deadly virus is concerned. "Saving their reverence," he concluded, "those who have criticized and condemned a corrective action which, as God is my witness, proceeded from a love of souls and a great fear for their salvation, are more taken up 'with the things that are their own than with the things that are of Christ Jesus' "—citing a passage from 1 Philippians (2:21) which we shall hear of again in a more explosive context.

From this first extant letter of Grosseteste's episcopate three principles emerge which may be said to have governed his whole approach to pastoral matters over the next eighteen years:

1. A bishop is directly responsible to God for every soul in his diocese.
2. A man lacking ability or a full respect for the law of the Church is no safe shepherd of a flock.
3. The rejection of an unworthy presentee is not enough. The evils inherent in the system of presentation must be struck at precisely where they are rooted, in those, that is, who presume to present. These must be made aware of their responsibility to present proper people, and to present them properly.

In one form or another these principles were to be invoked or acted upon by Grosseteste on every possible occasion and without respect of person. The basic principle, of course, is his conviction that a bishop is personally responsible to God for each and every soul in his diocese. In fact he was so possessed by it that he was moved on occasion to preach it to his brother bishops, and, indeed, to archbishops of Canterbury and to papal legates. It finds its fullest expression perhaps in a famous letter to the chapter of Lincoln some four years after his election.[43] Of course this lengthy letter (nearly eighty pages when printed) was not conceived in an entirely disinterested spirit, for Grosseteste's

Robert Grosseteste and the Pastoral Care

own rights over the chapter were at stake. Yet there is very little rancor in the letter, and very little intrusion of self. All Grosseteste's energies may be concentrated on proving that a bishop has a right to make a visitation to the chapter of his cathedral church, but his arguments rest on an objective consideration of the office of bishop. If he felt sorely tried, as must have been the case, he apparently kept personal considerations in the background. He was convinced, naively perhaps, that his only hope of asserting his authority was not to browbeat his wayward canons but to reason with them on purely impersonal grounds (drawing on the scriptures, Gregory the Great's *De cura pastorali*, and St. Bernard's *De consideratione*, for example), and to rely on the appeal and pungency of cases of common jurisdiction as supporting evidence.

In his letter to the chapter of Lincoln, Grosseteste sees the bishop as the *pastor ovium* who is so devoted to his charges that he is ready to die for each one of them. He will not let them stray; he must protect their pastures from any depredators, and will never be content to leave them wholly at the mercy of subordinate shepherds. The bishop must be the light of his diocese in exactly the same way that the pope sheds his light on the bishops at large. He is wed to the souls of his diocese, and like any husband will not be bashful to correct any signs of loose living or unseemly conduct in his spouse, the diocese. The bishop, above all, is the ruler of souls, the watchman of the vineyard of the Lord, the shepherd who must feed his flock on judgment and justice as well as on knowledge and doctrine.

The principle of personal responsibility has in this letter its most elaborate expression. But it is to be seen more forcefully, perhaps, in the many instances of its application in letter after letter during the rest of Grosseteste's episcopate. It underlies his reply in June, 1235, to Walter Raleigh, treasurer of Exeter, whose candidate Grosseteste had refused because he was "scarcely in his Ovid" ("puer videlicet adhuc ad Ovidium epistolarum palmam porrigens"), and his institution to a cure of souls would "open the way to hell for both of us."[44] Grosseteste acted on the same principle in 1236 when he rejected a relative of John Blund, the scholarly chancellor of York, stating that to admit him to a cure of souls would incur the stain of sin, since the young man was not only insufficiently educated but also effectively illiterate.[45] It is explicitly present in a letter of 1239 in which Grosseteste states that he "does not dare" institute an "almost illiterate" nephew of John Romeyn, subdean of York, "for the very good reason that there are none more worthy to be damned than those who advance or procure the preferment of persons to a *cura animarum* who are incapable or ignorant, or are unwilling to look after their charges."[46]

Poor Romeyn. Four years before this, when quite reasonably he had asked permission of Grosseteste to farm out his parish in the Lincoln diocese because he was subdean of York and could not attend properly to it, Grossesteste would not allow that this was sufficient reason, for, as he put it, "farming entails the servile subjection of the Church of Christ and would make me a traitor to the souls entrusted to me." It is possible that Romeyn's position was not at all helped by the fact that the papal legate Boezio had attempted to intervene on his behalf. Grosseteste told Romeyn, rather sharply, that he was to inform the legate that he had not, as the legate had implied in his letter, arbitrarily refused permission to farm but had based his decision on decrees of the Council of Oxford. He was also to let the legate know that Grosseteste was not at all impressed by threats such as the legate had indulged in in his letter.[47]

The successor of Boezio as legate, the able and well-liked Otto of Tonengo, did not fare any better. Although Otto had invited him to preach at the Council of London in 1237, shortly after the legate's arrival in England, Grosseteste in the year following refused to give a prebend specified by Otto to a clerk in his service, an Italian named Master Atto. There were excellent reasons, Grosseteste wrote, for not being able to accede to the legate's request. The first and most pertinent was that the prebend in question had already been allotted to someone else. The second was equally good—he simply could not accept Atto. The legate well knew, Grosseteste went on, that he would do anything in the world for the Pope and for the legate which would

Robert Grosseteste and the Pastoral Care

promote faith and charity, but not anything which would lead to the disruption of charity. And since he was obliged to live by the Gospel, he was going to speak plainly and clearly. No fear of the legate's power would stop him: "non coercebit me vestrae potestatis timor."

He was fully aware, he assured Otto, that the Pope and the Roman Church had the power freely to dispose of benefices. He was also more than aware that the abuse of that power brought with it a danger of hellfire, and that the use of that power for purposes other than the promotion of faith and charity was an abuse. Now, he argued, to confer an ecclesiastical benefice without consulting its patron, as the legate had done when he specified what benefice his clerk should have, was surely to disrupt faith and charity. He was always ready to consider candidates of the legate if only Otto would go the right way about things. All that he could do at the moment, however, was humbly to ask Otto to withdraw the present candidate.[48]

Otto seems to have taken the rebuke to heart. Shortly afterwards he sent letters in a proper *forma deprecatoria* to Grosseteste on behalf of Thomas, son of the Earl of Ferrers. Grosseteste was more polite this time, but he turned Thomas down all the same, on the grounds that he was under the canonical age and not in orders.[49] Three years later, the legate was rash enough to present his clerk Atto once more. Grosseteste's reply was as neat as it was pointed. He was aware, he told the legate, that Atto was a good fellow and was generally held in high esteem for learning as well as morals. But he seemed to remember that the legate had once told him that Atto had no dispensation for a plurality of benefices, especially for those with a *cura animarum*. This was too bad, he said. Once upon a time he himself had been in a similar position and had had to take the hard way out. In any case, he went on, it was very doubtful whether the Italian Atto would really take to Lincoln. He was a plant used to the sun and the warmth of southern regions; the northern clime would hardly suit him. There was always a danger that such a plant would not bear fruit away from its natural habitat: "A wise gardener in a cold region will know that he should choose plants from that region, for although they are not equal in quality to the luxuriant plants of warmer climes, they will at least bear fruit." All the same, Grosseteste concluded, he himself would prefer not to have to take the final decision on Atto. Given the circumstances, he would leave the whole thing to the "stronger sanctity, the fullness of power, the more illuminated wisdom, the invincible vigor" of the legate himself.[50]

Application of the principle of personal responsibility for every soul in a diocese was not, however, confined by Grosseteste to the context of presentation. In the vexed question of the appointment of priests and clerics as itinerant justices, Grosseteste opposed the King's mandate to the abbot of Ramsey in 1236, largely because the abbot's soul was in his care. Shortly afterwards he appealed to the Archbishop of Canterbury—later St. Edmund of Abingdon—to do something about clerical itinerant justices, "because the souls of those appointed are in danger of hellfire." And when Edmund hesitated and suggested that it would be better to wait until a council was called, Grosseteste wrote him again, this time asking for a straight answer to the question, "If religious sin when they act as judges, and clerics, too, who submit themselves to secular courts, how are we, who have the care of souls, to escape sin when we allow them to sin in this way even once?"[51]

But Edmund, it appears, remained irresolute, so Grosseteste in that same year (1236) abandoned pleas for direction from Edmund in favor of a statement of fact, the result being a long letter on violations of the liberties of the Church in England. It was abominable, he wrote to Edmund, that a man dedicated by office to the pastoral care should become involved in secular affairs. In his opinion all those guilty of such anomalies, and all those who choose to ignore them, sin gravely, as does the King when he compels the execution of mandates to abbots and other clergy to act as itinerant justices. And what excuse, he asked Edmund, will be made before the divine tribunal by bishops who do not contest these practices with all their might?[52]

In particular, Grosseteste kept an eye on episcopal elections. Five years after his own election to Lincoln, when an election to

Robert Grosseteste and the Pastoral Care

Hereford was pending, he wrote Edmund of Abingdon on the perils of bribery and influence at elections, and, quoting Ovid ("Sero medicina paratur, cum mala per longas invaluere moras"), concluded that a pastor elected in this way can bring only death to the flock over which he is put in charge.[53]

Two years before this, when rumors were circulating that the King was forcing his own nominee on the electors at Winchester, Grosseteste once more trained his sights on the legate Otto and opened up on him with intent. Otto must know, he wrote, that a person who occupies a pastoral post and does not feed his flock on knowledge and doctrine brings nothing but death to himself and his flock. If this type of bishop is elected at Winchester, all those who connive in any way in that election are accessories to that death. "God forbid," he wrote, "that a ship of the magnitude of Winchester should be handed over to a captain who is ignorant, negligent, or laboring under some disability, or that anyone should procure or consent to such an appointment, or that anyone in a position to stop the appointment should not raise a hand."[54]

Needless to say, the usually urbane legate took offense at the sting in the tail of a letter which, as it happens, mystified him completely. Grosseteste, in replying, thanked Otto for his elegant letter ("dulcifluo diligentique stylo"), but admitted that his own letter had been, in a Horatian sense, somewhat cloudy: "Brevis esse laboro et obscurus fio." However, he went on, if things were left unsaid, they should have been all the more evident for their omission. The sentiments expressed in his letter, he said, could be compared to the exhortation of spectators at a fight or a horse race. Every sentence, every word of that letter, was written in order to spur Otto on in the contest which was in progress over the Winchester bishopric. What he wanted to do in that letter was to bring out the best of Otto's zeal for the things of God so that eventually, with Otto's cooperation, God would provide Winchester with that quality of pastor which Grosseteste knew to be necessary there.[55]

If this letter to the legate was delicately devious, the letters to Edmund of Abingdon on justiciars and elections were almost insultingly direct—a call to the Archbishop to stand up like a man of God to the King. It is as though Grosseteste's own personal zeal for the good of souls had broken out of the confines of his own diocese in a spirited (some might say meddling) attempt to communicate the vitality of his concept of the episcopal office to those of his confreres who, flagging in their resolve, were all too easily overawed by majesty. His blithe self-confidence was encouraged, perhaps, by the ease with which he had circumvented Henry III at an early stage of his episcopate. Writing to excuse himself for rejecting a certain nobleman's presentee as prior of Kyme monastery, Grosseteste asked the nobleman not to take the rejection badly. He should not be shy, Grosseteste said, of imitating the King's example, for, "as I may confide to you, when I squelched elections in several royal monasteries and, without a word to the King, appointed one of my own men on the authority of the General Council [4 Lateran], the King took it all without a murmur."[56]

It would not always be so. Although Henry seems to have had a warm regard for Grosseteste, there were times when, understandably, he was vexed with him. And if Grosseteste, on the other hand, had on one occasion in 1242 to apologize to the King for his seeming neglect of him and his family,[57] this did not prevent him a year later from taking the King to task for writing an encouraging letter to a rebellious group in Bardney monastery, Lincolnshire. Asking the King to retract his letter, Grosseteste stated plainly that no non-ecclesiastical power, no matter how exalted, had the right to nullify or modify something done by a bishop in his own diocese.[58]

Some two years later, in 1245, Grosseteste once more had a brush with King Henry when he refused to admit a Forest Judge, Robert Passelewe, whom the King had presented to the church of St. Peter, Northampton. Explaining to Henry that he had done this out of "fatherly love for the royal person and for the salvation of the judge and the souls of the said parish," Grosseteste told him that he had informed Passelewe himself that to admit him to a *cura animarum* would be to go against divine and

Robert Grosseteste and the Pastoral Care

canon law, and to commit a breach of the profession of faith he had made at his consecration as bishop.[59]

The Passelewe affair, however, did not rest there. The judge made an appeal to the Archbishop of Canterbury, now Boniface of Savoy, to compel Grosseteste to institute him to Northampton —an action that drew a splendid letter from Grosseteste in that same year, 1245. The duty of the Archbishop of Canterbury, he wrote Boniface, is, as head of the bench of bishops, to applaud enthusiasm and reprimand negligence; it is not to attempt anything iniquitous. The Archbishop was well aware, he continued, that Grosseteste had refused repeatedly to admit Passelewe to Northampton, for the very good reason that Passelewe would not resign his appointment as a Judge of the Forest. Yet the official of the Archbishop, who had been sent by Boniface with an order to Grosseteste to admit Passelewe, had now seen fit to command Grosseteste to institute the judge to Northampton within eight days. Otherwise the institution would be done by the official himself.

Grosseteste implored the Archbishop to restrain his headstrong official and to help rather than hinder the pastoral care in which the suffragans of the Archbishop were engaged. He repeated to Boniface what he said he had already written to the official: that indeed he would obey an order of the Archbishop in all things lawful, but not in a matter so clearly contrary to divine and human sanctions. To Grosseteste, the Forest Judge was engaged in secular pursuits, and was so incapacitated canonically by these and other concerns that he was not only unfit for the pastoral care in Northampton but utterly unworthy of any pastoral office whatever. To order the admission of such a man to the *cura animarum*, as Boniface the Archbishop had done, was, Grosseteste felt, nothing other than the crime of idolatry. The only possible outcome would be the eternal damnation of the judge and the loss of all the souls in the parish of St. Peter in Northampton. And, he reminded Boniface, there would always remain a suspicion that it was fear of the King and not zeal for justice which was at the back of the action of the Archbishop.[60]

It is a lengthy step from attacking noblemen, canons, archbishops, papal legates, and a king to reprimanding the papacy itself in the interests of the *cura animarum*, but Robert Grosseteste eventually took it. Given his obsession with the pastoral care and his horror at the evils of presentation and provision, it was inevitable.

In 1250 the papal curia, then at Lyons, had a foretaste of what was to come when Grosseteste's pointed criticisms of curial venality and insensitivity to the needs of the pastoral care caused a considerable flurry.[61] In a memorandum presented personally to the Pope (Innocent IV) and his cardinals on 13 May 1250, Grosseteste charged that the curia was "the prime cause, font and origin" of all the evils that beset the pastoral care: "Sed quae est huius tanti mali prior et originalis causa, fons et origo? Dicere vehementissime tremesco et expavesco. . . . Causa, fons et origo huius est haec curia." Not only did the curia not prevent abuses, but by its dispensations, provisions, and collations it multiplied bad pastors and handed precious souls over to destruction.[62]

Three years later, in 1253, Grosseteste descended from the general to the particular in a manner that startled some but should not have been a surprise to anyone. He flatly refused to accept a provision of a canonry at Lincoln which had been made to a nephew of Pope Innocent, Federico da Lavagna. Grosseteste's letter rejecting the provision survives in some nineteen manuscripts and is also to be found in the *Chronica maiora* of Matthew Paris, the Annals of Burton, and the letters of Roger Marsh.[63] It is as pointed as it is brief. All obedience, Grosseteste allowed at the beginning of his reply, is due to apostolic mandates. Certain conditions, however, govern these mandates, he went on. The first is that the mandates must respect the teaching of Christ, whose representative the Pope is, and that of the apostles. The second is that they must be in accord with the "most divine sanctity" of the apostolic see, a sanctity which can never contradict Christ's teaching.

Now, Grosseteste argued, the tenor of the letter that provided the Pope's nephew to a prebend in Lincoln was not in harmony with that sanctity. Rather it was off-pitch and dissonant. For one

Robert Grosseteste and the Pastoral Care

thing, since it was strewn with "notwithstanding" clauses, which have no necessary basis in natural law, it could only lead to "a cataclysm of inconstancy, audacity, lying, distrust, and the like," thus dissolving the purity of the Christian religion and disrupting peace. For another, if one omits the sin of Lucifer, there was not, in Grosseteste's opinion, a genus of sin so far removed from the teaching of the gospels and the apostles and so abominably pernicious as that of the condemnation of souls to death and perdition by defrauding, cheating, the pastoral office and ministry. The pastoral ministry should be the way to life and to salvation. Those, therefore, who minister the cure of souls in a slipshod way stifle the life of God in the sheep committed to their care, and approximate Lucifer and Antichrist more closely than any other murderers. And the greater the divinely given power of ministers such as these, the more urgent is the duty of the Church to exclude and to extirpate them.

This being the case, the Holy See, endowed as it is by Christ with the highest possible power, cannot conceivably order or connive at a sin so pernicious to the human race and abominable to Christ as that of cheating and defrauding the pastoral care. If it should, it would join the other two princes of darkness, Lucifer and Antichrist, on the seat of pestilence. An order such as this from the Holy See, or for that matter from the highest in the angelic hierarchy, could not be obeyed for a moment. The only course to be followed in such an event would be absolute and relentless rebellion.

Because of this, Grosseteste concluded, and "because of the obedience by which I am bound to the Holy See as to my parents, and out of my love of my union with the Holy See in the Body of Christ, as an obedient son I disobey, I contradict, I rebel against, the things contained in the letter of provision in question, and particularly because they clearly verge upon the aforementioned sin which is so pernicious to the human race and so detestable to Christ."

It was impossible, Grosseteste was sure, for those to whom he had addressed his letter to make things difficult for him because of what he had written. And this for the very simple reason that "my every word and deed in this position I have taken are neither from contradiction nor rebellion but from the honor due by God's command from a son to a father and mother." What he had tried to say, he repeated briefly, was that the holiness which is present in the Holy See cannot be for destruction but only for building up, because "this is the fullness of power: to be able to do everything constructively." The "so-called provisions" do not build up, but make for destruction. It is not possible, therefore, for the Holy See to act on them. It is "flesh and blood," which shall not possess the kingdom of God, that "hath revealed" them and not "the Father" of Our Lord Jesus Christ "who is in Heaven."

This is a very famous letter, and it has had many interpretations. To some the letter makes Grosseteste a sort of pre-Wycliffite "Morning Star" of the Reformation. To others it is heroic though illogical. To still others, Powicke and Pantin for example, it is psychologically understandable, proceeding out of the nature and demands of the pastoral care as seen by Grosseteste.[64]

A recent explanation is that of Professor Tierney, who has shown that far from being illogical in "rebelling obediently," Grosseteste was in fact perfectly consistent with the prevailing opinion of his time (an opinion shared by Innocent IV himself) that "there was no certain presumption that every papal command was consistent with the divine will nor supported by divine authority." In effect, Grosseteste was making a distinction between the person of the ruler and the institution that he represented, a distinction which had been a well-known one of canonists for the half-century before his seemingly astonishing letter.[65]

It may be useful, however, to take a look once more at Grosseteste's letter (128 in Luard's edition) and at the so-called papal provision that occasioned it. As I shall suggest, both letters have been taken too much for granted in the long history of the interpretation of Grosseteste's action.

Let us consider the "papal provision" first, since it is crucial to an understanding of what Grosseteste was about in letter 128. Contrary to what one would gather from various writers over the past hundred years, the original provision to the Pope's nephew,

Robert Grosseteste and the Pastoral Care

Federico da Lavagna, is not extant. What survives is not a provision as such but a confirmation of a provision which Innocent IV included in a mandate to two designated executors ("provisors") of the provision, the then-Archdeacon of Canterbury (Stephen de Montival) and the papal scriptor, Master Innocenzo, an Italian then resident in Yorkshire: "archidiacono Cantuariensi et magistro Innocentio scriptori nostro in Anglia commoranti."[66] What this mandate has to say is as important as the fact that it has been overlooked, for the provision it confirmed was not as straightforward as is commonly assumed. There were, it turns out, two stages in the provision of Federico to a Lincoln canonry and prebend. First of all, and at an unspecified date, Guglielmo Cardinal of Sant'Eustachio, at the mandate of Pope Innocent, had formally invested Federico with a canonry at Lincoln, and also had provided him to a prebend there if one were vacant at the time Federico presented his letters of provision, or, if there were not, then as soon as one became vacant. The investiture and the provision, Innocent informs us in his mandate, were embodied in a letter of Cardinal Guglielmo.

It was not by chance that Innocent had entrusted this Cardinal with the investiture and the provision of his nephew Federico. Guglielmo was also a nephew of Innocent's, and a Fieschi at that, as Innocent was. But Federico (about whom we know nothing except that he was a cleric and a papal scriptor, and came from Lavagna, the native place of the Fieschi on the Ligurian coast south of Genoa)[67] was not satisfied with his cousin's handling of the affair. He begged his uncle for a confirmation.

Innocent did not disappoint him. He confirmed explicitly (and this is our second stage) what Cardinal Guglielmo had done: "Nos ipsius Federici devotis precibus inclinati, quod ab eodem cardinale super hoc factum est ratum et gratum habentes, illud auctoritate apostolica duximus confirmandum"; and then he commissioned the two provisors whom he was addressing to put Federico or his procurator into corporal possession of the canonry and prebend, and to excommunicate all who opposed him.

This should have been sufficient for Federico, but apparently it was not. Innocent added a comprehensive list of "notwithstanding" clauses and stated that the provision was to hold good "notwithstanding that the Bishop of Lincoln or the chapter may have had papal letters which exempt him or it from being compelled to accept any provision." No matter what the tenor of these or other apostolic letters, they were to have no effect whatever in the case of Federico: ". . . viribus omnino carere." There was no loophole. And should anyone oppose the provision he was to be summoned before the Pope himself within two months, no matter what privileges or exemptions he claimed to possess.

It was to this mandate of 26 January 1253 to the two provisors that Grosseteste's celebrated letter was directed a few weeks later. In Luard's edition of the letters of Grosseteste (1861) the reply is not addressed to the two provisors noted above but to "magistro Innocentio domino papae," a manuscript inscription which obviously was a garbled version of "magistro Innocentio domini papae scriptori."

Most authors today therefore speak of letter 128 as "the letter to Master Innocent." This in itself, however, is hardly correct. The inscription "magistro Innocentio domino papae" is not only garbled but also out of place, even in its corrected form. And this is for the simple reason that the letter printed by Luard as No. 128 (and which exists in some manuscripts with mistaken inscription) is only the second half of Grosseteste's original letter.

Luard, when editing letter 128 ("Noverit discretio vestra. . .") with the inscription "magistro Innocentio domino papae," prints in a footnote a letter from Grosseteste which, he observes, usually precedes letter 128 (or, as Harrison Thomson, repeating Luard, says, "The letter is usually preceded by a copy of the pope's letter to Master Innocent").[68] Now that letter in Luard's footnote which "usually" precedes letter 128 in manuscripts is, in fact, the first half of Grosseteste's reply to the papal mandate. It is addressed not to one but to two provisors ("Cantuariensi archidiacono et magistro Innocentio domini papae scriptori"), and contains a rehearsal of the papal mandate of 26 January 1253 to those two provisors: "Intelleximus vos litteram domini papae recepisse in haec verba: Innocentius . . . archidiacono Cantuariensi et magistro Innocentio domini papae scriptori, salutem et apostolicam

Robert Grosseteste and the Pastoral Care

benedictionem. Cum dilectus filius noster. . . . Datum Perus. vii Kal. Feb. pontificatus nostri anno decimo."[69] It is, indeed, to this rehearsal of Grosseteste that we owe our knowledge of the papal mandate. And if it "usually" precedes letter 128 in manuscripts, this is precisely because it was meant to.

What happened, I suspect, and misled Luard, Thomson, and others, was that as soon as it began to be copied, that part of the letter ("Noverit discretio vestra") which followed the rehearsal of Innocent's mandate was detached both from it and from the original inscription to the two provisors (as in the *Chronica* of Matthew Paris), and somewhere along the line (probably by the late thirteenth century), acquired the muddled inscription "magistro Innocentio domino papae" in some codices instead of the original, double inscription.

Such a conjecture is not farfetched. As it stands in Luard's footnote the rehearsal of the papal mandate is patently incomplete. It demands a follow-up. Besides, and in spite of the assertions of Luard and Harrison Thomson, there are manuscripts (at least three of which are from the second half of the thirteenth century) where the two "letters" follow each other without the intrusive "magistro Innocentio" inscription found in some other codices.[70] If further proof were needed, then one could turn to the contemporary Burton Annals. These state that when Grosseteste had received the Pope's letter from the two provisors, the archdeacon of Canterbury and Master Innocenzo, he replied to the provisors as follows:

Robertus, Dei permissione Lincolniae episcopus, Cantuariensi archidiacono et magistro Innocentio domini papae scriptori salutem et benedictionem. Intelleximus vos literam domini Papae recepisse, in haec verba: Innocentius episcopus, etc. Dilectis filiis archidiacono Cantuariensi et magistro Innocentio scriptori nostro in Anglia commoranti, salutem, etc., et infra [= beginning of rehearsal of the mandate].

Noverit autem discretio vestra. . . [= letter 128].

The text of the papal mandate is not given at this point, but there is enough here to show that the inscription and rehearsal are those in the letter in Luard's footnote and in the "first"

Grosseteste letter as it appears in the various manuscripts that carry it. As well, the conventional "et infra" (as distinct from "etc.") proves beyond all doubt that the rehearsal of the papal letter and letter 128 are but the first and second part of one and the same letter, for the text of the letter to the provisors, including all of the papal mandate, is to be found further on in the Annals with a reference back to the passage above and with an answering "*ut supra*" after "Noverit discretio vestra quod mandatis apostolicis affectione filiali omnino devote et reverenter obedio. His quoque quae mandatis apostolicis, etc., *ut supra*." [71]

What does this "restored" letter of Grosseteste (see *Appendix*) contribute towards an understanding of his reaction to the papal provision by executory mandate? From the fact that Grosseteste's letter is addressed to the two provisors and not to Pope Innocent himself, it now seems clear that Grosseteste had not had any direct communication from the Pope about the provision but only a letter from one or both of the provisors in which a copy of the Pope's mandate was included. This, I feel sure, is what is implied by the opening phrase of Grosseteste's letter to the provisors ("Intelleximus vos litteram domini papae recepisse in haec verba") and by his rehearsal of the papal mandate immediately afterwards. The Annals of Burton certainly confirm this point, stating that Grosseteste replied to the provisors after he had received the executory letters which they had had on their appointment as provisors:

Eodem anno cum dati essent provisores auctoritate Apostolica dominus et magister Cantuariensis archidiaconus, et quidam Romanus nomine Innocentius, ad providendum cuidam Romano puero parvulo de prima [praebenda] vacante in cathedrali Lincolniae, acceptis eorundem literis in eodem negotio executoriis, dominus et magister Robertus, eiusdem loci episcopus, eisdem in haec verba rescripsit. . . .[72]

It was, then, from a copy of the papal mandate to these provisors that Grosseteste learned for the first time that the Pope's nephew Federico da Lavagna not only had been provided to a canonry at Lincoln but also had been, as Pope Innocent put it to the provisors, "invested bodily, personally, and by ring as a canon

Robert Grosseteste and the Pastoral Care

of Lincoln with full legal rights by Cardinal Guglielmo." He would have learned further, and again for the first time, that the same Cardinal had also, at the Pope's behest, provided Federico to a prebend in the same church.

It goes without saying that this high-handed approach to the pastoral care must have irked Grosseteste. As he had told the legate Otto in 1237, when he rejected his clerk Atto, no one should confer a benefice without first consulting its patron. Because of this rebuke, Otto had made his next provision in a request form, *in forma deprecatoria*.[73] This was the proper procedure. The standard teaching on provisions was that there first should be a letter of request (*litterae rogatoriae*) from the provider to the patron, then a letter of admonition (*monitoriae*), followed by an order to provide (*praeceptoriae*), and, finally, if the patron refused to budge, by executory letters (*executoriae*) to one or two trustworthy outsiders (provisors) who would compel the patron to provide. In the words of the contemporary *Glossa ordinaria* on the Decretals (*X.* 1. 3, 37, *v. De monitoriis*): "ordo et consuetudo curiae est quod primo [i.e., after the initial *litterae rogatoriae*] monitoriae, secundo praeceptoriae, ultimo executoriae conceduntur."

Barraclough has noted that it was precisely in the pontificate of Innocent IV that the practice began of "granting all categories" of letters simultaneously, that is, of providing someone to a benefice by sending out executory letters to the provisors at the same time as the letters of provision to the bishop or patron.[74] All the same, Innocent himself in his commentary on the Decretals (*X.* 3. 5, 27, *v. assignari proventus*) seems to have preferred the normal procedure. Some have asserted, Innocent says, that one can act at once on monitory letters, but this idea "does not appeal to him." Such a procedure, he goes on, would make executors redundant. Besides, the fact that the Pope sends out monitory letters does not necessarily mean that he will follow them up with executory ones.[75] In the present case, however, there is nothing to suggest that Cardinal Guglielmo had had any consultation with Grosseteste before making the original provision, nor that any kind of deprecatory, admonitory, or peremptory letters were sent to Lincoln when the executory letters were dispatched to the two provisors. This was a grave lapse on the part of Innocent and his chancery. Given Grosseteste's notorious views on presentation, it was a very silly one.

What really moved Grosseteste to anger, however, was the series of "notwithstanding" clauses. Most of the writers who have discussed this letter of Grosseteste give the impression that he rebelled against the papal provision as such. To be accurate (and it may be noted that Pantin, Powicke, and others omit the operative words in their translations and summaries), what Grosseteste rebelled against was "the things contained in this letter": "his quae in praedicta littera continentur . . . filialiter et obedienter non obedio, contradico et rebello."

From this point of view it is of importance that the "heaped up *Non obstante* clauses" form the first of the two reasons that Grosseteste gives as proof that the "tenor of the letter" was not consonant with the holiness inherent in the Apostolic See: "Non est igitur praedictae litterae tenor apostolicae sanctitati consonus sed absonus plurimum et discors, primo, quia de illius litterae . . . supercumulato *Non obstante* . . . scatet cataclysmus. . . ."For these *Non obstante* clauses only beget a "cataclysmus inconstantiae, audaciae, et procacitatis etiam inverecundae mentiendi et fallendi, diffidentiae cuiquam credendi vel fidem adhibendi."

This was not a new position. In 1250, and in almost exactly the same words, Grosseteste had made the same point in his tough memorandum to Innocent and his cardinals at Lyons with respect to the curia's use of *Non obstante* clauses: "Huius quoque curiae, verbi huius non obstante frequentia, mundum replevit inconstantia, mentiendi fugavit verecundiam, adhibendi fidem chartis omnem abstulit evidentiam, et non observandi fidem eisdem omnem contulit audaciam."[76] What was new was that Grosseteste now found himself to be a victim of those same "shifty, shameless, and soul-destroying" practices of which he had accused the curia some three years before, for in 1239 he had been granted a special privilege by Pope Gregory IX that he would

Robert Grosseteste and the Pastoral Care

not be bound to respect any papal provision unless the letter made "full mention" of that privilege:

Exigentibus devotionis tuae meritis ut a nobis specialem gratiam consequaris, fraternitati tuae praesentium auctoritate concedimus ut in Lincolniensi ecclesia de mandato nostro plurium sicut dicitur provisione gravata, non tenearis alicui per nostras litteras providere nisi de concessione huiusmodi plenam fecerint mentionem.[77]

Now in a papal mandate of 1253 which bristled with *Non obstante* clauses and was not even addressed to him but to provisors, this privilege of 1239 was not only not mentioned explicitly but ignored as though it had never been granted.

This, in my opinion, was the root of Grosseteste's rebellion. And without giving credence to everything that Matthew Paris relates of Grosseteste's last days, it is surely significant that in one of his last discourses, as reported by Matthew, Grosseteste precisely accuses the Pope of "shamelessly annulling" the privileges of his predecessors by *Non obstante* clauses: "Privilegia sanctorum pontificum Romanorum praedecessorum suorum Papa impudenter annullare per hoc repagulum *Non obstante*, non erubescit."[78]

If, as I have suggested, the *Non obstante* clauses in the papal mandate of 1253 were the immediate cause of Grosseteste's refusal to accept it, this was not so much because these clauses "annulled" a privilege which he had had from Gregory IX as because they represented in this particular case, and perhaps in general, a grievously sinful abuse of power. This seems clear from Grosseteste's second reason why the "tenor" or "content" of the papal letter was not consonant with the innate holiness of the Apostolic See of which he had spoken at length in the preceding paragraphs: "After the sin of Lucifer," he wrote, "there is not, nor can there be, a type of sin so contrary to the teaching of the Gospel and of the apostles, so detestable to the Lord Jesus Christ, and so pernicious to the human race, as to maim and kill souls whom the office and the ministry of the pastoral care should enliven, by cheating that pastoral office and ministry."

"Pastoralis officii et ministerii defraudatione": coupled with

Grosseteste's accusation that the heap of *Non obstante* clauses gave rise to deceit, treachery, and breach of faith, the sin here that is second only to Lucifer's cannot simply be that of "depriving" souls of due pastoral care, as Mr. Pantin and others render the word "defraudatione." It must mean something more than that. If the sin were simply a question of "depriving" the pastoral care of competent ministers, then Grosseteste would surely have said something, as he had said on so many other similar occasions, about the fact that Federico was a foreigner and therefore unsuitable, or that he was illiterate and therefore a menace. But he does not. Federico is not even mentioned. What Grosseteste attacked was not the young, unseen Italian who had been provided but "what is contained in this letter." For once it was not a deprival of the pastoral care as such that he was worried about. It was a *defraudatio* that was present in the very mandate itself.

When he rebelled against and obediently refused to obey "the things contained in this letter," it was, he said, "particularly because they clearly verge on the aforementioned sin." For "the things contained in this letter" cheated, defrauded, his own pastoral care and ministry. They came from a system that countenanced deceit, a system that could grant a privilege on the one hand and ignore it on the other. The present letter of provision was a perfect example of what he had had in mind at Lyons, for with its *Non obstante* clauses that unblushingly set aside a papal privilege it was audacious and shameless, and destroyed all credibility. And it was sinful because it cheated and played fast and loose with the ministry of the cure of souls which had been committed to him. A pernicious sin at any time, double-dealing was abominably so when perpetrated by the Apostolic See, which by definition was supremely holy: "Haec autem quas vocant provisiones non sunt in aedificationem sed in manifestam destructionem. Non igitur eas potest beata sedes apostolica."

Grosseteste was an old man now, with his eightieth birthday well behind him. He had trusted the positive law and the curia when, in the interests of the *cura animarum* and because Lincoln was "plurium provisione gravata," he had sought for and obtained his privilege in 1239. Now in 1253, and on the verge of

Robert Grosseteste and the Pastoral Care

the grave after eighteen years of dedicated service, he felt deceived, betrayed, disillusioned. The curia had failed to keep its faith. And because he considered himself entitled to invoke the privilege the curia had ignored, he rejected the mandate and all that it contained out of hand. That privilege had been invoked successfully on a lesser occasion in 1241. Admittedly that was while Gregory was still alive,[79] but the privilege had not been revoked since, and there was no reason, or so it may have seemed to him, why it should not have been respected.

Yet Grosseteste made no mention of this privilege in his letter to the provisors, nor, for that matter, did he mention at least two other related privileges which he had had from Innocent himself.[80] Instead, he wrapped his refusal up in the circular, evangelical prose that is characteristic of his pastoral letters. Predictably, absolutely true to form, Grosseteste now lectured the two provisors (and through them the Pope and the curia) as he had lectured anyone who had crossed his path during his eighteen years as bishop, and as he had lectured the Pope and his cardinals at Lyons three years before. A schoolmaster for most of the sixty-seven years before he became bishop, he remained a schoolmaster, chiding and more than a little brusque, to the day of his death.

But the tone is shrill now, the reasoning strained. There is an incomprehension that borders on panic. He has been hurt to the quick, and by, of all people, his "Father and Mother," the Pope and the papacy. The privilege may never be mentioned, but it is none the less present for that. It is not for nothing that as he lay dying at Buckden in the early days of the following October, he is reported to have said of Innocent IV, "Privilegia sanctorum pontificum successorum suorum papa impudenter annullare per hoc repagulum *Non obstante* non erubescit. . . . Quis eius privilegia custodebit?"[81] The wound was still open.

Seven or eight months after this tortured letter—which, the Burton Annals say, the two provisors "sent on at once under their own seals to Pope Innocent and his cardinals"—Robert Grosseteste died at his manor at Buckden, Huntingdonshire, on 9

October 1253. Some three weeks later Innocent IV sent to the prelates of Christendom a remarkable letter, *Postquam regimini*, with which Grosseteste's letter of refusal may have more to do than hitherto has been suspected.

In this encyclical letter, described by Innocent himself as "proprio motu" or totally unsolicited, the Pope ruled that from now on all prelates, chapters, convents, and patrons in general could themselves confer on persons of their own choice any prebends, benefices, and incomes which might be granted by the papacy or others in the service of the papacy to foreigners ("oriundis extra regna in quibus habentur canonicatus et praebendae"), although those who were in possession of such benefices at present were not to be disturbed.

Scholars in general have not paid much attention to this lengthy letter or "statute," as Innocent himself terms it.[82] Grosseteste scholars who have adverted to it at all have been content to describe it with Matthew Paris as a "mitigation" of previous practice.[83] Of course it was much more. As A. L. Smith rightly noted over sixty years ago, though he did not pursue the matter further, it was "a complete restoration of the old rights of patronage to their old owners."[84]

What, to my knowledge, no one has remarked upon is the frank, uncurial language of the letter. It was, indeed, "proprio motu." For one thing, Innocent bluntly states that from now on prelates are to "tear up" any papal or legatine letters that go against this new statute on the provision of foreigners: ". . . licitumque sit vobis universis et singulis, tamquam nostris in hac parte ministris, nostras sive legatorum nostrorum lacerare litteras, si quae statuto ipsi contrariae vobis aut alicui vestrum fuerint praesentatae." For another thing, and this is still more astonishing, Innocent admits in his opening remarks that there have been mistakes made in the past in the system of provisions to foreigners, whether because of dishonest petitioners, or because of prevailing roguery all round, or, worse still, because he himself had been forced on occasion, and against his better judgment, to grant certain provisions:

Robert Grosseteste and the Pastoral Care

Postquam regimini generalis ecclesiae nos licet immeritos divina pietas voluit praesidere, cordi semper habuimus quod honestatem et ordinem in omnibus servaremus, ac in provisionibus faciendis haberemus illius providentiae modum per quem ecclesiis et monasteriis sive aliis piis locis honor et comodum proveniret. Quod autem quandoque contrarium accidisse dinoscitur, tum propter malitiam temporum, tum propter improbitatem nimiam petitorum, saepe nobis dolorem intulit et cordi nostro suspiria cumulavit, maxime cum post multa diffugia et excogitatae resistentiae studium, provisiones quasdam prorsus inviti fecerimus quas potuisse vitare pro magno et sollempni gaudio duceremus.

A papal letter that allows that there have been mistakes in policy or in practice is a rare event, but for a pope to admit to having had his arm twisted on occasion is quite unusual, if not a landmark in the history of the papacy: "maxime cum . . . provisiones quasdam prorsus inviti fecerimus quas potuisse vitare pro magno et sollempni gaudio duceremus." Yet these opening statements of *Postquam regimini*, not to speak of the dramatic order "to tear up" contrary papal letters, have not attracted any attention. Even the usually perceptive Powicke misses the point when he writes that this letter of 3 November 1253 "expounded a mitigation, which had caused him anxious thought, of a deplorable state of affairs. Owing to the evil of the age and the unscrupulous avidity of petitioners, the system of provisions had not had the healthy and salutary effect which he had hoped for."[85]

It is surprising, moreover, that Powicke, Pantin, and others make no connection whatever between Grosseteste's letter to the provisors and *Postquam regimini*. Of course, as Powicke rightly notes, *Postquam regimini* was "addressed to the whole Church," but it is at least curious that this encyclical letter seems to survive, outside of the register of Innocent's letters in the Vatican Archives, only in copies made by the contemporary English chroniclers Matthew Paris and the Burton annalist. What is more, and unlike Matthew Paris upon whom Powicke relied in this matter, the Burton annalist states quite explicitly that the letter of Grosseteste was the occasion of *Postquam regimini*: "At that time," the annalist notes just before the text of *Postquam regimini*, "as soon as the aforesaid letter of the Lord Bishop of Lincoln had been received, read, and understood, the Pope sent thirty copies or more of the following letter over his bull to the archbishops, bishops, and some abbots in England."[86]

It would be too much to claim that the letter of Robert Grosseteste was the sole cause of *Postquam regimini*, for other complaints about papal provisions had been made during Innocent's pontificate, notably those from England at the first council of Lyons in 1245, and the "Gravamina ecclesiae Gallicanae" (the so-called "Protestation of St. Louis") in 1247.[87] All the same, given the long lapse of time between those complaints and the papal letter of 1253, the statement of the Burton Annals that *Postquam regimini* was in answer to Grosseteste's letter cannot be discounted. The display of papal candor in the exordium of the letter, with its straight acknowledgment of occasional dishonesty in the system of provisions, could be taken as an admission that Grosseteste was right when he said that the presence of layer upon layer of *Non obstante* clauses "in the present letter, as in so many others all over the place, only leads to a cataclysm of inconstancy, shameless lying, and deceit, and to begetting a diffidence in believing or trusting anyone." The point would not have been lost on Innocent, to whom a copy of the memorandum of 1250, with its stark accusation of curial abuse of these clauses, had been handed personally by Grosseteste before the memorandum was read out in the presence of the Pope and cardinals. The order at the end of *Postquam regimini* to tear up any future papal or legatine letters which contradicted what the Pope now had to say could be seen as a condoning of Grosseteste's action in refusing a provision which did not respect but rather ran counter to a previous papal privilege. And what of Innocent's confession that he had sometimes "and after tenacious resistance, granted provisions against my will which gladly I would have avoided if I could"? May it not be that in Grosseteste's case Innocent had been browbeaten into an injudicious and offensive mandate to provisors by his nephews Cardinal Guglielmo Fieschi and Federico da Lavagna, especially in the light of the latter's known in-

Robert Grosseteste and the Pastoral Care

sistence on a papal confirmation of the original and rather innocuous provision?

What seems clear from *Postquam regimini* is that Innocent was not always in complete control of documents issued from his chancery, and that there had been, as he was sure there would be again in the future, unfortunate mistakes. Perhaps he was not even aware of the full tenor of the Lincoln provision when he sanctioned its confirmation or of the tactless range of the *Non obstante* clauses that went out in the mandate to the provisors. The pained rebuke from Grosseteste must have pulled Innocent up short. A striking account in Matthew Paris, repeated by Powicke and others, has the Pape raging at Grosseteste's letter and asking in his anger, "Who is this old man, as deaf as he is absurd [surdus, et absurdus], who dares so rashly to judge my acts"? He calmed down, Matthew relates, only when Cardinal Gil de Torres, Archbishop of Toledo, and others reminded him how zealous, holy, and learned a bishop Grosseteste was, and then suggested to him that the best thing to do was to ignore it all, lest there be a public outcry.[88]

Anger or not, there hardly was any need to remind Innocent who Grosseteste was. He was only too aware of Grosseteste's crusty integrity and of his unwillingness to be pushed around by anyone where the *cura animarum* or anything else was concerned. He had heard him out patiently at Lyons in 1250 when Grosseteste presented a most militant if rambling memorandum to the papal curia and had stated *tout court* that "the prime and original cause of all the evil in the Church" was "the papal curia itself." Had Innocent taken this or the subsequent crude response to the cardinals' objections very badly,[89] he would have sent the old, unpolished Bishop packing back to England at once. He did not. Grosseteste, indeed, remained at Lyons for another six months until his business there was complete.

If there was any anger when Grosseteste's letter to the provisors reached Innocent, it probably was directed not so much at Grosseteste as at the ineptitude of a chancery which had allowed such executory letters to be sent out, and at the expense of such a bishop. It was an anger which had cooled down, perhaps, by the following November to give way to the resigned but tight-lipped language of *Postquam regimini.*

It must, indeed, have been quite a shock to Innocent in the spring of 1253 to find that the letter confirming his nephew to a Lincoln benefice had overlooked Grosseteste's papal privilege so crassly and caused Grosseteste, who, as Pantin has put it, "was probably the most fervent and thoroughgoing papalist among medieval English writers,"[90] to denounce both the letter and the system that had spawned it.

We do not know whether any letters were exchanged between the Bishop and the Pope in the interval between Grosseteste's reply to the provisors and his death, but we do know that Innocent sent what amounts to an apologetic letter to the archbishops and bishops of England on 25 May 1253 in which he averred that he had ceased for years to provide benefices in England and did not wish to insist on keeping to the agreed sum of 8,000 marks a year in provisions. All that he asked was that the prelates should carry out his provisions in such a way that there would be no complaints.[91]

Postquam regimini, six months later, went further. With its clean sweep of many grievances at the provision of foreigners, its frank admissions, and its complete lack of recrimination, it is as eloquent a testimony, short of a personal letter of apology, as one could wish for, both to the effect of Grosseteste's letter and to the respect which Innocent came to have for him.

Grosseteste, of course, had been dead for some three weeks by the time *Postquam regimini* and its thirty or more copies were expedited to England. Matthew Paris, inventive as ever when it came to discussing Innocent, Italians, or friars, would have it that Innocent was overjoyed when he heard of Grosseteste's death, and in fact ordered Henry III to throw the remains of Grosseteste out of the church at Lincoln so that it might be proclaimed far and wide that Grosseteste was a recalcitrant pagan. The chronicler from St. Albans then goes on to relate that Grosseteste appeared to Innocent the night following and dug him in the ribs with his pastoral staff saying, "Sinibaldo, you miserable Pope, what do you think you are up to? The Lord

Robert Grosseteste and the Pastoral Care

does not suffer you any more to have power over me. I wrote to you in a spirit of love and humility so that you might correct your errors, but you, with your proud eye and your encumbered heart, spurned my words." With that he disappeared, quoting Isaias: "Woe to you that despise; your own moment will come." When, Matthew continues, the papal attendants, hearing a cry from Innocent, rushed in to his chamber, they found the Pope holding his side, trembling, and sweating. From that night onwards, Matthew assures us, Innocent was beset by sleepless nights, and when he died a year later it probably was from pleurisy that had set in after the blow from the pastoral staff.[92]

As a story, it does catch some of the implacable quality of Grosseteste, whom Matthew knew well. But it is highly unlikely. And since Matthew had gone to the trouble of including *Postquam regimini* in his "Additamenta," he could at least have acknowledged that far from spurning Grosseteste's words, Innocent had made a brave attempt to make amends to a formidable pastoral bishop.[93]

I

Appendix

Letter *128 Restored*

[This is not a critical edition of letter 128, but simply a working copy established from the text printed in Luard's note at pp. 432–433 of *Epp*. ("Robertus ... Intelleximus vos ... anno decimo.") and from his text of "Noverit" at pp. 432–437, with some small emendations from MS Bodley 42, fol. 283ʳ⁻ᵛ (late thirteenth century).]

Robertus, dei permissione Lincolniae episcopus, Cantuariensi archidiacono et magistro Innocentio domini papae scriptori, salutem et benedictionem. Intelleximus vos litteram domini papae recepisse in haec verba:

Dilectis filiis archidiacono Cantuariensi et magistro Innocentio scriptori nostro in Anglia commoranti, salutem et apostolicam benedictionem. Cum dilectus filius noster Guillelmus sancti Eustachii diaconus cardinalis dilecto filio Frederico de Lavania clerico, nepoti nostro, de speciali mandato nostro canonicatum Lincolniae cum plenitudine iuris canonice duxerit conferendum, ipsum per suum anulum corporaliter et praesentialiter investiens de eodem ut extunc canonicus Lincolniae existat et plenum nomen et ius canonici consequatur ibidem, ac praebendam, si qua vacaverit in ecclesia Lincolniae a tempore quo dudum litterae nostrae super receptione ac provisione facienda sibi in eadem ecclesia de praemissis venerabili fratri nostro episcopo Lincolniensi praesentatae fuerint, alioquin post vacaturam conferendam sibi donationi apostolicae reservaverit, decernendo irritum et inane si quid de praebenda huiusmodi a quoquam fuerit attentatum, necnon et in contradictores et rebelles excommunicationis sententiam nihilominus promulgando, prout in litteris eiusdem cardinalis exinde confectis plenius continetur: nos, ipsius Frederici devotis precibus inclinati, quod ab eodem cardinale super hoc factum est ratum et gratum habentes, illud auctoritate apostolica duximus confirmandum. Quocirca discretioni vestrae per apostolica scripta mandamus quatinus eundem Fredericum vel procuratorem suum eius nomine in corporalem possessionem praedictorum canonicatus et praebendae auctoritate nostra inducatis et defendatis inductum, contradictores per censuram ecclesiasticam appellatione postposita com-

Robert Grosseteste and the Pastoral Care

pescendo, non obstantibus aliquibus consuetudinibus vel statutis iuramentis vel confirmationibus sedis apostolicae seu quacunque alia firmitate roboratis, vel quod dictus Fredericus praesens non fuerit ad praestandum iuramentum de observandis consuetudinibus eiusdem ecclesiae consuetum, sive si episcopo praefato vel capitulo ipsius ecclesiae communiter vel singulatim seu aliis quibuscunque personis a dicta sede indultum existat quod ad receptionem vel provisionem alicuius compelli nequeant sive quod quivis alius in eorum ecclesia nemini providere valeat, vel quod interdici suspendi aut excommunicari non possit per litteras apostolicas sub quacunque forma verborum obtentas vel etiam obtinendas, etiam si totus tenor indulgentiarum huiusmodi de verbo ad verbum in iisdem litteris sit insertus, sive quibuslibet aliis indulgentiis quibuscunque personis dignitati vel loco sub quacunque forma verborum concessis a sede apostolica vel etiam concedendis per quas effectus huiusmodi provisionis posset impediri aliquatenus vel differri, cum volumus eas de certa scientia quantum ad provisionem factam et faciendam Frederico praedicto in ecclesia Lincolniensi viribus omino carere. Caeterum si aliqui praedicto Frederico vel procuratori suo super praemissis vel aliquo praemissorum aliquatenus duxerint opponendum, illos ex parte nostra citari curetis peremptorie ut infra duorum mensium spatium post citationem vestram personaliter compareant coram nobis, eidem Frederico super paremissis legitime responsuri, non obstantibus privilegiis sive quibuslibet indulgentiis personis regni Angliae generaliter vel cuivis alii personae dignitati vel loco specialiter a praedicta sede sub quacunque forma verborum concessis quod non possint ultra mare seu extra civitatem vel diocesim suum in iudicium evocari per litteras apostolicas sub quacunque forma verborum obtentas, quae privilegium et indulgentiae eisdem personis de certa scientia nullatenus volumus suffragari, et constitutione edita de duabus dietis in concilio generali non obstante. Diem autem citationis et formam nobis, vestris litteris tenorem praesentium continentibus, fideliter intimetis. Quod si non ambo his exequendis interesse poteritis alter vestrum nihilominus exequatur. Datum Perusiis vii kal. februarii pontificatus nostri anno decimo.

Noverit autem discretio vestra quod mandatis apostolicis affectione filiali omnino devote et reverenter obedio, his quoque quae mandatis apostolicis adversantur parentelam zelans honorem adversor et obsto: ad utrumque enim similiter et aequaliter teneor ex divino mandato. Apostolica enim mandata non sunt nec possunt esse alia quam apostolorum doctrinae et ipsius domini nostri Iesu Christi, apostolorum magistri et domini, cuius typum et personam maxime gerit in ecclesiastica hierarchia dominus papa, consona et conformia. Ait enim ipse dominus noster Iesus Christus, *Qui non est mecum, contra me est*. Contra ipsum autem nec est nec esse potest apostolicae sedis sanctitas divinissima. Non est igitur praedictae litterae tenor apostolicae sanctitati consonus sed absonus plurimum et discors, primo, quia de illius litterae et aliarum ei consimilium longe lateque dispersarum superaccumulato *Non obstante* non ex legis naturalis observandae necessitate inducto, scatet cataclysmus inconstantiae audaciae et procacitatis etiam inverecundae mentiendi et fallendi, diffidentiae cuiquam credendi vel fidem adhibendi, et ex his consequentium vitiorum quorum non est numerus christianae religionis puritatem et socialis conversationis hominum tranquillitatem commovens et perturbans. Praeterea, post peccatum Luciferi (quod idem erit in fine temporum ipsius filii perditionis Antichristi *quem interficiet dominus Iesus spiritu oris sui*) non est nec esse potest alterum genus peccati tam adversum et contrarium apostolorum doctrinae et evangelicae et ipsi domino Iesu Christo tam odibile detestabile et abominabile et humano generi tam pernecabile quam animas curae pastoralis officio et ministerio vivificandas et salvandas pastoralis officii et ministerii defraudatione mortificare et perdere. Quod peccatum evidentissimis scripturae sacrae testimoniis committere dinoscuntur qui in potestate curae pastoralis constituti de lacte et lana ovium Christi suis carnalibus et temporalibus desideriis et necessitatibus prospiciunt et pastoralis officii ministeria in aeternam Christi ovium salutem operandam debita non administrant; ipsa enim ministeriorum pastoralium non administratio est, scripturae testimonio, ovium occisio et perditio. Quod autem haec duo genera peccatorum, licet dispariter, sint pessima et omne alterum genus peccati inaestimabiliter superexcedentia, manifestum est ex hoc quod ipsa sunt duobus existentibus et dictis, licet dispariter et dissimiliter, optimis directe contraria. Pessimum enim est quod optimo est contrarium. Quantum autem est in dictis peccantibus unum peccaminum est ipsius deitatis superessentialiter et supernaturaliter optimae vilipensio, alterum vero deformitatis et deificationis ex divini radii

Robert Grosseteste and the Pastoral Care

gratifica participatione essentialiter et naturaliter optimae interemptio. Et quia sicut in bonis causa boni melior est suo causato, sic et in malis causa mali peior est suo causato, manifestissimum est quantum talium pessimorum interemptorum deiformitatis et deificationis in ovibus Christi in ecclesiam dei introductores ipsis pessimis interemptoribus sunt peiores et Lucifero et Antichristo proximiores; et in hac peioritate gradatim magis superexcellentes qui ex maiore et diviniore sibi divinitus potestate, in edificationem et non in destructionem tradita, magis tenentur ab ecclesia dei tales interemptores pessimos excludere et extirpare.

Non potest igitur sanctissima sedes apostolica cui a sancto sanctorum domino Iesu Christo tradita est omnimoda potestas, testante apostolo, *in aedificationem et non in destructionem*, aliquid vergens in huiusmodi peccatum domino Iesu Christo tam odibile, detestabile, abominabile et humano generi summe pernecabile vel mandare vel praecipere vel quoquo modo ad aliquid tale conari. Hoc enim esset evidenter suae sanctissimae potestatis et plenissimae vel defectio vel corruptio vel abusio et a throno gloriae Iesu Christi summa elongatio et in cathedra pestilentiae poenarum gehennalium duobus praedictis tenebrarum principibus proxima coassessio. Nec potest quis immaculata et sincera obedientia eidem sedi subditus et fidelis et a corpore Christi et eadem sancta sede per schisma non abscisus, huiusmodi mandatis vel praeceptis vel quibuscunque aliis conaminibus undecunque emanantibus, etiam si a supremo angelorum ordine eveniret, obtemperare, sed necesse habet totis viribus totum contradicere et rebellare.

Propter hoc, reverendi domini, ego ex debito obedientiae et fidelitatis quo teneor ut utrique parenti apostolicae sanctissimae sedi, et ex amore unionis in corpore Christi cum ea, his quae in praedicta littera continentur—et maxime quia in praetactum peccatum domino nostro Iesu Christo abominabilissimum et humano generi perniciosissimum evidentissime vergunt et apostolicae sedis sanctitati omnino adversantur et contrariantur catholicae unitati—fideliter et obedienter non obedio, contradico et rebello. Nec ob hoc potest inde vestra discretio quicquam durum contra me statuere, quia omnis mea in hac parte et dictio et actio nec contradictio est nec rebellio sed filialis divino mandato debita patri et matri honoratio. Breviter autem recolligens dico quod apostolicae sedis sanctitas non potest nisi quae in aedificationem sunt et non in destructionem. Haec enim est potestatis plenitudo omnia posse in aedificationem. Hae autem quas vocant provisiones non sunt in aedificationem sed in manifestissimam destructionem. Non igitur eas potest beata sedes apostolica. Etenim *caro et sanguis* quae regnum dei non possidebunt *eas revelavit* et non *Pater* domini nostri Iesu Christi *qui in caelis est.*

Notes

1. On Grosseteste in general, see F. S. Stevenson, *Robert Grosseteste: Bishop of Lincoln* (London, 1899); *Robert Grosseteste: Scholar and Bishop*, ed. D. A. Callus (Oxford, 1955) (henceforth Callus, *Grosseteste*); A. B. Emden, *A Biographical Register of the University of Oxford to A.D. 1500*, II (Oxford, 1958), 830–833. Grosseteste's letters, the main source of this paper, are edited in *Roberti Grosseteste episcopi quondam Lincolniensis Epistolae*, ed. H. R. Luard (Rolls Series, London, 1861) (henceforth *Epp.*). For a spurious letter in that collection (no. 130), see F. A. C. Mantello, "Letter CXXX of Bishop Robert Grosseteste: A Problem of Attribution," *Mediaeval Studies*, 36 (1974), 144–159.

2. D. A. Callus, "The Oxford Career of Robert Grosseteste," *Oxoniensia*, 10 (1945), 42–72. A newly discovered poem by a Brother Hubert, possibly one of the friars in the service of Grosseteste, is disappointing in its information on his early life; see R. W. Hunt, "Verses on the Life of Robert Grosseteste," *Medievalia et Humanistica*, n.s. 1 (1970), 241–251.

3. F. M. Powicke, "Robert Grosseteste, Bishop of Lincoln," *Bulletin of John Rylands Library*, 35 (1953), 486–487.

4. Canon 3 in *Conciliorum oecumenicorum decreta*, ed. J. Alberigo, etc. (Basle-Barcelona, 1962), p. 188; and in the Decretals of Gregory IX (henceforth *X*), 1. 6, 7.

5. *Councils and Synods with Other Documents Relating to the English Church*, Pt. 1 of Vol. II, *A.D. 1205–1313*, ed. F. M. Powicke and C. R. Cheney (Oxford, 1964), p. 112 (c. 19) (henceforth Powicke and Cheney, *Councils*).

6. D. A. Callus, "Robert Grosseteste as Scholar," in Callus, *Grosseteste*, pp. 10–11.

7. *Rotuli Hugonis de Welles episcopi Lincolniensis*, Canterbury and York Society, ed. W. P. W. Phillimore and F. N. Davis, II (London, 1907), 32, 235, 280–301, 308–321 (as archdeacon); *Rotuli Roberti Grosseteste episcopi Lincolniensis*, Lincoln Record Society, ed. F. N. Davis (Lincoln, 1914), pp. 390–391 (as rector of St. Margaret; and see n. 12 below).

8. The date of resignation is usually given as 1232, but the year 1231 is more likely. The letter to Juetta (*Epp.* 8, pp. 43–44) is after the feast of All Saints in an unspecified year and after his illness and resignation; that to Adam Marsh (*Epp.* 9, pp. 45–47) is also after these events and after Grosseteste had had a reply from Juetta (hence his reference in the Marsh letter to the reaction of his family). Since there is no record of any act of Grosseteste as archdeacon after mid-1231, the feast of All Saints in question is probably that of 1 November 1231.

9. Swayed, he says, by the opinion of people who held that it was lawful to hold at one and the same time a parish church and a prebend with a cure of souls, "nos . . . tenuimus aliquandiu simul huiusmodi praebendam et parochialem ecclesiam" (*Epp.* 74, p. 242). Presumably the "prebend with a cure of souls" is that of St. Margaret, Leicester, since he makes a clear distinction between that and his "parochial church" (Abbotsley).

10. *Epp.* 8, pp. 43–44.

11. *Epp.* 9, pp. 45–47.

12. Had Grosseteste retained the rectorship of St. Margaret, and therefore a *cura animarum*, his critics would hardly have had a case. Master John of Basingstoke was rector of St. Margaret by 1 April 1236, when Grosseteste, now bishop, gave an *inspeximus* of an agreement which he himself had negotiated while rector. There is nothing, however, to suggest just when that was, since the *inspeximus* refers to Grosseteste vaguely as "quondam rector" (*Rotuli Roberti Grosseteste*, pp. 390–391).

13. *The Registrum Antiquissimum of the Cathedral Church of Lincoln*, Vol. III

of the Lincoln Record Society, ed. C. W. Foster (Lincoln, 1935), 235–236 (12 November 1232).

14. *Ibid.*, Vol. II, ed. C. W. Foster (Lincoln, 1933), 70, 72.

15. Powicke, *Bulletin of John Rylands Library*, 35 (1953), 498, repeated in his introduction to Callus, *Grosseteste*, pp. xviii–xix.

16. *Epp.* 40, pp. 131–133. Jordan's Oxford sermon is edited in A. G. Little and D. L. Douie, "Three Sermons of Friar Jordan of Saxony, the Successor of St. Dominic, Preached in England, A.D. 1229," *English Historical Review*, 54 (1939), 1–13.

17. J. H. Srawley, "Grosseteste's Administration of the Diocese of Lincoln," in Callus, *Grosseteste*, pp. 146–177; W. A. Pantin, "Grosseteste's Relations with the Papacy and the Crown," *ibid.*, pp. 178–215.

18. *Epp.* 22, pp. 72–76; see also *Epp.* 50, pp. 146–147 and 107, pp. 317–318, both also edited in Powicke and Cheney, *Councils*, Pt. 1 of Vol. II, pp. 263–264, 479–480.

19. See the "Propositum" at Lyons in 1250 in S. Gieben, "Robert Grosseteste at the Papal Curia, Lyons 1250. Edition of the Documents," *Collectanea Franciscana*, 41 (1971), 375–377, and in Powicke and Cheney, *Councils*, Pt. 1 of Vol. II, p. 264 (first half only of "Propositum" as edited by Gieben).

20. See M. Gibbs and J. Lang, *Bishops and Reform, 1215–1272* (Oxford, 1934); C. R. Cheney, *English Synodalia of the Thirteenth Century* (2nd ed., Oxford, 1968), and the many synodal statutes edited in Powicke and Cheney, *Councils*.

21. For these English and Continental manuals in general, see P. Michaud-Quantin, *Sommes de casuistique et manuels de confession au moyen âge* (Louvain, 1962); L. E. Boyle, "The *Summa confessorum* of John of Freiburg," *St. Thomas Aquinas Commemorative Studies* (Toronto, 1974), II, 245–268.

22. S. Harrison Thomson, *The Writings of Robert Grosseteste, Bishop of Lincoln, 1235–1253* (Cambridge, 1940), pp. 121–147. See also S. Gieben, "Robert Grosseteste on Preaching, with the Edition of the Sermon 'Ex rerum initiatarum,' " *Collectanea Franciscana*, 37 (1967), 100–141; "Bibliographia universa Roberti Grosseteste," *ibid.*, 39 (1969), 362–418.

23. The *Speculum confessionis* was written for a friend, a monk perhaps: "Ecce dilectissime speculum confessionis . . . ut simpliciores fratres illud legendo . . . festinent se sanciare poenitentiae remedio" (Bodleian Library, Oxford, MS Laud misc. 527, fol. 262ᵛ), and it ends in another manuscript (British Library, MS Harley 5441, fol. 147ᵛ): "Explicit tractatus de confessione secundum magistrum Robertum Lincoln. episcopum in quo non solum saecularibus sed etiam religiosis et perfectis patet speculum verae confessionis."

24. See M. Deanesley, *The Lollard Bible* (Cambridge, 1920), pp. 141, 442; C. F. Bühler, "A Lollard Tract: On Translating the Bible into English," *Medium Aevum*, 7 (1938), 167–183, particularly 181–182.

25. British Library, MS Royal 7 F II, fols. 78ᵛ–83ᵛ.

26. There is a critical edition of these constitutions in Powicke and Cheney, *Councils*, Pt. 1 of Vol. II, pp. 265–278.

27. The date cited here for the constitutions is that of Professor Cheney in Powicke and Cheney, *Councils*, Pt. 1 of Vol. II, p. 266. The *terminus ante quem* is suggested by the fact that Walter of St. Edmund, Abbot of Peterborough and a friend of Grosseteste (see *Epp.* 57, pp. 173–178), was in possession of a "Templum Domini cum arte confessionaria" before his death in 1246; see M. R. James, "Lists of Manuscripts Formerly in Peterborough Abbey Library," *Supplement to the Bibliographical Society's Transactions*, 5 (1926), 22.

28. Bodleian Library, Oxford, MS Rawlinson A 384, fols. 98ʳ–106ᵛ. To the sixty-five MSS listed by Thomson, *Writings*, pp. 138–140, the following may be added: Kues, Hospital 233; London, British Library: Arundel 507, Cotton Vespasian D. V., Egerton 665, Harley 209; Longleat House; Metz, Bibl. de la Ville, 521; Ox-

Robert Grosseteste and the Pastoral Care

ford, Bodl. Library: Bodley 440, Tanner 110; Balliol College 228, Magdalen College 109, St. John's College 93; Paris: Bibliothèque Nationale Lat. 543; Wisbech Town Library 5.

29. For some other contemporary schemata of this kind, see A. Dondaine, "La Somme de Simon de Hinton," *Recherches de théologie ancienne et médiévale*, 9 (1937), 5–22, 205–218.

30. A common rubric of this sermon is "Quomodo examinandus est poenitens cum venerit ad confessionem," as in British Library MS 7 F II, fol. 83v. The sermon, now edited by Siegfried Wenzel, "Robert Grosseteste's Treatise on Confession, 'Deus est,'" *Franciscan Studies*, 30 (1970), 218–293, may possibly be the "Ars confessionaria" which Walter of St. Edmund owned (see n. 27).

31. Thomson, *Writings*, p. 126, gives the extant MSS of this tract, to which National Library of Scotland MS 18. 3. 6, fols. 132r–134r ("Diversitates poenitentiae secundum magistrum Robertum Grosseste") may be added. It occurs in this MS (which formerly belonged to the Advocates' Library) with the *Oculus sacerdotis* of William of Pagula (ca. 1320–26). A note on the flyleaf in a late hand states mistakenly, "In hoc volumine continentur opera magistri Roberti Grossete . . . scripta in 1305, primum quod inscribitur Oculus sacerdotum, secundum Diversitates."

32. For example, the verses "Haec sunt praecipue sacerdotibus insinuenda" (Bodleian Library, MS Rawl. A 384, fol. 99r; cf. 101r) are to be found in the opening section of the "Qui bene praesunt" of Richard Wethersett (e.g., British Library, MS Royal 4 B VIII, fol. 222r). The dependence on Flamborough is not explicit. It was first noted by an anonymous *Speculum iuniorum* of about 1250: "Casus in quibus committitur simonia quos ponit magister Robertus Lincoln. in Templo. Et extractae sunt de poenitentiali magistri Roberti de Flaveny qui incipit sic: Res grandis" (Bodleian Library, MS Bodley 655, fol. 20v). The borrowings are most obvious in the sections on simony (Rawl. A 384, fol. 103v) and matrimony (fol. 104v). On Robert of Flamborough ("de Flaveny") see J. J. F. Firth, *Robert of Flamborough: Liber Poenitentialis* (Toronto, 1971).

33. See L. E. Boyle, "Three English Pastoral Summae and a 'Magister Galienus,'" *Studia Gratiana*, 11 (1967: *Collectanea S. Kuttner I*), 135–144.

34. *Epp.* 37, p. 128 (ca. 1237): "Ex fido relatu mores vestros et opera sapientialia referentium."

35. The *Summa de casibus* was written ca. 1224 and was revised some ten years later; see S. Kuttner, "Zur Entstehungsgeschichte der *Summa de casibus poenitentiae* des hl. Raymund von Pennafort," *Zeitschrift der Savigny-Stiftung für Rechtsgeschichte*, kan. Abt., 83 (1953), 419–448.

36. On these translations, see D. A. Callus, "The Date of Grosseteste's Translations and Commentaries on Pseudo-Dionysius and the Nichomachean Ethics," *Recherches de théologie ancienne et médiévale*, 14 (1947), 186–210; Thomson, *Writings*, pp. 42–71; K. Hill, "Robert Grosseteste and His Work of Greek Translation," in *The Orthodox Churches and the West*, ed. Derek Baker, Studies in Church History, 13 (London, 1976), 213–222.

37. *Epp.* 112, pp. 329–333 (November, 1244).

38. See *Epp.* 14, pp. 59–60; 15, p. 61; 16, pp. 62–63; 20, pp. 69–71; 31, pp. 117–118; 58, pp. 179–181; 100, pp. 304–305.

39. *Epp.* 13, pp. 57–59 (April–June, 1235, while still bishop-elect).

40. *Epp.* 51, pp. 147–151 (1237?).

41. *Epp.* 46, pp. 138–40 (1237?). On Richard, see Emden, *A Biographical Register of the University of Oxford*, I (Oxford, 1957), 490–491.

42. *Epp.* 11, pp. 50–54 (27 March—3 June 1235).

43. *Epp.* 127, pp. 357–431. The work of E. B. King, *Robert Grosseteste and the*

Pastoral Office (Ann Arbor, Michigan, 1970), shows how all the administrative acts of Grosseteste were dictated by his teaching on the pastoral care, which King finds in its basic form in this letter to the Dean and Chapter; see also *Dissertation Abstracts*, 30A (1969–70), 3384–85.

44. *Epp.* 17, pp. 63–65.

45. *Epp.* 19, pp. 68–69 (1236?). On Blund, see Emden, *op. cit.*, n. 41 above, I, 206, and D. A. Callus and R. W. Hunt, *Iohannes Blund: Tractatus de Anima* (Oxford, 1970).

46. *Epp.* 72, pp. 203–204 (1239?).

47. *Epp.* 18, pp. 65–67 (1235?).

48. *Epp.* 49, pp. 144–148. On Cardinal Otto, see A. Paravicini-Bagliani, *Cardinali de Curia e "Familiae" Cardinalizie dal 1227 al 1254* (Padua, 1972), pp. 76–97.

49. *Epp.* 52, pp. 151–154 (1238?).

50. *Epp.* 74, pp. 241–243 (1241?). On Atto, see Paravicini-Bagliani, *op. cit.*, pp. 93–94. Another chaplain in Otto's suite, the young Ottobono Fieschi (later cardinal, legate to England, and Pope Hadrian V), was more successful. He was granted the living of Twywell by Grosseteste (*Rotuli R. Grosseteste*, p. 182; Paravicini-Bagliani, *op. cit.*, p. 359).

51. *Epp.* 27, pp. 105–108 (1236).

52. *Epp.* 72*, pp. 205–234 (1236). On Grosseteste's relations with St. Edmund, see C. H. Lawrence, *St. Edmund of Abingdon: A Study in Hagiography and History* (Oxford, 1960), p. 158, and n. 1.

53. *Epp.* 83, pp. 264–266 (1240); Ovid, *Remedium amoris*, 91.

54. *Epp.* 60, pp. 182–185 (1238).

55. *Epp.* 61, pp. 185–188 (1238); Horace, *Ars poetica*, 25–26.

56. *Epp.* 30, pp. 116–117 (1236).

57. *Epp.* 101, pp. 306–308 (1242?).

58. *Epp.* 102, pp. 308–309 (1243).

59. *Epp.* 124, pp. 348–351 (1245).

60. *Epp.* 126, pp. 353–356 (1245). Grosseteste had examined Passelewe in theology in 1244; see M. Paris, *Chronica Majora*, ed. H. R. Luard, IV (London, 1877), 401. On the Passelewe family, see F. M. Powicke, *The Thirteenth Century, 1216–1307* (Oxford, 1953), pp. 51, 52, 58, and, on the question of the clergy acting as judges, J. R. H. Moorman, *Church Life in England in the Thirteenth Century* (Cambridge, 1946), pp. 150–151.

61. The best discussion of this episode is Pantin, "Grosseteste at Lyons, 1250," in Callus, *Grosseteste*, pp. 209–215. The edition of the Lyons documents in E. Brown, *Fasciculus rerum expetendarum et fugiendarum* (London, 1690), is now superseded by S. Gieben, "Robert Grosseteste at the Papal Curia, Lyons 1250: Edition of the Documents," *Collectanea Franciscana*, 41 (1971), 340–393. See also "Grosseteste at the Papal Curia," in Harrison Thomson, *Writings*, pp. 141–147.

62. Gieben, *loc. cit.*, p. 355. The whole memorandum is in Gieben at pp. 350–370.

63. *Epp.* 128, pp. 432–437; *M. Parisiensis Chronica Majora*, ed. H. R. Luard, V. (London, 1880), 389–392; *Annales Monastici*, ed. H. R. Luard, I (London, 1864), 311–313; *Monumenta Franciscana*, ed. J. S. Brewer (London, 1858), pp. 382–385. For manuscripts of the letter, see Harrison Thomson, *Writings*, pp. 143, 193–194, 212–213. A copy of the letter in the Red Book of the Exchequer (Public Record Office, London, MS E. 164/2, fols. 196^v–197^r) escaped Thomson's list. See further n. 70 below.

64. F. M. Powicke, *King Henry III and the Lord Edward* (Oxford, 1947), I, 284–287, and introduction to Callus, *Grosseteste*, pp. xxii–xxiv; W. A. Pantin in Callus, *Grosseteste*, pp. 180–181, 188–195.

Robert Grosseteste and the Pastoral Care

65. B. Tierney, "Grosseteste and the Theory of Papal Sovereignty," *Journal of Ecclesiastical History*, 6 (1955), 1–17, esp. 10.

66. In his edition of the Burton Annals in *Annales Monastici*, Luard identified the archdeacon as Hugh de Mortuomari and in this has been followed by many authors. In fact the archdeacon was Stephen de Montival, who held that office at Canterbury from ca. 1248 to 1269; see J. Le Neve, *Fasti Ecclesiae Anglicanae, II: Monastic Cathedrals*, ed. D. E. Greenway (London, 1971), p. 15. Master Innocenzo, the papal scriptor, was in England from at least June, 1249, and was given a prebend in York on 8 March 1252: P. Herde, *Beiträge zum päpstlichen Kanzlei- und Urkundenwesen im 13. Jahrhundert* (Kallmünz, 1961), p. 31.

67. See Herde, *op. cit.*, p. 29. Federico does not occur as a member of any of the households of the cardinals of the period in Paravicini-Bagliani, *op. cit.*, n. 48 above, who has an interesting account of Cardinal Guglielmo (cardinal of Sant'Eustachio in Rome, 1244–56) and his "famiglia" at pp. 329–340.

68. Harrison Thomson, *Writings*, p. 212, and see p. 143 (2).

69. This letter is not to be found in the registers of Innocent's letters nor in any other collection of Innocent's correspondence, for example, G. Abate, "Lettere *secretae* d'Innocenzo IV e altri documenti in una raccolta inedita del sec. XIII—Regesto," *Miscellanea Franciscana*, 55 (1955), 317–373.

70. MSS: London, British Library, Vesp. A. XIII, fols. 90^r–92^v; Oxford, Bodleian Library, Bodley 42, fol. 283^{r-v}, and Merton College 82, fols. 90^v–100^v, are all from the second half of the thirteenth century. Other MSS which give the full letter are Cambridge: University Library, Ii. i. 19, fols. 208^r–209^v, Corpus Christi College 156, fols. 121^r–122^r, and 385, pp. 84–87 (but with only *incipit* of mandate); London, British Library: Lansdowne 458, fols. 147^v–148^r, Royal 6 E V, fol. 128^{r-v}, 7 E II, fols. 385^r–386^v, 7 F II, fols. 108^r–110^r; Oxford, Bodleian Library: Bodley 52, fols. 137^r–138^v, 312, fol. 117^{r-v}. In some of these MSS Grosseteste's rehearsal of Innocent's letter is separated from his own continuation, "Noverit," by a space or by some rubric such as "Responsum domini Lincolniensis," creating the impression that two letters were in question. E. Brown in his *Fasciculus* of 1690 (II, 399–401; see n. 61 above) therefore printed the letter as two letters from a now-destroyed Cotton MS. Luard followed suit in 1861, basing his work on Cambridge University Library MS Ii. i. 18 (a defective MS, in fact; see the angry note in a fourteenth-century hand at fol. 208^v [col. a]: "Pro amore Ihesu, quaere copiam aliam istius litterae m. Roberti Grostest doctoris sacrae theologiae, quia haec littera vitiose est scripta"), and on Bodley 312 (a copy corrected by Thomas Gascoigne about 1440 "from Grosseteste's own autographs in the library of the Franciscans at Oxford": *Epp.* p. xcvi). Harrison Thomson, following too readily in the steps of Brown and Luard, further complicated things by giving a list of MSS for "Intelleximus" at p. 143 and another for "Noverit discretio" at pp. 193–194; yet although all the "Intelleximus" MSS at p. 143 of *Writings* also carry "Noverit," five of these are not noted as such at pp. 193–194. Adding to the muddle, Thomson did not note that almost *all* the MSS of his "Noverit" also have the text of "Intelleximus." On Gascoigne and Grosseteste, see S. Gieben, "Thomas Gascoigne and Robert Grosseteste: Historical and Critical Notes," *Vivarium*, 8 (1970), 56–67.

71. *Annales Monastici*, I, 311–313, 437–438. On the character of the Burton Annals, see A. Gransden, *Historical Writing in England c. 550 to c. 1307* (London, 1974), pp. 408–410.

72. *Ibid.*, p. 311.

73. *Epp.* 52, p. 151.

74. G. Barraclough, *Papal Provisions* (Oxford, 1935), pp. 137–138.

75. "Dicunt quidam quod conditione ex hac decretali potest quilibet pro quo

scribuntur monitoriae agere et consequi quod in hac decretali continetur, sed certe hoc non placet nobis, quia iam frustra ecclesia daret executores, et licet quandoque papa det monitorias non tamen dat executorias" (*Commentaria super libros quinque decretalium*, Frankfurt, 1570). It may be noted in Innocent's registers that he appears to have observed due form in practice. See, for example, a mandate to provisors to provide Thedisio da Lavagna (another relative, presumably), papal scriptor, because a previous letter of provision to the Archbishop of Armagh had been ignored: *Pontificia Hibernica*, ed. M. P. Sheehy, II (Dublin, 1965), 209–210, no. 386 (21 July 1254).

76. Ed. Gieben, *loc. cit.* (n. 61 above), p. 367, no. 37.

77. Vatican Archives, Reg. Vat. 19, fol. 69^v, no. 374; calendared in *Calendar of Entries in the Papal Registers Relating to Great Britain and Ireland: Papal Letters*, I, ed. W. H. Bliss (London, 1893), 178.

78. *Chronica Majora*, V, 403. As Richard Vaughan, *Matthew Paris* (Cambridge, 1958), p. 149, notes, Matthew often put words into the mouth of Grosseteste in order to air his own grievances. On the other hand, Matthew may have learned a lot about Grosseteste's last days and ramblings from the Dominican physician John of St. Giles, who attended Grosseteste in his last illness (*Chronica Majora*, V, 400).

79. In 1241 John Mansel, a clerk of the King, had obtained a papal provision, as a result of which Henry nominated him to the prebend of Thame. When it was pointed out that the papal letters were defective inasmuch as they made no mention of Grosseteste's privilege ("Sed in hujus Papalis mandati tenore, quo utitur praedictus Johannes, . . . nulla fit dicti mentio privilegii"), the King agreed to a compromise with Grosseteste, who, in fact, found another benefice for Mansel (M. Paris, *Chronica Majora*, IV, 152–153).

80. On 27 April 1245 Grosseteste was granted an indult by Innocent that he could not be compelled to bestow benefices, etc. without a special papal mandate which made full mention of this privilege:

> Paci et tranquillitati tuae paterna volentes in posterum sollicitudine providere, auctoritate tibi praesentium indulgemus ut ad receptionem vel provisionem alicuius in pensionibus praebendis seu aliis ecclesiasticis beneficiis auctoritate sedis apostolicae vel legatorum ipsius minime compelli valeas absque speciali mandato sedis eiusdem faciente plenam de hac indulgentia mentionem. . . (Vatican Archives, Reg. Vat. 21, fol. 179^v, no. 841, calendared in *Papal Letters*, I, 216).

This indult, of course, was not quite as forceful as that granted by Gregory IX. On 13 June 1247 another indult was granted, this time to the effect that Grosseteste could not be summoned to a distance of more than one day's journey from his diocese, which, reputedly, was five days' journey in length, unless special mention were made of this privilege in the apostolic letters that summoned him:

> . . . Tuis igitur supplicationibus inclinati, auctoritate tibi praesentium indulgemus ut ultra unam dietam extra tuam diocesim, quae in longitudine per quinque dietas durare dicitur, nequeatis per litteras apostolicas conveniri, nisi litterae ipsae plenam fecerint de hac indulgentia mentionem. . . (Vatican Archives, *ibid.*, fol. 404^v, no. 833; *Papal Letters*, I, 234).

The last part of Innocent's mandate of 1253 ignored this indult also: "non obstantibus privilegiis, . . . quod non possint ultra mare seu extra civitatem vel diocesim suam in judicium evocari per litteras apostolicas sub quacunque forma verborum obtentas. . . ."

81. M. Paris, *Chronica Majora*, V, 403.

Robert Grosseteste and the Pastoral Care

82. *Postquam regimini* is to be found in the Burton Annals (*Annales Monastici*, I, 314–317) and in the "Liber Additamentorum" of Matthew Paris in British Library MS Nero D. 1, fol. 118ʳ⁻ᵛ, from which it has been printed by Luard in his edition of the *Chronica Majora*, VI (London, 1882), 260–264. It is also printed in the Turin edition of the *Bullarium Romanum* (Turin, 1857–85), III, 217, and in the *Epistolae saeculi XIII e regestis Pontificum Romanorum*, ed. G. H. Pertz and C. Rodenberg, III (Berlin, 1894), 200–202, of the *Monumenta Germaniae Historica*. There is a copy of the encyclical in the registers of Innocent IV in the Vatican Archives, Reg. Vat. 23, fol. 30ʳ⁻ᵛ. The text quoted here is that of the registered copy.

83. *Chronica Majora*, VI, 260: "Literae Papales aliquantulum mitigatoriae." Matthew's text of *Postquam regimini* (here, pp. 260–264) is that addressed to his own monastery of St. Albans.

84. A. L. Smith, *Church and State in the Middle Ages* (Oxford, 1913), p. 130.

85. F. M. Powicke, *King Henry III and the Lord Edward* (Oxford, 1947), I, 281. However, H. K. Mann, *Lives of the Popes*, XIV (London, 1923), 262–265, notes the "tearing up" of papal letters.

86. *Annales Monastici*, I, 314. Stevenson's *Life*, p. 317, notes the Burton annalist's remark and accepts the connection.

87. See Barraclough, *Papal Provisions*, pp. 10–13; C. H. Lawrence, "The Thirteenth Century," in *The English Church and the Papacy*, ed. C. H. Lawrence (London, 1965), pp. 119–156; and texts in Powicke and Cheney, *Councils*, Pt. 1 of Vol. II, pp. 392–401.

88. *Chronica Majora*, V, 393. Grosseteste had corresponded many times with Cardinal Gil de Torres; see *Epp.* 36, 45, 46, 67, pp. 125–128 (1236?), 137–138 (1237?), 138–139 (1237?), 196 (1239?). Presumably the two had met at Lyons in 1250.

89. Text in Gieben, *loc. cit.*, n. 61 above, pp. 380–385.

90. Pantin in Callus, *Grosseteste*, p. 183 (and see pp. 183–188).

91. Vatican Archives, Reg. Vat. 22, fol. 272ʳ⁻ᵛ, no. 696, calendared in *Papal Letters*, I, 286 (but inaccurately). Innocent's letter is a reply to a request for alleviation of provisions sent by the English bishops. He apologizes for overburdening them, saying, though not as strongly as in *Postquam regimini*, that owing to the malice of the times and the importuning of many, he has been forced, sometimes unwillingly and at other times barely willingly, to give out provisions.

92. *Chronica Majora*, V, 460, 429–431, 470.

93. It is not clear at present what impact *Postquam regimini* had in England or on the Church at large. It does not appear among the decretals in collections of Innocent's legislation as noted by P. J. Kessler, "Untersuchungen über die Novellen-Gesetzgebung Papst Innozenz' IV.," *Zeitschrift der Savigny-Stiftung für Rechtsgeschichte*, kan. Abt., 31 (1942), 142–320; 32 (1943), 300–383; 33 (1944), 56–128; and "Wiener Novellen. Supplementum Novellisticum," *Studia Gratiana*, 12 (1967: *Collectanea S. Kuttner II*), 91–110, nor in M. Bertram, "Aus kanonistischen Handschriften der Periods 1234 bis 1298," *Proceedings of the Fourth International Congress of Medieval Canon Law, Toronto 1972* (Vatican City, 1976), pp. 27–44. Possibly *Postquam regimini* was included in an encyclical letter of Alexander IV, Innocent's successor, on 9 April 1255, revoking certain general letters of Innocent on benefices: see *Epistolae saeculi XIII a regestis Pontificum Romanorum selectae*, ed. G. M. Pertz and C. Rodenburg, III (Berlin, 1894), 351–352 (n. 392).

II

THE QUODLIBETS OF ST. THOMAS AND
PASTORAL CARE

A S THE NAME SUGGESTS, the *Quodlibet* or *Quaestio de quolibet* was an open, " free for all," debate in which the questions discussed were not, as in the *Quaestio disputata*, announced and specified beforehand, but were put at random from the floor on the day of the debate.[1]

The procedure of the medieval quodlibetal disputation was first established by P. Glorieux in his pioneer work, *La littérature quodlibétique*, in 1925, and his findings were later refined in articles over the next forty-five years, as well as in his second volume on *La Littérature quodlibétique* in 1935.[2] According to Glorieux, this type of unprepared public discussion first came to be used at Paris in the Mendicants' schools, and probably during the student strike of 1229-1231. From Paris it later spread to Oxford, Toulouse, Cologne, and the Roman curia. Altogether some 356 Quodlibets are extant from the Paris schools, and some Paris and Oxford masters, e. g., Henry of Ghent, Geoffrey of Fontaines, and Roger Marston, became so enamoured of the form that they made the Quodlibet their chief means of literary expression.[3]

---

[1] " de quolibet ad voluntatem cuiuslibet," as the General of the Dominicans, Humbert de Romanis, put it in his *Instructiones de officiis ordinis*, c. 12, ed. J. J. Berthier, *Beati Humberti de Romanis Opera de Vita Regulari*, II (Rome, 1889), p. 260.

[2] P. Glorieux, *La littérature quodlibétique de 1260 à 1320*. I (Kain, 1925), pp. 11-95, II (Paris, 1935), pp. 9-50 " Le Quodlibet et ses procédés rédactionnels," in *Divus Thomas* (Piacenza) 42 (1939), 61-93; " Où en est la question du Quodlibet? ", in *Revue du moyen âge latin* 2 (1946), 405-414.

[3] P. Glorieux, " L'enseignement au moyen âge. Techniques et méthodes en usage à la Faculté de Théologie de Paris au XIIIe siècle," in *Archives d'histoire doctrinale et littéraire du moyen âge* 43 (1968), 65-186 at pp. 128-134. Quodlibets were not confined to university circles but were common where the various orders of friars had schools and at chapters of these orders: see L. Meier, " Les disputes quodlibétiques en dehors des universités," in *Revue d'histoire ecclésiastique* 53 (1958) 401-442.

Like the more formal *Quaestio disputata*, the Quodlibet was held under the direction of a regent-master of the University, after whom the Quodlibet was named ("Quodlibet Petri," "Quodlibet Thomae," etc.). It was held twice a year, in Advent before Christmas and in Lent towards Easter, and seems to have been designed to test both the bachelors who were preparing for the degree of master and the regent-masters themselves. That the Quodlibet was a rough test there can be no doubt, for only an exceptional bachelor would be able to field without flinching a series of unpredictable questions from an audience composed of masters, students, and visitors.[4]

Some modern authors, however, give the impression that the Quodlibet was first and foremost a test of the regent-master, and that it was such a formidable test that "many a master refused to risk himself at it, or felt satisfied when he had done so once in his career."[5] There is possibly some exaggeration here. For one thing, a Quodlibet involved two really distinct sessions, a "Disputatio generalis de quolibet" and a "Determinatio de quolibet." In the General Disputation the master's role was hardly more than that of referee, immediate answers to questions from the floor being left to the *Responsalis*, that is, to the bachelor who was being put through his paces in public. If the regent-master entered at all into the discussion, it was probably only to stress a point here or make more explicit a point there, in the replies of the *Responsalis*. Sometimes, indeed, the master might throw in a question himself, as Robert Holcot certainly did in the early part of the 14th century: "In disputatione generali de quolibet proponebantur a sociis decem questiones praeter duas quas proposui ego ipse."[6]

From the regent-master's point of view the second stage of

---

[4] For some examples, with names, of those who were bachelors or who submitted objections at Quodlibets at Oxford, see A. G. Little and F. Pelster, *Oxford Theology and Theologians, c. A.D. 1282-1302* (Oxford, 1934), pp. 335-362.

[5] M.-D. Chenu, *Toward understanding St. Thomas*, trans. A. M. Landry and W. D. Hughes (New York, 1964), p. 92.

[6] Oxford, Balliol College, MS. 246, f. 257v. On the Quodlibets of Holcot see Glorieux, *La littérature quodlibétique* (henceforward cited as Glorieux, *Littérature*, I or II), II, pp. 258-261.

the Quodlibet, the "Determinatio de quolibet," was much more important. For if the purpose of the General Disputation seems to have been to expose a bachelor or bachelors to random questions from the audience, the scope of the Determination was to demonstrate to the bachelors and the master's immediate students how best to handle these questions. What is more, the Determination did not take place on the same day as the General Disputation but rather on the day following or on the next teaching day, so the master had a chance in the meantime to ponder the questions and to reduce them to some sort of logical order. As James of Viterbo put it at a Determination in 1293-1295, "In disputatione de quolibet *praehabita* quaesita sunt in universo viginti duo, que ut enumerentur *non ordine quo fuerint proposita* sed secundum ordinem alicuius connexionis . . . procedendum est."[7] In a word, the regent-master was not expected to provide an exhaustive answer off the cuff to the questions proposed at the General Disputation. Rather, the General Disputation was an occasion on which the master was presented through his bachelor or bachelors with a series of questions which he had to "determine" or answer definitively at a Determination at a later date.[8]

Glorieux and others are inclined to think that this second or "determining" session of the Quodlibet was not as open to the general public as the first or General Disputation session and that the Determination took place "in the quiet of the classroom" with only the master's own students present. This seems a little odd, since it was only at the second session that the master delivered his measured reply to the questions to which he had given only the sketchiest of responses (or no

---

[7] Glorieux, *Littérature*, I, p. 216.

[8] See the preface of Nicholas de Vaux-Cernay to his Quodlibet (c. 1324) in S. Axters, "Le maître cistercien Nicholas de Vaux-Cernay et son Quodlibet," in *New Scholasticism* 12 (1938), 242-253 at pp. 244-245: "Haec quaestiones *propositae fuerunt* die lunae tertiae septimanae adventus domini *coram* magistro Nicholao in scholis sancti Bernardi Parisius, *qua die* dictus magister de quolibet *disputavit*. Et dictas quaestiones prout in isto libello recitentur *determinavit die sabbati insequenti*."

response at all) on the day of the General Disputation. Since Quodlibets were held only twice a year, and the Determination followed hard on the General Disputation, it seems reasonable to suppose that the audience of the first session made it a point to be present at the second session in order to hear the magisterial replies to the questions posed at the first. That this indeed was the case seems clear from a 14th-century story about Albert the Great. As the story has it, at a " generalis disputatio de quolibet " in the presence of a " maxima comitiva magistrorum et scolarium " Albert was at such a loss for a ready and convincing reply to three questions about angels put to him by the devil in the guise of a scholar that he spent the whole night awake trying to find an answer (which he did eventually, but by divine inspiration) before the Determination on the next day. What is important is that the story states that it was the same audience that turned up next day for the Determination: " *omnes* cras revertuntur . . . Et totum in crastino *coram omnibus* refert et dicit in scolis." [9]

Most of our unpublished or published Quodlibets record the proceedings of the Determination, not those of the first stage of the Quodlibet. Hence the Quodlibets as we know them do not really represent the heat of the debate that followed on the questions thrown at the bachelors by the audience but rather the considered reply of the master after he had had time to sort the questions out, to consult some sources, and to marshal his arguments. However, what we find in the Quodlibets of St. Thomas and others is not exactly the Determination as such but a version which was reworked and refined for publication. After the " Disputatio generalis " and the " Determinatio " there came the " Ordinatio," as may be seen in Quodl. III, q. 5, a. 4 of St. Thomas, where there is the cross-reference, " sicut supra dictum est," to the first article of the same *quaestio*.

[9] James of Aqui, *Chronicon imaginis mundi*, cited by P. Mandonnet, " Thomas d'Aquin, Créateur de la dispute quodlibétique," in *Revue des sciences philosophiques et théologiques* 16 (1927), 9 n. 1. (= RSPT henceforward).

236

Some Quodlibets, of course, survive in an unpolished state. A good case is that of Quodlibet III of the Dominican Bernard of Trilia, who died in 1292. According to Bernard Gui some twenty or thirty years later, this Quodlibet was in such a jumbled state on Bernard's death that his executors were quite confused: "Sed quia illa [quodlibet] *nondum* quando obiit *ordinaverat* ad votum suum ad plenum, et quaedam quaestiones particulares et sexterni dispersi manebant, illi qui nimis praeoccupaverunt pro magna parte confuderunt et truncaverunt." [10] Quodlibet XII of St. Thomas, too, has an unfinished look about it when compared with his other Quodlibets and clearly had not had the benefit of "Ordinatio" before his death in 1274. Some questions (e. g., 4, 6, 8-11, 21-24) entirely lack objections and replies, containing only the corpus ("Respondeo dicendum"); others (e. g., 2) carry nothing more than drafts of replies to objections. Perhaps the truth is that what we now possess of Quodlibet XII of St. Thomas is not, as has been suggested, a student's "Reportatio" of, or St. Thomas's own notes towards, the Determination,[11] but rather, for the most part, the text of the Determination precisely as it was held in 1270 or 1272 and before he had had time to prepare more than a few questions for eventual publication. If this is so, then it may also be true that a Determination did not consist in much more than the master's main reply ("Respondeo dicendum") to the questions raised at the General Disputation and that the replies to the objections were not drawn up until the "Ordinatio" stage of the Quodlibet.

*   *   *   *   *

The Quodlibets of St. Thomas, of course, present some special problems of their own. Until Denifle discovered the dates of

---

[10] J. Quétif and J. Echard, *Scriptores ordinis praedicatorum,* I (Paris, 1719), p. 432.

[11] See J. Destrez. "Les disputes quodlibétiques de saint Thomas d'après la tradition manuscrite," in *Mélanges Thomistes* (Kain, 1923) 61-66; P. Pelster. "Wann ist das Zwölfte Quodlibet des hl. Thomas von Aquin entstanden?," in *Gregorianum* 5 (1924), 278-286; P. Glorieux, "Le Quodlibetum XII de saint Thomas," in *RSPT* 14 (1925), 20-46.

two of the Quodlibets (III, V) in 1907,[12] there was very little interest in the Quodlibets as literary productions or as part of the Thomistic corpus. Denifle's discovery enabled Mandonnet in 1910 to establish for the first time ever a chronology of Quodlibets I-VI (1269-1272).[13] Mandonnet, however, on the authority of the 14th-century English Dominican, Nicholas Trivet, continued to assign Quodlibets VII-XI to the " Italian period " of the teaching career of St. Thomas, dating them vaguely between 1264 and 1268.[14] In this he was followed by Destrez (1923) in his catalogue of the manuscripts of the Quodlibets and by Synave (1924) and Glorieux (1925).

It was not until 1926 that Mandonnet turned his full attention to Quodlibets VII-XI, proving beyond all doubt (and to the confusion of Synave and Glorieux, who had just published an elaborate ' Italian ' chronology) that they belonged to the first teaching period of St. Thomas at Paris (1256-1259).[15] Since then his conclusions about certain individual Quodlibets within this group have been challenged or refined by scholars such as Synave, Glorieux, and Isaac. For what it is worth, the following schema attempts to summarize the twists and turns of chronological research on the Quodlibets of St. Thomas from 1910, when Mandonnet published the revised edition of his *Siger de Brabant,* to the present day, here represented by Marc's introduction to an edition of the *Summa contra Gentiles* (1967) and by the most recent biography of St. Thomas, that of Weisheipl (1974). The schema (in which C stands for

---

[12] H.-S. Denifle, " Die Statuten der Juristen-Universität Bologna, I," in *Archiv für Literatur und Kirchengeschichte des Mittelalters* 3 (1907), 196-347, at p. 320.

[13] P. Mandonnet, *Siger de Brabant et l'averroïsme latin au 13e siècle,* second ed., I (Paris, 1911), pp. 85-87.

[14] P. Mandonnet, *Les écrits authentiques de saint Thomas d'Aquin,* second ed. (Fribourg, 1910), p. xvi; P. Mandonnet and J. Destrez, *Bibliographie Thomiste* (Paris, 1921), p. xvi.

[15] P. Mandonnet, " Thomas d'Aquin, créateur de la dispute quodlibétique," in *RSPT* 15 (1926), 477-506, 16 (1927), 5-38. The conclusions about the new chronology of Quodlibets VII-XI in this article had been stated briefly the previous year, but without any documentation, in his introduction to the " Lethielleux " edition of the Quodlibets: S. *Thomae Aquinatis Quaestiones Quodlibetales* (Paris, 1925), pp. v-viii.

Christmas and E for Easter) is not exhaustive,[16] but it does suggest where the chronology proposed by Mandonnet for individual Quodlibets in the two series has not met with universal acceptance.[17]

[16] Some studies of individual Quodlibets are not included, e. g., P. Glorieux, " Le plus beau Quodlibet de S. Thomas (IX) est-il de lui? ", in *Mélanges de science religieuse* 3 (1946), 235-268, answered in the affirmative by Pelster (1946— see next note) and by J. Isaac, " Le Quodlibet 9 est bien de S. Thomas," in *Archives d'histoire doctrinale et littéraire du moyen âge* 16 (1947-1948), 145-186. Nor is there any mention of P. Castagnoli, " Le dispute Quodlibetali VII-XI di S. Tommaso," in *Divus Thomas* (Piacenza) 31 (1928), 276-296, who held that these Quodlibets belonged to the " Italian " period and could be dated as a block between 1259 and 1268. There are good summaries of the conclusions of chronological research on the Quodlibets in the appendix by I. T. Eschmann, "A Catalogue of St. Thomas's Works," in E. Gilson, *The Christian Philosophy of St. Thomas Aquinas* (New York, 1956), pp. 381-439, at p. 392.

[17] The following abbreviations are used in this table:

Mandonnet I = P. Mandonnet, *Siger de Brabant*, sec. ed. I (Paris, 1911), 85-87.

Mandonnet 2 = P. Mandonnet, " Chronologie sommaire de la vie et des écrits de Saint Thomas," in *RSPT* 9 (1920), 142-152, at p. 148.

Destrez = J. Destrez, " Les disputes quodlibétiques de saint Thomas d'après la tradition manuscrite," in *Mélanges Thomistes* (Kain, 1923), 49-108, at p. 51.

Synave 1 = P. Synave, review of Destrez in *Bulletin Thomiste* I (1924) [32]-[50].

Glorieux 1 = P. Glorieux, *La littérature quodlibétique* I (Kain, 1925), pp. 276-290.

Mandonnet 3 = P. Mandonnet, " S. Thomas d'Aquin, créateur de la dispute quodlibétique," in *RSPT* 15 (1926), 477-506, 16 (1927), 5-38.

Synave 2 = P. Synave, " L'ordre des Quodlibets VII à XI de S. Thomas d'Aquin," in *Revue Thomiste*, n. s., 9 (1926), 43-47.

Pelster 1 = F. Pelster, " Beiträge zur Chronologie der Quodlibeta des Hl. Thomas von Aquin," in *Gregorianum* 8 (1927), 508-538; 10 (1929), 52-71, 387-403, on which see Synave, *Bull. Thomiste* 2 (1930) [114].

Glorieux 2 = P. Glorieux, *La littérature*, II (Paris, 1935), p. 272.

Van Steenberghen = F. Van Steenberghen, *Siger de Brabant dans l'histoire de l'Aristotelisme*, II (Louvain, 1942), p. 541.

Glorieux 3 = P. Glorieux, " Les Quodlibets VII-XI de S. Thomas d'Aquin. Étude critique," in *Recherches de théologie ancienne et médiévale* 13 (1946), 282-303.

Pelster 2 = F. Pelster, " Literarische Probleme der Quodlibeta des hl. Thomas von Aquin," in *Gregorianum* 28 (1947), 78-100; 29 (1948), 62-87.

Isaac = J. Isaac, review of Pelster 2 in *Bull. Thomiste* 8 (1947-1953), 169-172.

XII	VI	V	IV	III	II	I	XI	X	IX	VIII	VII	QUODLIBET
1964–1968		1271C	1270C 1271E	1270E	1269C	1269E	8	2 6	1 • • • • •	4 6	1 2	Mandonnet 1 1910
	1272E											Mandonnet 2 1920
			1271E				8	2 6	1 • • • • •	5 9	1 2	Destrez 1923
1271E 1270C			1270C 1271E				1267E	1266C	1266E	1267C	1265C	Synave 1 1924 / Glorieux 1 1925
1270C			1271E				1259E	1258C	1258E	1257C	1256C	Mandonnet 3 1926
1271E			1270C								1257C	Synave 2 1926
1272 Naples			1269C	1270C		1271E			1265 Rome			Pelster 1 1927
											1255C	Glorieux 2 1935
1270C Paris			1271E									Vansteenberghen 1942
								1256C?	1256?	1254C?	1255C	Glorieux 3 1946
			1271E	1270C	1269C					1258–59		Pelster 2 1947
									1256C		1257C	Isaac 1948
								1257 –60		1257 –60	1257C?	Marc 1967
1270C			1271E									Weisheipl 1974

In spite of some uncertainties of chronology these Quodlibets of St. Thomas have a fascination all their own in comparison with his other works. This fascination is not peculiar to the Quodlibets of St. Thomas but is rather something that flows from the nature of a Quodlibet. For even in its final, polished state at some distance removed from the excitement of the original General Disputation, a Quodlibet reflects the interests of the audience that attended the General Disputation and not those of the master. The question that then came from the floor are the questions that the master answers, the pragmatic (" Utrum melius sit facere phlebotomiam in novilunio quam in plenilunio ") with the deeply theological (" Utrum emanatio Filii sit ratio emanationis creaturarum ").[18]

The type of question asked at the General Disputation seems to have depended very much on the reputation or speciality of the master. The Quodlibets of the Augustinian Giles of Rome (1286-1291) are quite " speculative " from start to finish whereas the Quodlibet (5 March 1282) of Berthaud of Saint Denis, canon of Paris, is severely practical: " Utrum clerici teneantur solvere pedagia vel tributa. . . . Utrum molere dominicis diebus sit peccatum mortale." [19] By and large, however, the extant Quodlibets from Paris and Oxford are a mixed bag of speculative and practical questions, ranging from the heavily practical Quodlibets (1262-1272) of Gerard of Abbeville to the long and rather contorted Quodlibets attributed to Peter John Olivi from the end of the 13th century.[20] The audience, clearly, was a mixed one, too. A master with a reputation for practicality would attract a different audience from that of a master known for a speculative approach. All the same, the presence of a number of practical questions in most

Marc = P. Marc, C. Pera, F. Caramello, *S. Thomae Aquinatis Summa contra Gentiles*, I (Turin, 1947), p. 412.

Weisheipl = J. A. Weisheipl, *Friar Thomas d'Aquino* (New York, 1974), p. 367.

[18] Henry of Lübeck, Qdl I. 33 (1323) in Glorieux, *Littérature* II, p. 136; Giles of Rome, Qdl. I.3 (1286), *ibid.*, I, p. 141.

[19] See the list of Giles' quodlibetal questions in Glorieux, *Littérature*, I, pp. 141-147, and that of those of Berthaud, *ibid.*, pp. 105-106.

[20] For Gerard's see *ibid.*, I, pp. 112-117; for those of Olivi, ibid., II, pp. 205-211.

of the Quodlibets suggests that there really was no hard and fast rule about what questions might be asked.

An air of immediacy is rarely absent. A Quodlibet gave the students a chance to take the floor for a change, and they made the most of the moment. Some questions are somewhat pointed, like that in the Quodlibet of an anonymous (English?) Franciscan about 1300 (" Utrum frater minor peccat mortaliter portando pecuniam alicuius "),[21] or that in an Oxford Quodlibet of Thomas Wylton about 1312: " Utrum sit magis licitum magistro in theologia tenere plura beneficia quam alteri." [22] Others have all the openended quality of a High School debate of " The Pen is Mightier than the Sword " type: " Utrum melius sit regi ab optimo viro quam ab optimis legibus." [23] And if there are questions which sound a tired, perfunctory note, being repeated from Quodlibet to Quodlibet, there are others which bear upon burning issues or events of the day. The question of where to bury the body of Philip III of France, who died on 5 October 1285, was the subject of a question in a Quodlibet of Geoffrey of Fontaines the following Christmas.[24] The resignation of Celestine V in December 1294 came up in a Quodlibet of Peter of Auvergne some two years later: " Utrum summus pontifex possit cedere vel renuntiare officio suo in aliquo casu." [25] The implications of Boniface VIII's *Clericis laicos,* issued in February 1296, were considered at a Quodlibet of Eustace of Grandecourt at Paris the following Christmas or Spring.[26] A prevailing conviction that the end of the world was at hand in 1300 is present in a Quodlibet of Peter of Auvergne in that same year.[27]

From time to time the students were moved to question the teaching methods. Some clearly felt that the Universities

---

[21] Listed *ibid.,* II, p. 217.

[22] *Ibid.,* II, p. 279.

[23] *Ibid.,* II, p. 147.

[24] Qdl. I. 11, ed. M. de Wulf and A. Pelzer, *Les quatre premiers Quodlibets de Godefroid de Fontaines* (Louvain, 1904), pp. 27-31.

[25] Qdl. I.15, listed in Glorieux, *Littérature,* I, p. 259.

[26] Qdl. II. 5, *ibid.,* II, p. 82.

[27] Qdl. V. 15, *ibid.,* I, p. 262.

242

and the teachers should be doing more for the ordinary clergy
and for their education ("Utrum ignorantia sacerdotum doctoribus imputetur in peccatum "); [28] others that too much
emphasis was being placed on advancement and on academic
honors and not enough on the pastoral care ("Utrum melius
est manere in studio seu scholis, spe plus proficiendi, quam ire
ad animas, intentione salutem eis procurandi ").[29] Although
Henry of Ghent, in another context, furnished a classic answer
to the latter question ("Audientiam intelligo non tam praesentium quam etiam illorum ad quos per audientes doctrina illa
poterit pervenire "),[30] there were many students who were less
than enchanted with the teaching. If one may judge from a
question that occurs in at least three different Quodlibets, there
were masters who were reluctant to answer any and every
question at a Quodlibet: "Utrum magister in theologia dis-
putans de quolibet, qui renuit accipere quaestionem sibi pro-
positam quia tangit aliquos quos timet offendere, peccat in hoc
mortaliter." [31] There were others, too, who were more adept
at parrying questions than facing up to them squarely: "Utrum
doctor sive magister determinans quaestiones sive exponens
scripturas publice, peccet mortaliter non explicando veritatem
quam novit." [32] Still others devoted too much time to exotic
questions at the expense of those of greater import: "Utrum
magistri tractantes quaestiones curiosas, dimittentes utiles ad
salutem, peccent mortaliter." [33]

* * * * *

" Utiles ad salutem " : most strikingly of all, the Quodlibets
reflect an abiding interest among the students in the cura

[28] William de Falegar, Qdl. I. 15 (1280-1281), ibid., II, p. 126.

[29] Henry of Ghent, Qdl. I.35, (1276C) in Henrici Gandavensis Quaestiones
Quodlibetales (Paris, 1518), f. 23 v.

[30] Henry of Ghent, Qdl. X. 16 (1286 C), ed. cit., f. 437.

[31] Q. 55 of Quodlibet of Gervase of Mont Saint-Eloi (1282-1291) in Glorieux,
Littérature, I, p. 137. See also Qdl. III. 23 (1287) of Richard of Middleton
(ibid., I. p. 270), and Qdl. XII. 6 (1295) of Geoffrey of Fontaines (ibid., I, p. 270).

[32] Henry of Ghent, Qdl. X. 16 (1286 C), ed. cit., f. 437.

[33] Qdl. II. 16 (1308) of Hervé Nédellec, in Glorieux, Littérature, I. 202.

animarum. This is only natural. For a large proportion of the students in the theological faculties of Paris, Oxford, and elsewhere, was engaged in or destined for pastoral care at one level or another. What the proportion exactly was is not ascertainable, but until the constitution *Licet canon* of the second council of Lyons disrupted the practice, many of the clergy were able to take leave from their *curae animarum* for a few year's study at Universities. Certainly after 1298, when Boniface VIII's educational constitution, *Cum ex eo*, was issued, the number of parochial clergy attending the Universities must have been appreciable.[34]

The preoccupations of these students are reflected in questions about residence and study, benefices and beneficial obligations, the sacraments and pastoral responsibilities. The imposition on rectors of personal residence in their livings at the second council of Lyons naturally occasioned a number of questions, for example, concerning the obligation of becoming a priest within a year of taking possession of a rectory.[35] And when the constitution *Cum ex eo* of Boniface had relaxed the Lyons legislation in 1298, allowing rectors to be supported from the revenues of their parishes while studying at a University, there were rectors who were not too scrupulous about observing the conditions of their licences to study, as may be gathered from a question in a Quodlibet of James of Ascoli in 1311-1312: "Utrum clericus beneficiatus qui habet licentiam standi in studio, si stet in studio sine spe proficiendi ita quod studio non vacet sed potius ludat, discurrat et sit vagabundus, utrum teneatur ad restitutionem fructuum perceptorum tempore intermedio pro quo debuit vacare studio." [36]

---

[34] See L. E. Boyle, " The Constitution *Cum ex eo* of Pope Boniface VIII," in *Mediaeval Studies* 24 (1962), 263-302.

[35] Thus Qdl. III. 18 of the Franciscan Roger Marston at Oxford in 1283: " Utrum aliquis legitime institutus in beneficio habente curam animarum si non fuerit ordinatus infra annum possit illud beneficium licite retinere post concilium Lugdunense," ed. G. F. Etzkorn and I. C. Brady, *Fr. Rogerus Marston: Quodlibeta Quatuor* (Quaracchi, 1968), p. 346.

[36] Bibliotheca Apostolica Vaticana, MS. Vat. lat. 932, f. 68r-v (Qdl. I. 16); Glorieux, *La littérature*, II, p. 142.

244

If a certain distaste for the way of life of the Parisian clergy may be detected in a question about the size of the stipends demanded by the " rich curates " of Paris,[37] a distinct pride in the quality of the parochial clergy vis-à-vis the privileged friars is to be noticed in a question put to Henry of Ghent in 1287 about preaching: " Si sacerdos curatus in parochia sua paratus sit et velit praedicare, et similiter frater habens privilegium ut possit praedicare, nullo eum impediente, uter eorum potior sit in iure, et utri cedere debeat alter? "[38] The friars and their privileges, particularly those of hearing confessions and preaching, were, of course, very sore points, and provoked a number of queries, as in this question in a Quodlibet of Geoffrey of Fontaines four or five years after Martin IV had endowed the friars with some unpopular privileges: " Utrum confessus ab aliquo habente potestatem audiendi confessiones et absolvendi confitentes virtute privilegii Martini VI, teneatur eadem peccata proprio sacerdoti iterum confiteri."[39]

On the whole, the practical questions, such as one from a Quodlibet of John of Naples at the beginning of the 14th

[37] See q. 8 of Quodlibet (1282-1291) of Gervase of Mont Saint-Éloi in Glorieux, La littérature, I, p. 134: " Utrum divites curati peccent in accipiendo quando administrant sacramenta, ut in ista villa, scilicet Parisius, quando accipiunt duodecim denarios in administratione sacramenti extremae unctionis, duos solidos vel tres in desponsatione coniugum."

[38] Qdl. VII. 21, ed. Paris, 1518, f. 272.

[39] Qdl. III. 7. ed. de Wulf and Pelzer, Les quatre premiers Qoodlibets de Godefroid de Fontaines (Louvain, 1904), p. 214. A similar question was put in 1283 to Roger Marston at Oxford (Qdl III. 25): " Si ex privilegio nobis concesso possumus audire confessiones si praelati prohibeant " (ed. Etzkorn and Brady, Fr. Rogerus Marston: Quodlibeta Quatuor, pp. 359-388). In one form or another the question crops up time and again over the next centuries, e. g., in the late 14th century when the Irish Cistercian Henry Crump was arraigned at London on seven charges involving confessional jurisdiction, one of which was that he held that those were " damned for eternity " who did not confess to their own parish priest after confessing to a friar. Obviously it was possible to approach the question from all sorts of angles, as in this version in Quodlibet IV. 24 (c. 1286) of the English Dominican Thomas Sutton at Oxford: " Posito quod sacerdos parochialis sit sufficiens in scientia et moribus ad curam animarum, quaeritur utrum debeat licentiare subditum si petat ut possit confiteri sacerdoti alieno, nisi exprimat causam rationabilem et evidentem suae petitionis.": Thomas von Sutton Quodlibeta, ed. M. Schmaus and M. González-Haba (Munich, 1969), pp. 655-658.

century, are as vital and pertinent as those with which the
pastoral clergy in any age is faced: " Utrum medicus debeat
dare medicinam mulieri praegnanti ex qua sequeretur mors
filii, et si non daret eam, sequeretur mors utriusque." [40] At
times, indeed, the questions in some Quodlibets have more
the look of *casus* in moral theology than that of classic *quaestiones*.

*   *   *   *   *

The casus-type question appears in Quodlibets as early as
those of Guerric of Saint-Quentin (1233-1242). [41] It was, of
course, a very common method of teaching in the law schools
of the late 12th century, from which, in fact, the schools of
theology borrowed the technique of both the Disputed Question
and the Quodlibet. Here in the theological Quodlibets from
Paris and Oxford in the second half of the 13th century the
presence of these *casus* is quite striking. Though there is little
evidence of practical " moral " theology in the works of the
main scholastic writers of the 12th, 13th, and 14th centuries,
there is plenty of evidence in these Quodlibets that a discussion
of practical *casus* was not left entirely to authors of *Summae de
casibus* like Raymund of Peñafort (1234) or to writers of
Summae confessorum such as John of Freiburg (1298). Indeed,
as will be suggested later, it was precisely because of these
casus and practical moral conclusions that the *Quodlibets* of
some of the greater scholastics of the 13th century were almost
as well-known to the manualists and summists as the *Summa*
of St. Thomas or the *Repertorium* of Durandus.

A typical *casus is to be found in* Qdl. III, 49 (1277) of the
Franciscan John Pecham: " Posito quod Titius promisit locare
seu ad firmam dare concedere Gaio fundum usque ad quinquennium pro decem aureis, sed non fecit quod promisit, pro
quo Gaius dicit se lucra plurima perdidisse, quaeritur an Titius
teneatur aliquid dare pro damno ipsi Gaio." [42] Variants on this

---

[40] Qdl. X. 27 in Glorieux, *Littérature*, II, p. 170.
[41] Qdl. IV. 18, *ibid.*, p. 109.
[42] *Ibid.*, p. 179.

246

"Posito quod" statements of a *casus* are to be found in many Quodlibets, for example, in those of John de Pouilly.[43] On many occasions, however, the *casus* is presented with all the terseness of a "problem" in mathematics (to which, in any case, legal and theological *casus* and *quaestiones* reach back in origin), thus: "Ponatur: Aliquis commisit decem peccata. Confitetur novem non recolendo de decimo. Sufficienter est contritus et bene confiteretur decimum si recoleret. Absolvitur a sacerdote. Post aliquod tempus recordatur. Utrum teneatur confiteri?"[44]; or again, "Item, ponitur *talis casus*: Iste scholasticus habet conferre scholas grammaticales. Quidam clericus dat ei argentum hac intentione ut possit eas obtinere. Obtinet. Utrum sit simonia?".[45]

* * * * *

Although there are none of these *casus-quaestiones* in the Quodlibets of St. Thomas, there is the usual quota of practical questions. In fact, there is scarcely one of his Quodlibets that does not carry a question or two bearing directly on the *cura animarum*. As is common in quodlibetal literature, the practical questions generally come at the end of each Quodlibet, where they were placed when the questions from the General Disputation were being sorted out for the Determination. After the questions "De Deo" and De angelis," to take the simplest division of a Thomistic Quodlibet, there are those "De homine."

The very first Quodlibet of St. Thomas (VII) is devoid of practical questions, apart from two very long questions on manual work (VII. 7 and 8) which appear to be Disputed Questions and to have been tacked on to this Quodlibet when the first Parisian group of Quodlibets were put in circulation long after the death of St. Thomas.[46]

[43] Qdl. III. 12 (1309): "Ponamus quod aliquis sit excommunicatus pluribus excommunicationibus et quod absolvatur ab una illarum. . . .": Glorieux, *Littérature*, I, p. 227.

[44] Qdl. I. 4 (1287-1288) of John de Weerde: *ibid.*, II, p. 188.

[45] Qdl. II. 8 (1300-1301) of Renier of Clairmarais: *ibid.*, II, 255.

[46] See P. Glorieux, "Les Quodlibets VII-XI de S. Thomas d'Aquin," in *Recherches de théologie ancienne et médiévale* 13 (1946), 286-289; C. Molari, "I luoghi

From the next Quodlibet (VIII) onwards, however, matters of practical morals become more prominent, e. g., " Utrum ille qui vadit ad ecclesiam propter distributiones, alias non iturus, peccet." (VIII.1,1) There is also a brief reply to a question about pluralism (VIII.6,3) where there is a discussion of the difficulty pluralists encounter in forming their consciences because of the varying opinions of masters. The same point about a pluralist's conscience is made at much greater length in the next Quodlibet (IX.7, 2: "Utrum habere plures praebendas sine cura animarum absque dispensatione sit peccatum mortale ") .

Prebends, according to some authorities, are so many apples to be plucked at will; according to others, a plurality of prebends offends against the natural law, and a dispensation is impossible. So far as St. Thomas is concerned, it is an extremely dangerous thing to give a straightforward decision about mortal sin in a question such as this where the truth of the matter is not clear and unambiguous and where jurist contradicts jurist and theologian is at odds with theologian: " inveniuntur enim theologi theologis et juristae juristis contrarie sentire." The controversy over whether the ancient laws prohibiting pluralism have been abrogated or not is, he feels, something that " should be left to the jurists." If the laws still hold, then, customs to the contrary notwithstanding, it is his view as a theologian that several benefices cannot be held without a dispensation. But if, on the other hand, it is certain that these laws have been abrogated by custom, then there is no question of having to seek a dispensation.

*   *   *   *   *

On the whole, however, practical questions are not as thick on the ground in these Quodlibets (VII-XI) from St. Thomas's first Parisian period of teaching (1256-1259) as they are in those (I-VI, and possibly XII) from his second (1269-1272) .

The audience, perhaps, was a little more varied then than in the first period; and the presence of influential "practical" theologians such as Gerard of Abbeville has also to be taken into account. When St. Thomas arrived in Paris in 1269, Gerard had been teaching for some seven or eight years and had a wide following.[47] His nineteen Quodlibets (1262-1272) are probably the most pastoral of the Quodlibets of the 13th century and include a splendid example of a *casus-quaestio*: "Quoddam cimiterium a praelato loci fuit benedictum. Per multa vehicula illi terrae benedictae addita et adiecta et superposita fuit terra non benedicta usque ad altitudinem unius stagii vel duorum, in qua terra non benedicta sepeliuntur funera quae in parte tangit terram prius benedictam. Utrum illa corpora sunt sepulta in cimiterio benedicto, vel utrum tale cimiterium iterum sit benedicendum? ".[48]

None of the questions in the Quodlibets I-VI of St. Thomas are quite as "casuistic" as this, but there are a few which are not as innocent as they seem. If, in answer to a straight question, there is a reply (later repeated *ad litteram* in his *Summa*: II-II, q. 10, a. 12) that calmly and firmly establishes that Jewish children should not be baptized behind their parents' backs (II.4, 2), there is a long and over-emphatic defence (with answers to twenty-three objections) of the admission of "callow youths" to religious orders (IV.12, 1). St. Thomas clearly regarded the question and the objections as mischievous, since he begins his reply rather testily: "Respondeo dicendum quod hoc quod pro quaestione hic inducitur, dubitationem non habet, nisi quod quidam contentioni studentes veritatem obnubilare conantur."[49] This is almost the only occasion on which

---

[47] Gerard headed a group of very vocal anti-mendicant masters at Paris. Some of the questions in the Quodlibets of St. Thomas (especially Qdl. I. 14; III. 11-12, 17; IV. 23-24) were inspired by or aimed at the "Geraldine" circle: see P. Glorieux, "Les polémiques 'contra Geraldinos'," in *Reherches de théologie ancienne et médiévale* 6 (1934), 5-41.

[48] Qdl. IV. 12 (1265) listed in Glorieux, *Littérature*, I, p. 115.

[49] Probably he had some of the "Geraldines" in mind, since this question in Qdl. IV and that following (IV. 12, 1-2) are noted in MS. Vat. lat. 799 in the Vatican Library as follows: "Isti duo articuli fuerunt disputati a fratre Thoma contra Geroldum in principio quadragesimae [1271]": Glorieux, *art. cit.*, pp. 34-36.

he drops his guard a little, though a question in Quodlibet I
(9, 4) on whether monks who eat meat sin mortally, moves
him to make comparisons between the rules of various religious
orders and to blow a trumpet for the admirably balanced
legislation of his own Dominican Order: " in ordine fratrum
praedicatorum est cautissima et securissima forma profitendi
qua non promittit [frater] servare regulam sed obedientiam
secundum regulam." [50]

At events, this second Parisian group of Quodlibets is full
of good, practical, everyday questions covering many aspects
of the pastoral care: almsgiving (III.6, 1; VI.7; VI.8, 1), baptism (II.4, 2), benefices and beneficial practice (I.7, 1; IV.8,
4; IV.12, 1; V.11, 3; VI.5, 3), bigamy (IV.8, 2), buying and
selling (II.5, 2), conscience (III.12, 1-2), crusades and in-
dulgences (II.8, 2; IV.7, 2; V.7, 2), death (III.9, 2), the
Eucharist (V.6, 1-2), excommunication (IV.8, 3), fasting (V.9,
2), hell (III.10, 2), ignorance (I.9, 3), lies (VI.9, 3), loans
and restitution (V.9, 1), martyrdom (IV.10, 1-2), matrimony
(III.7; IV.8, 2; V.8, 1-2), penance and confessional practice
(I.5; I.6, 1-3; III.13, 1-2; IV.7, 1; V.7, 1), perjury (I.9, 2),
precepts (V.10, 1-2), priests and their obligations (I.7, 1; III.
13, 2; V.14; VI.5, 2), purgatory (II.8, 2), study and teaching
(I.7, 2; III.4, 1-2), tithes (II.4, 3; VI.5, 4), usury (III.7, 2),
vows (III.5, 1-3), wills and executors' responsibilities (VI.8,
1-2).

Generally these questions are answered with courtesy and
learning and out of a conviction (echoed later by Henry of
Ghent) that teachers of theology have no mean place in the
salvation of souls: [51] " Theologiae doctores sunt quasi principales artifices [aedificii spiritualis] qui inquirent et docent

---

[50] The edition of the Quodlibets used here is " Marietti " edition: *S. Thomae
Aquinatis Quaestiones Quodlibetales*, ed. R. Spiazzi (Marietti: Rome-Turin, 1956),
where parallel passages in other works of St. Thomas are clearly indicated and
where the alternative methods of citing the Quodlibets (by question and article
within the question, as in the present essay, or by the consecutive number of the
article in the Quodlibet) are used side by side, most conveniently.

[51] See J. Leclercq, " L'idéal du théologien au moyen âge," in *Recherches de
science religieuse* 21 (1947), 121-148.

qualiter alii debeant salutem animarum procurare " (I.7, 2).
Teaching was so important, in fact, that, given a proper disposition on the part of the teacher, it was a higher and better
occupation than pastoral care: "Ipsa enim ratio demonstrat
quod melius est erudire de pertinentibus ad salutem eos qui et
in se et in aliis proficere possunt quam simplices qui in se
tantum proficere possunt " (*ibid.*). And to those who were of
the opinion that study was a waste of time and should take
second place to the *cura animarum*, he answered drily, " nullam
iacturam temporis patitur qui quid est melius operatur docendo
vel qui ad hoc per studium se disponit " (*ibid.*). St. Thomas
took his teaching very seriously indeed. Certainly he had no
time for those who in a " Disputatio magistralis " (presumably
he is speaking here of the Determination stage of the Quodlibet)
answer questions with a battery of authorities and leave the
hearers dazed and no wiser than they were before. The duty
of a teacher is to instruct and not to send his students away
empty, as he says in this interesting passage in Quodlibet IV
(9, 3):

Quaedam vero disputatio est magistralis in scholis, non ad re-
movendum errorem sed ad instruendum auditores ut inducantur
ad intellectum veritatis quam intendit: et tunc oportet rationibus
inniti investigantibus veritatis radicem et facientibus scire quomodo
sit verum quod dicitur; alioquin si nudis auctoritatibus magister
quaestionem determinet, certificabitur quidem auditor quod ita
est, sed nichil scientiae vel intellectus acquiret et vacuus abscedet.

True to the conviction expressed in Quodlibet IV, St. Thomas
never answers questions, however simplistic, with anything approaching glibness, from " Utrum sufficiat confiteri scripto "
(I.6, 1) to " Utrum habens duas ecclesias teneatur utriusque
officium dicere " (I.7). And he rarely lets slip an opportunity
to instruct, as in the question, " Utrum sacerdos parochialis
teneatur credere suo subdito dicenti se alteri esse confessum "
(I.6, 3), where he nicely sets the confessional off from civil
courts and combats a tendency in confessional practice to turn
confessionals into tribunals: " In foro iudiciali creditur homini

contra se sed non pro se. In foro autem poenitentiae creditur homini pro se et contra se." In some of the replies there is a down-to-earth realism that allows that matins may be anticipated "propter necessitatem et licitarum honestarum occupationum, puta si clericus vel magister debet videre lectiones suas de nocte" (V.14), and that it is not a sin for a preacher "to have an eye on earthly things," provided he is simply looking to the necessities of life, "sicut ad stipendia pro necessitate sustentationis vitae" (II.6 2). On the question of the support of the clergy, indeed, he is uncompromising, arguing that to support the clergy is of divine and natural law (II.4, 3) and that the question of tithes has nothing to do with whether a priest is poor or rich (VI.5, 4).

But for all his humanity and his sympathetic understanding of the problems of pastoral care, St. Thomas made no attempt to court the favor of the parochial clergy in his audience. He was totally convinced of the relative superiority of the teaching office over the pastoral, and he said so more than once. In his opinion the pastoral clergy are simply the "manual workers" in the spiritual edifice, where the doctors of theology are the "skilled workers" showing how things should be done: "In aedificio autem spirituali sunt quasi manuales operarii qui particulariter insistunt curae animarum. . . . Sed quasi principales artifices sunt et episcopi. . . . Et similiter theologiae doctores sunt quasi principales artifices, qui inquirunt et docent qualiter alii debeant salutem animarum procurare." (I.7, 2) He was no less adamant on the point that the parochial clergy belonged to a lower grade of perfection than religious (I.7, 2; III.6, 3). Which is why, he explains rather finely, religious and not parish priests become bishops (I.7, 2).[52]

* * * * *

[52] Qdl. III. 6, 3 is explicitly devoted to this question of relative perfection: "Utrum presbiteri parochiales et archidiaconi sint maioris perfectionis quam religiosi." The Quodlibet was held towards Easter of 1270, some four or five months after a similar question ("Utrum sacerdotes curati sint in statu perfectiori quam religiosi": Glorieux, *Littérature*, I, p. 122) had been answered rather differently by Gerard of Abbeville. Some of the objections put to St. Thomas echo Gerard's position.

252

At least 127 manuscripts of the Quodlibets of St. Thomas are extant from the Middle Ages, and they mostly come from college libraries, monasteries, and Dominican houses.[53] What possible impact, then, could these Quodlibets have had on pastoral care at large from which so many of the questions were drawn and to which the replies were of some interest? Oddly, an appreciable impact, albeit indirectly. For, although there is nothing to indicate that the first Parisian Quodlibets (VII-XI) or Quodlibet XII were ever known outside a small, narrowly professional circle, it is otherwise with the second Parisian block, Quodlibets I-VI. The pastoral teaching in these Quodlibets of 1269-1272 was known and quoted all over Europe from about 1300, finding its way into all sorts of small pastoral manuals, from the *Oculus sacerdotis* of William of Pagula in England about 1320 [54] to the *Manipulus curatorum* of Guido de Monte Rocherii in Spain about the same time,[55] and into more authoritative works such as the *Confessionale* of Antoninus of Florence in the middle of the 15th century [56] and the *Summa* of Sylvester Prierias at the beginning of the 15th.[57]

This, as it happens, was not because these Quodlibets I-VI of St. Thomas were widely known as such, but because of the industry if not the perceptiveness of a German Dominican called John of Freiburg or John the Lector.[58] A pupil at one

[53] J. Destrez, " Les disputes quodlibétiques de saint Thomas d'après la tradition manuscrite," in *Mélanges Thomistes* (Kain, 1923), pp. 49-108, who lists 96 MSS. Another 31 are listed by S. Axters, " Où en est l'état des manuscrits des questions quodlibétiques de saint Thomas d'Aquin?," in *Revue Thomiste* 41 (1936), 505-530.

[54] New College, Oxford, MS. 292, f. 76r, etc.

[55] *Manipulus curatorum*, ed. Louvain, 1552, e. g., f. 128r: " Sanctus Thomas in quadam quaestione de quolibet ponit casus in quibus tenetur existens in peccato mortali confiteri."

[56] *Confessionale*, ed. Paris, 1516, f. 21v: " Item secundum Thomam in quolibet et Innocentium contritus debet magis diligere Deum quam seipsum."

[57] *Summa summarum quae Sylvestrina dicitur*, ed. Cologne, 1518, ff. 35v, 165v, etc.

[58] For a more specific discussion of John of Freiburg, his *Summa confessorum* and the place of St. Thomas in popular theology, see L. E. Boyle, " The *Summa confessorum* of John of Freiburg and the popularization of the moral teaching

time of Ulrich Engelbrecht of Strasbourg, John of Freiburg
accompanied Albert the Great to Mecklenberg in 1269 and
may, indeed, have attended some of the Quodlibets of St.
Thomas at Paris in 1279-1272, when Albert went there to assist
St. Thomas. After his appointment as Lector in the Dominican
house at Freiburg-im-Breisgau about 1280, John decided to
bring his textbook of practical theology, the *Summa de casibus*
of Raymund of Peñafort, up to date and supplemented it with
excerpts from the *Secunda secundae*, Quodlibets I-VI, and other
works of St. Thomas, and from other theological and canonical
sources that had appeared in the interval of some fifty years
since the *Summa de casibus* was published in its final edition
(1234). In a *Summa confessorum* of his own which he published in 1298 [59] John incorporated most of the material from
St. Thomas and others which he had collected in this way,
including the corpus of at least 22 *quaestiones* from Quodlibets
I-VI. If Quodlibets VII-XI and Quodlibet XII seem to be unknown to him (thus, incidentally, confirming the view of many
scholars that these Quodlibets were not put into circulation
until sometime after 1300), John was thoroughly familiar with
all of Quodlibets I-VI and had searched them thoroughly (together with another Quodlibet which he thought was by
Thomas but which really was by John Pecham) [60] for moral
teaching.[61] Hardly one of the " pastoral " questions in these

---

of St. Thomas and some of his contemporaries," in *St. Thomas Aquinas, 1274-1974:
Commemorative Studies*, ed. A. A. Maurer (Toronto, 1974) II, pp. 245-268.

[59] There are various editions of the work, e. g., that at Nuremberg, 1517. Incunabula of the *Summa* are in L. Hain, *Repertorium bibliographicum* (Stuttgart-
Paris, 1826-1838), nn. 7365 (1476) and 7366 (1498).

[60] Pecham's Quodlibet occurs in at least 2 MSS. of the Quodlibets of St. Thomas
but is attributed to St. Thomas in only one of these MSS: see Destrez, *art. cit.*
in 53 above, pp. 59-81. It is interesting to note that the 14th-century English
Dominican Robert Holcot, when quoting one of these Pecham questions attributed
to St. Thomas by the *Summa confessorum,* suspected that there was something
wrong: ". . . sicut dicitur in Summa confessorum et imponitur sancto Thomae
in quodam quaestione de quolibet. Sed puto quod non est suum. . . .": *In IV
libros Sententiarum*, ed. Lyons, 1518, I D. 7, casus XVI.

[61] John of Freiburg also uses Quodlibets of Peter of Tarentaise (*Summa confessorum* 3.33, 8 and 3.34, 254) and Ulrich of Strasbourg (*ibid.*, 3. 34, 272). He

254

Quodlibets has been missed, and no one quotation is repeated twice, as may be seen from the following summary table of borrowings (which does not claim to be exhaustive):

Quodlibet		Summa C.	
I	5	3.34.26	Utrum contritus debeat magis velle esse in inferno quam peccare
	6 2	3.34.69	Utrum confessio differri possit usque ad quadragesimam
	6 3	3.34.48	Utrum sacerdos parochialis teneatur credere suo subdito dicenti se alteri esse confessum
	7 1	1. 7.19	Utrum habens duas ecclesias teneatur utriusque officium dicere
	7 2	3. 5. 4	Utrum vacans saluti animarum peccet, si circa studium tempus occupat
	9 2	1. 9.23	Utrum periurium sit gravius peccatum quam homicidium
II	4 2	1. 4. 4	Utrum pueri Iudaeorum sint baptizandi invitis parentibus
III	4 1	3. 5. 5	Utrum liceat alicui petere licentiam pro se docendi in theologia
	4 2	3.32.18	Utrum discipuli sequentes diversas opiniones magistrorum excusentur a peccato erroris
	6 2	3.34.249	Utrum religiosus possit egredi claustram absque licentia sui praelati ut patri subveniat in necessitate existenti
	9 2	1.11.23	Utrum liceat requirere ab aliquo moriente ut statum suum post mortem revelet
	13 1	3.34.110	Utrum satisfactio universaliter iniuncta a sacerdote sit sacramentalis
IV	7 2	1. 8.62	Utrum vir possit accipere crucem uxore nolente, si de eius incontinentia timeatur
	8 3	3.33.194	Utrum debeant vitari illi excommunicati circa quorum excommunicationem est apud peritos diversa sententia
V	7 2	3.34.192	Utrum melius moriatur crucesignatus qui moritur in via eundi ultra mare quam qui moritur redeundo

was not the only one of the manualists to comb the Quodlibets for practical doctrine. The Franciscan *Summa astesana* (1317) uses Quodlibets of Henry of Ghent: *Summa astesana*, ed. Regensburg, 1480, f. 20 r, etc. Guido de Monte Rocherii used Quodlibets of Geoffrey of Fontaines: *Manipulus curatorum*, ed. Louvain, 1522, f. 142 v, etc.

	11 3	3.34.237	Utrum praelatus qui dat beneficium alicui suo consanguineo ut exaltetur, simoniam committat
	14	1. 7.20	Utrum liceat clerico qui tenetur ad horas canonicas dicere matutinas sequentis diei de sero
VI	5 2	1. 7.21	Utrum clericus beneficiatus teneatur in scholis existens dicere officium mortuorum
	5 3	3.34.236	Utrum episcopus peccet dans beneficium bono si praetermittet meliorem
	8 1	2. 5.113	Utrum mortuus aliquod detrimentum sentiat ex hoc quod eleemosynas quas mandavit dari retardantur
	8 2	2. 5.114	Utrum executor debeat tardare distributiones eleemoysynarum ad hoc quod res defuncti melius vendantur
	9 3	1.10. 5	Utrum maius peccatum sit cum aliquis mentitur facto quam cum aliquis mentitur verbo

Armed with the corpus of these *quaestions,* each introduced by the phrase, " secundum Thomam in quadam quaestione de quolibet," the *Summa confessorum* spread all over Europe and was the dominant *summa* for confessors over the next two centuries. It was copied, abbreviated, arranged in alphabetical order, translated into German and (partly) into French. And it became a prime source for the moral teaching of St. Thomas (especially as found in the *Secunda secundae* and these Quodlibets) in scholastic as well as in unprofessional circles—so much so, indeed, that, if one finds in a scholastic writer or confessor's manual a quotation from St. Thomas, " in quadam quaestione de quolibet," the source almost invariably proves to be John of Freiburg's *Summa confessorum* or a derivative and not the Quodlibets of St. Thomas themselves. Thus when Ranulph Higden, monk of Chester and author of the well-known *Polychronicon,* states in his *Speculum curatorum* (1343), " Sanctus Thomas in quadam quaestione de quolibet dicit quod in foro contentioso creditur homini pro se et contra se et sine probationibus," the source, if a little garbled in this particular manuscript of the *Speculum,* is not St. Thomas but

256

John of Freiburg (*Summa* 3.34.48) .[62] The same is true when the English canonist and parish priest, William of Pagula, writes in his *Summa summarum* in about 1320, "An clericus praebendatus in scholis existens tenetur dicere officium mortuorum? . . . . Sciendum . . . secundum Thomam in quadam quaestione de quolibet." [63]

These and a host of other manuals of the 14th and 15th centuries were written for and generally circulated among those engaged in the *cura animarum*. It is surely not inappropriate that the replies furnished so carefully by St. Thomas in Determinations at Paris in 1269-1272 to chance questions from pastoral care should have reached, however indirectly, over the next two centuries and more, that very milieu from which these practical questions had come in the first instance.

Pontifical Institute of Mediaeval Studies
Toronto, Canada

[62] Cambridge University Library, MS. Mm. i. 20, f. 188 v.
[63] Oxford, Bodleian Library, MS. Bodley 293, f. 140 v, from *Summa confessorum* I. 7. 19.

III

THE *SUMMA CONFESSORUM*
OF JOHN OF FREIBURG AND THE POPULARIZATION
OF THE MORAL TEACHING OF ST. THOMAS
AND OF SOME OF HIS CONTEMPORARIES

JUST as in the wake of the theological and legal advances of the twelfth century there was a demand for popularization at the beginning of the thirteenth that produced, for example, the *summae* of Robert of Flamborough, Thomas Chobham or Raymund of Peñafort, so in the years that followed the age of Aquinas, Bonaventure and Hostiensis, there was another, and possibly more spectacular, wave of popular treatises that was, for the most part, to endure until about 1500.

Summaries of Bonaventure's commentary on the *Sentences* were numerous by 1300;[1] while as early as 1272, material from the commentary of Aquinas on the *Sentences* was incorporated into a popular *Dialogus de quaestionibus animae et spiritus*[2] by the Dominican, John of Genoa ("Januensis", the author of the influential *Catholicon*, in which there is also much of the moral theology of Aquinas). Later, between 1280 and 1288, the General of the Dominicans, John of Vercelli, commissioned Galienus Ozto to make an abbreviated version of the *Secunda secundae*.[3]

Lesser works of Bonaventure and Aquinas also had their share of popularity, in particular Bonaventure's *Breviloquium* and the *De articulis fidei et de sacramentis* of Aquinas.[4] The most popular work of all, however, was a product of neither Aquinas nor Bonaventure,

---

1 S. Alzeghy, "Abbreviationes Bonaventurae. Handschrifliche Auszüge aus dem Sentenzenkommentar des hl. Bonaventure im Mittelalter," *Gregorianum* 18 (1947) 474-510. See also K. Ruh, *Franziskanisches Schrifttum im deutschen Mittelalter*, (Munich 1965), pp. 192-197, 214-221.

2 M. Grabmann, *Mittelalterliches Geistesleben*, I (Munich 1926), pp. 369-373, and "Die Weiterleben und Weiterwerken des moraltheologischen Schrifttums des hl. Thomas von Aquin im Mittelalter," *Divus Thomas* (Freiburg in d. Schweiz) 25 (1947) 10.

3 Grabmann, art. cit., pp. 5-6.

4 J. Hartzheim, *Concilia Germaniae*, V (Cologne 1763), pp. 401, 414, 423. See also F. W. Oediger, *Ueber die Bildung der Geistlichen im späten Mittelalter* (Leiden-Cologne 1953), p. 123.

246

although it often circulated under their names: the *Compendium theologicae veritatis* of Hugh of Strasbourg. Written between 1265 and 1270 on a basis of Albert the Great's *Summa de creaturis* and Bonaventure's *Breviloquium*,[5] it had a remarkable influence on popular theology in the 14th and 15th centuries, in England, for example, where it is prominent in William of Pagula's *Speculum praelatorum* (c. 1320), and in the anonymous *Regimen animarum* (1343) and *Speculum christiani* (1360-1370).[6] And if the *De instructione sacerdotum* which Albert of Brescia compiled about 1300 "ex libris et quaestionibus et tractatibus fratris Thomae de Aquino" had no great success,[7] the *Dialogus de administratione sacramentorum* which William of Paris put together between 1300 and 1313 "de scriptis fratris Thomae...ac Petri Tarentoize", proved so useful that it survives in very many manuscripts and in numerous printed editions.[8]

I

Aquinas and Peter of Tarentaise are also at the centre of the subject of the present essay, the *Summa confessorum* of John of Freiburg. Its author was a contemporary of William of Paris, and died a year or so after William. Like William, who also produced several compilations of canon law, he was an indefatigable compiler.

Born at Freiburg-im-Breisgau towards the middle of the 13th century, John was to spend most of his life there as Lector in the Dominican priory. Even when he was unwillingly elected prior of the house about 1290 he was allowed to retain his lectorship by Hermann of Minden, the provincial of Germany, "ne conventus vestrae doctrinae salutaris interim accipiat detrimentum."[9] Until his death in 1314, John continued

---

5　G. Boner, "Ueber den Dominikanertheologen Hugo von Strassburg," *Divus Thomas* (Fr.) 25 (1954) 268-286. In the middle ages the *Compendium* was variously attributed to Albert, Bonaventure, Thomas, Giles of Rome, Peter of Tarentaise, etc. Some of the medieval uncertainty about authorship is reflected in a 15th-century English treatise on the seven deadly sins (Oxford, Bodleian Library, MS. Rawlinson C. 288, f. 5r): 2 "To this answereth a grete clerk (et est sanctus Thomas secundum quosdam, et sanctus Albertus secundum alios) in Compendio theologiae, lib. 3, cap. de avarita."

6　*Speculum praelatorum*: Oxford, Merton College, MS. 217, f. 5r-v; *Regimen animarum*: Oxford, Bodleian Library, MS. Hatton 11, f. 4r; *Speculum christiani*, ed. G. Holmstedt (London 1933), p. 182.

7　M. Grabmann, "Albert von Brescia O.P. (ob. 1314) und sein Werk *De officio sacerdotis*," *Mittelalterliches Geistesleben*, III (Munich 1956), pp. 323-351.

8　A. Teetaert, "Un compendium de théologie pastorale du XIIIe-XIVe siècle," *Revue d'histoire ecclésiastique* 26 (1930) 66-102.

9　H. Finke, *Ungedruckte Dominikanerbriefe des 13. Jahrhunderts* (Paderborn 1891), p. 165.

to combine these offices of "prior per se" and "lector per accidens", as Hermann of Minden nicely put it.[10]

A pupil of Ulrich Engelbrecht, under whom he had studied at Strasbourg before 1272,[11] John the Lector (as he was often known) had accompanied Albert the Great to Mecklenburg in 1269,[12] and may have studied for a time at Paris, perhaps while Aquinas and Peter of Tarentaise were lecturing there.[13] When he entered about 1280 on his function as Lector at Freiburg (which was mainly to hold public lectures which his own brethren and those of the local clergy who so desired would attend),[14] John soon found that Raymund of Peñafort's *Summa de casibus*, the standard work of confessional practice, and other similar compilations, were badly in need of revision.[15] Raymund had written his *Summa* at Barcelona about 1225,[16] and although it had been revised by Raymund himself some ten years later and had been glossed extensively by William of Rennes about 1241,[17] it was, inevitably, very much out of date by 1280. Given his background, it is not surprising to find that when John of Freiburg came to the conclusion after some years of teaching that the *Summa de casibus* would have to be revised, he turned at once to the writings of Ulrich Engelbrecht, Albert the Great, Thomas Aquinas and Peter of Tarentaise, for material which would bring the *Summa* up to date.

As we know from John himself (first prologue to his *Summa confessorum*), the earliest form of his revision of Raymund's *Summa* was a

10 See H. Flamm, "Die Grabstätte des Dominikaners Johannes von Freiburg," in *Zeitschrift der Gesellschaft für Beförderung der Geschichts-, Altertums- und Volkskunde von Freiburg* 31 (1916) 272.

11 A. Fries, "Johannes von Freiburg, Schüler Ulrichs von Strassburg," *Recherches de théologie ancienne et médiévale* 18 (1951) 332-340.

12 H.-C. Scheeben, "Albert der Grosse. Zur Chronologie seines Lebens," *Quellen und Forschungen zur Geschichte des Dominikanerordens in Deutschland* 27 (1931) 53.

13 A. Walz, "Hat Johann von Freiburg in Paris studiert?," *Angelicum* 11 (1934) 245-249.

14 See H.-M. Feret, "Vie intellectuelle et vie scolaire dans l'ordre des Prêcheurs," *Archives d'histoire dominicaine* 1 (1948) 11, 20-24.

15 "Quoniam dubiorum nova quotidie difficultas emergit casuum, doctores moderni tam theologi quam iuristae plures casus et legendo et scribendo determinaverunt qui in antiquioribus compilationibus non habentur,...": John of Freiburg, first prologue to the *Summa confessorum*. — The edition of the *Summa confessorum* (here cited, where convenient, as *SC*) used in the present essay is that of Nuremberg 1517. Since John of Freiburg has arranged his work very carefully, and it is very easy to locate a given reference in any of the editions of the *SC*, it will not be cited here by the page of the Nuremberg edition, but simply by book, *titulus* and *quaestio*, thus: 1.7,1 (Book One, title 7, question 1).

16 S. Kuttner, "Zur Entstehungsgeschichte der *Summa de casibus poenitentiae* des hl. Raymund von Pennafort," *Zeitschrift der Savigny-Stiftung für Rechtsgeschichte*, kan. Abt., 83 (1953) 419-448. The edition of the *Summa de casibus* (cited on occasion as *SdC*) used in this essay is that of Paris 1603, but the work is cited only by book and title, e.g. *SdC* 3.24.

17 A. Walz, "Sanctus Raymundus auctor Summae casuum," in *Acta Congressus iuridici internationalis, Romae 1934*, III (Rome 1936) 25-34.

Registrum: an alphabetical index that combined the matter in the *Summa de casibus* with that in the *Apparatus* of William of Rennes. Then, spreading his net a little, he began to collect *casus* which were not covered by the *Summa* and the *Apparatus*, the result being a *Libellus quaestionum casualium* that followed the order of Raymund's *Summa* but contained much more material. Finally, he embarked on a full-blown *Summa confessorum* of his own, the first *summa*, in fact, to be so called.[18]

The date usually assigned to this *Summa confessorum* by bibliographers and others is 1280 x 1298, the *terminus ante quem* being determined by the fact that John added a supplement to the *Summa* when the *Liber sextus* of Boniface VIII was issued in 1298.[19] This span of years may now be narrowed considerably. For example, John (*SC* 3.13, 12, etc.) quotes Garsias Hispanus on the second Council of Lyons, a commentary written in 1282;[20] he also refers (*SC* 3.35, 5) to the *Summula* of "frater Burchardus", a work that is probably to be dated 1290 x 1295;[21] further, he speaks of a treatise on excommunication by "Hermannus, ordinis praedicatorum, *quondam* provincialis Teutoniae" (*SC* 3.22, 219, etc.), who can only be Hermann of Minden, the provincial who confirmed John as prior about 1290 and who was in office from 1286 to 1290.[22]

If these references take us much nearer to 1298 than to 1280, a further important reference enables the *Summa* to be dated even closer to 1298. In that year Boniface VIII published the *Liber sextus*, and John therefore appended a section correlating his *Summa* with the *Sext*, "ne *libri qui* de Summa confessorum *iam scripti erant* appositione statutorum domini Bonifatii nuper in suo sexto libro decretalium de novo editorum destruerentur." This, I take it, means that when the *Sext* came to John's attention, a large part of his *Summa* ("libri qui de Summa confessorum iam scripti erant") had already been completed and he was loth to tamper with it, preferring to add "utiles indices in fine ipsius summae sub titulis eiusdem summae." Certainly John was in

---

18 The use of this title in editions of pre-1300 works for confessors is anachronistic, as in F. Broomfield, *Thomae de Chobham Summa confessorum* (Louvain 1968).

19 For example, in H. Finke, "Die Freiburg Dominikaner und der Münsterbau," (Freiburg in Breisgau 1901), pp. 163-171; J. Dietterle, "Die Summa confessorum," *Zeitschrift für Kirchengeschichte* 25 (1904) 257-260; M.-D. Chenu in *Dictionnaire de théologie catholique* VIII.1 (1924), cols. 701-702; A. Teetaert, *La confession aux laïques* (Louvain 1926), pp. 440-444; P. Michaud-Quantin, *Sommes de casuistique et manuels de confession au moyen âge* (Louvain 1962), p. 44 ("vers 1290").

20 London, British Museum, MS. Royal 9 C 1.

21 Dietterle, art. cit., p. 208.

22 P. von Loë, "Statistisches über die Ordensprovinz Teutonia," *Quellen und Forschungen...Dominikanerordens* 1 (1907) 13.

a position fully to analyze the *Sext* before he compiled the index to his *Summa*, since he states expressly in his preamble to the index that he is including there "additiones quas de sexto libro decretalium collectas in fine summae in speciali tractatu addidi." Given that the *Sext* was published in March 1298, a date 1297/1298 may therefore be suggested for the composition of the *Summa confessorum*.

II

In character, the *Summa confessorum* is a mixture of practical theology and canon law. Like the *Summa copiosa* of the canonist Hostiensis (d. 1271), upon which John draws extensively, the *Summa* is in question and answer form, each question being answered "according to" one or other of several of John's main authorities: Raymund, William of Rennes' *Apparatus*, Hostiensis, Geoffrey of Trani, William Durandus the Elder (*Speculum* and *Reportorium*), the *glossa ordinaria* on the Decretals, Albert, Aquinas, Peter of Tarentaise, Ulrich of Strasbourg.

Following the plan of Raymund's *Summa de casibus*, John's *Summa* is divided into four books, each of which reproduces the chapter-headings in Raymund, from *De symonia* in Book One to *De donationibus* in Book Four. Like Raymund, John also breaks each chapter into numbered *quaestiones*, but John's *quaestiones* do not always coincide with those of Raymund. And where Raymund often discusses several subjects under a single heading, John gives each new subject a special *rubricella*, without, however, disturbing the consecutive numeration of the *quaestiones*.[23] Thus in *SC* 1.1 (= *Summa confessorum, libro* 1, *titulo* 1), where there are 92 *quaestiones* in all, the full *titulus* (from Raymund, *SdC* 1,1), is *De symonia et de iure patronatus*, but qq. 1-79 are entitled *De symonia*, and qq. 80-92 are given a *rubricella, De iure patronatus*. Again, where Raymund (*SdC* 3.24) has 70 paragraphs for *De poenitentia et de remissionibus*, John of Freiburg (*SC* 3.34) has a large number of *rubricellae* embracing some 288 *quaestiones*. On occasion, as in *SC* 3.33, q. 34, John sets up special but unnumbered *quaestiones* within a single numbered *quaestio*. The overall impression of the *Summa* as a well-planned and carefully-executed piece of work is heightened by the author's numerous and very

---

23 John often cites Raymund by paragraph, e.g. *SC* 3.34, 6: "Post haec quaero quot et quae sunt actiones poenitentiae. Respondeo secundum Raymundum, par. 5."

explicit cross-references, for example, in *SC* 1.4,3, where the reader is referred from the beginning of the First Book to the middle of the Third: "vide de hoc infra libro 3, titulo 38, *De transitu clericorum,* 'utrum aliquis'."

Since much of the method and material of the *Summa confessorum* derives from his earlier compilation, the *Libellus quaestionum casualium,* John of Freiburg included the preface to the *Libellus* in the *SC,* immediately before the preface to the *SC* itself. His purpose, he explains in the first (*Libellus*) preface, was to aid his own Dominican brethren in the pastoral care:

> Cum igitur quamplurimae quaestiones ad consilia animarum perutiles diversorum doctorum per volumina sint dispersae, ego frater Iohannes lector de ordine praedicatorum minimus, aliquas ex illis quas magis utiles iudicavi in unum decrevi colligere ad meum et aliorum fratrum profectum, ut si qui forte librorum copiam non habuerint, vel ad tot summas et scripta transcurrenda non vacaverint, hic collecta sub compendio multa de his inveniant quae requirunt...

To that end he had written his earlier *Registrum* of the *Summa* of Raymund and of the *Apparatus* of William of Rennes. Now in the *Libellus* he has put together *quaestiones casuales* which elaborate upon Raymund's or are not to be found in Raymund, and which he has taken from certain canonists and from four theologians of his own Order:

> ...in isto libello quaestiones casuales quae vel non continentur vel minus plene continentur in ipsa praedicta summa fratris Raymundi et apparatu eius, quas in pluribus doctorum libris et scriptis invenire potui, in unum collegi easque sub titulis eiusdem summae et eorumdem librorum et titulorum ordine disposui, aliquas insuper rubricellas de specialibus materiis quibusdam titulis supponendo. Sunt autem haec collecta maxime de libris horum doctorum memorati ordinis, videlicet, fratris Alberti quondam Ratisponensis episcopi, fratris Thomae de Aquino, et fratris Petri de Tharantasia, postmodum summi pontificis Innocentii quinti, magistrorum solemnium in theologia. Item, fratris Ulrici, quondam lectoris Argentinensis eiusdem ordinis, qui quamvis magister in theologia non fuerit, tamen magistris inferior non extitit, ut in libro suo quem tam de theologia quam de philosophia conscripsit evidenter innotescit, et famosorum lectorum de scholis ipsius egressorum numerus protestatur: unde et postea provincialatus Theutoniae laudabiliter administrato officio, Parisius ad legendum directus, ante lectionis inceptionem ibidem a domino est assumptus. Item ponuntur hic aliqua de summa Goffredi et plura de summa domini Ebrudunensis quae dicitur Copiosa, qui postmodum fuit cardinalis Hostiensis: unde et a quibusdam nominatur summa domini Hostiensis. Adduntur quoque hic aliqua de novis statutis summorum pontificum sive in modernis conciliis editis sive in curia publicatis. Sed et hic considerandum est quod cum secunda pars secundae

de summa fratris Thomae praedicti quasi pro maiori parte sit moralis et casualis, plurima de illa sumpta in hoc opusculo posui: et ideo ubicumque solum dicitur "Respondeo secundum Thomam in summa" vel simile, nullo addito, semper intelligendum est de secunda secundae nisi alia pars specialiter exprimatur.

The preface to the *Summa confessorum* itself presumes that one has read the above preface to the *Libellus,* although there is a slight variation on the warning about references to the *Summa* of Aquinas: "quod cum nominatur hic 'in summa Thomae', semper intelligitur de secunda parte secundae nisi alia pars specialiter exprimatur." John is also careful to point out that when he states at the beginning of a reply that he is following a given author, then all of that reply is to be understood as coming from that author:

Nota etiam quod cum cuiuscumque doctoris nomen vel liber ponitur in principio responsionis ad quaestionem, puta cum dicitur "Respondeo secundum Raymundum vel Thomam" aut similia, ab illo accepta est tota solutio quaestionis usque in finem nisi alius doctor interponatur. Cum vero duo vel plures doctores simul ponuntur in principio quaestionis, ut cum dicitur "Respondeo secundum talem et talem," solutio totius quaestionis communis est illis doctoribus, licet aliqua verba ponat unus ad explanationem quae non ponit alius, sed in sententia non discordant.

John explains, too, what precisely he means when he adds (typically, as it happens) at the end of a citation from an author that several other authors (e. g. Thomas and Albert and Peter) support this position:

Verum cum in fine alicuius quaestionis sic dicitur "Concordat" vel "Idem dicit talis et talis", et nullus alius doctor interpositus est, concordia intelligitur totius solutionis vel in sententia et quasi in verbis vel saltem in sententia, nisi solutio plura membra et plures articulos habeat; tunc enim respondet illi versui vel sententiae cui immediate adiungitur, nisi per aliquid additum designetur ad omnia praecedentia vel ad aliqua plura de praedictis esse referendum...

Again, as in the *Libellus,* the audience to which the *Summa* is directed is the "animarum medici". John now hopes that in this present work "multa de his quae requirunt inveniant, et ex diversorum concordia doctorum sciant quid sit probabilius et securius iudicandum."

Now, although John does not claim to be doing anything more than bringing Raymund up to date ("... de summa fratris Raymundi quam quasi totam huic operi includo...": *SC* 3.34,84), his *Summa* is, in fact, a much different work from that of Raymund. For one thing, his range of canonical authorities naturally goes far beyond that of the *Summa de casibus* to include the chief legal writers between 1234 and 1298: Innocent IV, Peter Sampson, Geoffrey of Trani, Garsias Hispanus,

Hostiensis, William Durandus. For another, the tone of the *Summa* is much more theological than that of Raymund. This is largely because of John's adroit use of theological authorities, and in particular of his four Dominican sources. John claims that he is simply filling out Raymund's *summa* with "casus morales", but in fact he presents the reader with quotation after quotation from his "doctores moderni", and thus places some of Raymund's legal solutions in a wider, theological framework.

A good example is Raymund's chapter *De sacramentis iterandis et de consecrationibus ecclesiarum* (*SdC* 3. 24). Raymund is entirely preoccupied with irregularities in this chapter, and only a few lines are allowed to the sacraments as such: "Quoniam quorundam sacramentorum iteratio irregularitates inducit, merito post praedicta impedimenta (sexus, etc.) de hoc aliqua sunt tangenda, pauca sacramentorum generatim praemittendo." As usual, John repeats the opening words of Raymund, "Quoniam...tangenda", but then adds, "et quia de aliquibus sacramentis non ponuntur—puta de baptismo, confirmatione, eucharistia et extrema unctione—quarum notitia non modicae est utilitatis, de his in hoc titulo aliquantulum latius prosequamur, maxime secundum theologos a quibus haec materia perfectius determinatur" (*SC* 3. 24, prologue). As a result, John now devotes 149 elaborate *quaestiones*, with replies mostly from Aquinas, to the four sacraments in question, and a further 14 to a separate *rubricella De consecratione*.

Of course, John never forgets that his primary text is that of Raymund. It was, in its way, sacred in the Dominican Order. For Raymund, who had been a General of the Dominicans for a brief period, was the known compiler of the *Decretales* promulgated by Gregory IX in 1234; besides, his *Summa* was one of the few books to be singled out for mention in the *Ratio studiorum* which a committee composed of Albert, Thomas, Peter of Tarentaise and two others had drawn up for the Order in 1259.[24] This reverence is reflected in the care with which John of Freiburg quotes the *Summa* at length at the beginning of each chapter and keeps to the order of Raymund's paragraphs. Here and there it restrains him when he is tempted to jettison parts of Raymund: "...praetermissa vero hic posui, ne de summa fratris Raymundi...viderer partem notabilem detruncasse" (*SC* 3. 34, 84).

Yet John was quite aware of Raymund's limitations. For example, Raymund has nothing at all on the sacrament of Orders. In fact, under the title *De aetate ordinandorum et de temporibus ordinationum*, he plunges into impediments, without as much as a glance at the nature of

---

24 *Acta capitulorum generalium*, I, ed. B. M. Reichert (Monumenta ordinis praedicatorum historica 3), (Rome 1898), p. 99; see pp. 110, 174.

the sacrament: "Repellitur quis ab ordinatione et electione propter defectum aetatis, dist, 77" (*SdC* 3. 22). John, on the other hand, will have none of this too legalistic approach: "De hoc titulo circa ordines, ordinantes et ordinatos magis specialia exequens, primo quaero...quid sit ordo...."; and proceeds in some 54 *quaestiones* to give long quotations from Thomas, Peter of Tarentaise and others, on the meaning of order, character, etc. Again, in the title *De bigamis (SC* 3. 3), John is content to repeat Raymund almost word for word for the first three *quaestiones*, but then breaks away with the question (q. 4): "Sed quare ad perfectionem sacramenti (matrimonii) non requiritur virginitas in viro sicut in muliere?" And his reply possibly has a sting in its tail: "Respondeo secundum Thomam in scripto (4 D. 27, cited earlier by John), quia defectus in ipso sacramento causat irregularitatem....Juristae tamen diversas rationes alias assignaverunt quae stare non possunt...."

By and large, there is scarcely one place where John is satisfied to repeat Raymund without some comment or addition. Sometimes it is simply a question of filling out a casual reference in Raymund, as when in *SC* 3. 34, 6 he adds a *Decretum* reference ("ab Augustino: De pe. dist. 1") where Raymund has a vague, "ut ait Augustinus". At other times, and especially on purely legal matters, there is an unexpected display (for a theologian) of legal learning. Thus, in the title *De negotiis saecularibus, et utrum de illicite acquisitis possit fieri elemosina (SC* 2. 81), John devotes four *quaestiones* (qq. 39-42) to *De iure emphiteosis* where Raymund has only a few desultory sentences.

Of course, John's command of legal sources was not entirely at first-hand. Most of his acquaintance with the finer points of law, and with the major Decretists and Decretalists, was due, as he admits in his prologues, to the *Summa copiosa* of Hostiensis, the *Apparatus* of William of Rennes on Raymund, and the *Summa* of Geoffrey of Trani (not to speak of the *Speculum iudiciale* of William Durandus, which he does not mention there). Thus, in *SC* 3. 33, 245, after what appears to be an uncommon familiarity with some of the Decretists, John admits disarmingly: "Haec omnia in glossa". All the same, John appears to have made a fair attempt to keep abreast of legal scholarship. If it is not unexpected to find him using the *Speculum* (1287) of Durandus, or the *Manuale* of his fellow-Dominican, Burchard of Strasbourg (*SC* 3. 33, 105, 135, etc.) and the *De interdicto* of his former superior, Hermann of Minden (*SC* 3. 33, 219, 226, 251, etc.), it is a little surprising at first glance to note the presence of the commentary (1282) of Garsias Hispanus on the legislation of the Second Council of Lyons (*SC* 3. 13, 12; 3. 34, 221, 227, etc.). But, then, as befitted an assiduous teacher of practical theology, John had more than a passing interest in the constitutions issued by that Council, for he quotes them often (*SC* 1. 7, 29; 2. 7, 71, 72; 4. 24, 149, etc.).

Since Raymund of Peñafort has many chapters of purely legal content in his *Summa de casibus*, there are, inevitably, some quite long stretches of almost unrelieved quotations from legal authorities in John of Freiburg's *Summa confessorum*. Otherwise, John never lets slip an opportunity of drawing extensively on the "doctores moderni" of theology. As John states in both his prologues, these theological sources are generally limited to the writings of Albert, Ulrich of Strasbourg, Peter of Tarentaise and Thomas Aquinas. Albert and Ulrich, however, are much less in evidence than Peter and Thomas.

The *Liber de missa* of Albert is quoted extensively on many occasions (e. g. *SC* 3. 24, 56, 60, 75, 85, 105, 110), but his *Summa de creaturis* is used sparingly (*SC* 1. 8, 47, 48; 4. 1, 21, etc.), though it is often cited in support of an opinion of one of the other theologians. One of the more notable instances of dependence upon it occurs in the *rubricella De consecratione et velatione virginum (SC* 3. 3, 14-24), where in q. 17 John shows that he is well aware of the relationship between Albert and Thomas: "Quid de virginibus occultis, si sine scandalo earum consecratio intermitti non potest? Respondeo secundum Albertum in Summa de quatuor coaequaevis, in tractatu de virtutibus cardinalibus, di. 58. Et quasi eadem verba sunt Thomae et Alberti, quia Thomas sumpsit de Alberto, qui doctor eius fuerat in studio Coloniensi." Although the "Summa de bono" of Ulrich of Strasbourg is cited more frequently than Albert's *Summa*, it ceases to be prominent after Books One and Two (e. g. *SC* 1. 1, 2, 3, 4, 6, 12: 2. 5, 64-99), and appears only fitfully in Book Three (where, as it happens, there is a citation from Ulrich "in quadam quaestione de quolibet": *SC* 3. 34, 272).

The two theological mainstays of the *Summa confessorum* are, in fact, Peter of Tarentaise and Thomas Aquinas. The *Quodlibets* of Peter are quoted only twice,[25] but his commentary on the *Sentences* is almost as frequently invoked as the *Summa* or the commentary on the *Sentences* of Thomas. Sometimes there are long runs of citations from Thomas, but just as often there are passages of equal length from Peter,

25 "Utrum religiosus teneatur obedire praelato suo praecipienti sibi aliquid contra regulam. Respondeo secundum Petrum in quadam quaestione de quolibet" (*SC* 3.33, 8). This is Qdl. 1.34 in P. Glorieux, *La littérature quodlibetique*, II, (Paris 1935), p. 227, and is printed in Glorieux, "Le Quodlibet de Pierre de Tarentaise," *Recherches de théologie ancienne et médiévale* 9 (1937) 270. A second reference, "Respondeo secundum Petrum in quaestionibus de quolibet" (*SC* 3.34, 254), may really be to Peter's *Quaestiones de peccato*, on which see Glorieux, "Questions nouvelles de Pierre de Tarentaise." ibid., 14 (1947) 98-103.

one after the other. Thus, in *SC* 3. 34, qq. 144-148 (*Pro quibus peccatis requiratur poenitentia?*), all five replies are from Peter; and this block of questions is followed by *De remissione venialium* (qq. 149-158), where Peter is the source called on for qq. 149-152, Thomas for q. 153, Peter again for q. 154, Thomas for qq. 155-156, Peter for 157, and so on. Unless one were to count, and then add up the lines of explicit borrowings from these two authors, it would be difficult to state with any exactitude which one of them is relied upon more than the other in John's *Summa*. But in view of John's own remarks in his prologues, it is not unfair to suggest that Thomas would possibly prove the winner.

Of the works of Thomas quoted in the *Summa confessorum*, the least expected is that known as *De regimine Iudaeorum ad ducissam Brabantiae*. It first occurs in *SC* 1. 4, 9 ("Utrum liceat dominis terrarum aliquam exactionem facere in Iudaeos? Respondeo secundum Thomam in quadam epistola ad ducissam Lotharingiae et Brabantiae..."), and is cited at length on at least 10 occasions — practically all of the letter, in fact (*SC* 1. 4, 9, 10, 11, 12, 13, 14; 2. 5, 34, 36, 40, 41).

John's use of the *Quodlibets* of Thomas is even more striking, for he cites Thomas "in quadam quaestione de quolibet" on at least 33 occasions, and generally in full. Obviously he had searched through the *Quodlibets* and had utilized as much as possible of those with a "pastoral" bearing,[26] e. g., "Utrum clericus praebendatus in duabus ecclesiis, in die quo diversum est officium in utraque ecclesia, debeat utrumque officium dicere...Respondeo secundum Thomam in quadam quaestione de quolibet..." (*SC* 1. 7, 19 = Thomas, *Qdl.* I. 7, 1: all of corpus); "Utrum executor debeat tardare distributionem elemosinarum...Respondeo secundum Thomam..." (*SC* 2. 5, 114 = *Qdl.* VI. 8, 2: all of corpus): "Utrumque aliquis teneatur dimittere studium theologiae, etiam si aptus ad docendum alios, ad hoc quod intendat saluti animarum. Respondeo..." (*SC.* 3. 5. 4 = *Qdl.* I. 7, 2: all of corpus).

Curiously, not all of the *Quodlibets* which John attributes to Thomas prove to be really his. Here and there one's suspicions are aroused by passages which do not have the ring of Thomas, as in *SC* 3. 28, 23: "Utrum periculum sit claustralibus monachis si cura ecclesiarum spectantium ad claustrum negligatur a monachis officialibus? Respondeo secundum Thomam in quadam quaestione de quolibet....Et si esset mihi notum aliquid tale monasterium, non auderem consulere quod aliquis in tali collegio eligeret monachatum." As it happens, this quotation comes

---

26 See L. E. Boyle, "The Quodlibets of St. Thomas and the Pastoral Care," *The Thomist* 38 (1974).

from q. 24 of the first *Quodlibet* (1270) of John Peckham.[27] This is quite interesting, when one remembers that, beginning from 1279, this *Quodlibet* of Peckham occurs in at least 23 MSS of the *Quodlibets* of Thomas, but that only one of these MSS explicitly attributes it to Thomas. This is a late 13th-century MS (Paris, BN, lat. 15351), and it seems reasonable to suppose that the manuscript of the *Quodlibets* of Thomas to which John of Freiburg had access, belonged to that same tradition.[28] At all events, in 11 of the following 33 instances, John of Freiburg turns out to be quoting from Peckham's first *Quodlibet* and not at all from Thomas "in quadam quaestione de quolibet":

	S. confessorum		St. Thomas		Peckham
* 1.	1:	1,66			I.20a
2.		4,4	II.4,	2	
3.		7,19	I.7,	1	
4.		20	V.13,	3	
5.		21	VI.5,	2	
6.		8,62	IV.7,	2	
* 7.		78			I.26
* 8.		79			I.26
9.		9,23	I.9,	2	
10.		10,5	VI.9,	3	
11.		11,23	III.9,	2	
*12.	2:	5,93			I.17
13.		113	VI.8,	1	
14.		114		2	
15.	3:	5,4	I.7,	2	
16.		5	III.4,	1	
*17.		24,23			I.22
*18.		28,23			I.24
19.		32,18	III.4,	2	
*20.		33,6			I.19
*21.		10			I.25
22.		194	IV.8,	3	
23.		34,26	I.5		
24.		48	6,	3	
25.		69		2	
*26.		73			I.23
*27.		74			I.23a
28.		110	III.13,	1	
29.		192	V.7,	2	
30.		236	VI.5,	3	
31.		237	V.11,	3	
32.		249	III.6,	2	
*33.		289			I.18

27   For the quodlibets of Peckham see P. Glorieux, *La littérature quodlibétique* I (1925), pp. 220-222, II (1935), pp. 174-175.

28   See J. Destrez, "Les disputes quodlibétiques de Saint Thomas d'après la tradition manuscrite", *Mélanges Thomistes*, (Paris, 1923), pp. 49-108, at pp. 59-61. The MS. is Paris, Bibliothèque nationale, MS. lat. 15351 (n. 69 in Destrez).

Needless to say, the work of Thomas that is used most of all in the
Summa confessorum is the *Secunda secundae* of his *Summa*. Other parts
of the *Summa*, of course, are cited: the *Prima secundae* occasionally;
the *Tertia pars* (with the commentary on 4 *Sentences*) frequently in *SC*
3. 33, qq. 24-167, on Baptism, Confirmation, Eucharist and Extreme
Unction. But pride of place is given to the *Secunda secundae*, "cum (as
John states in his first prologue) secunda pars secundae de summa
fratris Thomae praedicti pro maiori parte sit moralis et casualis..." And
in both of his prologues he warns the reader, "quod cum nominatur hic
in summa Thomae, semper intelligitur de secunda parte secundae, nisi
alia pars specialiter exprimatur."

The *Secunda secundae* is present right from the opening title of the
Summa (*De symonia*) and it is invoked on every occasion that some
moral point is being considered, even in the midst of long legal
passages. If it is very notable in sections on the *De lege et consuetudine*
(*SC* 2. 5, 203-208), or *De emptione et venditione* (*SC* 2. 8, 7-19), or *De
sententia praecepti* (*SC* 3. 33, 5-26, etc.), it is at its most evident in the
rubricella De iudiciis peccatorum (qq. 196-288) of *SC* 3. 34 (*De
poenitentiis et remissionibus*). After some quotations from Raymund,
and one from the *Prima secundae*, John introduces a long selection
from the *Secunda secundae* with the words, "Post haec descendendo ad
spiritualia, de fide primo quaero..." (q. 202). There now follow the
essentials of the teaching of Thomas on most of the theological and
moral virtues:

S. confessorum	St. Thomas	Subject
q. 202	2.2 2. 6, 7	explicit faith
203	8	"
204	3, 2	confession of faith
205	10, 6	infidelity
206	7	infidels
207	13, 1	blasphemy
208	2	"
209	15, 1	torpor
210	2	despair
211	20, 1	"
212	21, 2	presumption
213	25, 8	charity
214	9	"
215	10	"
216	12	"
217	26, 2	"
218	7	"
219	34, 2	hate
220	35, 1	sloth
221	2	"

258

222	36, 1	envy
223	2	"
224	3	"
.	.	"
.	.	"
.	.	"
288	168, 2	games

In all of the *Summa confessorum*, however, there is very little to be seen of John of Freiburg himself, apart, that is, from a few asides such as "in hoc tamen casu credo quod..." (*SC* 3. 33, 61), "Ego sine praeiudicio credo" (3. 33, 86), "Fateor dictum fratris Thomae, cum ex ratione procedat, mihi magis placere" (2. 8, 25), "Prima opinio benignior et communior" (3. 30, 12), and from a possibly autobiographical glimpse when he speaks of John de Varzy, a Dominican who taught at Paris in 1266: "Et hanc formam (absolutionis) exposuit magister Iohannes de Verziaco in scholis..." (3. 34, 89).

For all that, it would be a mistake to dismiss the *Summa* as a mere, if gifted, compilation. Rather, it may prove not to be an exaggeration to state that the *Summa confessorum* was the most influential work of pastoral theology in the two hundred years before the Reformation. Certainly it was endowed by its author with a doctrinal character which few manuals before it had possessed — and one which would be imitated but rarely improved upon by the manuals and manualists of the next two centuries. [29]

III

Whatever its originality, the *Summa confessorum* was an immediate success. It attracted followers from professional theologians such as Rainerius of Pisa (*Pantheologia*, c. 1330) [30] and legists such as Albericus de Rosate (*Repertorium iuris*, c. 1338) [31] to humble manuals such as the *Fasciculus morum* (1320 x 1340), [32] the *Cilium oculi* (1330 x 1340), [33] the *Speculum christiani* (1370 x 1400), [34] the *Lucerna conscientiae* (c.

---

29 For a slightly different opinion, see P. Michaud-Quantin, *Les Sommes de casuistique*, p. 50. While allowing that the *SC* has a theological character, he feels that it is so faithful to Raymund that there is no new direction there.

30 *Pantheologia* (Louvain 1570), I, p. 384a; II, p. 896b, etc. The *SC* is not cited as such.

31 See R. Abbondanza in *Dizionario biografico italiano* 4 (Rome 1962), cols. 463-465.

32 Oxford, Bodleian Library, MS. Bodley 332, f. 142vb, etc. The *SC* is not cited by name.

33 Oxford, Balliol College, MS. 86, f. 233rb, etc. Again, there is no explicit reference to the *SC*.

34 Oxford, Bodleian Library, MS. Rawl. C.19, ff. 7v, 8r, etc., but again not by name. This MS. contains a larger, if not an original, version of the *Speculum* as printed by G. Holmstedt (London 1933).

1400),[35] the ethico-medical *Florarium Bartholomaei* (1395 x 1407) of John Mirfield,[36] and the *Speculum iuratorum* (c. 1450) of Thomas Wygenhale.[37] And if we are to believe the *Summa rudium* (c. 1338), Pope John XXII held the *Summa confessorum* in such high esteem that he remarked on one occasion of its author, "Qui istam summam collegit, reputo unam esse de melioribus personis totius ecclesiae."[38] There may be some truth in this report, for, as we know from an inventory of 1327, the *Summa* was indeed among the books in John XXII's study.[39]

Not unexpectedly the Dominicans of the 14th and 15th centuries responded with enthusiasm to the new, up-to-date, pattern of confessional manual set by John of Freiburg. From the earliest days of their Order there had been a sturdy tradition of manuals for confessors, mainly because Honorius III had commissioned them in 1221 to hear confessions and had commended them as confessors to the bishop of Christendom. As a result, the Dominicans had entered the field of theology for the very first time, when manuals of practical theology were hurriedly put together at various points of the expanding Order. At Bologna, a *Summa* by Conrad Höxter was possibly ready by May 1221; in 1222 the Dominicans at St. Jacques combined to produce a handy vademecum for the Paris area; another handbook appeared at Cologne in 1224; and in 1225 a first version of a *Summa de casibus* was composed at Barcelona for the Dominicans of Spain by Raymund of Peñafort.[40] It was in this way that a tradition began which Raymund was to dominate in the thirteenth century, and John of Freiburg from 1300 onwards. Raymund, of course, was a great name all through the middle ages,[41] but it is not unlikely that some of the fame attached to Raymund and the *Summa de casibus* is to a large extent due in the later middle ages to the fact that John of Freiburg's ubiquitous *Summa*, with its superficial likeness to that of Raymund, was sometimes mistaken

---

35 Oxford, Bodleian Library, MS. Bodley 801, *passim*, but not by name.

36 Cambridge University Library, MS. Dd. xi. 83, f. 82v, etc., but not explicitly. There is a general study of the *Florarium* in P. Hartley and H. R. Aldridge, *Johannes de Mirfield* (Cambridge 1936).

37 Cambridge University Library, MS. Ii. vi. 39, ff. 3v, 4r, etc., but not by name.

38 *Summa rudium*, (Reutlingen 1487), prologue. The 15th-century chronicler Johann Meyer also reports this eulogy, but his source is probably the *Summa rudium*. See H.-C. Scheeben, "Johannes Meyer O.P., *Chronica brevis ordinis praedicatorum*," in *Quellen und Forschungen...Dominikanerordens* 29 (1933) 53.

39 A. Maier, "Annotazioni autografe di Giovanni XXII in codici vaticani," *Ausgehendes Mittelalter* II (Rome 1967), pp. 81-96, at p. 94, n. 28.

40 See P. Mandonnet, *Saint Dominique*, ed. M.-H. Vicaire and R. Ladner (Paris 1938), I, pp. 249-269.

41 A. Walz, "S. Raymundi de Penyafort auctoritas in re paenitentiali," *Angelicum* 12 (1935) 346-396.

(especially by library catalogues) for the *Summa de casibus*, and cited as "Raymundi *Summa confessorum*", through ignorance of its real author.[42]

The readiness with which the Dominicans abbreviated, translated or simply used the *Summa confessorum* leaves little doubt that John had taken over the field from Raymund. The *Summa rudium*, with its eulogy of John, is largely a simplified version of the *Summa* by an anonymous Dominican;[43] another Dominican, William of Cayeux, published an abridgement about 1340;[44] in 1338, Bartholomew of S. Concordio composed at Pisa an influential *Summa de casibus* (often called *Pisanella* or *Magistruccia*) that is basically an alphabetical arrangement of the *Summa confessorum*;[45] about a hundred years later a small Dominican *Tractatus de sacramento altaris* is described by its author as "ex Summa confessorum quasi totaliter extractus."[46]

Dominicans, too, contributed to vernacular versions of the *Summa*. Berthold of Freiburg, John's successor as superior, made a German translation which was to find its way into print at least four times before 1500.[47] In the middle of the 14th century the *Summa* is used, if not directly translated at times, by the *Tugenden Buch*, a work which translates selections from the *Secunda secundae* of Thomas, and with which John of Freiburg himself is credited in some three manuscripts.[48] At the end of the 15th century a French translation was printed of a *Regula mercatorum* which Guy of Evreux had pulled together about 1320 from John of Freiburg's chapters on usury and just price in the *Summa*.[49]

---

42 Thus the *Regimen animarum* (1343): "Compilavi enim hoc opusculum ex quibusdam libris, videlicet, Summa summarum, Raymundi Summa confessorum,...." (Oxford, Bodleian Library, MS. Hatton 11, f. 4r). John of Freiburg himself is partly to blame for any mistake of identity. Shorn of its two prologues, the *SC* could easily have been taken for the *Summa de casibus*. The incipits of both works are largely identical, as are the prologues to each *titulus*.

43 J. F. von Schulte, *Geschichte der Quellen und Literatur des canonischen Rechts*, II (Stuttgart 1877), pp. 528-529; R. Stintzing, *Geschichte der populären Literatur des römisch-kanonischen Rechts in Deutschland* (Leipzig 1867), p. 514; J. Dietterle, "Die Summae....," in *ZKG* 27 (1906) 78-80. Since this article of Dietterle, "Die Summae confessorum...von ihren Anfängen an bis zu Silvester Prierias....," is cited often in the following notes, it may be useful to note here that the whole article runs through five volumes of the *Zeitschrift für Kirchengeschichte* (*ZKG*), as follows: 24 (1903) 353-374, 520-548; 25 (1904) 248-272; 26 (1905) 59-81, 350-362; 27 (1906) 70-83, 166-188, 296-310, 431-442; 28 (1907) 401-431.

44 Schulte, II, p. 423; Dietterle, *ZKG* 26 (1905) 59-63.

45 Schulte, II, pp. 428-429; Dietterle *ZKG* 27 (1906) 166-171.

46 Cambridge University Library, MS. Ee. iii. 58, ff. 80r-88r.

47 Dietterle, *ZKG* 26 (1905) 67-77; R. Stanka, *Die Summa des Berthold von Freiburg* (Vienna 1937).

48 K. Berg, *Der tugenden Buch. Untersuchungen zu mittelhochdeutschen Prosatexten nach Werken des Thomas von Aquin* (Munich 1964), pp. 77-78, 97-100, 109-112. The *Summa confessorum* is also present in German works of Nicholas of Dinkelsbühl (ob. 1433), one of the great 15th-century popularizers of scholasticism (ibid., pp. 30-32, 41-52).

49 P. Michaud-Quantin, "Guy d'Evreux, technicien du sermonnaire médiéval," *Archivum Fratrum Praedicatorum* 20 (1950) 216-217.

Finally, if the influence of the *Summa confessorum* is to be seen in the two great Franciscan *Summae* of the end of the 15th century, the *Rosella casuum* of Baptista de Salis[50] and the *Summa angelica* of Angelo Carletti,[51] it is even more present in the last, and perhaps the most ambitious, of the medieval Dominican manuals, the *Summa summarum Sylvestrina* (1516) of Sylvester Mazzolini de Prierio.[52] A man of formidable learning, Sylvester nevertheless draws, as so many others had done for over 200 years, on the *Summa* of John of Freiburg for quotations from the *Quodlibets* and the *Secunda secundae* of Thomas, from the *Summa* of Raymund, from the *Apparatus* of William of Rennes and, need it be said, from the writings of Albert the Great and Peter of Tarentaise. At the end of the *Sylvestrina* there is a long catalogue of the main "summistae" of the preceding centuries. It is surely not inappropriate that the *Summa confessorum* of John of Freiburg should appear there simply and anonymously as "Summa confessorum ordinis praedicatorum".[53] If anything, the impact of the *Summa confessorum* on the manualist tradition at large was as pronounced as that on the Dominican manualists. As early as 1303 it was used (but without acknowledgement) by the Franciscan, John of Erfurt, in the second edition of his *Summa de poenitentia*.[54] About the same time there also appeared the first Franciscan counterpart to the *Summa*, an anonymous *Labia sacerdotis*. While this leans heavily on the pre-1300 manualists, and on Bonaventure, it also cites Thomas, Peter of Tarentaise and Raymund. The *Summa confessorum*, however, is never mentioned. Yet it is clear from the whole layout of the *Labia*, and from its citations from these Dominican sources, that the author had John of Freiburg's work before him.[55]

The most successful attempt to do for Franciscan moralists what John of Freiburg had done for Ulrich, Albert, Peter and Thomas, comes some ten years later with the *Summa Astesana* of Astesanus of Asti.[56]

50   Schulte, II, pp. 448-450; Dietterle, *ZKG* 27 (1906) 431-442.

51   Schulte, II, pp. 452-453; Dietterle, *ZKG* 27 (1906) 296-310; Michaud-Quantin, *Sommes*, pp. 99-101.

52   Schulte, II, pp. 455-456; Dietterle, *ZKG* 28 (1907) 416-431; Michaud-Quantin, *Sommes*, pp. 101-104.

53   *Summa summarum quae Sylvestrina dicitur* (Cologne 1518), ff. xxxvv, clxvr, etc.

54   A first edition of this *Summa* was written c. 1296 (see F. Doelle, "Johann von Erfurt," in *ZKG* 31 (1910) 225-238). A second edition in 1302 (e.g. Oxford, Oriel College, MS. 38) uses the *Summa confessorum*, for example at f. 150r, where, citing Aquinas on the Eucharist through the *SC*, John of Erfurt says, "Ego tamen credo cum Bonaventura...".

55   For example, Oxford, Bodleian Library, MS. Hamilton 34, f. 279r: "Numquid participans excommunicato in casibus non concessis peccat mortaliter? Respondetur. Quidam dicunt sic, ut Ray. et Gau., et istud durum est dicere. Sed Bon., Thomas et Petrus dicunt..." (= *Summa confessorum*, 3.33, 165, without, of course, the reference to Bonaventure).

56   For an account of Astesanus see G. Giorgino, *Sponsalium institutum in fr. Astesani de Ast Summa de casibus* (Caiazzo 1942), pp. 4-17. See also Schulte, II, 425-427; Dietterle, *ZKG* 26 (1905) 35-62; Michaud-Quantin, *Sommes*, pp. 57-60.

Written in 1317, and dedicated to cardinal Giovanni Caetani, it was probably as influential as John's *Summa* over the next two centuries. The preface, which is not unlike that of John of Freiburg,[57] carries a massive list of authorities, mostly Franciscan moralists and theologians such as Bonaventure, William de la Mare, Alexander of Hales and John Scotus ("Famosissimus et subtilissimus"). If there are also the *Quodlibets* of Henry of Ghent, the commentary on the *Sentences* of Richard of Middleton, and the recently-published *Apparatus* of Iohannes Andreae on the *Sext*, the *Astesana*, nevertheless, has a batch of authorities in common with John of Freiburg: Thomas ("famosissimus"), Raymund, William of Rennes, Peter of Tarentaise, Hostiensis, Garsias Hispanus and William Durandus. There is no sign, however, of the *Summa confessorum* among the sources cited, whether in the prologue or the text. This is a little strange. For although the *Astesana* does appear to show some independent knowledge of Raymund, Thomas and Peter of Tarentaise, there are sections where quotations from these authors are undoubtedly through John of Freiburg's work.[58]

The unacknowledged use of John of Freiburg's *Summa* was, in fact, widespread. One of the most striking instances is that of the Berkshire vicar, William of Pagula. In three of his works, and particularly in his very popular *Oculus sacerdotis* (1320-1327), Pagula quietly uses the *Summa confessorum*, without once mentioning it by name, for matter from various canonists and, on many occasions, for quotations from Albert, Thomas, Raymund and Peter of Tarentaise.[59] One small example will suffice to illustrate the point:

Oculus[60]	*Summa* (3. 34, 28)
Tanta potest esse contritio quod tota poena remittitur absque confessione. Nichilominus tamen confessio et poenitentia iniuncta ex-	Utrum contritio possit tollere totum reatum poenae? *Respondeo secundum Petrum*:... Tantum potest incendi contritio

---

57 "...exhortatione ven. patris et domini supra memorati, et etiam plurium fratrum, summam de casibus deo auxiliante compilavi," prologue.

58 Compare, for example, *Summa astesana* (Regensburg 1480), 4.3, 4, with *SC* 3.24, 13. Often, as in *Astesana* 4.3, 4 and 4.3, 5, the author gives a precise reference to Aquinas and Peter of Tarentaise where the *SC* has only a general reference. Anonymous borrowings from John of Freiburg are also to be found in the *Summa de casibus* (c. 1315) of the Franciscan Durandus de Campania: see Dietterle, *ZKG* 27 (1906) 70-78.

59 On the *Oculus* see L. E. Boyle, "The *Oculus sacerdotis*... of William of Pagula," in *Transactions of the Royal Historical Society*, 5th series, 5 (1955) 81-110.

60 Oxford, New College, MS. 292, f. 76r.

pleri debent non propter remedium sed propter praeceptum.

Et non solum propter praeceptum tenetur quis confiteri et satisfacere, sed etiam propter incertitudinem, quia non est certus quod
sua contritio fuit sufficiens ad totum reatum tollendum, *secundum
Thomam et Petrum.*

quod tota poena remittitur. Nichilominus tamen confessio et poenitentiae iniunctae expletio requiritur etiam, non propter remedium
sed propter praeceptum.

Concordat his Thomas, et addit
quod non solum propter praeceptum tenetur confiteri et satisfacere
sed etiam propter incertitudinem,
quia, scilicet, non est certus quod
sua contritio fuerit sufficiens ad
totum reatum tollendum.

The same unacknowledged dependence on John of Freiburg is again
to be noted in William of Pagula's *Summa summarum,* a massive and
not unsuccessful compilation of law and theology which was put
together between 1319 and 1322. The same is true of his *Speculum
praelatorum* of much the same period.[61] And when Pagula's *Oculus
sacerdotis* was revised, and in part re-written, some sixty years later by
John de Burgo, chancellor of Cambridge, there is an even greater ex-
ploitation of the *Summa confessorum.* But there is a difference. Like
William of Pagula, the *Pupilla oculi* (1384) of de Burgo cites Albert,
Aquinas, Peter, Raymund, etc. through the *Summa confessorum,* but
unlike Pagula, de Burgo explicitly admits that the *Summa* of John of
Freiburg is his source, as when he states in his tract on the Eucharist,
after a series of quotations from Aquinas: "Haec omnia notat Iohannes
in Summa confessorum, lib. 3, tit. xxiiii, c. xxix."[62] Again, his debt to
the *Summa confessorum* is obvious, even though he does not explicitly
acknowledge it, when he says that his exposition of the Peckham
"Syllabus of pastoral instruction" (1281) comes "ex dictis sancti Thomae
in secunda secundae, diversis articulis."[63]

Borrowings from the *Summa confessorum,* whether explicit or implicit, were not at all confined to popular manuals. Thus, John Bacon-

---

61 Thus, at the end of the *Summa summarum* (Oxford, Bodleian Library, MS. Bodley 293, f.
83r): "Quare requiritur maior numerus testium contra episcopos et superiores quam contra alios
simplices homines? Dic quod triplex est ratio...secundum Thomam in Summa" (= *SC* 2.5, 183);
"Quid si testis producatur super re de qua non est omnino certus? Dic secundum Thomam in
Summa...." (= *SC* 2.5, 183), etc. See L. E. Boyle, "The *Summa summarum*...," in *Proceedings of
the Second International Congress of Medieval Canon Law, Boston 1963,* ed. S. Kuttner and J. J.
Ryan, (Vatican City 1965), pp. 415-456, at p. 423.
62 *Pupilla oculi,* 4.10 (Strasbourg 1518), f. xxxiii.
63 Ibid., 10.5 (Strasbourg 1518), f. clxxvr.

thorpe, the English Carmelite theologian, whom one would have expected to have known his Thomas at first-hand, is content in his Postill on St. Matthew (1336-1337) and *Quaestiones canonicae* on the 4th book of the *Sentences* (c. 1344) to draw on the *Summa confessorum* for many passages from Aquinas.[64] What is more interesting, perhaps, is the fact that although Baconthorpe possessed John of Freiburg's *Summa*, he often quotes Thomas, Peter, etc., not through the *Summa confessorum* but through William of Pagula's *Summa summarum* which, in turn, was totally dependent upon the *Summa confessorum*. There are occasions, indeed, when he prefers to quote Thomas from the *Summa summarum* rather than from Thomas himself, or, for that matter, from the *Summa confessorum,* the source of the *Summa summarum*. Thus when he writes, "In Summa summarum et Summa confessorum habes multos casus expressos necessitatis excusantes (a ieiunio)....Primo quid de laborantibus in vineis....Respondetur ibidem (i. e. Summa summarum) ....Sic tenet Thomas in secunda secundae q. 174, art. iv," the wording of the passage from Thomas is that of the *Summa summarum* and not of the *Summa confessorum* or Thomas himself. Yet John Baconthorpe clearly had the *Summa confessorum* of John of Freiburg open before him at the same time. For where Pagula's treatment of fasting ends simply "secundum Thomam in Summa",[65] Baconthorpe proceeds to give a more precise reference to Thomas, taking it straight from the *Summa confessorum*.[66]

While one can understand that a canonist such as William of Pagula (or, a hundred years later, William Lyndwood in his *Provinciale*)[67] would have found the *Summa confessorum* convenient for quotations from the great theologians, it is otherwise in the case of John Baconthorpe or of equally professional theologians such as Antoninus of Florence (d. 1459) and Robert Holcot (d. 1349). If, for example, the *Confessionale* of Antoninus is based mainly on the *Pisanella* of Bartholomew of Pisa, a derivative of the *Summa confessorum,* there are numerous instances when Antoninus turns (sometimes without acknowledgement) to the *Summa confessorum* itself for references to Thomas, Peter of Tarentaise, etc., thus: "Duplex est contritionis dolor secundum Thomam et Petrum in 4 d. xvii.... Item secundum Petrum in 4 d. xvii, dolor maior intellectualis debet esse de maiori peccato

---

64 See B. Smalley, "John Baconthorpe's Postill on St. Matthew," *Medieval and Renaissance Studies* 4 (1958) 99-110, 119, 143.

65 *Summa summarum*, MS. Bodley 293, f. 149v.

66 Baconthorpe, Commentary on 4 *Sent.* 20.2, 2 (Cremona 1616, II, p. 446). The same passage is also to be found in the *Postilla in Matthaeum*, Trinity College, Cambridge, MS. 348, f. 120v.

67 *Provinciale* 3.23 (Oxford 1679), pp. 227-235, on Penance, etc. Thus at p. 229, note 1: "In hac materia dicunt beatus Thomas et Petrus in scriptis, et idem recitat Jo. in Summa confessorum, tit.

habitualiter et non actualiter si considerentur peccata in communi.... Item secundum Thomam in quolibet et Innocentium, contritus debet magis diligere Deum quam seipsum" (= *Summa confessorum* 3. 34, 22-26).[68] Robert Holcot, in his commentary on the fourth book of the *Sentences*, also uses the *Summa confessorum* extensively, but with a certain amount of caution. Citing the *Summa confessorum* for a *Quodlibet* of Aquinas which is, in fact, one of John Peckham's, Holcot voices his suspicions as follows, "Numquid debet baptizari (monstrum) ut unus homo an ut duo? Dicendum est...sicut dicitur in Summa confessorum et imponitur sancto Thomae in quadam quaestione de quolibet. Sed puto quod non est dictum suum. Tamen satis bene dicit...."[69]

Holcot's fellow Dominican and exact contemporary, John Bromyard, probably makes the greatest use of the *Summa confessorum* of all the writers of the 14th and 15th centuries who borrowed from John of Freiburg. Both in Bromyard's *Opus trivium* (c. 1330)[70] and the massive *Summa praedicantium* (1330-1348), there are passages through the *Summa confessorum* "ex responsione sancti Thomae ad ducissam Lotharingiae" (*Summa praedicantium* M. 8, 36; U. 12, 27), from Raymund and the canonists, as well as from Albert, Ulrich of Strasbourg and Peter of Tarentaise. At times Bromyard acknowledges his source, thus "Contrariae vero opinionis sunt sanctus Thomas et Petrus et Ulricus, qui volunt .... Nota s. Thomam ad hoc, prima secundae, q. 64, art. 4. Vide in Summa confessorum, lib. 3, tit. 34, q. 321" (*Summa praedicantium* D. 5, 5). But there are other moments when there is no reference to the *Summa confessorum*, and an unwary reader might be led to conclude that Bromyard had consulted all the numerous sources which he lists, as when he states, "Ad omnia namque haec secundum Hostiensem, Raymundum,...Tancredum, Ulricum, tenentur..." (*Summa praedicantium* R. 6, 2 = *Summa confessorum* 2. 5, 91), or again, "Quibus concordat sanctus Thomas de Aquino in scripto super 4 sent. d. 25.... His etiam concordat idem in Summa q. 100, art. 4. Et Petrus et Albertus in scripto super 4 dist. 25..." (ibid., S. 9, 1 = *Summa confessorum* 1. 1, 1).[71]

---

de penitentiis et remissionibus, rubrica de suffragiis, q. 163...;" p. 232n.: "Sed numquid contritus, non tamen confessus, recipiendo corpus Christi, peccat? Dic secundum Petrum....Et his concordat Albertus d. 16...Notantur haec secundum Jo. in Summa confessorum, lib. 3, c. 24, q. 78."

68 *Confessionale* (Paris 1516), f. 186v.
69 *In quattuor libros Sententiarum* (Lyons 1518), 1.7, casus XVI.
70 *Opus trivium*, R 7 B-C, S 1 C, etc.; London, British Museum, MS. Royal 10 C X, ff. 123v, 125v, etc.
71 *Summa praedicantium* (Venice 1586). On Bromyard see L. E. Boyle, "The Date of the *Summa praedicantium* of John Bromyard," *Speculum* 48 (1973) 533-537.

IV

If the general influence of the *Summa confessorum* of John of Freiburg on canonists, theologians and manualists is impressive, there is, in respect of the works of Aquinas and Peter of Tarentaise, a further point that has not been fully appreciated by scholars. This is the fact that much of the knowledge of the moral teaching of Aquinas and Peter (not to speak of Albert, Ulrich of Strasbourg, Raymund and the others) in the 14th and 15th centuries is due to a great extent to the *Summa confessorum*.[72] So ubiquitous, indeed, was the *Summa* that it is not surprising to find references to Albert or Aquinas or Peter in places as unlikely as the jottings of a confessor's notebook in St. John's College, Cambridge,[73] or the notes scribbled at the end of a Canterbury copy of the *Summa de casibus* of Thomas Chobham,[74] or in the interlinear gloss of the *Manuale confessorum metricum* of a Cologne Dominican towards the end of the 15th century.[75] And if the name of one of John of Freiburg's teachers, John de Varzy, was known to John Gerson in the early 15th century, this is precisely because, as he himself tells us, he possessed a copy of the *Summa confessorum*:

> Petis primo, si apud aliquem doctorem reperiatur forma authentica absolutionis sacramentalis. Respondeo quod sic. Et de hoc videatur Summa confessorum....Tenor quaestionis de qua fit superius mentio in Summa confessorum, lib. 3, tit. 34, q. 91, *secundum quotationem libri mei* sic se habet: ... Respondeo secundum Albertum....Et hanc formam exposuit magister Iohannes de Varziaco....Thomas etiam in ultima parte summae..."[76]

Leaving John de Varzy aside, there is no doubt that Albert, Thomas and Peter of Tarentaise were known in their own right by many scholastics. But where their moral teaching is concerned, and particularly in non-professional circles, the evidence seems to point to the

---

72 Thus, many of the works cited by Grabmann, "Das Weiterleben und Weiterwerken des moraltheologischen Schrifttums des hl. Thomas von Aquin im Mittelalter," in *Divus Thomas* (Fr.) 25 (1947) 3-28, as evidence of the influence of the moral theology of Aquinas in the middle ages, in fact derive much of their knowledge of Aquinas from John of Freiburg, e.g. the *Summa astesana*, the *Summa rudium*, the *Consolatorium* of John Nider (ob. 1438).

73 Cambridge, St. John's College, MS. 355, f. 84r. 15th c.

74 For example, "Utrum satisfactio possit fieri per opera extra caritatem facta? Respondeo secundum Petrum in scriptis d. 15, et Iohannem in Summa, lib. 3, c. de satisfactione...Dicit Thomas...:" Canterbury, Dean and Chapter Library, MS. B.10, f. 23r. 14th century.

75 (Cologne 1498), f. cxxxvii, etc.

76 J. Gerson, *De absolutione sacramentali*, in *Opera omnia*, ed. E. du Pin (Antwerp 1706), II, cols. 406-407.

Summa confessorum and its many derivatives. In the case of Peter and Thomas one has to allow, of course, for the influence of the very popular *Dialogus de administratione sacramentorum* which the Dominican William of Paris compiled between 1300 and 1314 "de scriptis fratris Thomae principaliter...ac Petri Tarentoize."[77] In practice, however, one can rule it out, since, unlike John of Freiburg, William of Paris rarely identifies his quotations.

But even when the *Summa confessorum* is not mentioned by name, it is fairly easy to recognize its presence where there are citations from Albert, Aquinas, Peter of Tarentaise, Ulrich of Strasbourg or Raymund of Peñafort. The juxtaposition of two or more of these names is usually a good indication. The phrase, "ut dicit Thomas in quadam quaestione de quolibet", also provides a strong hint, as in the *Summa summarum* of William of Pagula (1319-1322),[78] the *Manipulus curatorum* of the Spaniard Guido de Monte Rocherii (c. 1330),[79] or the *Speculum curatorum* of the Benedictine Ranulph Higden (c. 1340).[80]

The key, however, is in the formula by which John of Freiburg cites his authorities. He drew attention to it in his second prologue ("Verum cum in fine alicuius quaestionis sic dicitur *Concordat...*"), and he is unfailingly true to it from the very opening chapter of the *Summa*, thus:

> Quaestio prima. Quaero quid sit symonia. Respondeo. Symonia est studiosa voluntas emendi vel vendendi aliquid spirituale vel annexum spirituali. Sic diffinitur communiter a theologis et iuristis. Communiter enim addunt "vel spirituali annexum", ut Thomas in scripto super 4 sent.. dist. xxv, et Petrus de Tarentasia, etiam Albertus, eadem distinctione, et Thomas in Summa q. 100, art. 1....Quare etiam symonia dicitur haeresis? ....Respondeo secundum Thomam in Summa art. i et art. x. Ideo symonia dicitur haeresis quia sicut protestatio fidei exterior quaedam religio est....*Concordat* his Petrus in scripto et Ulricus par. ii....Quare symoniaci dicuntur a Symone...quam Giezite?....Respondeo secundum Ulricum, par. Dicuntur autem, quod completior huius ratio peccati fuit in actu Symonis quam in facto Giezi, nam ille solum vendidit donum Dei....*Concordant* his Thomas et Petrus..."

77   A. Teetaert, "Un compendium de théologie pastorale," *Revue d'histoire ecclésiastique* 26 (1930) 66-102

78   For example (MS. Bodley 293, f. 140v): "An clericus praebendatus in duabus ecclesiis in die quo diversum est officium in ecclesia debeat dicere utrumque officium vel unius ecclesiae officium dicere debet? Dic...*secundum Thomam in quadam quaestione de quolibet*" (= *SC* 1.7, 19); "An clericus praebendatus in scholis existens tenetur dicere officium mortuorum?... Sciendum...*secundum Thomam in quadam quaestione de quolibet*" (= *SC* 1.7, 21).

79. *Manipulus curatorum* (Louvain 1552), e. g. at f. 128r : "Sanctus Thomas *quadam quaestione de quolibet* ponit aliquos casus in quibus tenetur existens in peccato mortali statim confiteri" (= *SC* 3. 34, 69).

80. Cambridge University Library, MS. Mm. i. 20, f. 188v : "Sanctus Thomas *in quadam quaestione de quolibet* dicit quod in foro contentioso creditur homini pro se et contra se et sine probationibus" (= *SC* 3. 34, 48).

268

Armed with this key, and remembering in particular John of Freiburg's variations on the "Concordat" theme, it is not too difficult to suggest what must be the source, directly or at a remove, of, for example, a gloss that begins, "Declarantur praefati versus quoad restitutionem secundum beatum Thomam, Albertum et Ulricum, sic...."[81] Above all, it allows us to estimate just how widespread was the direct influence of Thomas or Albert in certain areas of scholasticism, and to cut down to size some of the supposed influence of Peter of Tarentaise and Ulrich of Strasbourg.[82] And if an author claims rather plausibly, as a certain Henricus de Belle of Löwenich does in a fifteenth-century treatise, that he has compiled his work from notes taken "dum studueram in 4 lib. sententiarum", and, further, goes on to urge his readers to study "in libris Thomae et Alberti", this seeming evidence for the availability of certain works of Albert and Thomas to the common clergy of the Rhineland crumbles away when one discovers the said Henricus using phrases such as "et concordant Albertus et Thomas."[83]

As for Raymund and his well-known, if not axiomatic, domination of the penitential theory and practice of the middle ages, much of this was just as vicarious from 1300 onwards as the reputed influence of Albert and Thomas and Peter of Tarentaise on popular (and some nonpopular) theology. Sylvester de Prierio was not far from the truth in 1516 when he gave the label "Summa confessorum *ordinis praedicatorum*" to John of Freiburg's work. For although it never had the blessing of official approval in the Dominican Order that Raymund's *Summa* had had, the *Summa confessorum* was *the* Dominican manual in as much as it had distilled the moral teaching of the greatest of the Dominican theologians, and had placed it at the disposal of a vast audience. From 1300 onwards, Raymund was, in fact, obsolete. It is surely not without some significance that whereas John of Freiburg's *Summa confessorum* was printed twice before 1500[84] and repeatedly in the following century, the *Summa de casibus* of Raymund did not appear in print until 1603.

---

81 *Manuale confessorum metricum* (Cologne 1498), f. cxxxviiv. For the *Manuale* see Dietterle, *ZKG* 27 (1906) 177-183.

82 J. Daguillon, *Ulrich de Strasbourg, O.P., 'Summa de bono'* (Paris 1930), pp. 3*-5*, and H.-D. Simonin, "Les écrits de Pierre de Tarentaise," in *Beatus Innocentius Papa V* (Rome 1943), pp. 163-335, make no allowance whatever for the *Summa confessorum* when discussing the influence of their respective authors in the later middle ages.

83. Cambridge University Library, MS. Kk. i. 9, ff. 54r-65v, at ff. 54r, 58r. Henricus de Belle was pastor of Löwenich, and his treatise is addressed to his curate, John. Another copy, dated 1470, is in Brussels, Bibliothèque Royale, MS. 2070 (2434-52), ff. 64r-81v.

84. L. Hain, *Repertorium bibliographicum* (Stuttgart-Paris 1826-1838), nn. 7365 (1476) and 7366 (1498). Incunabula of the German translation by Berthold of Freiburg are at nn. 7367-7377.

THE *OCULUS SACERDOTIS*
AND SOME OTHER WORKS OF
WILLIAM OF PAGULA

ONE of the results of the Fourth Lateran Council in 1215 was a heightening of interest in the cure of souls, and the years that followed the Council saw a generous effort on the part of prelates to provide, in accordance with the Lateran directives, a better-educated clergy who could bring the laity to a reasonable understanding of the essentials of Christian belief and practice. In England, during the reign of Henry III, nearly every diocese contributed to the movement for reform, chiefly by statutes modelled upon or deriving from decrees of Innocent III's great council. The Council of Oxford in 1222, the Council and Constitutions of the Legate Otto at London in 1237 and of the Legate Ottobono at London in 1268, catered in varying degrees for the Church in England as a whole.[1]

By 1260 the great wave of diocesan pastoral legislation seems almost to have spent itself, and some twenty lean years of pastoral effort were to follow until the Council of Lambeth in 1281. There, the Franciscan John Pecham promulgated his *Ignorantia Sacerdotum*, an outline of Christian doctrine and morals which the priests of the province of Canterbury were ordered to expound in the vernacular four times each year.[2] This may be said to represent the high point of pastoral legislation in medieval England, not because there is anything great or original about the Lambeth outline but because it was the first programme of pastoral instruction

---

[1] Cf. M. Gibbs and J. Lang, *Bishops and Reform, 1215–1272* (Oxford, 1934), especially pp. 94–179; and, for the synodal statutes of the period, C. R. Cheney, *English Synodalia of the Thirteenth Century* (Oxford, 1941).

[2] D. Wilkins, *Concilia Magnae Britanniae et Hiberniae* (London, 1737), ii. 54–6. The outline occupies a chapter of the Lambeth Constitutions to which Wilkins gives the title *De Informatione Simplicium*. We shall refer to the outline by its *incipit*: *Ignorantia Sacerdotum*.

in pre-reformation times to emanate from Canterbury, the ecclesiastical centre of England. As such it was to exercise influence in the two centuries preceding the Reformation.[1]

The character of the Lambeth outline has not always been clearly rendered by historians. Some, beguiled perhaps by the famous opening sentence about the ignorance of priests, seem to represent Pecham's enactment as a manual of practical theology designed to combat that ignorance.[2] This is precisely what it is not. For the *Ignorantia Sacerdotum* is simply a Syllabus which lists or defines what responsible parish priests should preach to their parishioners: it presumes rather than imparts knowledge, and, far from providing, demands a companion volume of practical theology comparable to the *Templum Domini* with which Robert Grosseteste supplemented his pastoral legislation.[3] Unaided, it could have done little to relieve clerical ignorance.

Forty years were to elapse before any elaboration of Pecham's Syllabus would emerge. In the meantime those priests who took the Lambeth programme seriously could implement their knowledge of the points they were required to preach from one or other of the handbooks of popular theology which the thirteenth century had produced. The *Summula* of Bishop Quivil of Exeter in 1287, for instance, although it is primarily a manual for the examination and instruction of penitents in the confessional, incidentally covers some of the ground of the programme.[4]

But with the flowering of pastoral theology in the fourteenth

---

[1] Thus, as late as 1520, an Oxford bookseller, John Dorne, may be seen doing a steady trade in an English adaptation of the outline called the *Exhonoratorium Curatorum*, thirty copies of which were sold during about ten months of that year. Cf. F. Madan, *The Daily Ledger of John Dorne, 1520* (Oxford Historical Society, *Collectanea*, i. 1885), where the entries for the period are printed pp. 79–138.

[2] E.g. M. Deanesly, *The Lollard Bible* (Cambridge, 1920), p. 196; D. Douie, *John Pecham* (Oxford, 1952), p. 138. F. Barlow, reviewing Miss Douie's book (*Journal of Ecclesiastical History*, iv (1953), 229–30), calls it 'a handbook for confessors' akin to the *Summula* of Quivil.

[3] The *Templum Domini* is extant in some 70 manuscripts, 65 of which have been listed by S. H. Thomson, *The Writings of Robert Grosseteste* (Cambridge, 1940), pp. 138–40.

[4] I.e. the ten commandments and the seven deadly sins. The text is printed in Wilkins, *Concilia*, ii. 162–8. In the prologue Quivil states his purpose: ' . . . insufficientia presbyterorum saecularium confessiones audientium compatiens . . . praesentem summulam eisdem assigno ut eam sciant ad utilitatem

century, manuals began to appear in Latin and in the vernacular which featured expositions of the Syllabus. The first of these manuals came appropriately from the pen of a parish priest. This was the *Oculus Sacerdotis*, commonly attributed to a Berkshire parish priest, William of Pagula. Written about 1320, part of it is an explicit elaboration of the *Ignorantia Sacerdotum* of Pecham, and all of it must have helped to make the fulfilment of the requirements of that Syllabus easier for the parochial clergy of the next two centuries. Our concern in this essay is with this manual, with its probable author and with the largely unsuspected richness of its setting.

As the name suggests, the *Oculus Sacerdotis* deals with matters which should come within the vision of a priest; and, in the form in which it is normally found, consists of three parts, the first, from which the whole often took its title,[1] being called the *Pars Oculi*, the second the *Dextera Pars*, the third the *Sinistra Pars*. At first, these titles may seem somewhat unusual until one remembers the great vogue of the *Oculus Moralis* of Petrus de Lacepiera which, about the time when the *Oculus Sacerdotis* came to be written, may have been circulating under the name of Grosseteste or Pecham, either of 'which commanded respect.[2] This *Oculus Moralis* of Lacepiera analysed the moral significance of the eyes. The right eye, for example, was the eye of action and morals; the left eye that of knowledge and speculation.[3] The plan, therefore,

suam et confitentium'. Although Miss Douie, *John Pecham*, pp. 138–9, says that Quivil used the Pecham programme 'as the source of the little *Summa*', the programme and the *Summula* differ in character and purpose.

[1] Thus the first catalogue of Dover Priory (M. R. James, *Ancient Libraries of Canterbury and Dover* (Cambridge, 1903), p. 418, nos. 95, 96) twice describes as *Pars Oculi* what the second catalogue (*ibid.*, p. 445) reveals to be all three parts of the *Oculus Sacerdotis*.

[2] The *Oculus Moralis* is ascribed to Grosseteste in many fourteenth-century MSS. listed in Thomson, *Writings of Robert Grosseteste*, pp. 256–7, and to Pecham in one MS. of the next century. The colophon of the Augsburg edition of 1477 reads: 'Tractatus (Johannis Pitsham Archiepiscopi Cantuariensis) . . .' For Petrus de Lacepiera (Pierre de Limoges), cf. H. Spettmann, 'Das Schriften "De Oculo Morali" und sein Verfasser', *Arch. Franc. Hist.*, xvi (1923), 309–22.

[3] *De Oculo Morali*, Augsburg (A. Sorg), 1477, fo. 11: ' . . . in nobis duplex oculus: intellectus videlicet et affectus. . . . Oculum intellectus illuminat veritas, oculum affectus caritas. . . . Sed in multis sinister oculus multum illuminatus est cum dexter sit obscuratus . . . O quot sunt hodie . . . qui multum intendunt circa quaestiones sed modicum circa mores'.

84

of at least two parts of the *Oculus Sacerdotis* may well have been suggested by the contents of this little treatise. The moral or teaching part is significantly called the *Dextera Pars Oculi*, and the dogmatic or semi-speculative part the *Sinistra Pars Oculi*; while the part on confessional practice, the *Pars Oculi*, although it has no obvious source in the *Oculus Moralis*, may be taken to represent a function of the eye, the capacity to scrutinize. At all events, later supplements to the *Oculus Sacerdotis* were to continue the image, a *Cilium Oculi* about 1330–40 adding an eyelash to make up, no doubt, for a certain lack of finish[1]; the *Pupilla Oculi*, later still, being an explicit attempt to refocus the *Oculus* after some sixty years of use.

In purpose, therefore, the *Oculus Sacerdotis* was meant to embrace all aspects of the *cura animarum* to which a parish priest was committed; and in secular literature it has an interesting parallel, the *Oculus Pastoralis*, a manual written to instruct a future ruler of a state in the *cura rerum* which Muratori prints under the year 1222.[2] However, in electing to approach the pastoral care from the three angles of confessional practice, sacramental theology and preaching matter, the author of the *Oculus Sacerdotis* involves himself in much repetition which has led some authors to question the competence of the work. Thus Professor Davis, the only writer who has studied the *Oculus* to any depth, concluded in 1913 that the treatise was the work of an author who was diffuse, repetitive and incapable of arranging his material in an orderly fashion; that it was, in fine, the product of a less scientific school of jurisprudence than the *Pupilla Oculi* of a Chancellor of the University of Cambridge, John de Burgh, which in 1384 improved upon it.[3]

It would seem, however, that in charging the author of the *Oculus Sacerdotis* with a lack of method Davis was only accepting

[1] It is called 'quoddam additamentum Oculi Sacerdotis' in MS. Balliol College 86, fo. 231r, and on occasion is found as a fourth part of the *Oculus*, as in MS. 249, Guildhall, London.

[2] *Oculus Pastoralis* sive *Libellus erudiens futurum rectorem populorum anonymo auctore conscriptus circiter annum 1222*, in L. A. Muratori, *Antiquitates Italicae Medii Aevi*, ix (1776), 792–858.

[3] H. W. C. Davis, 'The Canon Law in England', *Zeitschrift der Savigny-Stiftung f. Rechtsgeschichte*, xxxiv (1914), 349–50, reprinted in J. R. Weaver and A. L. Poole, *H. W. C. Davis, A memoir* (London, 1933), pp. 123–43.

at their face value some statements of de Burgh himself in his preface to the *Pupilla*. The *Oculus*, de Burgh allowed, may be a very
popular manual of pastoral theology, but the treatment it gives
to its subject seems to involve a certain disorder: this he would
remedy by pruning and redistributing the matter.[1] On the other
hand, a later writer, whose pastoral manual has recently come to
light, seems on the contrary to imply that de Burgh in his *Pupilla*
missed some of the point of the *Oculus*. This manual, a further
Pupilla Oculi, restores much of the *Oculus* that de Burgh had
deemed redundant and, superficially at least, shows a greater
understanding of the plan of the original *Oculus*.[2] For although
in the *Oculus Sacerdotis* there is considerable repetition of matter,
it is in each part approached from a different point of view. Thus,
in the *Sinistra Pars*, when the priest is making himself familiar
with sacramental theology, there is one approach; there is a second
in the *Dextera Pars* when he is presenting the fruits of his study
to his parishioners; and there is still a third in the *Pars Oculi*, when
he is applying the matter in the confessional. Each part of the
Oculus Sacerdotis was in fact designed to be complete for its purpose, and as such is often to be found on its own in manuscripts;
indeed, as we shall see later, there is evidence that the first of the
three parts of the *Oculus Sacerdotis* as it commonly circulated was
in reality the last to be written. But even in the normal tripartite
Oculus which Davis and de Burgh had before them, the seemingly endless repetition of which they complained does in fact
eliminate cross-reference. The *Oculus Sacerdotis*, on that score
at least, would thus as a whole be highly acceptable to readers
of whose capacities the author may have had an unflattering but
scarcely an inaccurate opinion. An analysis of the three parts
of the *Oculus* indicates that he knew his potential public only
too well.

The first part of the *Oculus Sacerdotis*, the *Pars Oculi*, was
written to enable confessors to examine penitents thoroughly, to
suggest to them appropriate remedies for their weaknesses and

[1] 'Modus tamen et ordo tractandi ob quorundam in eo contentorum
inordinatam replicationem non videtur doctrinaliter ordinatus': *Pupilla
Oculi*, London (impensis Bretton), 1510, fo. iir.

[2] MS. Corpus Christi College, Oxford, 145, fos. 121r ff.: 'Incipit libellus
qui dicitur Pupilla Oculi summarie compilatus. . . .' The text itself begins
with the prologue to the *Pars Oculi*: 'Cum ecclesiae quibus praeficiuntur
personae minus idoneae. . . .'

to assign salutary penances. It is, in fact, a modest *Summa de Poenitentia*.

The twelve opening chapters are devoted to a method of examining penitents from many walks of life on aspects of the articles of faith, the ten commandments, the seven deadly sins and the venial sins. Then follows a model setting of a confession in which the penitent accuses himself of the various sins and faults which have been the burden of the priest's interrogation. John Myrc, in part of his *Instruction for Parish Priests*, has rendered most of the contents of these chapters into English verse, though with an appreciable rearrangement.[1] The *Pars Oculi*, however, proceeds from this point with some twelve chapters on the penances which a priest, prudently withal, should assign to certain types of sin, homicide, harlotry and the like. By and large, this second block of chapters summarizes or embodies some ten chapters of the *Summa de Casibus* of Thomas de Chabham, a priest of the Salisbury Diocese a century earlier.[2]

Thus far the contents of the *Pars Oculi* closely resemble those of any standard penitential manual of the period. Some personal experiences of the author now inspire him to make a contribution of his own. While engaged in the office of a penitentiary, he tells us in his prologue to the *Pars*, he was appalled to find how many parish priests seemed to have no inkling where the jurisdiction that they exercised over consciences in the confessional began or ended. Some were absolving from sins and censures over which they had no control, while others were denying absolution and referring penitents to the diocesan penitentiaries when in fact the remedy was theirs to apply. This state of affairs revealed an ignorance of the penitential canons of the Church in general and of the

---

[1] J. Myrc, *Instructions for Parish Priests*, ed. E. Peacock (Early English Texts Society, Old Series, xxxi, 1868), ll. 976–1096, 1107–1286, etc.

[2] *Pars Oculi*, MS. New College 292, fos. 8v–11r: Thomas de Chabham, *Summa* (MS. Oriel College 17), Pars VIIa, cc. 114, 127, 128, 130, 131, 140, 170, 175, 185, 186. For Master Thomas de Chabham, subdean of Salisbury between about 1208 and 1228, cf. J. C. Russell, *Dictionary of writers of thirteenth-century England* (Bulletin of Institute of Historical Research, special supplement no. 3, London, 1936), pp. 158–9; and A. Teetaert, *La confession aux laiques dans l'église latine* (Paris, 1926), pp. 347–51. It is not generally known, however, that he was also perpetual vicar of Sturminster Marshall, Dorset, between 1206 and about 1220 (Muniments of the Dean and Chapter, Salisbury, Press 4, Box C, doc. 4, 5).

Church in England which could not reasonably be pleaded by those who by profession were committed to the execution of this discipline.[1]

To offset this dismal situation, and to render happier the lot of parishioners, many of whom had often to go for a year on end without absolution, the author draws up for the guidance of the parochial clergy the great catalogue of censures, reserved and unreserved, which occupies the central chapters of the *Pars Oculi*.[2] Based on general and provincial legislation, this catalogue includes an account of the occasions on which a priest himself may absolve from censures, and of those on which the absolution is reserved to the pope, to bishops or to penitentiaries whom they have delegated; and, among other matters, 140 ways in which greater excommunication may be incurred, fifty of which are the articles of *Magna Carta* and the *Carta de Foresta* to which an excommunication *ipso facto* had been attached in the previous century.

As a whole, the catalogue depends largely on the manuals of continental canonists, but the achievement of the author is none the less remarkable. For the first time, it would seem, a manual was at the disposal of the parochial clergy of England in which the censures imposed by the Church in England were analysed and placed within the framework of the established classification

---

[1] 'Et licet animae hominum pretiosiores omnibus aliis rebus et corporibus ... ipsae tamen animae per praelatos et sacerdotes minus idoneos multipliciter sunt deceptae, prout experientia didici in officio poenitentiarii constitutus. Nam multoties scivi et inveni quamplures sacerdotes parochiales errasse in modo confessionis audiendae et etiam in absolutione inpendenda ac etiam in poenitentiis iniungendis, et absolventes parochianos suos de facto quos absolvere non possunt de iure ... et in multis casibus mittentes eos poenitentiariis episcoporum in quibus ipsi sacerdotes absolvere possunt bene. Et sic quandoque propter negligentiam parochianorum et ignorantiam presbiterorum remanebant quidam parochiani per annum et ultra non absoluti de peccatis de quibus idem sacerdos parochialis absolvere possit ... et hoc propter iuris ignorantiam quae non poterit eos excusare cum nulli sacerdotum liceat poenitentiales canones ignorare nec quicquam facere quod patrum regulis possit obviare: XXXVIII D, 1, 2 et 3, et cap: *Nulli Sacerdotum.* ... Valde tamen necessarium est sacerdotibus parochialibus scire poenitentias in canonibus diffinitas, ut sic scire possint pro maioribus peccatis maiorem poenitentiam inponere, ... et casus in quibus absolvere non possunt. ... Et quia in praedicitis quamplures scio errare, (cupio) ... quantum possum Dei gratia eos ... ab huiusmodi erroribus revocare. ...' (MS. New College 292, fo. 2r–2v.)

[2] MS. New College 292, fos. 13r–27v.

of censures binding the Church universally.[1] At all events, the catalogue was to become classic, being repeated in one form or other by manuals of the next two centuries. Thus, as late as 1523, we find among the articles of the Great Sentence in the printed edition of the Sarum *Manuale*: 'Also all those that breke any poynt of the Kynges Grete Chartre . . . or of the Chartre of the forest. . . . In the Grete Chartre be xxxv poyntes and the Chartre of the forest comprehendeth xv poyntes (ut in tractatu qui vocatur Pars Oculi in prima parte plenius continetur).'[2] The penitentiary-class which the author of the *Oculus* may be taken to represent must have rejoiced in the drop in claims on their services which doubtless followed on the publication of the *Pars Oculi*. Yet there are indications that poor and ignorant parish priests were not the only ones at fault in this matter of moral jurisdiction. The prologue to the *Pars* tactfully makes the parochial clergy the main offenders, but the fact remains that the catalogue of censures also covers 'Cases which a bishop's penitentiary may not absolve', and 'Cases which may not be absolved by a bishop'.

The second part of the *Oculus Sacerdotis*, the *Dextera Pars*, is concerned with the parish priest precisely as pastor, and with the manner in which he should educate those committed to his care in the essentials of dogma and morals, and familiarize them with the legislation which council or synod had devised to protect them from misbelief or from misdemeanour.[3]

First, the author deals with matters which should be preached or expounded from time to time, such as the vernacular form of baptism; the use of the baptismal form in cases of danger of death;

[1] There were, of course, many excommunication-lists current in the thirteenth century in England, but few of the range of the *Pars Oculi* catalogue. In passing, we may mention Grosseteste's use of the excommunications pronounced at the Council of Oxford in 1222 in his constitutions (*Roberti Grosseteste Epistolae*, ed. H. R. Luard (Rolls Series, 1861), pp. 162–4); and his 'Casus quibus excommunicatur ipso iure', etc., in the *Templum Domini* (MS. Rawl. A 384, fo. 101).

[2] Sarum *Manuale*, 1523, fo. cxxv, quoted by C. Wordsworth, *Ceremonies and Processions of the Cathedral Church of Salisbury* (Cambridge, 1901), pp. 252–3.

[3] 'Ne quis igitur praelatus seu sacerdos parochialis de hiis per aliqualem ignorantiam se excuset, omnia praecipua quae per canones (et) constitutiones provinciales praecipiuntur parochianis exponi et inter parochianos in ecclesia praedicari in hac modica summa breviter et faciliter continentur' (MS. New College 292, fo. 35r).

the rôles and responsibilities of sponsors; the variety of forms in which homicide can occur: mothers, for instance, should make sure that there is no danger of their children being overlaid and smothered in bed; the meaning of confirmation, matrimonial consent, banns; the importance of annual confession in obedience to the decree of the Fourth Lateran Council; the significance of the sacrifice of the Mass; the obligation to pay tithes, and the manner of collecting these in the province of Canterbury; the iniquities and forms of usury; reverence for the Holy Name; the impropriety of loud behaviour or secular gatherings in churches or in cemeteries. Most of these points are taken from the *Decretals* and provincial legislation, but some of them derive directly from the Salisbury constitutions of Richard Poore and Robert of Bingham in the first half of the thirteenth century.[1]

After this outline of occasional preaching matter which Myrc, in his *Instructions*, has adapted into English,[2] there follows a list of thirty-four excommunications of more frequent occurrence to which people are liable *ipso facto*, and which therefore should be brought to their notice on occasions throughout each year. Nineteen of these censures come from the universal discipline of the Church, and the remaining fifteen from excommunications peculiar to the Church in England.[3] Like the longer catalogue of censures in the *Pars Oculi*, this excommunication-list was to have a wide vogue, and has found its way into print in Wilkins' *Concilia* as an appendix to the constitutions of Archbishop Greenfield of York in 1311.[4] Indeed the whole of the two sections of the *Dextera*

---

[1] Poore's constitutions (ed. W. D. Macray, *Charters and Documents of Salisbury* (Rolls Series, 1891), pp. 128–63) are cited once, and those of Bingham (B.M. Harl. MS. 52, fos. 119v–126r) at least four times. Indeed, the sequence of this section of the *Dextera Pars* seems to be closely related to that of Bingham's 'quae sunt principalia sacramenta et quot propter simpliciores'.

[2] Lines 69–86, 119–263, 304–403.

[3] Two excommunications from the *Decretum*, three from the *Decretals*, eight from the *Sext*, six from the *Clementines*; two from the Lambeth Council of Boniface of Savoy in 1261, one from the constitutions of the Legate Ottobono in 1268, one from the Reading Council of Pecham in 1279 and eleven from his Lambeth Council of 1281.

[4] Wilkins, *Concilia*, ii. 413–15, but with two notable alterations: the two references in the *Dextera Pars* to the *Speculum Praelatorum* become references to the *Pupilla Oculi* (written 1384).

Pars thus far described was to enjoy an existence separate from the *Oculus Sacerdotis* in pastoral miscellanies of the late fourteenth and early fifteenth centuries.[1]

The remaining and greater part of the *Dextera Pars* is taken up with the Pecham Syllabus, the *Ignorantia Sacerdotum*, by which priests were obliged to instruct the laity in the fourteen articles of the Creed, the seven sacraments, the ten commandments, the seven deadly sins, the seven works of mercy and the seven virtues. This programme of moral instruction is now elaborated from an extensive acquaintance with Fathers and theologians, with Provincial legislation and the latest glosses on the *Decretals*, the *Sext* and the *Clementines*. The exposition, however, has little in common with Lyndwood's glosses on the articles of the Creed from the *Ignorantia Sacerdotum* in the first chapter of his *Provinciale*.[2] Its simple purpose is to suggest matters of theological or legal import which a parish priest would find useful when faced with the quarterly problem of expanding Pecham's Syllabus for the instruction of his parishioners. Only once is there anything approaching a ready-made sermon. This is a fine and perhaps original sermon on the Last Judgement which the author includes in his exposition of the seventh article of the Creed, the Resurrection from the Dead, as a model illustration of the way in which a particular point of the Pecham programme could profitably be developed. It will appear again in the fourteenth century in one or more manuals, notably in the *Judica me* treatise of Richard Rolle which incorporates many passages from the *Pars Oculi* and from this *Dextera Pars*.[3]

[1] Of the instances of this which have been noted to date, the more interesting are five to which C. R. Cheney's *English Synodalia* (p. 147; and pp. 112, 115) has drawn our attention. In each of these instances the extract from the *Dextera Pars*, which Professor Cheney describes as 'a short series of instructions to parish priests' and of uncertain origin, is found accompanying, or as an appendix to, the *Pupilla Oculi* of de Burgh. For the extract represents one of the sections of the *Oculus* which de Burgh, in revising it, had omitted or redistributed. In fact, the extract may really be an appendix to the *Pupilla*: some of the Salisbury references have been dropped, several points are abbreviated and the reader referred to the *Pupilla*, and, as in the work referred to in the preceding note, references to the *Speculum Praelatorum* are replaced by references to the *Pupilla*.

[2] W. Lyndwood, *Provinciale* (Oxford, 1679), pp. 1–8. Myrc, *Instructions*, ll. 454–525, represents the *Dextera Pars* on the articles of faith.

[3] Cf. H. E. Allen, *The Writings ascribed to Richard Rolle* (New York–

A part of the Pecham programme comes up for consideration once again in the *Sinistra Pars* of the *Oculus Sacerdotis* which is entirely devoted to a study of the seven sacraments. This third part of the *Oculus* is prefaced by a long discussion of clerical ignorance which begins with a phrase, *Ignorantia sacerdotum populum decipit et multoties ducit in errorem*, which might be taken for a memory of the famous opening sentence of Pecham's *Ignorantia Sacerdotum*. Some caution, however, must be exercised when assessing the historical significance of this prologue, of the prologues to the *Pars Oculi* and *Dextera Pars* which likewise accuse clerics of ignorance, and of the Pecham prologue. Pecham, for instance, is probably adapting a passage from the Fourth Council of Toledo in 633 with which the medieval cleric would be familiar from the 38th Distinction of Gratian's *Decretum* of which it is the opening chapter.[1] Similarly the whole prologue to the *Sinistra Pars* is mainly a mosaic of quotations from this same Distinction.

It is possible, then, that an apparent witness of this kind to contemporary clerical backwardness may not be uncoloured by a certain convention. Certainly this seems true of Pecham's prologue, the full import of which cannot be evaluated independently of the real character of its correlative, the Syllabus. For if Pecham's remedy for a widespread ignorance of a vital part of Christian teaching, the sacraments, is merely to name the seven of them and leave it at that, then what has been called Pecham's 'groan . . . at the illiteracy of the parish clergy'[2] must lose some of the dark significance with which it is commonly credited.

On the other hand, the prologues of the *Oculus Sacerdotis* probably reflect an actual condition of the clergy if we are to judge

London, 1927), pp. 101–4. Miss Allen's dating of Rolle's treatise *ante* 1322 may be a few years out, since *Judica B2* uses the *Pars Oculi*, which appears to have been written about 1327–9.

[1] 'Ignorantia mater errorum cunctorum maxime in sacerdotibus vitanda est, qui docendi officium in populo Dei susceperunt' (*CIC.*, ed. A. Friedberg, Leipzig, 1879, i. 141). Pecham's words are: 'Ignorantia sacerdotum populum praecipitat in foveam erroris . . .' (Wilkins, *Concilia*, ii. 54). Cf. the preamble to Quivil's synodal statutes of 1287, where the *Decretum* passage is repeated almost *ad verbum* (*ibid.*, ii. 143).

[2] 'Giraldus Cambrensis might laugh, and Pecham and Grosseteste groan, at the illiteracy of the parish clergy, but it is only fair to remember that the facilities for receiving any sort of education were very meagre' (J. R. H. Moorman, *Church Life in England in the thirteenth century* (Cambridge, 1946), p. 94).

from the explicit attempt each part makes to cater in a realistic fashion for ill-educated parish priests. Thus the *Sinistra Pars* provides them with an excellent *summa* of basic sacramental theology on which to improve themselves. This, naturally, demands a more elaborate treatment of the sacraments than in the *Dextera Pars* where the sacraments were dealt with as part of the programme of lay instruction. The sacrament of Order, for instance, which was passed over there because, the author said, it was no business of the laity, now gets full attention. Similarly, the Eucharist is handled at greater length: there is a chapter in which every rubric and action of the Mass is examined and explained, selections from which were later incorporated into the rubrics of the Canon of the Mass in some missals and manuals of the Salisbury usage.[1] In the tract on Order the detail is close enough to take us into the examination-room of a candidate for orders. 'Ordinands', the author says, 'are not to be examined too rigidly, but rather in a summary fashion, and leniently. Too great perfection is not required as long as a reasonable literacy, a legitimate age and a good character are not wanting'; 'the good opinion in which a candidate is publicly held can be equivalent to an examination: indeed it is clear (from the *Decretum*) that local candidates of good repute are to be spared examination.'[2]

This brief description of the *Oculus Sacerdotis* at least throws into relief some of the qualities which may have made it an attractive, if not imperative, purchase for the parish priests of the fourteenth century. There were, of course, many manuals of varying excellence to choose from, these being a legacy of the thirteenth century, but few if any of these showed the scope and realism of the *Oculus*. In character, indeed, the *Oculus* seems to belong to a *genre* of pastoral literature which embodies many features of, but clearly is distinct from, the better-known homiletic, penitential and moralizing treatises of the thirteenth and fourteenth centuries with which it is sometimes confused. In the *Oculus* the pastoral care is seen as a whole, while only certain aspects of that care are covered in compendia of virtues and vices, in *summae* of penance and confessional practice, in manuals of sermons and sermon-

[1] Cf. J. Wickham Legg, *Tracts on the Mass* (Henry Bradshaw Society, xxvii, 1904), pp. 270–4.
[2] MS. New College 292, fo. 94.

making. The *Oculus*, with its wider and often more sensitive vision of the needs of a priest in his parish, contrives to comprehend the essentials of the specialized treatises while embracing the education of the priest as well as of his parishioners. If, however, the *Oculus Sacerdotis* is to be considered in this light, this is not to set aside or minimize the value or the significance of the narrower expressions, continental or English, vernacular or Latin, of the literature of pastoral theology. The tradition which the *Oculus* represents is but one facet, however important or realistic, of the endeavour of the thirteenth and fourteenth centuries to better the training and education of clergy and laity.[1]

The *Oculus Sacerdotis*, nevertheless, was not the first manual of its kind to be composed for the convenience of the parochial clergy of England. Rather is it the culmination of an interesting series of manuals which, attempting to treat of the pastoral care in the wider sense that we have suggested above, seems to have had its beginnings in the *Summa de Casibus* of Thomas de Chabham about 1220.[2] But the *Oculus* differs from these on one important point. For although the manuals of Chabham, Wetherset and Simon Hinton, to name the more popular, run parallel to the great provincial and synodal legislation of the thirteenth century, little, if any, reference to this local legislation is to be found in them.[3] The

---

[1] The specialized literature of the thirteenth century is discussed in E. J. Arnould, *Le Manuel des Péchés* (Paris, 1940), pp. 1–59; and that of the thirteenth and fourteenth centuries in H. G. Pfander, 'Some medieval manuals of instruction in England and observations on Chaucer's "Parson's Tale" ', *Journal of English and Germanic Philology*, xxxv (1936), 243–58.

[2] Although the *Summa 'Cum miserationes'* of Thomas de Chabham, subdean of Salisbury, and perpetual vicar of Sturminster, is professedly 'de poenitentia', it ranges beyond the confines of manuals such as Raymund of Peñafort's *Summa de Casibus*, including, for instance, a chapter on the conduct of priests which begins 'Est etiam officium periculosum officium sacerdotum vel aliorum clericorum habentium curas animarum, et tamen nesciunt animas regere vel, si sciunt, negligunt' (MS. Oriel College 17, fo. 60r).

[3] It is perhaps unfair to include Thomas de Chabham in this general statement since he was writing before the wave of pastoral legislation had gathered force: no doubt he was composing his *Summa* about the same time as his diocesan, Richard Poore, was framing his synodal statutes, but, as Professor Cheney says, 'whether one stimulated the other to write it is impossible to say' (*English Synodalia*, p. 54). Chabham, however, senses the importance of a knowledge of local excommunications: 'secundum diversas regiones sunt diversi canones et diversae institutiones latae

94

Oculus, for reasons we have seen, looked back from the first quarter of the fourteenth century to the Lateran Council of 1215 and took in a century of particular applications of that Council's decrees in England. In this, and in its high theological content, would lie its appeal to the parochial clergy of the two centuries following.

If the recurrence of the work in wills and visitational records of the fourteenth and fifteenth centuries may be taken as an indication, the *Oculus Sacerdotis* was widely appreciated. Thus, in the register of church goods in the archdeaconry of Norwich which was compiled in 1368, the *Oculus Sacerdotis* occurs, in whole or in part, no less than eleven times,[1] while a brass at Emberton (Bucks.) depicting a priest in vestments has an inscription which might suggest that the *Oculus* had won a place for itself as a regular item of church furniture: 'Pray for the soul of Master John Mordon, once rector of this church, who, during his lifetime, gave to his church a Missal, an *Ordinale* and a *Pars Oculi*.'[2] The glimpses, however, that are afforded of the personal life of priests who possessed the *Oculus* are few and slight. But on one priest at least the work may have made a strong impression. For in leaving his copy of the *Oculus* to the church he had served, this priest also leaves seventeen shillings 'in memory of the ten commandments and the seven deadly sins'.[3]

Although the popularity of the *Oculus* declined gradually after the publication of its revision, the *Pupilla Oculi*, in 1384, some fifty manuscripts of it still survive in this country, and it is to be

sententiae, ut in aliquibus regionibus vel episcopatibus excommunicati sunt ipso facto omnes sortiarii et omnes sortiarie et omnes qui pervertunt testimonia defunctorum et omnes falsi testes et omnes usurarii. . . . Unde oportet quod quilibet sacerdos sciat constitutiones synodales factas in episcopatu suo . . .' (MS. Oriel College 17, fo. 50v). The synodal excommunications instanced bear a marked resemblance to those in Poore's synodal constitutions (cap. xlix).

[1] A. Watkin, ed., *Archdeaconry of Norwich, Inventory of Church Goods temp. Edward III.* (Norfolk Record Society, xix, 1947), ii. p. xlviii. Copies at Thwaite, Sall, Stiffkey St. John, Mileham, Gayton Thorpe, Tilney All Saints, Dersingham, West Newton, Merton, Swanton Abbot, Ashby.

[2] 'A fifteenth-century library list', *Records of Buckinghamshire*, xii (1927–33), 365–7. Mordon died in 1410.

[3] Will of Roger Shirreve, clerk, of St. Martin (near Ludgate ?), proved 1392: R. R. Sharpe, *Calendar of Wills proved and enrolled in the Court of Husting* (London, 1889), ii. 296–7.

found in wills and inventories as late as, and even after, 1500.[1] It was never printed, however, though the *Pupilla* was printed at least three times between 1510 and 1518, at London, Rouen and Paris. But the spirit of the *Oculus* persisted in the *Pupilla* which, as de Burgh expressly says, was 'for the most part dependent on the *Oculus Sacerdotis*, a manual more widespread than other manuals that have been inspired by a zeal for souls'.[2]

One notable feature of this tribute of de Burgh is that the *Oculus Sacerdotis* is cited anonymously. But although this could mean that the work was so commonplace by 1384 that no ascription was thought to be necessary, there are indications that the author may indeed have been unknown. There is not, for example, any mention of an author in the *Cilium Oculi*, which was issued as a supplement a decade, perhaps, after the *Oculus*[3]; nor in the *Regimen Animarum* of 1343, which makes explicit and very extensive use of the work.[4] Further, the manuscripts of the *Oculus* that belong to the fourteenth century are no more helpful, and generally limit themselves to something such as *Summa quae vocatur Oculus Sacerdotis*. No ascription of the *Oculus* seems to occur in any

---

[1] E.g. the will of Ralph Busby, vicar of the parochial church of Great Baddow, dated 1492: H. C. Malden, 'Ancient Wills: 2', *Trans. Essex Archeological Society*, vi (1896), 122; and that of Thomas Mawdesley, clerk of Myddleton, 1554: *History of the Chantries I* (Chetham Society, lix, 1872), 123–4. The copy of the *Oculus* in the Dean and Chapter Library, Canterbury (MS. D. 8), belonged, the flyleaf tells us, to Dom. W. Ingram, 'penit(entiarius) ecclesiae . . . Cant' olim'. A note in pencil on the MS. states that Ingram was penitentiary from 1511–1532.

[2] '. . . precursores nostri quidam zelo animarum permoti de his que regimen animarum concernunt sententias seu tractatus varios contexerunt, inter quos ille qui sacerdotis oculus intitulatur ceteris communior . . . (nostrum compendium) quia de predicto tractatu qui dicitur Oculus Sacerdotis pro magna parte excerptum est . . . Pupillam Oculi censui nuncupandum' (J. de Burgh, *Pupilla Oculi*, London, 1510, fo. ii).

[3] The purpose of the *Cilium Oculi* is clear enough, e.g. (on reserved censures): 'Sunt autem casus episcopales sufficienter recitati in Oculo Sacerdotis. . . . Item, casus papales in eodem libro satis patent praeter quos hos duos iniungendos decrevi . . .' (MS. Balliol College 86, fo. 232v), but whether the work is by the author of the *Oculus Sacerdotis* or by some contemporary is not easy to decide. Certainly it would seem to have been written within the period 1330–40.

[4] 'Incipit liber qui vocatur Animarum Regimen compilatus in anno Domini millesimo tricentesimo quadragesimo tertio. O vos omnes sacerdotes qui laboratis onerati et curati animarum attendite et videte libellum

form until the next century, when it appears in the *Catalogus* of John Boston, a monk of Bury who is said to have flourished about 1410. There the *Oculus Sacerdotis* is assigned to a William of Pagula, vicar of Winkfield in the Forest of Windsor, who would seem to have lived during the reign of Edward III.[1]

With the possible exception of Coxe, who betrays a little exasperation at times by describing the *Oculus* as *opus Willelmi de Pagula sive Iohannis de Burgo sive cuiuscumque sit*,[2] most bibliographers of later ages have accepted this ascription, and there is evidence to hand that Boston may not have misled them. This, in the main, is provided by four other works with which Boston credits Pagula, a *Summa Summarum*, a *Speculum Praelatorum*, a *Speculum Religiosorum* and an *Epistola ad Regem Angliae Edwardum III*.[3]

istum. . . . Compilavi enim hoc opusculum ex quibusdam libris, videlicet, Summa Summarum, Raymundi, Summa Confessorum, Veritatis Theologiae, Pars Oculi Sacerdotis, et de libro venerabilis Anselmi De Concordia Praescientiae et Praedestinatione et Gratiae Dei cum Libero Arbitrio . . .' (MS. Hatton 11, fo. 4r).

[1] The full William of Pagula entry in Boston's *Catalogus* will be given in the next note but one. But it may be noted here that a century after, and, perhaps, independently of, Boston, the catalogue of the books of Syon Monastery explicitly ascribes the three copies of the *Oculus Sacerdotis* that the monastery possessed to 'Magister Willelmus de Pagula' (*Catalogue of the Library of Syon Monastery, Isleworth*, ed. M. Bateson, Cambridge, 1898, p. 188, nos. T. 11, T. 32, T. 43).

[2] H. O. Coxe, *Catalogus Codicum Manuscriptorum* . . . (Oxford, 1852), e.g. MS. New College 292; Trinity 18.

[3] Boston of Bury *apud* T. Tanner, *Bibliotheca Britannico-Hibernica* (London, 1748), introduction, p. xl:

Wilhelmus de Pagula, vicarius de Wingfeld, prope forestam de Windesor, floruit A.C. . . . et scripsit

Summam Summarum de jure canonico pariter et divino et continet lib. v. Pr. *Ad honorem*. Fin. *respondendum*.

Speculum Prelatorum.

Speculum Religiosorum. Pr. *Accipite*. Fin. *passionem Christi*.

Summam quae dicitur Oculus Sacerdotis. Pr. *Ignorantia*. Fin. *coronam vitae*.

Ad regem Angliae Edwardum iii epist. i.

From this entry Bale, Tanner (*op. cit.*, p. 570) and later writers derive their basic information about William of Pagula. But in Bale's case there are some curious discrepancies. Here, for instance, Boston, in listing the *Oculus*, gives the *incipit* of the *Sinistra Pars* only. Bale, in his *Index* (*Index Britanniae Scriptorum*, ed. R. L. Poole and M. Bateson, Oxford, 1902, p. 143), repeats

For although all of these works, when identified, prove to be as anonymous as the *Oculus Sacerdotis*, their contents and character suggest immediately that Boston is at least correct in attributing four of the total five works to a single author. Thus, the *Pars Dextera* and *Pars Sinistra* of the *Oculus Sacerdotis* and the *Speculum Religiosorum* prove to be, by and large, a few chapters of the massive *Speculum Praelatorum*; one-third of the *Speculum Praelatorum* itself is explicitly dependent on the *Summa Summarum*; while half of the first part of the *Oculus Sacerdotis*, the *Pars Oculi*, is made up of passages woven together from both *Summa Summarum* and *Speculum Praelatorum*.[1] The strong impression of a unity of purpose and authorship created by this interlacing is put beyond reasonable doubt by a passage towards the end of the third book of the *Summa Summarum*. There, in a chapter 'De expositione Missae', the author excuses himself from developing this

this and the whole entry ('ex Bostoni Buriensis Catalogo'), but in his *Scriptorum Illustrium Maioris Brytanniae Summarium* (Basle, 1559, p. 448), where he says his information comes from Boston 'in magno doctorum Catalogo', he lists the *Oculum Sacerdotis Dextrum* and *Oculum Sacerdotis Sinistrum*, gives longer *incipits* than those in the above entry and produces a eulogy of Pagula which he says he is taking from Boston ('illa quidem sunt eius verba'). Since none of these details are to be found in the extract from a catalogue of Boston's which David Wilkins inserted in his preface to Tanner's *Bibliotheca* and which we have printed here, or in the only known version of a complete catalogue, Tanner's transcript in Camb. Univ. Lib., Add. MS. 3470, it is possible that there were, as Wilkins suggests in his preface (p. xv), two Boston catalogues, a 'major' and a 'minor', both or at least the 'major' of which Bale knew, while Tanner and Wilkins knew the 'minor' only. But for our purposes it must suffice to state that the information about William of Pagula which Bale claims to have taken from Boston of Bury 'in magno doctorum Catalogo' proves in fact to be as accurate as the basic details about Pagula and his works with which the only known version of Boston's *Catalogus* supplies us.

[1] A few examples of interdependence may be noted here. The MSS. quoted are as follows. *Oculus Sacerdotis*: MS. New College 292; *Summa Summarum*: MS. Bodley 293; *Speculum Praelatorum*: MS. Merton College 217; *Speculum Religiosorum*: MS. Gray's Inn Library 11.

Oc. Sac. (*Pars Oculi*)	fos. 13r–16v	: *Summa Summarum*	fos. 219r; 250v.
	fos. 16v–24r	: *Spec. Praelatorum*	fos. 162r–167r.
	fos. 24r–26r	: *Summa Summarum*	fos. 218v–219r.
Oc. Sac. (*Dext. Pars*)	fos. 34r–61v	: *Spec. Praelatorum*	fos. 142r–160r.
Oc. Sac. (*Sinistra Pars*)	fos. 66v–107v	: *Spec. Praelatorum*	fos. 30v–71r.
Spec. Religiosorum	fos. 25r–54r	: *Spec. Praelatorum*	fos. 90v–96v.
Spec. Praelatorum	fos. 30v–179v	: *Summa Summarum passim.*	

98

subject, because 'I have already dealt fully with the exposition of the Mass in my small sacramental *summula*, the *Sinistra Pars Oculi Sacerdotis*. In any case I shall return to the subject again in the *Speculum Praelatorum*'.[1]

But if Boston of Bury is thus far proved to be correct, is this author Boston's 'William of Pagula'? A William of Pagula really did exist in the fourteenth century, and the four works whose unity of authorship is thus attested, together with the fifth work, the *Epistola ad Regem Edwardum*, can be dated to a span of years, 1320–31, within his known lifetime, 1314–32.[2] This convenient dating is only one of six striking resemblances between inferences from, or conclusions about, the five works attributed to Pagula and the only known facts of his life. For although the five works are of a rigidly anonymous character, a clue to authorship has been extracted from each which matches, detail for detail, the career of William of Pagula who, from documentary evidence, is known to have been a Master, a penitentiary of the diocese of Salisbury in 1322 and perpetual vicar of the parish of Winkfield near the Forest of Windsor in that diocese between 1314 and 1332. The *Summa Summarum*, despite an express anonymity,[3] betrays a hint that the author's name is Doctor (or Master) William[4]; the *Pars Oculi* informs us that he has had experience as a penitentiary,[5] and, granting our dating of the *Pars*, therefore before 1327; in three of the

---

[1] 'De huius missae expositione . . . tractavi ad plenum in modica summula sacramentali quae vocatur Sinistra Pars Oculi Sacerdotis eodem titulo. Sed plenius de hoc tractabo in Speculo Praelatorum . . .' (MS. Laud. misc. 624, fo. 108v; MS. Exeter College 19, fo. 182v; MS. Christ's College 2, fo. 109v; MS. Pembroke College (Cambridge) 201, fo. 189r). But other MSS. abbreviate the passage and speak impersonally: 'De hac materia tractatur ad plenum in quadam nova summa quae vocatur Speculum Praelatorum' (MS. Bodley 293, fo. 144v; MS. Magdalen College 134, fo. 172v; MS. Royal 10 D x, fo. 179v; MS. Harl. 5014–5, fo. 164v; MS. Edinburgh University Library 136, fo. 157r; MS. Worcester Cathedral Library F131, fo. 213r; MS. Durham Cathedral Library C. 11.13, fo. 143r).

[2] The sequence and dating of the five works are considered briefly in Appendix A *infra*.

[3] 'nomen collectoris exprimere nolo ne collectio vilescerit cognito collectore' (MS. Bodley 293, fo. 1v).

[4] 'Sed quid si per alia etiam rescripto contenta constat de persona mea, ut impetrat contra me W(illelmum) doctorem iure canonico . . .' (MS. Bodley 293, fo. 251r; MS. Pembroke College (Cambridge) 201, fo. 32v; and all other MSS.).

[5] Cf. the prologue to the *Pars Oculi supra* p. 87, n. 1.

works there are indications that he is indeed a priest of the Salisbury diocese[1]; from the *Epistola ad Regem Edwardum* it may be inferred that he is a parish priest in or near the neighbourhood of Windsor Forest about 1330–1,[2] and from the works as a whole that he wrote his *opera omnia* between 1320 and 1331.

If this circumstantial evidence, when taken with the fact that four of the works are by the same author, seems to argue a case for William of Pagula's claim to the title of all five works which Boston of Bury attributes to him, then the matter is, perhaps, clinched by a late fourteenth-century note at the end of a copy of the *Summa Summarum* which James most effectively concealed some forty years ago under the title *Decretales Novae* in his *Catalogue* of the manuscripts of Christ's College, Cambridge. This *Summa Summarum*, alone of the seventy-seven extant manuscripts of the *opera omnia*, contributes the welcome information: *Hoc opus compositum fuit per Dominum Willelmum de Pabula*.[3]

A Yorkshire man, perhaps, and from Pagula (Paull) near Kingston-on-Hull, William of Pagula, then a deacon, was instituted perpetual vicar of the church of Winkfield, on the outskirts of the Salisbury diocese, in 1314 and towards the end of the episcopate of Simon of Ghent.[4] Sometime during the next seven years he was

---

[1] Because the only synodal constitutions he quotes are those of Salisbury bishops, e.g. *Oculus Sacerdotis*, MS. New College 292, fo. 35v; *Speculum Praelatorum*, MS. Merton College 217, fo. 142v; and cf. p. 89, n. 1, *supra*. The *Summa Summarum* (MS. Bodley 293, fo. 25r) says that he does not belong to the diocese of Lincoln.

[2] Cf. Appendix A (IV) *infra*.

[3] MS. Christ's College 2, fo. 269r. Cf. M. R. James, *A descriptive catalogue of the manuscripts in the library of Christ's College Cambridge* (Cambridge, 1905), pp. 2–3, where the above note, to which Mr. R. B. Bartle first drew my attention, is printed. 'De Pabula' seems near enough to 'de Pagula' to allow the conclusion that this is Boston's William of Pagula.

[4] *Registrum Simonis de Gandavo*, ed. C. T. Flower and M. C. B. Dawes (Canterbury and York Society, 1934), p. 822. This may be the same William of Pagula, clerk, to whom Archbishop Greenfield of York granted letters dimissory in November 1313 (*Register of William Greenfield*, ed. W. Brown and A. Hamilton Thompson (Surtees Society, cli. 1936), iii. 197–8), although the prevalence of the name Pagula or of its variants, Poul, Paul, Pole, Pawel, in fourteenth-century Yorkshire makes it unwise to press the identification. Thus Willelmus de Sancto Paulo or William Paul, Carmelite and bishop of Meath (1327–49), was also known as Willelmus de Pagula, and has in fact been confused by some bibliographers with Boston's de Pagula

ordained priest and took a Master's degree, for on his appointment as penitentiary for Reading in 1321/22 (and a few months later, perhaps, for the whole of Berkshire), he is noted in Mortival's register as *Magister Willelmus de Pagula*.[1] After 1325, when he is still at Winkfield,[2] all trace of him disappears. But since there is no record of an admission to Winkfield before 1332,[3] it seems safe to assume that the years 1314–32 represent our present knowledge of the career and life of William of Pagula. No further preferment appears to have come his way, and although a seemingly personal reference in the passage of the *Summa Summarum* which gave us the name 'William' would suggest that Pagula was professing canon law at Oxford and a canon of St. Paul's, London, no external support for this has been found to date.[4]

Yet William of Pagula must have been something out of the ordinary run of parish priest. If the *Oculus Sacerdotis* alone shows one possessed of a delicate feeling for his less-educated fellows, his works as a whole bear the marks of a fine canonist and a competent theologian. Each, if we except the *Epistola*, reveals the same mas-

(cf. *Dict. Nat. Biog. s.vv.* Pagula, William, and Paul, William). But Bale and Pits, although sadly misrepresented by the *D.N.B.* on this point, are very careful to distinguish between the bishop and the vicar. Bale (*Index*, p. 143) writes: 'Guilhelmus de Pagula, alius ab illo Midensi episcopo, . . .', and again (*Summarium*, 1559, p. 448): 'Guilhelmus de Pagula, alius ab illo eiusdem cognominis qui . . . Midensis episcopus fuit. . . .' Likewise Pits (J. Pitseus, *De rebus anglicis*, Paris, 1619), though not in his notice of Pagula, the parish priest (*s.a.* 1350, p. 476), which otherwise copies Bale, but in his notice of Pagula, the bishop (*s.a.* 1280, p. 363): 'Guilhelmus Paghamus (alius ab illo qui Paghanerus seu de Pagula dicitur, et circa annum Domini 1350, floruit). . . .'

[1] Salisbury Diocesan Registry, *Reg. Mortival*, ii, fo. 132r: 'Poenitentiarii constituti in Archidiaconatu Berk' 8 id. Mar. 1321, et anno consecrationis nostræ VII°. . . Decanatus Radyngg tantum: Magister Willelmus de Pagula Vicarius de Wynkefeld.' (*Add. later hand*: Postmodum habet potestatem per totum archidiaconatum Berk'.)

[2] Muniments of the Dean and Chapter, Salisbury, Press 4, Box E, doc. 2.6: 'In vigilia Sancti Iacobi Apostoli anno domini 1325 presentibus Domino Willelmo Poul perpetuo vicario Wynkefeld. . . .'

[3] *Reg. Wyvil* ii, fo. 19r: 'Iohannes de Lavyngton presbyterus admissus ad vicariam de Wynkefeld . . .'

[4] 'Sed quid si per alia etiam rescripto contenta constat de persona mea, ut impetrat contra me W(illelmum) doctorem iure canonico legentem Oxon. et canonicum Sancti Pauli London., et sic per huiusmodi indicia constat de persona mea, an valeat rescriptum?' (MS. Bodley 293, fo. 25r, and the ten other MSS. that are extant in England.)

tery of general Church law, the same sense of the place and importance of the legislation of the Church in England, the same balance
of law and theology which may be noted in the *Oculus Sacerdotis*.
Possessed of a seemingly tireless zeal for the education of his contemporaries, he would write four major works within a decade
and, perhaps, for the most part concurrently.[1] His *Summa Summarum* is a compilation of canon law and theology of five books
and almost 350,000 words designed to provide every cleric, from
parish priest to prelate, with an authoritative answer to every possible question that might arise out of his state or obligations. It is
the only manual of canon law from an English source that can
compare with the *Copiosa* of Hostiensis or the *Speculum* and *Reportorium* of Durandus, and it would commend itself to a variety
of clerics: to Acton, the glossator of the Legatine Constitutions[2];
to a notary public who willed his copy to Archbishop Arundel[3];
to the famous curialist, Thomas Polton, bishop of Worcester, who,
in his will, displays anxiety about its future.[4]

[1] There are many indications that Pagula had two or more of the works
in hand at the same time, the most interesting of which is that in a manuscript
of the *Summa Summarum* at Pembroke College, Cambridge (MS. 201,
fo. 189: 'De expositione Missae'): 'De huius missae expositione ... tractavi
ad plenum in modica summula sacramentali quae vocatur Sinistra Pars
Oculi Sacerdotis ... sed plenius de hoc tractabo in Speculo Praelatorum ...
rubrica De officio celebrantis Missam, per totum. De officiis autem divinis
... tractabitur ibidem in rubrica proxima praecedenti per totum. Quae
omnia nondum adhuc plenum complevi in quibus et in aliis iuvet nos
Omnipotens Deus.' (Cf. p. 98, *supra*.)

[2] In his *Septuplum* (1346), MS. Gonville & Caius Coll. 282, fos. 129r,
136r, a work written after his famous *Glossa*.

[3] *Testamenta Eboracensia* (Surtees Soc., xlv. 1864), iii. 1: will of John de
Scardeburgh, notary public, 1395.

[4] Register of Henry Chichele, ed. E. F. Jacob (Oxford, 1938), ii. 487:
'Similiter lego unum librum qui vocatur Summa Summarum precii vi
marcarum ... cum cathena ferrea in choro ecclesie ipsius prioratus (Sancte
Margarete virginis iuxta Marleburgh') aut in alio loco magis ad hoc apto
perpetuo ligandum et inibi sub pena anathematis perpetuo, remansurum et
scribatur in primo folio nomen conferentis et causa.' Polton, who was at the
Council of Basle from the end of 1432 until his death in 1433, may have been
responsible for introducing John Nider, prior of the Dominican convent
there in this period, to the *Summa Summarum* which Nider seemingly
knew when he was writing his *Manuale Confessorum* between 1434 and 1438.
Cf. J. Nider, *Johannis Nider ordinis predicatorum Manuale Confessorum* ...
(Paris, 1477), fos. 6–9. Miss B. Smalley has kindly drawn my attention to
the unexpected use of the *Summa Summarum* in the *Postilla in Mattheum*

But as though the *Oculus Sacerdotis* and this *Summa Summarum* were not enough for any one man, Pagula attempted to combine both in the *Speculum Praelatorum* which, swelling to a size twice that of the *Summa Summarum*, was never to command the same attention as these. Where eleven manuscripts of the *Summa Summarum* and fifty of the *Oculus Sacerdotis* are known to be extant in this country, the *Speculum Praelatorum* survives, solitary and incomplete, in a manuscript of 483 folios.[1] Yet, in a sense, it is his greatest work, not least in that it contains one of the finest sets of sermon *themata* of the fourteenth century.[2] Its offshoot, the *Speculum Religiosorum*, was more fortunate. Smaller, and a legal tract *de religiosis* of almost unique value at its time, it is extant in some ten manuscripts, accompanying five of the eight collections of legislation affecting monks which were made at Durham in the middle ages.[3]

But Pagula's first love was the parochial clergy. For them he wrote his *Oculus* and *Speculum Praelatorum*; they are not excluded from his *Summa Summarum*. And because of this, it is as a writer of pastoral theology that he deserves to be remembered. For he was that rare but ideal combination of canonist, theologian and parish priest. A canonist by training, perhaps, he knew intimately

of the famous Carmelite doctor, John Baconthorpe, which would appear to have been written about 1340.

[1] MS. Merton College 217. The actual text takes up 449 folios, the remainder consisting of an index, etc. Twenty-eight chapters of Part 2 are missing, and were not in the exemplar from which this copy was made: cf. fo. 179v, where the copyist writes 'Hic deficit de exemplari'.

[2] MS. Merton College 217, fos. 180r–449r, the third part of the *Speculum*. Besides *themata* (four or more) for every Sunday, festival and possible occasion of the liturgical year (fos. 180r–248r), there is an excellent set of sermon *Distinctiones* (*Aperire-Zelus*: fos. 248r–449r) from which the *themata* could be filled out.

[3] For a description of the manuscripts and a list of the contents of these collections see the introduction to *Chapters of the Black Monks*, ed. W. A. Pantin (Camden Society, 3rd ser., xlvii, 1933), ii, pp. viii–xvii. The *Speculum Religiosorum*, in its original form, accompanies only one of these collections; but the treatise *Abbas vel Prior*, which accompanies four of the others and was formerly thought to be a work of Uthred of Boldon, has turned out to be a rearrangement of the *Speculum*. The rearrangement was probably made before 1336, and thus before Uthred's day as a writer, since it makes no attempt to correlate the Constitutions of Benedict XII (1336) with the earlier legislation (Legatine Constitutions to *Clementines*) which the *Speculum Religiosorum* embodies.

the needs of parish priests; yet his desire and ability to better their legal education did not blind him to a deeper want, a knowledge of theology without which the executive side of the pastoral care may become mechanical and lifeless: with Decretal and provincial canon he gave them Aquinas and the *Stimulus Amoris*.[1] Seemingly abreast of the new devotional literature of the fourteenth century, he is in the vanguard of the new movement in pastoral theology begun by the German Dominican, John of Freiburg, in which moral theology has its place and law does not predominate.[2] For although Pagula never mentions the work by name, it is from the *Summa Confessorum* of John of Freiburg that his wide acquaintance with Albert, Aquinas and Peter of Tarentaise largely derives.[3]

It is possible, therefore, that Simon of Ghent, whose endeavour to raise the standard of education in the Salisbury diocese is well known,[4] may not have been unaware of the promise of the deacon, Pagula, when he instituted him perpetual vicar of Winkfield in place of a Master in Theology, lately resigned.[5] Nor can the dean and chapter who had the right of presentation have been lacking

[1] The whole of the *Stimulus Amoris* of James of Milan has been incorporated into the *Speculum Praelatorum*: the greater part of it occupies the second chapter of Part I entirely (MS. Merton College 217, fos. 11r—30v: *De contemplatione*; while the section on predestination appears in the middle of the first chapter, *De fide*, fo. 5r-v), which otherwise is composed of extracts from the popular *Summa Theologicae Veritatis* of Hugh of Strassburg. The *Stimulus Amoris* has been edited in the series *Bibliotheca Franciscana Ascetica*, iv (Quaracchi, 1905), and may also be found printed among the works of St. Bonaventure (*Opera omnia*, Paris (Vivès), 1868, xii). The *Summa Theologicae Veritatis* circulated in the middle ages as a work of Albert the Great, St. Thomas or St. Bonaventure, and is to be found printed in the Vivès edition of the *opera omnia* of each of these three writers.

[2] Cf. *Dict. Théol. Cathol.*, viii (i), 1924, 761–2, *s.v.* Jean de Fribourg (M. D. Chenu).

[3] These three authorities appear *passim* in the *Oculus Sacerdotis*, *Speculum Praelatorum* and *Summa Summarum* as they do also in many fourteenth-century works of general theology and canon law. I hope to prove later that the source of many quotations from these authorities in works of popular theology is the *Summa Confessorum* which, written about 1280–98, revised the *Summa de casibus* of Raymund of Peñafort, and, by an adroit use of the latest theological knowledge, gave the *Summa de Casibus* a new lease of life. Cf. John of Freiburg's prologue to his *Summa* printed in *Summa Confessorum reverendis patris Iohannis de Friburgo* (Lyons, 1518).

[4] Cf. K. Edwards, 'Bishops and learning in the reign of Edward II', *Church Quarterly Review*, cxxxviii (1944), 66–72, 78–9.

[5] *Reg. S. de Gandavo*, p. 822.

in confidence: a bare decade before, Winkfield had been the scene of grave and bitter disturbances.[1]

Towards the end of Pagula's known residence at Winkfield, the parish was to be disturbed once more, not this time by a wrangle over tithes, but by 'a great cry from the people of the neighbourhood of the Forest of Windsor' who were being sorely grieved by the demands made upon their labour and time by commissioners of the king. In this discontent, we possibly catch our only glimpse of Pagula, the parish priests' manualist, at home in his own parish. Moved to strike at the root of the trouble, Pagula turned his legal knowledge on the king in a fine appeal for letters of protection on behalf of his parishioners. Into this *Epistola ad Regem Edwardum* there are thrown Decretal—and, on occasion, Decretalist—the excommunications attached to *Magna Carta*, the Lambeth constitutions of Pecham, and even a quotation from the *Digest* in an attempt to persuade the king to relieve the distress of his parishioners who, for days on end, are compelled to hew and cart wood for a pittance and in violation of everything that the king at his coronation had sworn to observe.

Granted the authenticity of this *Epistola*, it is Pagula's last work. But when Archbishop Mepham, a year or two later in his *Speculum Regis*, took it up and gave it the character of a generalized indictment of the abuses of kingship,[2] there is no mention of William of Pagula. Already he has disappeared, submerged in his works. He will appear again only for a brief moment in Boston of Bury's eulogy of 'that great man, Pagula, who, skilled in both laws and in theology, smote the dissolute lives of clerics and priests with all his voice and power of pen: *sed non absque singulari modestia*'.[3]

---

[1] Cf. *Reg. S. de Gandavo*, pp. 180–4, 513.

[2] A treatise which is well known from Bishop Stubbs' use of it. Cf. W. Stubbs, *Constitutional History of England* (4th edition, Oxford, 1896), ii. 394, 423, 564, 567. Usually the *Speculum* is ascribed to Simon Islip, but we here accept Professor Tait's suggestion that Simon Mepham is a more likely author: cf. appendix A (IV), *infra*.

[3] Boston of Bury as quoted by Bale, *Scriptorum Illustrium Maioris Brytanniae Summarium* (Basle, 1559), p. 448. Cf. pp. 96–7, n., *supra*.

APPENDIX A

DATING AND SEQUENCE OF THE FIVE WORKS OF WILLIAM OF PAGULA

Two of Pagula's works, the *Oculus Sacerdotis* and *Summa Summarum*, were certainly in circulation by 1343, when both of them were used and referred to by the *Regimen Animarum*. On internal evidence, however, the *opera omnia* may be dated to the years 1320–31.

I. The *Sinistra Pars Oculi, Dextra Pars Oculi, Summa Summarum* and *Speculum Praelatorum* were written between 1320 and 1326, and probably between 1320 and 1322/3;

  (*a*) 1320–6. The latest source quoted in these works is the gloss of Willelmus de Monte Lauduno on the *Clementines* (1319). There is no sign of a knowledge of any of the legislation of Pope John XXII, twenty of whose *Extravagantes* were glossed by Zenzelinus de Cassanis in 1325, or of the gloss of Iohannes Andreae on the *Clementines* (1326).[1]

  (*b*) 1320–3. A note in the *Summa Summarum*[2] indicates that it was written after the *Sinistra Pars* and before the *Speculum Praelatorum*, but a longer version of that note suggests that the *Summa Summarum* and *Speculum Praelatorum* were being written together.[3] A date before 1322/3 is therefore suggested since the *Summa Summarum* does not show a knowledge of European events extending beyond 1322 or 1323.[4] The *Dextera Pars* may also be within the dating 1320–2/3, although it is possible that it was written a little after the *Sinistra Pars.*

---

[1] Cf. A. van Hove, *Prologomena ad Codicem Iuris Canonici* (2nd ed. Malines, 1945) for Willelmus de Monte Lauduno (p. 482) and Zenzelinus de Cassanis (p. 475). For the date of Iohannes Andreae, cf. J. F. Schulte, *Die Geschichte der Quellen und Literatur des canonischen Rechts* (Stuttgart, 1877), ii. 217.

[2] Cf. *supra*, p. 98, n. 1.

[3] Cf. *supra*, p. 101, n. 1.

[4] For example, in a chapter 'De Imperatore et eius electione' Pagula asks the question 'Quid iuramentum debet imperator facere papae' and answers 'Dic quod tale iuramentum: "Tibi Domino Iohanni Papae, ego, talis, promitto et iuro. . .."' (MS. Bodley 293, fo. 18r). The contrast between

II. The *Speculum Religiosorum* was written after the *Speculum Praelatorum* and the *Dextera Pars Oculi*,[1] probably 1320–6. Being mainly an extract from the *Speculum Praelatorum* it is not easy to date it with any great exactitude, but the dating and reasons given in I (*a*) above may certainly be applied to it.

III. The *Pars Oculi* was written after 1326 and probably before 1328.

(*a*) After 1326. It uses Iohannes Andreae's gloss on the *Clementines* (1326).

(*b*) Before 1328. The *Pars Oculi* does not refer to the provincial constitutions of Simon Mepham (1328). This is all the more striking since the author is a priest of the diocese of Salisbury. For Bishop Roger Mortival, within five weeks of the promulgation of these constitutions, had ordered them to be read publicly on Sundays and holy days throughout his diocese, laying stress particularly on those statutes to which an excommunication was attached. Remembering the catalogue of excommunications in the *Pars Oculi* and the care taken to include censures from provincial constitutions, it is unlikely that Pagula would have allowed this opportunity to pass of adding to his list or of bringing it up to the moment.[2]

the definite 'John' (XXII) and *talis* suggests that Pagula was writing while the issue between the rival claimants for the empire declared vacant by John XXII was still undecided, and before Lewis of Bavaria emerged victorious in 1322.

[1] Cf. *Speculum Religiosorum* (MS. Egerton 746, fo. 84r): 'De ceteris peccatis mortalibus . . . quaere in summa quae vocatur Oculus Sacerdotis scilicet in Dextera Parte'.

[2] Salisbury Diocesan Registry, *Reg. Mortival* II, fo. 243r: ' . . . Statuta in concilio provinciali ad diem veneris post festum conversionis Sancti Pauli Londoniis convocata edita suscepimus sub sigillo venerabilis patris Domini Simonis., continentia seriem hanc verborum "Zelari oportet", etc. Cum igitur parum prosit statuta condere nisi fiat executio eorumdem vobis et vestrum singulis auctoritate dicti concilii et ex dicti patris iniunctione firmiter iniungendo committimus et mandamus quatenus copiam praesentium absque mora assumentes, et statuta praedicta et praesertim ea in quibus maioris excommunicationis sententiam contrarium facientes incurrunt, vos . . . in vestris capitulis . . . et singulis ecclesiis infra iurisdictionem vestram consistentibus cum maior populi affuerit multitudo diebus dominicis et festivis solemniter et intelligibiliter . . publicantes . . .'

IV. The *Epistola ad Regem Edwardum III* is not later than 1331.

In 1891, when M. Joseph Moisant[1] published an edition of the well-known *Speculum Regis* which he attributed to Simon Islip, he also published what seemed to be a 'first recension' of the *Speculum*: it had the same *incipit* as the *Speculum*, and clearly was connected with the *Speculum Regis* which refers to it expressly on two occasions. Ten years later, Professor Tait published an article in which he dated the 'first recension' and the *Speculum Regis* more precisely than Moisant had done; the 'first recension', he proved, was not written later than 1331, and the *Speculum Regis* not later than 1332; and he proposed that Simon Islip did not qualify for the authorship as readily as Archbishop Simon Mepham.[2]

There are, however, grounds for believing that the 'first recension' thus published with the *Speculum Regis* of Islip or Mepham, and dated before 1331 by Professor Tait, is really the *Epistola ad Regem Edwardum* which is attributed to William of Pagula by Boston of Bury:[3]

1. The title given to Pagula's work by Boston agrees with the *explicit* of the 'first recension' which is: 'explicit epistola edita ad dominum E. regem angliae'. (The *explicit* of the Islip or Mepham *Speculum Regis* is always 'explicit Speculum Regis Edwardi'; the confusion between *Epistola* and *Speculum* has resulted from identical *incipits*.)

2. The 'first recension' differs in character from the *Speculum*:

(*a*) It is a localized appeal, from the locality of Windsor Forest, for letters of protection,[4] while the *Speculum* is a generalized indictment of the abuses of kingship.

(*b*) It is presumably written by a parish priest, since he

---

[1] J. Moisant, *De Speculo Regis Edwardi III ... quem ... conscripsit Simon Islip* (Paris, 1891). The 'first recension' is printed pp. 83–123.

[2] J. Tait, 'On the date and authorship of the "Speculum Regis Edwardi" ', *English Historical Review*, lxi (1901), 110–15.

[3] Professor Tait and M. Moisant were not aware of this ascription.

[4] E.g.: 'O domine mi rex, erubesce et contremisce quando a te petuntur huiusmodi litterae protectionis ... illi de familia tua capiunt de foresta de Widesore et locis vicinis homines carectas et equos pauperum et compellunt eos, recedere a domibus propriis ... et ibi carriare boscum ...' (*Epistola*, ed. Moisant, p. 100); ' ... et de hoc, fit magnus clamor populi, in partibus de Windesore, ubi traxisti originem ...' (*ibid.*, p. 106).

refers to those on whose behalf he is pleading as 'illi de parochia'; the *Speculum* could have been written by anyone.

(*c*) It is written by a canonist who can cite and employ Decretal, Decretalist and provincial legislation. There is no evidence of canon law in the *Speculum*.

William of Pagula qualifies, therefore, for the title of author of this printed 'first recension', the *Epistola ad Regem Edwardum*, because:

(*a*) Boston ascribes such a work to him.

(*b*) It bears the marks of William of Pagula, canonist and parish priest.

(*c*) It is written from a parish close to Windsor Forest at a time when Pagula was still parish priest of Winkfield.

APPENDIX B

MANUSCRIPTS OF THE *OCULUS SACERDOTIS* (COMPLETE OR INCOMPLETE) AND *SUMMA SUMMARUM*

KNOWN TO BE EXTANT IN GREAT BRITAIN OR IN AMERICA

Oculus Sacerdotis

BRAMSHILL HOUSE, Hants, 14.

CAMBRIDGE:
 University Library, Gg. 1. 13, Gg. 6. 10, Gg. 6. 12, Ii. 2. 7,
  Mm. 5. 33.
 Gonville and Caius College, 62, 87, 352, 443, 487.
 Pembroke College, 248, 281.
 St. John's College, 36, 93, 108.
 Trinity College, 398.

CANTERBURY:
 Dean and Chapter Library, D. 8, D. 9.

EDINBURGH:
 National Library of Scotland, 18. 3, 6.

HATFIELD HOUSE, 290.

HOLKHAM HALL, 159.

LEICESTER:
 Museum and Art Gallery, W. Hosp. 10.

LINCOLN:
 Cathedral Library, 213.

LONDON;
 British Museum:
  Egerton 655.
  Harley 233, 1307, 2379, 5021, 5444.
  Royal 6 E. i, 8 B. ii, 8 B. xv, 8 F. vii.
 Guildhall, 249.
 Lambeth Palace, 216.

MANCHESTER:
 John Rylands Library, lat. 339.

OHIO:
 University Library 1.

OXFORD:
  Bodleian Library;
    Bodley 828.
    Hatton 11.
    Rawl. A 361, 370.
    Rawl. C 84, 565.
  Balliol College, 83.
  New College, 292.
  Trinity College, 18.
  University College, 122.
SOTHEBY:
  Harmsworth Trust Library (6), 1945, nos. 2052, 2053.
WORCESTER:
  Cathedral Library, Q 92.

Summa Summarum

CAMBRIDGE:
  Christ's College, 2.
  Pembroke College, 201.
DURHAM:
  Cathedral Library, C. II. 13.
EDINBURGH:
  University Library, 145.
LONDON:
  British Museum:
    Harley 5014–15.
    Royal 10 D. x.
OXFORD:
  Bodleian Library:
    Bodley 293.
    Laud Misc. 624.
  Exeter College, 19.
  Magdalen College, 134.
SAN MARINO (California):
  Huntingdon Library, EL. 9, H. 3.
WORCESTER:
  Cathedral Library, F. 131.

V

WILLIAM OF PAGULA
AND THE *SPECULUM REGIS EDWARDI III*

The little treatise *Speculum Regis Edwardi III*, generally attributed to Simon Islip, archbishop of Canterbury (1349-1366), has been well known to writers on English constitutional history and to lexicographers from the middle of the 17th century. The great legal writer Edward Coke possessed a copy which had at one time belonged to William Warham, archbishop of Canterbury (c. 1450-1532), and used it in his *Institutes of the Laws of England*.[1] After Coke, who indeed seems to have been the first to draw attention to the *Speculum*, there are some references to the treatise in Spelmann's *Glossarium Archaiologicum*, Du Cange's *Glossarium* (citing Spelmann), Hook's *Lives of the Archbishops of Canterbury*, and notably in Stubbs' *Constitutional History*, where several passages are printed from MS. Bodley 624.[2]

It was not, however, until M. Joseph Moisant published his doctoral thesis *De Speculo Regis Edwardi III* seu tractatu quem de mala regni administratione conscripsit Simon Islip (Paris, 1891), that a full text of the *Speculum* first became available in print. Moisant, who had discovered some ten MSS of the work in England, was forced to the conclusion that two recensions of the *Speculum* had circulated in England in the Middle Ages, and he decided that it was better to publish both. The first recension ('Recensio A', printed by Moisant at pp. 83-123) bore the title *Epistola ad Regem Edwardum III*, and is extant in five MSS (Oxford, Bodleian Library, MS Digby 172, ff. 134v-141r; London, British Museum: MSS Cotton, Cleopatra D IX, ff. 87r-112r and Faustina B I, ff. 184r-191r, Royal 10 B XI; Cambridge, University Library, MS Kk. iv. 4. ff. 49r-54v). The second recension ('Recensio B', printed at pp. 127-169) is properly the *Speculum Regis*, and is to be found on its own in another five codices (Oxford, Bodleian Library: MSS Bodley 624, Rawlinson C.606; London, British Museum: MSS Add. 15673, Harley 2399 and 6237).

---

[1] See British Museum, MS. Harley 6237, a copy of the *Speculum* made in 1728, 'ex codice olim Willemi Warham archiepiscopi Cantuariensis, postea Edwardi Coke, militis, ... nunc penes Th. Coke, militem de Balneo.'

[2] E. Coke, *The Second Part of the Institutes of the Laws of England*, (London, 1633), 545; H. Spelmann, *Glossarium Archaiologicum*, 3rd ed. (London, 1687), 468-469, s.v. *Prisae regiae*; C. du Fresne du Cange, *Glossarium mediae et infimae latinitatis*, ed. L. Favre, 6 (Paris, 1938), 506-507; W. F. Hook, *Lives of the Archbishops of Canterbury*, 4 (London, 1865), 136; W. Stubbs, *The Constitutional History of England*, 2 (Oxford, 1880), 408, 439, 585, 587. See also M. McKisack, *The Fourteenth Century* 1307-1399 (Oxford, 1959), 296.

Although the two recensions — *Epistola* and *Speculum* — never occur together in any manuscript, Moisant felt confident that they were nothing more than two versions of the same work, and that their sole author was archbishop Simon Islip. He had good reason. For if the 14th century MSS of the *Speculum* (Bodley 624, Rawl. 606, Add. 15673) explicitly ascribe the work to Islip, so also do two of the three 14th century MSS of the *Epistola* (Cleo. D IX, Faustina B I). Besides, internal evidence showed a close relationship between the two recensions. The incipits are similar — 'O domine mi rex, ex quo respublica tibi committitur gubernanda' (*Epistola*); 'O domine mi rex, utinam saperes et intelligeres ac novissima provideres' (*Speculum*) — there are some common passages and, more significantly, there are two explicit references to the *Epistola* in the *Speculum*, e.g., 'Multe sunt alie cause de quibus tractatur in quadam summa modica que sic incipit, O domine mi rex, ex quo, etc.' (p. 132). Concluding therefore that the *Epistola* and the *Speculum* were two versions of the same work of Islip, Moisant allowed that there was an appreciable time-lag between them, the *Epistola* being written about 1337, some twelve years before Islip became archbishop of Canterbury, the *Speculum* shortly after he was made archbishop in 1349.

Ten years after the publication of Moisant's thesis, Professor James Tait argued convincingly against these dates, maintaining instead that the *Epistola* was not later than 1331, and that it preceded the *Speculum* by only a few months. Because of this early date, Simon Mepham, archbishop of Canterbury (1328-1333), seemed to Tait to be a more likely author of the *Speculum* than Simon Islip; and since the two treatises 'have hardly a passage in common', he doubted that the author of the *Speculum* was also the author of the earlier *Epistola*.[3] The present writer, in an article some years ago which suggested that the author of the *Epistola* was really William of Pagula, accepted without reserve these two conclusions of Tait.[4] Now, however, I am convinced that the author also of the *Speculum* is again none other than Pagula.

At the risk of repeating some points made in the previous article, a few remarks must be made about the authorship and date of the *Epistola* before going on to consider the *Epistola* and *Speculum* together.

A native of Paull (Pagula) in Yorkshire, William Poul of Pagula (or William of Pagula, as he is commonly known) was admitted as a deacon to the perpetual vicarage at Winkfield in Windsor Forest, some three miles to the south-west of Windsor, in March 1314, and was ordained priest on the Whit Saturday following (1 June) in Canterbury Cathedral by Archbishop Reynolds.[5] After some years at Oxford, where he obtained a doctorate in canon law in 1319-1320, Pagula returned to Winkfield, writing there most of his *Oculus sacerdotis*, an influential *summa* of canon law and sacramental theology for the parish clergy, and completing his *Summa summarum*, a lengthy compendium of law and theology.[6] In November

---

[3] J. Tait, "On the date and authorship of the 'Speculum Regis Edwardi'", *English Historical Review*, 61 (1901), 110-115.

[4] L. E. Boyle, "The *Oculus Sacerdotis* and some other works of William of Pagula", *Transactions of the Royal Historical Society*, 5th ser., 5 (1955), 81-110.

[5] Lambeth Palace Library, The Register of Archbishop Reynolds, fol. 11r. I owe this important reference to Dr John R. Wright.

[6] On Pagula see A. B. Emden, *Biographical Register of the University of Oxford*, III (Oxford

1332 he was succeeded at Winkfield by Master John de Lavyngham, and since no trace of him has been found after that, it may be presumed that he died sometime in the summer or autumn of 1332.[7]

The evidence for Pagula's authorship of the *Epistola* is very solid, and recently has been confirmed further by an entry in a list of books acquired for Glastonbury Abbey by Abbot Walter de Moynton (1341-1374: '(tractatus) magistri Willelmi Paul ad regem et ministros suos'.[8] For among the five works attributed to Master William (Poul) of Pagula, vicar of Winkfield 'prope forestam de Windesor', by the early 15th century writer known as 'Boston of Bury', there is a title, 'ad regem Angliae Edwardum III, epistola i', which corresponds exactly to the explicit of the *Epistola*: 'Explicit epistola edita ad dominum E. regem Anglie' (MS. Digby 172, f. 141r).[9] The *Epistola* itself corroborates Boston of Bury. Clearly it was written by a parish priest in the Forest of Windsor during the last eighteen months of William of Pagula's known tenure of the vicarage at Winkfield — and by one who had canon and civil law at his finger-tips: there are many references to Gratian and the Decretals;[10] Hostiensis and Joannes Monachus are cited;[11] and, as in so many passages in Pagula's other works, the excommunications attached to Magna Carta are invoked, together with the Lambeth constitutions of John Pecham.[12]

The precise date of Pagula's *Epistola* is at the centre of its relationship to the *Speculum regis*. The *Epistola* is an appeal from a priest in Windsor Forest for letters of protection for himself and his parishioners against the royal prerogative of purveyance[13] — against the right, that is, of the King and his family to buy provisions at the very lowest rate, to compel owners to sell, and to enforce personal labour. The King, obviously, has just begun his reign. Reminding him of his father's untimely end and of the fate that 'lately' has overtaken Roger Mortimer,[14] and

---

1959), 1536-1537; L. E. Boyle, "The *Summa summarum* and some other English works of canon law", *Proceedings of the Second International Congress of Medieval Canon Law*, ed. S. Kuttner and J. J. Ryan (New Haven-Vatican City, 1965), 415-456.

[7] Salisbury Diocesan Registry, Reg. Wyvil II (2), fol. 19r. Four months afterwards Lavyngham was given an office that Pagula had held, that of penitentiary of the Deanery of Reading (*ibid.*, fol. 15v); he did not vacate Winkfield until 1347 (*ibid.*, fol. 160v).

[8] Cambridge, Trinity College, MS 711, p. 246, n. 22. I owe this reference to the kindness of Mr N. R. Ker.

[9] Boston of Bury, *Catalogus Scriptorum Ecclesiae*, in T. Tanner, *Bibliotheca Brittannico-Hibernica* (London, 1748), introd., xl. On Boston see R. H. Rouse, "Bostonus Buriensis and the author of the *Catalogus Scriptorum Ecclesiae*", *Speculum*, 41 (1966) 471-499.

[10] *Epistola*, ed. Moisant, 87, 88, 91, 93, 98, 99, 104, 108-111 (Decretum); 104, 111, 112, 115 (Decretals); 110 (Sext).

[11] But not in Moisant's edition. The references to these writers will be found in the MS upon which he based his text, MS Digby 172, fols. 138ra, 139rb. Where Moisant does print legal references they are often inaccurately rendered, as when (p. 106) he omits a part of a reference to the civil Digest and considers what he has retained as a reference to the Decretals (*ibid.*, fol. 138rb). There is a reference to the Codex on fol. 139rb (see Moisant, 113). Throughout the *Epistola* there are references to or citations from Aristotle, Augustine, Cassian, Cassiodorus, Gregory the Great, etc.

[12] *Epistola*, ed. Moisant, 100.

[13] *Ibid.*, 116.

[14] *Ibid.*, 120: 'Nunc eciam ultimo, iste magnus dominus Roger le Mortimer captus et interfectus est'.

V

of his debt of gratitude to God who 'has freed him miraculously' from the control of Mortimer and Isabella (October 1330),[15] Pagula upbraids Edward for the fact that more abuses of purveyance have taken place 'in the short time' he has been reigning than in the whole reign of his father.[16] He therefore urges the 'ductores regis' to direct Edward's first steps in ruling on his own, asking them to make sure that the King and his household observe the common law in 'buying and selling'.[17] All through the *Epistola*, Pagula calls on the King to abolish the 'infamous prerogative' or at least to stem the abuses, warning him that ill-feeling was rife and could lead to serious consequences.[18] Here, I am sure, Pagula was not inventing. In November 1330, the month after Edward first assumed real power, the counties of Somerset and Dorset protested strongly against purveyance; and ten months later (September 1331), Parliament attempted to put a brake on the whole system.[19]

The *Epistola*, in fact, probably reflects the situation in England just at the beginning of 1331. For if Pagula were writing after the Peace of Amiens had been signed between Edward and Philip of France in April 1331, he would hardly have stated to Edward that England had had no peace within herself or with her neighbours since Edward I first introduced the 'devilish' prerogative of purveyance in the 18th year of his reign (1289-1290). What is particularly interesting about this passage of the *Epistola* is that it has a close parallel in the *Speculum*. But the *Speculum*, while making the same general point about purveyance as the *Epistola*, notes that the only time that the peace is broken now is when the 'prerogative' is put into practice by the King and his family; that otherwise a state of peace prevails in England 'in the past year', the like of which the country 'has not experienced since your grandfather Edward I introduced purveyances'. Here, of course, as on so many occasions, the *Speculum* is echoing the *Epistola*, but it is surely significant that in the common reference to the fateful effects on peace of Edward I's introduction of purveyance, the *Speculum* allows that there is general peace at last where the *Epistola* laments that the country has yet to experience it. The *Epistola* and *Speculum* thus appear to fall on either side of Edward III's homage to Philip of France at Amiens in April 1331: Pagula's *Epistola* sometime in the previous four or five months, the *Speculum* probably a year or so after the Peace:[20]

[15] *Ibid.*, 99.

[16] *Ibid.*, 105.

[17] *Ibid.*, 120: 'Et ideo moneo vos ductores regis, ex parte Dei, ut ipsum bene et sapienter ducatis, saltem ut ipse et illi de familia sua in empcionibus et vendicionibus observent ius commune'.

[18] *Ibid.*, 88: 'Sed nunc est clamor quasi per totam hanc terram quod rex et sui vivunt de huius rapina'; 96: 'propter huiusmodi rapinas et iniusticias, quasi totus populus tristatur contra adventum tuum ubicumque veneris in regnum tuum, et tecum non sunt mente licet tecum videantur corpore; et forte, si caput aliud haberent, insurgerent contra te, sicut contra patrem tuum fecerunt...'.

[19] *Rotuli Parliamentorum*, 1278-1503, II (London, 1768), 40, 62.

[20] If the peace 'after forty years' of which the *Speculum* speaks, does not refer to the period after April 1331 (the calm before the storm, as it turned out), it is not easy to see why the household administration of the King of France should be held up for Edward's imitation: 'Vide dominum regem Francie, quanto moderamine, quam sapienter, quam sagaciter, facit expensas domus sue...' (158).

Epistola (p. 115)

O domine mi rex, si predicta non poterint te movere, audi nunc quid actum fuerit de bonis illorum qui utebantur illo privilegio. ... Postmodum, tempore illius nobilis regis Edwardi avi tui, in principio regiminis sui, ut dicitur, nichil capiebat contra voluntatem dominorum rerum usque ad xviii annum regni sui, et toto illo tempore fuit pax et gaudium in regno isto. Sed in xviii anno regni sui incepit uti illo prerogativo diabolico, scilicet, capere oves, boves, fenum et avenam et alia multa pro minori precio quam venditor dare voluerit. Et tunc contra ipsum orta fuit guerra in Vasconia, Vallia et Scotia; et usque ad mortem utebatur illo prerogativo maledicto. Et ab eo tempore, nunquam fuit bona pax in terra ista.

Speculum (p. 167)

O domine mi rex, adverte diligenter

quod iam quadraginta annis elapsis, scilicet, ab illo tempore quo ille nobilis rex Edwardus, avus tuus, incepit uti illo predicto prerogativo, scilicet, capere res alienas pro minori precio quam venditor voluerat dare,

non fuerat tanta pax in hac terra sicut nunc et jam fuit anno lapso; preterquam in partibus illis in quibus tu transitum facis.

The passages cited above are sufficiently close to one another to suggest that the author of the *Speculum* had Pagula's *Epistola* before him. This is not at all surprising, for on two occasions he refers the King to the *Epistola* for details of abuses: 'Et qui sint illi errores (tue curie), vide in quadam summa modica que sic incipit: O domine mi rex' (p. 129); 'Multe sunt alie cause de quibus tractatur in modica summa que est: O domine mi rex, ex quo, etc.' (p. 132). Besides, there are numerous sentences and phrases which are common to the two treatises. Both speak of Edward's emancipation from Isabella and Mortimer in much the same terms: 'O domine mi rex, ex quo nunc, benedictus Deus, miraculose liberatus es a custodia illorum qui talia permiserunt' (*Epistola*, p. 94); 'Et ne tradas oblivioni quam graciose, quam miraculose, a custodia matris tue et aliorum fueras liberatus' (*Speculum*, p. 128). And both treatises have much the same admonition for the King: 'O domine mi rex, premissis auditis et intellectis, te moneo ex parte 'Dei omnipotentis et sancte ecclesie, et te deprecor ex parte populi tui Anglicani, quod in empcionibus et vendicionibus observari facias jus commune, videlicet, ut nullus de tua curia, nec alius quicunque, capiat res aliquas pro minori precio quam venditor voluerit eas dare, nec aliquis invito domino res aliquas capiat alienas' (*Epistola*, p. 122); 'Et ideo domine rex, ... te consulo, te rogo, ex parte Dei omnipontentis et sancte ecclesie, et ex parte populi anglicani, ... ut facias statui et ordinari ne quis, sub gravi pena, capiat bona alicuius contra suam voluntatem, sed res emat sicut cum venditore poterit convenire, ...' (*Speculum*, p. 133)

In fact, if the *Speculum* and Pagula's *Epistola* are examined side by side, it soon becomes evident that the *Speculum* is really a follow-up of the *Epistola*, if for no other reason than that the common phrase, 'O domine mi rex', with which the two works open, occurs time and again, and, indeed, introduces new chapters some thirteen times each in the *Epistola* and *Speculum*. Both treatises certainly have the same purpose, to persuade the King of the evils of the purveyance system, but where the *Epistola* is a documented attack on the 'maledictum prerogativum' from an historical, legal and moral point of view (with a wealth of citations from Scripture, the Fathers and legal sources), the *Speculum* is a more simple but no less effective meditation upon the words of Deut. 32, 39: 'Utinam saperes et intelligeres ac novissima provideres'.[21] This text is introduced at once in the incipit ('O domine mi rex, utinam...'), and it rings out at regular intervals (ten at least) throughout the *Speculum*, serving as a point of departure for each new complaint: lavishness, neglect of the poor, and especially the iniquities of purveyance, e.g., 'O domine mi rex, utinam saperes ac intelligeres ac novissima provideres. Saperes, id est, intime cogitaris quid prodest, et prodesse tibi poterit, habere amorem Dei et populi tui anglicani... Et ego dico tibi, coram Deo, quod nunquam habebis... quamdiu servientes tui, te consensciente, capiunt res alienas pro minori precio quam venditor velit dare' (*Speculum*, pp. 163-164).

If both treatises are obsessed by the 'maledictum prerogativum', their authors write out of the same harrowing experiences. Pagula's *Epistola* is precisely an appeal to Edward from the locality of Windsor ('where you were born') for protection for himself and his parishioners against the depredations of royal servants.[22] Commissioners of the King, Pagula says, and of the Queen and his son and daughter, are making outrageous demands upon the 'parochiani' of the Forest of Windsor, compelling them at times to neglect their households and tillage for days on end. They commandeer horses and carts, they appropriate victuals, fodder and bedding, yet pay grossly unfair prices (and sometimes nothing at all) for what they requisition or buy.[23] The *Speculum* makes more or less the same charges, speaking on several occasions of the terror which visits of the King and his party induce in the inhabitants of rural villages. Official after official will arrive before the King and demand hay and the like for the King's horses,[24] or take chickens 'for your table' from some poor woman.[25] This, indeed, is a sad state of affairs: 'Erubescere enim potest tota gens anglicana habere regem in cuius adventu populus contristatur communiter, et in recessu suo letatur' (*Speculum*, p. 131).

For William of Pagula in his *Epistola* (p. 103), all these things are 'notoria in partibus de Wyndesore'. The *Speculum* does not mention Windsor, but one passage,

[21] The *Speculum* confines itself more to Scripture than the *Epistola*, although there are a few citations from Ambrose, Augustine, Bernard, Gregory. A long section is taken up (150-159) with reflections (generally with reference to purveyance) upon the advice of St Louis of France to his son, Philip.

[22] *Epistola*, 106: 'et de hoc fit magnus clamor populi in partibus de Windesore ubi traxisti originem, quamvis racione originis tue, deberes illis magis parcere quam aliis qui alibi morantur...'.

[23] *Ibid.*, 100: 'O domine mi rex, erubesce et contremisce, quando a te petuntur huiusmodi littere protectionis. Nichil aliud est dicere in effectum nisi: domine rex, non a regendo sed a rapiendo concede michi litteras tuas, scilicet protectionis... Item, illi de familia tua capiunt de foresta de Wyndesore et locis vicinis, homines, carectas, et equos pauperum; et compellunt eos recedere a domibus propriis per x leucas, et ibidem carriare boscum non solum per tres vel quatuor dies sed per multos, et pro labore solvere promittunt sed nichil solvunt'.

[24] *Speculum*, 135: 'Recte consimiliter est de precursoribus tuis. Quandocumque audiuntur rumores de adventu tuo et auditur unum cornu, contremiscit fere quilibet qui est in villa. Postmodum venit precursor tuus ad villam, et omnes videntes eum tristantur et expavescunt. Non dicit eis: ne timeatis; sed dicit quod vult habere avenam, fenum, lituram pro equis domini regis... Postmodum venit alius eodem modo, et dicit quod vult habere aucas, gallinas et multa alia. Deinde venit tercius, et ipse vult habere frumentum, etc...'.

[25] *Ibid.*, 159.

where the writer tells the King exactly how much it costs to maintain his magnificent horses, does bring Windsor to mind.[26] And I think that Winkfield, some three miles away in the Forest, is the scene of one moving passage where the author sums up the dread people feel at the King's approach: 'As for myself, I am compelled in truth (which is God) to tell you that as soon as I hear your horn and know that you are near, I begin to tremble all over, no matter where I am, in the open, in church, at Mass, at home, or in my study. And if one of your servants knocks at my gate I tremble all the more; and still more if he is actually at my door. And this fear does not leave me while you are in the neighbourhood, because of the untold evil that those who say they belong to your curia may be doing to the poor' (*Speculum*, p. 134).

As vicar of Winkfield, some three miles from Windsor, William Poul of Pagula more readily than any other fills this vivid picture of the fear of the local priest at the approach of the King and his retainers. And after almost twenty years as parish priest, he certainly was in a position to know more than most ecclesiastics about the cost of the upkeep of the King's stables and the wages of the grooms. The numerous parallels, and the obvious continuity, between the *Epistola* and the *Speculum* are indeed so striking, that Pagula must be the author of the *Speculum* as he is without doubt the author of the *Epistola*.[27]

In early 1331 he had written the *Epistola* to protest the repeated acts of purveyance with which his parish at Winkfield was being ruined. The Peace of Amiens in the following April had, however, destroyed his nice point about the continual state of war and the lack of peace that had resulted from Edward I's introduction of purveyance. The *Speculum*, written about a year after that Peace, was Pagula's attempt to recover some ground, and to make sure that the *Epistola* did not go unread and unheeded by the King, now that the country appeared to be at peace. England, he says in the *Speculum*, may indeed seem to have peace now for the first time for over forty years, but the 'pax et gaudium huius terre, que iam fuerint anno isto' will surely come to nothing if purveyances are not put down. And just as he had warned the King in the *Epistola* (p. 96) that the people, given the leadership, 'insurgerent contra te, sicut contra patrem tuum fecerunt', if he does not redress grievances at once, so again in the *Speculum* (pp. 167-8) he voices the same fear: 'valde timendum est quod insurgeret contra te populus huius terre'.

Edward, of course, had grown up in years when purveyance was accepted as part of the royal way of life. Pagula, it seems, had little or no confidence that the well-placed 'iuris periti' (*Epistola*, p. 87) and 'clerici de curia' (*Speculum*, p. 162) would be very much inclined to encourage the King to change an established

---

[26] *Ibid.*, 143: 'Et nunc, domine rex, considera expensas quas facis per annum, circa unum magnum equum. Unus magnus equus habebit ad minus unum garcionem custodem qui recipiet, singulis diebus, denarium pro expensis suis; pro equo iterum capiet unum dimidium busselli avene, pretii i denarii, fenum, precii i denarii. Unde expense unius hebdomadae: ii solidi, vii denarii, obolum — de quibus quattuor pauperes vel quinque poterunt sustentari...'

[27] There is no point in discussing the fact that three late 14th century MSS. of the *Speculum* attribute the work to Simon Islip. Manuscript inscriptions are not infallible; and in any case there are also some 14th century MSS. which attribute Pagula's *Epistola* to the same Islip. Possibly Islip owned a copy of both works at some point (and he did castigate Edward for his expenditure), and copyists took his ownership for authorship.

and profitable sytem, although he does appeal in the *Epistola* (p. 120) to the 'ductores regis', and in the *Speculum* (pp. 162-163) to the 'viri litterati... cum domino morantes', to induce the King to do away with the 'prerogativum maledictum'. For his part, Pagula was determined that Edward should be left in no doubt about the just grievances — not to speak of hostile feelings — of the long-suffering people of Windsor Forest and elsewhere.

Pagula obviously felt that he was in a strong position to influence the young King and to better the condition of the people of Winkfield and the Forest. He had come to Winkfield when Edward was some two years old, and the paternal tone throughout the *Epistola* and *Speculum* suggests that he knew the King well, and was simply putting down in writing before it was too late what he had often told Edward in person: 'O domine mi rex, he says towards the end of the *Speculum* (p. 159), obsecro te ne irascaris si adhuc semel loquar tibi'. He had, he also notes in the *Speculum*, often before begged the King to abolish purveyances, but had had no satisfaction: 'Sed in brevi, timendum est quod nisi predicta facias emendari, ... timendum est quod Deus te non exaudiet, *quia multocies pro pauperibus ad te clamavi*, ut tolleres de terra ista illud maledictum prerogativum, ... *et non exaudisti me*' (p. 160). One such instance, surely, was the *Epistola* of early 1331. And when that weighty appeal appeared not to be producing its effect, Pagula returned to the attack a year or more later in the more meditative *Speculum regis*.

Pontifical Institute of Mediaeval Studies.

CLERICAL EDUCATION

NOTES ON THE EDUCATION OF THE *FRATRES COMMUNES* IN THE DOMINICAN ORDER IN THE THIRTEENTH CENTURY

Although the original mission of the Dominican order was that of preaching, within four years of its foundation the order became an Order of Confessors as well as an Order of Preachers.

This change, it appears, was not wholly the doing of Dominic, but was largely due to the attempts of pope Honorius III to implement certain constitutions of the Fourth Lateran Council in 1215, under his predecessor Innocent III.

The mandate of preaching itself was the direct result of the constitution *Inter caetera* of that Lateran Council, which stated that bishops who were overworked, or who were not up to the demands of preaching, should establish groups of preachers in their dioceses who would be their helpers and co-workers in the pastoral care. Dominic, who was at the council with bishop Fulk of Toulouse, his diocesan, had felt that in his band of diocesan preachers centred in Toulouse, he had the means of making sure that this constitution would not remain a dead letter. In January 1217 he therefore obtained from Honorius a mandate (*Gratiarum omnium*) that gave a general approval to "the work already begun of preaching the word of God".[1] This papal confirmation of Dominic's Toulouse Preachers as Preachers-in-general was followed over the next three years (1218-1220) by many letters to prelates urging them to make use of the Preachers and to encourage them in the office of preaching "ad quod deputati sunt".[2]

---

[1] *Monumenta diplomatica S. Dominici*, ed. V. J. Koudelka and R. J. Loenertz (Rome 1966), n. 79 (21 Jan. 1217).

[2] Ibid., nn. 86-8, 91, 101-3, 109, 112, 121-2. See also L. E. Boyle, "The Death of St Dominic in 1221: an anniversary note", *Doctrine and Life* 21 (1971) 438-46.

In the mandate *Gratiarum omnium* of 1217 and in these letters of recommendation there is no mention whatever of the hearing of confessions. Yet, logically, there should have been. For the constitution *Inter caetera* of the Lateran Council had explicitly allied the function of hearing confessions to that of preaching: "Unde praecipimus tam in cathedralibus quam in aliis conventualibus ecclesiis viros idoneos ordinari, quos episcopi possint coadiutores et cooperatores habere, non solum in praedicantium officio verum etiam in audiendis confessionibus et poenitentiis iniungendis ac caeteris quae ad salutem pertinent animarum".[3]   Possibly Honorius was waiting until the fledgling Preachers had proven themselves generally as they had proven themselves locally in Languedoc before entrusting to them the second function envisaged by the Lateran constitution. Dominic, indeed, may have been aware that the mission confided to the order in *Gratiarum omnium* entailed more than the office of preaching, for he took some trouble at once to ensure that his Preachers became learned men in the spirit of the Lateran Council which, in a celebrated constitution *Omnis utriusque sexus*, had laid down that a confessor should be "discreet and judicious and of a prudent understanding".[4]   Perhaps this was one of the reasons why in the month after the Preachers of Toulouse had been recognized by the papacy as Preachers-in-general, Dominic enrolled his six disciples in the course that Alexander Stavensby was giving at the Cathedral school in Toulouse[5]; perhaps this was why in the summer of 1217 he sent some of his young community to study at the university of Paris, and then arranged foundations in university centres such as Bologna (1218), Palencia (1220), Montpellier (1221), and, just before his death, Oxford (August 1221).

At all events, Honorius must have been satisfied by 1221 that in the order of Preachers he had not only the freelance preachers of the constitution *Inter caetera* but also preachers who would "hear confessions and enjoin penances". In an

---

[3] *Conciliorum oecumenicorum decreta*, ed. J. Alberigo, etc. (Bologna-Barcelona-Freiburg 1962), pp. 215-6 (c. 10).

[4] Ibid., p. 221 (c. 21).

[5] Humbertus de Romanis, *Legenda S. Dominici*, ed. A. Walz (Rome 1935), n. 40.

encyclical letter to "all archbishops, bishops and prelates" of 4 February 1221, Honorius reiterated the commendation of the Preachers which he had been issuing regularly since 1217, but added now that the bishops and prelates were to allow the Preachers where possible to hear confessions and enjoin penances:

> Hinc est quod dilectos filios fratres ordinis praedicatorum qui paupertatem et vitam regularem professi verbi dei sunt evangelizationi totaliter deputati vobis duximus propensius commendandos, universitatem vestram rogantes et hortantes attentius ac per apostolica vobis scripta mandantes quatenus [a] cum ad partes vestras accesserint, ad praedicandi officium ad quod deputati sunt caritative recipiatis eosdem..., [b] benigne permittentes presbiteris eorumdem cum expedierit penitentium confessiones audire et consilium eis iniungere salutare, cum iidem fratres animarum intendentes profectibus discretos et cautos dirigant sacerdotes per quos salutare potest consilium preberi et remedium adhiberi...[6]

By these words, with their clear echoes of both *Omnis utriusque sexus* ("*Sacerdos* autem sit *discretus et cautus...* diligenter inquirens et peccatorum circumstantias et peccati, per quas prudenter intelligat quale ille *consilium* debeat *exhibere* et cuiusmodi *remedium adhibere*") and *Inter caetera* ("non solum in praedicationis officio verum etiam *in audiendis confessionibus et poenitentiis iniungendis*"), the Preachers fully became the "suitable men" of the Lateran Council's constitution on preaching. Their preaching mission from now on was hearing confessions as well as straight preaching.

* * *

The young Dominican order probably had enough seasoned men to meet the new situation. The foundations in university cities such as Bologna and Paris had already attracted a number of masters to the Order. But in February 1221, when the papal commission to hear confessions was issued, the Order was about to open up new areas beyond the confines of France, Italy, Spain and the Rhineland, where it was already established. In May 1221, in fact, Preachers were sent out by the General chapter of Bologna to Britain, Ireland, Scandinavia, Poland, Hungary and the near

---

[6] *Cum qui recipit prophetam* in *Monumenta diplomatica S. Dominici*, n. 143.

East.   To provide some sort of handbook of penance for the brethren in general and for the pioneers in particular must have been Dominic's first concern after the promulgation of the confession mandate.

This concern probably accounts for the fact that shortly after the encyclical letter of February 1221, Paul of Hungary, a professor of law who had joined the Order from the university of Bologna, put a *summa* of penitential practice together at Bologna.   It is just possible that it was completed in time for the general chapter there in May of that year, and that the Preachers designated for the new fields in Britain, Scandinavia and Eastern Europe were in possession of copies of Paul's work before they set out.[7]

Perhaps the Order as a whole was a little taken by surprise. A general mandate to hear confessions was something new in the life of the Church.   The Preachers, of course, could have obtained copies of the new type of general manual which had recently appeared at Paris and elsewhere.   Robert of Flamborough, a penitentiary at St. Victor, had written an excellent *summa* at Paris in 1208 which had broken away from the traditional books of penitential canons.   At Salisbury in England Thomas Chobham had written a fine *Summa de casibus* shortly after the Fourth Lateran Council.[8]   But the Preachers probably felt that the new commission to hear confessions demanded some sort of guideline from within the Order as such.   This probably accounts for the fact that within four years of the encyclical letter of February 1221, four manuals of penance for Dominicans appeared

---

[7] Printed as "Rationes penitentie composite a fratribus predicatorum" in *Bibliotheca Casinensis* IV (Monte Cassino 1880), pp. 191-215, from Cassino MS. 184, it was definitively identified as the work of Paul of Hungary by P. Mandonnet, "La 'Summa de Poenitentia magistri Pauli Presbiteri S. Nicolai'", in *Aus der Geisteswelt des Mittelalters* [Festschrift Grabmann], (Münster 1935), I. 525-44, an essay later reprinted in P. Mandonnet, *St. Dominique*, ed. M.-H. Vicaire and R. Ladner (Paris 1938), I. 249-69.   The fact that Paul refers to "Magister Dominicus prior noster" (ed. cit. p. 197) makes it clear that the work was written before Dominic's death in August 1221; a remark a little earlier (ibid., p. 196) suggests that it was being composed in a hurry – perhaps for the General Chapter of May of that year.

[8] Robert of Flamborough, *Liber poenitentialis*, ed. J. J. Firth (Toronto 1971); *Thomae de Chobham Summa confessorum*, ed. F. Broomfield (Louvain-Paris 1968).

at what were then the focal points of the order.[9] Paul of Hungary wrote his manual at Bologna in 1221; in 1222 the Preachers of St. Jacques in Paris pooled their resources to produce a rudimentary vademecum called the *Flos summarum*[10]; at Cologne the German provincial Conrad Höxter (again a recruit from the law faculty at Bologna) wrote a *Summa confessionis* about 1224[11]; in 1225 a first version of his famous *Summa de casibus* was composed at Barcelona for the Preachers of Spain by another jurist of Bologna, Raymond of Pennafort.[12]

These four manuals represent the first literary activity of the Dominican Order. They were the forerunners of a remarkable number of pastoral manuals of various kinds over the three centuries before the Reformation, the high points for the thirteenth century (and for the fourteenth as well) being the revised edition of the *Summa* of Raymund in 1234 or 1235, the *Summa vitiorum* (c. 1236) and *Summa virtutum* (before 1248-50) of Guillaume Peyraut[13], and the *Summa confessorum* of John of Freiburg in 1297-98.

By and large the beneficiaries of these manuals within the Dominican Order were the "Fratres communes", those, that is, who were not selected for special studies at a *Studium provinciale* or a *Studium generale*. They were the men who were generally engaged in the day-to-day hearing of confessions or "common" preaching to which the Order was specifically committed.[14] The

---

[9] See in general, Mandonnet, *St. Dominique*, pp. 256-8; P. Michaud-Quantin, *Sommes de casuistique et manuels de confession au moyen âge* (Louvain-Lille-Montreal 1962), pp. 24-6, 34-42.

[10] "Summa supra virtutes et vicia cum confessione noviter composita a quibusdam fratribus sancti Iacobi quae dicitur Flos summarum": Paris, B.N. lat. 16433. First reported by Mandonnet (*St. Dominique*, p. 156), the *Flos summarum* is extant in some eight MSS., in one of which (Trinity College, Dublin, 326, fos. 28r-31v) it is entitled simply, "Summa penitencie fratrum praedicatorum".

[11] J. Dietterle, "*Die Summae confessorum*", *Zeitschrift für Kirchengeschichte* 24 (1903) 520-7, who records the prologue as stating "pro ipsorum minorum et pauperum eruditione", instead of "pro ipsorum *iuniorum*...".

[12] S. Kuttner, *Zur Entstehungsgeschichte der* Summa de casibus *des hl. Raymund von Pennafort*", *Zeitschrift der Savigny-Stiftung für Rechtsgeschichte*, Kan. Abt. 85 (1953) 419-48.

[13] A. Dondaine, "Guillaume Peyraut. Vie et œuvres", *Archivum Fratrum Praedicatorum* 18 (1948) 162-236.

[14] The term "Frater communis" is a 14th-century one: "Communes vero fratres singulis diebus ad scolas vadant lectoris principalis et ibidem lectiones

254

"Communes" were, in fact, the backbone of the Order and vastly outnumbered the Alberts and Thomases, the lectors and the masters. They are the "iuniores" of the prefaces of so many Dominican manuals and treatises (such as that of Conrad Höxter), to whom the more academic brethren were never slow to communicate their own learning or that of the schools. It was for them, principally, that Raymund, Guillaume Peyraut and John of Freiburg wrote. It was for them, explicitly, that Simon Hinton, probably when provincial of England, wrote his *Summa iuniorum*, [15] and Aag of Denmark, when provincial of Scandinavia, his *Rotulus pugillaris*. [16] They had to be well-trained, well-informed and alert if they were not to betray their calling. From that point of view the preacher and the confessor were as important in the Dominican scheme of education as the professional teachers. As the general chapter of 1259 put it: "Non fiant lectores vel praedicatores vel confessores nisi sint tam sufficientes quod possint sine periculo notabili huiusmodi officia exercere". [17]

From the earliest days of the Dominican Order, great care was taken to see that all the brethren, the "Communes" with the "Docibiles", "Lectores" and "Doctores", had a formal training, and that that training had a pastoral bearing. As the prologue to the first constitutions (1220) put it, "Studium nostrum ad hoc

audiant, alias illo die a vino vel a pictantia sine dispensatione abstineant", *Acta capitulorum generalium ordinis praedicatorum*, ed. B. M. Reichert, II (Rome 1899), 152-3. For the term "Praedicator communis" (as distinct from the more qualified "Praedicator generalis"), see Humbertus de Romanis, *Opera*, ed. J. J. Berthier, 2 vv. (Rome 1888-9), II. 369.

[15] "Ad instructionem iuniorum quibus non vacat opusculorum variorum prolixitatem perscrutari": prologue of Simon of Hinton as in J. Gerson, *Opera omnia* (Antwerp 1706), I. 233. See n. 31, below.

[16] "Ad laudem Iesu Christi pro instructione iuvenum fratrum ordinis Praedicatorum et aliorum qui pro tempore ob salutem animarum praedicationi et confessionum auditioni sunt exponendi, ea quae communia sunt et in sacra theologia magis necessaria simplicibus ad sciendum in unum quasi rotulum pugillarem breviter collecta redegi... Moneo vero iterum atque iterum ne aliqui fratres dicti ordinis Daciae ad praedicta officia praedicationis et confessionis assumantur priusquam de his quae hic conscripta sunt et aliis quae in constitutionibus praefati ordinis ponuntur ad memorata officia pertinentia diligenter examinati fuerint et approbati": A. Walz, "Fratris Augustini de Dacia, O.P., *Rotulus Pugillaris*", *Angelicum* 6 (1929) 254. The *Rotulus* was written while Aag was provincial of Scandinavia (1254-66; 1272-84).

[17] *Acta capitulorum generalium ordinis praedicatorum*, I (Rome 1898), 100

principaliter ardenterque summo opere debeat intendere ut proximorum animabus possimus utiles esse ". [18] The same constitutions specify that no house was to be founded without a superior (" prior ") and a teacher (" lector "), [19] and insist on the importance of study: " Qualiter intenti debeant esse in studio ut de die, de nocte, in domo, in itinere, legant aliquid vel meditentur, et quicquid poterint retinere cordetenus nitantur ". [20]

The emphasis was wholly on a theological training. A grounding in Latin and grammar was taken for granted. [21] Instruction in these subjects was by way of exception, though later the Chapter of 1259 would recommend the provision of courses in grammar in priories, where necessary. [22]

As a rule, all young Dominicans began their studies in a local priory under the local lector, and most never obtained any education other than that provided in these priories and by these lectors. Opportunities for higher studies were small. Only the brightest students found their way to a *studium generale*, the only one of which until 1248 was Paris (to which three were allowed to go from each province). And even after 1248, when four other *studia generalia* (Cologne, Oxford, Montpellier, Bologna) were added to Paris, a quota-system kept the number of students down to two from each province to each of the new *studia*. [23] By the middle of the century there were, of course, the *studia provincialia*, midway between the priory schools and the *studia generalia*. But again, although these also offered advanced work in theology, they were chiefly meant for those students who had been selected for training as lectors, and were mostly outside the reach of the generality of the *Fratres communes*. [24]

---

[18] Ed. A. H. Thomas, *De oudste Constituties van de Dominicanen* (Louvain 1965), pp. 311-12.

[19] Ibid., p. 358.

[20] Ibid., p. 324.

[21] Ibid., pp. 361-2: "Seculares scientias non addiscant, nec etiam artes quas liberales vocant, sed tantum libros theologicos tam iuvenes quam alii legant" See also A. Duval, "L'étude dans la législation religieuse de S. Dominique", *Mélanges Chenu* (Paris 1967), pp. 221-47.

[22] *Acta* I. 99.

[23] Ibid., I. 34, 38, 41.

[24] See W. A. Hinnebusch, *The History of the Dominican Order*, II (New York 1974), pp. 23-32.

Not that the *Fratres communes* (nine-tenths, perhaps, of the whole Dominican order in the 13th century) were thereby neglected or only received a spotty education from the lectors in the priories. Far from it. Study was as much a part of their lives as it was of those of their more gifted brethren. Even after they had become priests and had taken a place as preachers, confessors, administrators and missioners, only a dispensation could excuse them at any point from attendance at the lectors' classes, just as in their student-days. [25]

The General Chapter at Valenciennes in 1259 shows itself especially sensitive in their regard. Adopting the *Ratio studiorum* drawn up by a committee of five that included Albert the Great, Thomas Aquinas and Peter of Tarentaise, the Chapter ordered that each house with a lector should also have a tutor to assist him. No one, not even the prior, was to be absent from lectures; and while lectures were in progress the brethren should not, as a rule, be engaged in saying Mass or out about the town on business. Aware that many priories were finding it hard to obtain lectors, mainly because of the increase in houses all over Europe, the Valenciennes Chapter suggested that visitators should keep a look out for lectors or other teachers who were at a loose end from province to province, and attempt to induce them to spend two or three years on loan to provinces which were short of lectors. Priories without lectors were encouraged to take steps on their own. They should send some of their members, especially younger ones, to priories which already had lectors in residence, or, failing this, should set up a series of private classes for the brethren of their communities on the *Historia scholastica* (of Peter Comestor), the *Summa de casibus* (of Raymund) or some such material, lest the brethren should drift into idleness. Lectors, in turn, were urged to let nothing stand in the way of their teaching in the priories: " Ad promotionem studii ordinamus hoc quod lectores non occupentur in officiis vel negotiis per que a lectionibus retrahantur ". [26]

Humbert de Romanis, writing after he had retired as General in 1265, gives one of the clearest pictures of the office of lector and of the studies of the *Fratres communes* in the 13th century. In a chapter " De officio lectoris " in his *Instructiones de officiis*,

---

[25] *Acta* I. 39, 175, 196; Humbertus de Romanis, *Opera*, I. 45-6.
[26] *Acta* I. 99-100.

Humbert says that lectors should be totally at the disposition of the brethren. Their vacations should be taken only at those times when the greater part of the community was absent, during the Summer, for example, or during the busy preaching seasons of Advent and Lent. They should give freely of their time for private tuition of the better students. In their lectures they should always aim at practical instruction and should stick as closely as possible to their text, whether the Bible, the Histories (of Comestor) or the Sentences (of Peter Lombard). [27]   In their disputations they should confine themselves to "materia utilis et intelligibilis". Later, when speaking of the office of librarian, Humbert notes that it is up to the librarian to provide a convenient ready-reference area in which there are good, legible copies of, among other things, the Bible, the Decretum and the Decretals, *Distinctiones morales,* the *Summa de casibus* of Raymund, the *Summa [supra titulis]* of Geoffrey of Trani, the *Summa de vitiis et virtutibus* (of Guillaume Peyraut), "ut communitas fratrum in promptu possit illa habere". [28]

* * *

From the Valenciennes Chapter of 1259 and from Humbert it is clear that practical theology ("collationes de moralibus", as Humbert terms it) was the order of the day for the *Fratres communes,* the young with the old. And as befitted Preachers who were also Confessors, a treatise on moral practice stands at the centre of their training, the *Summa de casibus* of Raymund of Pennafort. Almost as soon as it was published it became the semi-official text-book of the Order in all that touched penance

---

[27] Humbertus de Romanis, *Opera* II. 254-61.

[28] Ibid., II 265: "Item, ad ipsum pertinet providere quod in aliquo loco silentii et apto, sit aliquis pulpitus magnus, vel plures, in quibus legentur aliqui libri bene legibiles, quibus frequentius fratres indigent cum habentur, ut est *Biblia* glossata in toto vel in parte, *Biblia* sine glossis, *Summae De casibus* et *Gaufredi* et *De vitiis et virtutibus* et *De quaestionibus, Concordantiae, Interpretationes, Decreta, Decretales, Distinctiones morales, Sermones varii de festis et dominicis* per totum annum, *Historiae, Sententiae, Chronica, Passiones* et *Legendae sanctorum, Historia ecclesiastica,* et similia multa, ut communitas fratrum in promptu possit illa habere".

and morals. [29]   As we know from John of Freiburg and other sources, it was commented on, synopsized, enlarged upon, all over the Order.

John of Freiburg himself, who for thirty years or more fulfilled the office of lector in the Dominican house at Freiburg-im-Breisgau, was perhaps the lector par excellence. He had begun his career, as every lector was doing at the time, by teaching straight from the *Summa* of Raymund. Then, for the convenience of his community, he made an index that combined the matter of the *Summa* with that of the *Apparatus* which William of Rennes had written to the *Summa* about 1241; as well, he compiled a *Libellus quaestionum casualium* from the *Summa* and supplemented Raymund's *casus* with some from other sources. But having been a student of some of the great theologians of the Order who had written since Raymund's day (certainly of Ulrich of Strasbourg, possibly of Albert, Thomas and Peter of Tarentaise), John gradually grew discontented with Raymund's *Summa*, which by his time was more than a little dated. Working through the writings of Ulrich, Albert, Thomas and Peter, John of Freiburg first made a supplement to Raymund, then embarked in 1297-98 on a *Summa* of his own that integrated what he had culled from his four theologians (and from canonists such as Hostiensis) into the scheme of Raymund's *Summa*. [30]

What John the Lector, as he was known, accomplished at Freiburg-im-Breisgau probably is a fair reflection of what was going on for the benefit of the *Fratres communes* in priories all over the whole Dominican order: lecturing on Raymund's *Summa* (" quae, as Simon of Hinton put it, passim apud fratres habetur "), expanding it here and there from later sources, collecting *casus* by which to broaden the experience of the *Fratres* or to drive home the points of law and theology found in their text-book, the *Summa de casibus*.

Apart from the *Summa confessorum* of John the Lector and his other writings, only one other example, so far as I know,

---

[29] See A. Walz, "S. Raymundi de Penyafort auctoritas in re paenitentiali", *Angelicum* 12 (1935) 346-96.

[30] See L. E. Boyle, "The *Summa confessorum* of John of Freiburg", *St Thomas Aquinas 1274-1974 Commemorative Studies*, ed. A. A. Maurer (Toronto 1974), II. 245-68.

survives from the 13th century to illustrate the method of teaching followed by a conventual lector in his lectures to and teaching of the *Fratres communes*. This is a miscellany, dating probably from a little after 1260, which is now in the British Library (formerly Museum), London, as Additional MS. 30508. Because it is an interesting witness, the remainder of this article is devoted to a description and summary of it.

* * *

Additional MS. 30508 is a small, pocket-size volume which was purchased for the British Museum (as it then was) in 1877. Taken without its over-large 19th-century binding, the volume measures 15 × 12 cms. The folios are of two columns, each 12 × 3 cms., with, as a rule, 21 lines to a column. Two wormholes from the back of the volume disrupt the text of columns rb and va for some twenty folios, one ending at o.f. 258rb, the other at o.f. 261rb.

An original foliation (= o.f.) runs in Arabic numerals from 1 - 279, but since folios 105, 106 and 198 are now missing, and, as well, since the medieval foliator forgot the number 233 and did not bother to number three folios at the end, the total volume today consists of 278 original folios (and two flyleaves which are later additions to the beginning of the volume). The modern foliation of 1878 (= n.f.) also arrives at 278 folios for the volume, but with a total disregard of the original foliation (to which the contemporary index at the end, with its folio references, is a splendid witness). Because it begins from the unoriginal flyleaves and, further, fails to record two of the present folios (194, 196, o.f.), the only place where the modern foliation keeps step with the original is at fos. 107-193, where the absence of the original folios 105-106, compensates for the two intrusive flyleaves at the beginning and brings the two foliations unwittingly into line for a while.

The volume is a homogeneous collection of pastoral tracts and notes, here listed in the original foliation, with the modern in brackets after it:

a. 1 - 104 (3 - 106): Anon. treatise on Creed, Sacraments, etc. Inc.: "Notandum est quid sit simbolum... Simbolum est omnium credendorum ad salutem spectantium compendiosa collectio...". This is an abbreviation of the *Summa iuniorum* (1250 × 1260) of the English Dominican Simon of Hinton (see n. 31 below).

    b. 105 - 106: now missing.

    c. 107 - 112: sermon-notes in pencil (109-112r); verses in ink over pencilled notes (112v).

    d. 113 - 168r: Anon. tract on Commandments, Creed, Confession, etc. Inc.: "De primo precepto supraposito...".

    e. 169 - 190: Tract on Confession. Inc.: "Animetur primo confitens brevi exhortacione...". At 179v-190v there is a long Latin formula of confession, followed, 191-193r, by a French formula.

    f. 194 (-): blank. 195 (194): riddles. 196 (-): blank. 197 (195): scribbles. 198: now missing.

    g. 199 - 246r (196 - 242r): Unacknowledged synopsis of all four books of Raymund's *Summa de casibus.* Inc.: "Simonia est studiosa voluntas emendi vel vendendi...".

    h. 246v - 279r (242v - 275r): Series of "problems" or *casus.* Inc.: "Aliquis iurat se restituturum gladium alicui...". At the end, 279rb, there is a note: "Pro anima Agnetis de Winterseth xiid".

    i. 279v (275v): Brief contemporary subject-index to whole volume, with folio and column references (see n. 35 below).

    j. ---: (276): riddles; 277v: "Hec sunt suffragia capituli generalis celebrati Oxon. anno domini m° cc° lxxx°. Summa missarum pro vivis xxxii. Summa pro defunctis x"; 278v: 15th-century notes of expenses.

Even without the presence of Raymund and the *Summa iuniorum* of Simon of Hinton [31], the whole volume conjures up

---

[31] In an article, "La Somme de Simon de Hinton", *Recherches de théologie ancienne et médiévale* 9 (1937) 5-22, 205-18, A. Dondaine has shown that the *Compendium theologiae* printed in the 1706 edition of the works of John Gerson is really the *Summa* of Simon of Hinton, *Excerptiones* from which were published from Sidney Sussex College, Cambridge, MS. 73 by A. Walz, "The *Exceptiones* from the *Summa* of Simon of Hinton", *Angelicum* 13 (1936) 263-368 (text at 290-368). Dondaine lists the present Add. MS. 30508 as one of the many manuscripts of the *Summa*, but in fact the text here is not exactly that printed among Gerson's works, nor is it exactly that of the *Exceptiones.* Although basically the text in Add. MS. 30508 is that of Hinton's *Summa*, there are points at which it is

a Dominican setting, and an English one at that. There are references in the texts to " fratres " (257ra, 266ra: o.f.) and to preachers (257ra), to London (255vb) and to priests who " come to these parts " from Ireland (250rb, 251ra). And at the end of the volume there is the note of the Dominican General Chapter at Oxford in 1280: " Hec sunt suffragia capituli generalis celebrati Oxon . . . ".

This note probably provides a *terminus ante quem* for the volume, just as the version of Hinton's *Summa* probably gives a *terminus post quem* of 1250 × 1260. The date, then, of the volume as a whole is probably 1260 × 1280, but since there are no references whatever to canonists or theologians after the time of Hinton, the date of compilation may be nearer to 1260 than to 1280. The script, a good, well-formed textual Gothic of 1250 × 1300, does not at all conflict with this dating. Nor does the presence, both in the text and the foliation, of Arabic numerals, though they were not in general use in England until the end of the century.

The combination of Hinton's *Summa* (1 - 104), snippets from the *Summa* of Raymund (199-246) and a set of " Problems " (246-79), strongly suggests that the volume was compiled by or for a lector in one or other of the English Dominican houses (possibly, indeed, at Pontefract in the north of England)[32]. The writing appears to be the work of a professional scribe. It is competent and secure, and takes some pains to maintain an even edge to the lines of the columns, resorting time and again throughout the volume to fillers (generally a cancelled 1) to avoid

---

fuller than the printed texts of the *Summa* and the *Exceptiones*   For other abbreviations of the *Summa*, see L. E. Boyle, "Three English pastoral *Summae* and a Magister Galienus", *Studia Gratiana* 11 (1967) 133-44.

[32] The evidence for Pontefract is indirect, but none the less persuasive. The Dominican house at Pontefract, in Yorkshire, was founded in 1256, just before the date of our volume, and had a community of 31 by 1300: see W. A. Hinnebusch, *The Early English Friars Preachers* (Rome 1951), pp. 95-6, 274. Here, on fol. 278v (n.f.), the place-names Houghton and Barnsley, not very far from Pontefract, occur in a late 15th-century list of expenses. What is more, a note in a clear, 13th-century hand on fol. 279r (o.f.), just at the end of the "problems", yields the name of Wintersett, a village midway between Pontefract and Barnsley: " Pro anima Agnetis de Winterseth xiid ".

unseemly gaps at the end of lines [33]. But the various texts were not copied without some mistakes – mistakes which are corrected in a clear, notular script by the same hand, it seems, as that which compiled the index at fol. 279v (o.f.). This same hand, presumably that of the lector-owner, was also responsible for the sermon-notes in pencil on fos. 109-112, as well as for the riddles and other notes at fos. 195 (o.f.) and 276 (n.f.).

The only parts of the volume which concern us here are those that carry the extracts from Raymund's *Summa* (199-246) and the series of "Problems" or *casus* (246-79). Although the compiler does not state that he is drawing on Raymund for his extracts, the borrowing is beyond doubt [34]. The selection follows each of the four books of the *Summa de casibus* from the opening chapter *De simonia* to that *De divortiis* at the very end. In all, the compiler compresses the whole *Summa* into less than fifty folios. His method generally is to begin with Raymund's definition of a topic or with the heading, and then to retell one of Raymund's examples in the form of a *casus*, thus: "De periurio. Aliquis captus ab hostibus propter metum qui potest cadere in virum constantem, iurat se daturum x. Queritur utrum obligatur ex tali iuramento? Et videtur multis auctoritatibus quod non. Tamen fere omnes doctores dicunt quod obligatur... Tamen Iohannes [Teutonicus] excipit iiii casus in quibus sic iurans non tenetur..." (fol. 197r o.f.). Here the compiler jumps from the title (*Summa*, ed. Paris 1603, 80a) to the middle of the chapter (87b, 88b), completely ignoring the whole first part (80a-87a).

In effect, this synopsis of Raymund is nothing more than a series of *casus* plucked straight (without even changing Raymund's first person) from the *Summa de casibus*. It was, no doubt, a very handy collection by which to illustrate the various topics discussed by Raymund or to test a student's understanding of

---

[33] See C. Jeudy, "Signes de fin de ligne et tradition manuscrite...", *Scriptorium* 27 (1973) 252-62, for some interesting notes on fillers. The examples in the present MS. would appear to antedate by some years the earliest known instances of the phenomenon.

[34] Although the title *Summa de Casibus* appears nowhere, there are clues to the fact that the collection of *Casus* is from Raymund. At one point (fol. 207ra) there is a rubric, "De tercio libro", exactly at the change-over from book two to book three of the *Summa*. Besides, the helpful index on 279v (o.f.) states, "De casibus reimundi a 199° usque ad 246", putting the matter beyond doubt.

them. Some twenty or thirty years later John of Freiburg would do the same sort of thing in his *Libellus quaestionum casualium*. All the same, the series of problems here is entirely dependent on Raymund, and is not at all as interesting as the series which immediately follows it in the volume (246-79). There is more variety now, and there is a local flavour which is absent from the borrowings from the *Summa de casibus*.

The range, too, of the problems is wider, and the (by my count) 216 questions cover most of the practical aspects of the pastoral care with which an ordinary Dominican or *Frater communis* would be expected to be familia: abstinence, adultery, almsgiving, betrothal, bigamy, burial, concubinage, confession and the seal of confession, consanguinity and affinity, degradation, domicile, the eucharist, excommunication, fear, falsification of letters, fortune telling, homicide, irregularity, loans, manumission, matrimony, cases of necessity, oaths, occult sins, orders, penance, perjury, religious life, restitution, shipwreck, simony, spiritual daughters, sponsors, stole fees, theft, tithes, usury, violence and vows.

Most of the subjects in this long catalogue are presented in the *casus* or « problem » form which the summists and moralists of the late 12th and the 13th centuries had adopted from Gratian's *Decretum*, where Gratian sometimes uses the « problem » technique to get to the roots of the law on some matter or other, e.g., « Duo clerici ad monasterium transire volunt; uterque licentiam ab episcopo suo petiit; unus relicta propria ecclesia eo inito, alter dimissa regulari canonica cenobio se contulit. Modo queritur, si episcopus debeat permittere ut relicta propria ecclesia clericis monasterium ingrediatur?... » (C. 19, proem.).

But although the 216 problems (some of which include follow-up questions) have all the appearances of the *quaestiones* of the Decretists and Decretalists, they are much more like the type of problem which a teacher would use in class to test his students, or at an examination. There is the smack of the examination for confession faculties about some of them, e.g., « Aliquis furatus est duas vaccas. Unam statim interficit, aliam equalis valoris reservat et percipit magnum emolumentum. Post quinquennium confitetur. Quod consilium dabitur ei quoad restitutionem utriusque – et quid iuris sit? » (fol. 248ra o.f.). More often than not only the question is given, or simply the bones of a question, without any suggestion of what the answer is or could be.

In all likelihood what we have here is a set of problems which a resourceful English lector had compiled or had himself dreamed up over a number of years of teaching practical theology from the *Summa de casibus*. The careful layout, the marginal corrections and the intelligent index (with folio references, too) [35] testify that the volume as a whole was highly regarded and that the collection of problems was far from casual. The lector could fall back on his bank of problems when the *Fratres communes* were short of a topic for the periodic disputations. He could draw on them for the regular *collationes de moralibus* and revision sessions, during which, as Humbert de Romanis says, the lector was expected to quiz the brethren « de lectionibus, vel quaestionibus auditis a fratribus, ut videatur de profectu eorum » [36].

Here and there the questions plumb a student's general knowledge (« Queritur si confirmacio vel ordo vel aliquod tale sacramentum possit precedere baptismum, cum baptismus sit ianua sacramentorum »: fol. 250va), but others are of the tricky variety which only an alert student would answer without some hesitation: « Aliquis aufert sacrum de non sacro, alius non sacrum de sacro: quis istorum magis peccat? » (fol. 249rb); « Iste aufert garbas de decima repositas in horreo, alius aufert garbas de decima iacentes in campo: quis magis peccat? » (ibid.). In some of the questions one can almost see the lector putting the main question, waiting for some answer, and then pouncing on any fuzziness in the reply: « Quidam coniugatus contrahit matrimonium cum quadam soluta. Post, audito rumore de morte sue legitime, contrahit matrimonium cum alia. Quid iuris? Vel si stet cum ipsa, quid iuris? Vel si possit stare cum ipsa? » (fol. 250ra). Of course, not all the matrimonial questions (and there are many) are as direct as this one. Some are quite labyrinthine and require

---

[35] The index is interesting in that it not only gives folio numbers but also notes the columns for each folio, using a and b for the *recto*, c and d for the *verso*, thus: "Nota de simbolo in primo folio usque ad undecimum... De casibus reimundi a 199° usque ad 246. Item de casibus [preter?] reimundum a 246° usque ad 279... De peccato contra virtutes theologicas 99ᵃ. Contra virtutes cardinales 99 c et d. Contra sacramenta 100, 101, 102, 103...".

[36] Humbertus de Romanis, *Opera* II. 260.

a great deal of expertise, e.g.: « Mulier separata est a marito propter arctitudinem. Nubit alteri auctoritate ecclesie. Effecta est habilis per secundum amplexibus primi. Restituta est primo marito et cognita a primo. Si secundus peccavit cognoscendo eam? Vel si primus postea cognoscendo ipsam sit irregularis ita quod post mortem eius non potest promoveri ad ordines? Quid si concipiat a secundo: si partus ille sit legitimus necne? Et si sit legitimus alterius, cui habet succedere? » (fol. 251va).

Since the volume is Dominican, some problems bear on religious life or on the activities of Dominicans. One involves a Dominican's power to absolve (« possit frater absolvere? ») from reserved censures, in this case from that incurred by those who obtain a false papal letter or accept a reputed papal letter from anyone but the pope or his deputy; the answer, citing *Extra. De crimine falsi,* c. *Dura sepe* (= X. 5. 20, 4), is that this excommunication is reserved to the pope and is outside the competence of a friar (fol. 266ra). A second problem touches on a point which may not have been at all academic, and, indeed, occasions a « Nota » in the margin. A religious is so dangerously ill that he cannot recover unless meat is placed on his diet. A skilled doctor examines him and states emphatically to the man's superior that there is no hope of recovery without meat, but fails to move the superior, as a result of which the religious dies. Does the superior thereby incur irregularity? (fol. 256rb). A third « Dominican » problem is in the best tradition of the academic conundrum. A Dominican is going along a road and chances on an unbaptized child on the point of death. There is a deep well nearby but there is not enough water in it to allow some to be drawn for baptism. What should the Dominican do? Should he throw the child into the well? Or should he allow him to die unbaptized and to be damned for ever? (fol. 257ra).

It is not unlikely, of course, that many of the questions in this collection were stock ones which passed from province to province within the Dominican Order in much the same way as the *Quaestiones* of the Decretists and Decretalists were repeated from area to area all over Europe [37], or as « international » jokes are today. There is, for example, a problem about Greek

---

[37] See G. Fransen, "Les *questiones* des canonistes. Essai de dépouillement et de classement (1)", *Traditio* 12 (1956) 566-92, and succeeding issues.

priests which was hardly indigenous to England (fol. 266va). All the same, some of the problems in this English Dominican volume do have a nicely local flavour to them.

There is, for example, the trader who has a domicile and family in a certain town but spends a full year in London, where he makes a tidy profit on his transactions there (the question being to which church, that at home or that in London, should he pay his tithes?: fol. 255vb). And there are some priests from Ireland who engage in dubious dealings in England. One approaches a bishop in England and slips him ten shillings for permission to exercise his ministry in the bishop's diocese (Is he a simoniac? : fol. 250rb). Another « transfers himself to these parts » from Ireland but is not allowed by a certain bishop to function as priest in his diocese unless he pays him a certain sum of money (Is he a simoniac if he gives in to the bishop? : fol. 251va).

Then there are the married people who get into difficulties in Paris. One, a married man, goes over (« peregre vadit ») to Paris, and while he is on his way his wife dies without his being aware of it. In Paris he becomes engaged to a spinster and has sexual relations with her. Later, when he has heard of his wife's death, he becomes engaged with the same consequences to a second spinster. (Which of the two is he bound to marry? : fol. 262va). Two married persons, a man and a woman, land themselves into a similar predicament. They go to Paris, contract a clandestine marriage and commit adultery, each being ignorant of the fact that the other is married. Shortly after this, the abandoned wife and husband at home die. As soon as the two in Paris hear the news they solemnize their marriage. (« Queritur quid agendum? : fol. 262vb).

* * *

Quid igitur agendum? To Dominicans and others all the above will have a familiar ring. The approach of this English Dominican of the second half of the 13th century is not so very different from that of the *Collationes morales* and *Casus conscientiae*, which until recently were such a regular feature of the teaching of practical theology in most studentates, scholasticates and seminaries.

As witnessed by John the Lector and by this anonymous Lector from the English Dominican province, the tradition of this sort of practical theology in the Dominican Order is a very old one, and it reaches back in fact to the *Summa de casibus* of Raymund of Pennafort and the three other manuals of confessional practice which were written for Dominicans between 1221 and 1225 and were the first literary productions of the Order. This tradition was a remarkably successful part of the Dominican educational system from the very beginning, a system that was designed, through its provisions for students, lectors and *Fratres communes*, to produce both the well-informed Preachers-at-large commissioned by Honorius III in 1217 and the « discreet, judicious and prudent priests » to whom the same pope entrusted the twin function of the hearing of confessions universally in 1221.

E cathena et carcere: *The Imprisonment of Amaury de Montfort, 1276*

SOME time around Christmas 1275 and some ten years after the defeat and death of Simon de Montfort, earl of Leicester, at the battle of Evesham, a French ship was stopped and boarded off the coast of Cornwall or perhaps close to the mouth of Bristol Channel by four ships out of Bristol.[1] Discovering that it carried, among others, two outlawed cousins of King Edward I, Amaury de Montfort, the younger son of Simon, and his sister Eleanor, the sailors forced the ship into Bristol, where Eleanor and Amaury and all on the ship were handed over with much rejoicing to agents of Edward.[2]

Edward, in turn, as he explained to Pope Hadrian V in a letter on 8 August 1276, looked upon the 'chance capture' as an act of divine providence,[3] and he rewarded the various sailors who had seized the ship with royal protection and safe-conducts for three years.[4] For he was at war with Llywelyn of Wales, to whom he now discovered his cousin Eleanor to be betrothed; what was more, the de Montfort party was actually on its way from Normandy to Wales for her marriage to Llywelyn when the ship was intercepted. Edward therefore placed Eleanor in detention at Windsor Castle,[5] and the two Welsh Dominicans who were found on the

---

[1] The account followed here is that of W. Rishanger, *Chronica et Annales*, ed. H. T. Riley (R.S., 1865), p. 87.

[2] *Annales monastici*, ed. H. R. Luard, iv (R.S., 1869), p. 267, according to which the ship was becalmed outside Bristol Channel and excited the curiosity of the locals, who handed over the de Montfort party to the king, 'triumphali laetitia'.

[3] *The Liber epistolaris of Richard of Bury*, ed. N. Denholm-Young (Roxburghe Club, 1950), pp. 14–17 (n. 23).

[4] *Calendar of Patent Rolls, 1272–1281*, p. 161.

[5] *Annales monastici*, iv. 266–7.

ship with the de Montforts were released from jail in Bristol into the hands of the Dominican archbishop of Canterbury, Robert Kilwardby, who was instructed to question them closely in order to find out who had arranged or connived at the marriage.[1]

What to do about Amaury de Montfort was quite another thing. If he was a son of Simon de Montfort, the discredited baron, and a brother of Guy,[2] the author of the recent murder at Viterbo of Henry of Almaine (a cousin of both Edward and the de Montforts) he was also a cleric, and a papal chaplain at that, as well as a respected intellectual.[3] To proceed against him with any severity would brand Edward as vindictive and would certainly rouse the bishops and the papacy to anger. To release him unconditionally, as Edward told Hadrian he was quite prepared to do if the Pope insisted, would surely draw the fire of many who had suffered at the hands of his father.

Shortly after Amaury's arrest, indeed, the bishops of England had proposed that Amaury should be released into their custody, but when they found themselves unprepared to guarantee a firm watch over Amaury, as Edward demanded, both the king and the bishops decided to refer the matter to Pope Hadrian. Edward wrote him to that effect on 8 August, but Hadrian died some ten days later, and it was only in the following January of 1277 that his successor, John XXI, produced an acceptable solution.

By then, Amaury had been for the best part of a year in Corfe Castle in Dorset, where, as Edward delicately put it to Hadrian, he had been placed in 'private custody', probably on 1 February 1276. And while all the diplomatic activity was going on, probably without his knowledge, he had been far from idle. By the time Edward was writing to Hadrian in August, Amaury in fact had put together a couple of treatises on theology. He had always

---

[1] *The Liber epistolaris of Richard of Bury*, p. 46.

[2] For Guy, the Almaine murder, and its consequences see F. M. Powicke, *Ways of Medieval Life and Thought* (London, [1950]), pp. 69–83.

[3] When Amaury became a papal chaplain is not certain, but he is so described by John XXI in his mandate of 28 January 1277 to the English bishops; *C.P.L.* i. 452. Although, as C. Bémont, *Simon de Montfort, Comte de Leicester* (Paris, 1884), p. 255, has shown, he was given a licence by Archbishop Rigaud of Rouen to be ordained to major orders (subdeacon, deacon, priest) by any bishop anywhere, there is nothing to support Bémont's conclusion that he took these orders in 1268 or at any other time. There is nothing in his general confession (Appendix B) to suggest that he was anything other than a cleric in minor orders.

been studious and had had one of the best mathematicians in Europe as his tutor.[1] A bare five years before, he had completed the last of his three or four years in the Faculty of Arts in the University of Padua.[2] He was not yet stale. His training and habit of study now stood him in good stead. He read much, took careful notes, meditated on what he read, prepared drafts of his treatises on bits of parchment, and finally wrote fair copies in a clear, assured hand.

For all his scholarly industry, there were moments, in the summer months in particular, when he brooded a little over his position, and this finds expression here and there in his pages. In that summer of 1276 he was in his thirty-fourth year of age, and perhaps for the first time in his life he felt isolated if not rejected. He had been born into a large family, the fourth child, and the youngest son, of the six children of Simon de Montfort and Eleanor, the sister of Henry III.[3] He had had many honours, not least a canonry at the age of eighteen from the distinguished and zealous prelate Eudes Rigaud, archbishop of Rouen. He had been, though only because of his father's pressure on Henry III while Henry was a prisoner of his, treasurer and canon of York. But now his father's memory was execrated, his mother had died at Montargis shortly before the bridal party set out for Wales, his brother Guy was still an outcast in Tuscany because of the Almaine murder, he and his sister were in prison in England.

Above all else he felt that he had been let down badly by a close friend, possibly one of the two French knights who were on the ship with him. In the opening phrases of some fascinating pages (here printed in Appendix A) on his methodology, his fears and hopes, towards the end of the volume he composed at Corfe

---

[1] Roger Bacon, writing in 1267: *Opus tertium*, ed. J. S. Brewer (R.S., 1859), p. 35.

[2] See Bémont, *Simon de Montfort*, pp. 365–7, who cites an attestation by the University of Padua and other notables to the presence of Amaury ('quasi a triennio citra in studio Paduano laudabiliter conversatus') at Padua, where he was at death's door with fever, on the day Henry of Almaine was assassinated at Viterbo by Amaury's brother Guy. Amaury is listed as having studied at Bologna in 1269 by M. Sarti and M. Fattorini, *De claris archigymnasii Bononiensis professoribus*, ed. C. A. Albicini and C. Malagola (Bologna, 1888–96), ii. 309.

[3] Details of Amaury's life will be found in the entry in *D.N.B.*, in Bémont's *Simon de Montfort*, or in Margaret Wade Labarge, *Simon de Montfort* (London, 1962). The 1884 edition of Bémont is to be preferred to that upon which the English translation by E. F. Jacob (London, 1930) is based since Bémont prints many valuable documents there which were later dropped.

Castle, he complains bitterly, in a nice concatenation of verses from different psalms, about his betrayal by someone who clearly was an intimate of his: 'Traditus sum et non egrediebar [Ps. 87: 10] . . . etenim homo pacis mee in quo speraui, qui edebat panes meos, magnificauit super me supplantacionem [Ps. 40: 11], tradens me fallaciter et nefande in manus querencium animam meam [Ps. 34: 4].' Whoever this monstrous friend was, he was not rewarded as he had expected to be but rejected ignominiously by Amaury's captors, and Amaury gloats biblically over his fate: 'Cuius tradicionis supplicium ab hiis quibus me tradidit iusto dei iudicio reportauit, proiectus in tenebras exteriores [Matt. 8: 12]: in lacu miserie et in luto fecis [Ps. 39: 3].'

The autograph of the works that Amaury de Montfort put together at Corfe Castle in the spring and summer of 1276 survives today as part of a codex from Cerne Abbas, also in Dorset, which is now in the Bodleian Library as MS. Auct. D. 4. 13. The codex itself is bulky and ungainly. It measures 232 × 155 mm. and contains 225 folios. There are three separate works in the codex, one in a later twelfth-century hand, the other two in hands of the second half of the thirteenth century. These works were bound together and given continuous pagination in the fourteenth or fifteenth century, probably at the Benedictine monastery of the Blessed Virgin Mary, Saint Peter, and Saint Ethelwold at Cerne Abbas, to which the codex certainly belonged in the fifteenth century (ex-libris, fol. 225). According to the *Summary Catalogue* of the Bodleian Library (2571), the codex was probably acquired by the Bodleian Library between 1605 and 1611.

The first work in the codex (fols. 1–62)[1] is a pastoral manual in Latin, 'Signaculum apostolatus mei', composed in England in the second half of the thirteenth century;[2] the second (fols. 63–128) is a glossed Canticle of Canticles which was written out about 1200; the third (fols. 129–224) is what is described by the *Summary Catalogue* as 'works by Amalricus (Aimeric), probably the writer's autograph, who may have been a monk of Cerne'.[3]

---

[1] Three half-sheets at the beginning, foliated in Roman numerals, form a separate gathering. They carry a late 12th-century copy of Macrobius on the *Somnium Scipionis*.

[2] See L. E. Boyle, 'Three English Pastoral *Summae* and a Magister Galienus', *Studia Gratiana*, xi (*Collectanea S. Kuttner*, i, 1967), 138–9.

[3] The name 'Almaricus' also occurs on the spine of the codex, where there is

This last is in fact the autograph of Amaury de Montfort and is the only part of the codex that concerns us here. Nowhere in this autograph, of course, does Amaury describe himself plainly as 'Amalricus de Monteforti' or state that the place of composition is Corfe Castle. But the evidence for his authorship is well-nigh watertight. The writer is a cleric, though not a priest (fol. 218). He is in prison (fol. 136^v, etc.), and he began to write there 'in carcere et cathena' at Easter 1276 (fols. 136^v, 213va). His sister (unnamed) is also in detention somewhere (fol. 213ra). Their mother (equally unnamed) has died recently (fol. 131). He claims to have placed his name on the opening page of his treatises (fol. 214ra), and the name that appears at the beginning of two of these treatises (fols. 129, 137) is 'Amalrici' (Amalricus or Amaury).

If the make-up of the autograph does not at once bring to mind a castle or a prison, it does at least suggest that the author had not a ready supply of regular parchment to hand. For although the sheets are pricked and ruled, they are of varying sizes. The gatherings, likewise, are not at all uniform, and there are bits and pieces of parchment, some foliated, some not, in between some of the gatherings:

1^8	fols.	129–136	*De principiis et partibus theologie.*
2^5		137–141	*Distinctiones ewangeliorum.* Fol. 137 is a half-sheet which overlaps the fold of sheet 138/141 and binds the gathering.
3^8		142–149	*Tabulae,* embracing gatherings 3–9 (fols. 142–211).
4^6		150–155	Continuation of *Tabulae.*
5^{11}		156–166	Continuation of *Tabulae.* Fol. 156 is a long, uneven piece with notes towards an index (*Abbas–Ordo*), strips of which overlap the fold of sheet 157/166. Fols. 157–166 are very scrappy and much indented.
6^8		167–174	Continuation of *Tabulae.* Between fols. 167^v and 168 there is a jagged, unfoliated piece of vellum with notes towards an index (*Pacificus–Xtus*), tags of which peep out between fols. 173^v and 174.
7^{11}		175–85	Continuation of *Tabulae.* Fol. 185 is a

a cryptic list of contents, and on the inside of the front cover, on the parchment binding (over boards).

384   E cathena et carcere: *The Imprisonment of*

		half-sheet, with a fold overlapping that of sheet 175/184.
8^{17}	186–202	Continuation of *Tabulae*.
9^{9}	203–211	End of *Tabulae*. Two unfoliated strips, carrying medical prescriptions, act as binders of the gathering. There is a rough 'file-card', with Biblical references to *Peccatum*, between sheets 206/209 and 207/208.
10^{6}	212–218	Fol. 212: blank; 212^{v}: note on use of concordance; 213–214: *De composicione, diuisione, et ordine tabularum*, printed below as Appendix A; 214–215: Table of chapters; 215^{v}–216^{v}: Index: *Abissus–Zelus*. Fol. 218 is an irregular quarter-sheet, the recto containing Amaury's '*Confessio*' (Appendix B), the verso being blank. Three side-tags, which are to be seen at the beginning of the gathering, keep it in place as the outer sheet of the gathering.
11^{6}	219–224	A later index, but not in the same hand as the other gatherings.

Although these gatherings have an adventitious look about them, the sheets, half-sheets, and scraps were gathered together with patience and care. And they were the result of months of devoted, tenacious work. Conscious of the fact that he had no theological training, Amaury resolved shortly after his removal from Bristol to Corfe Castle to comb the Bible for the themes of classical theology and, as well, to attempt to compose for himself an introduction to the subject. As he informs us in the colophon (fol. 136^{v}) to his first treatise, *De principiis et partibus theologie*, (fols. 129–136^{v}), this work was begun and completed in the Easter season (5 April–24 May) of 1276, 'in carcere et cathena':

Hoc opus ad memoriam et inuencionem facilem scripturarum infra quadraginta dies resurectionis dominice, ex solo textu biblie, sine copia scripture alterius, breuiter compilaui anno incarnacionis dominice M.CC.LXXVI, uite mee XXXIIII in carcere et cathena. Peto autem errata corrigi, omissa suppleri, et michi ueniam indulgeri, quia nec theologie studium attigi nec scholas intraui, licet a puericia legerim sacras literas inter sciencias seculares.

Amaury is probably not exaggerating when he says that the only book he had to study was the Bible, though he is surely drawing a long bow when he states some months later that his jailors were reluctant to allow him even a Bible: 'magna precum instancia, textu biblie michi uix concesso, legi continue in sacra pagina . . .' (fol. 213ᵛᵃ: Appendix A, lines 71–2). The imprisonment seems to have been quite mild (with eight grooms, four valets, and a single guard),[1] so any delay he experienced was probably due to a dearth of Bibles at Corfe Castle and not to stringencies of discipline.

Clearly the provision of a Bible stretched the Castle to its limits, for Amaury on occasion laments the fact that no other books are available to him (fol. 213ᵛᵃ: 'nec scripturam aliquam habere potui preter textum biblie'), and, when writing out his *Tabulae* (fols. 142–211ᵛ), he leaves blanks against the day when he would be able to consult other books: 'In tabulis spacia relinquuntur, ut plures forsitan auctoritates addantur ex libris . . .' (fol. 142).

For the moment, however, he had to make do with the Bible and with a memory now and then of what he had been taught by his tutors or in the schools at Padua (Avicenna: fol. 129ᵛ; Cicero: 129; Seneca: 212ʳᵃ, 213ʳᵃ). And it must be admitted that he did not do too badly. The opening treatise (fols. 129–136ᵛ) on the principles and divisions of theology may not be a masterpiece, but it does suggest a man who knew now to organize his materials and to deploy with some success the techniques of exposition that he had learned at Padua and elsewhere.

The very first chapter, on the insufficiency of secular sciences, shows that Amaury, for all his protestations, must have picked up a fair amount of incidental theology in his thirty-four years. Some of what he has to say is, no doubt, elementary, but there are moments when he rises above this. Commenting, with a reasonably controlled style, on the limitations of natural philosophy, he writes that even the greatest and most perceptive of the natural philosophers did not, in the long run, achieve anything more than the application of their science to ethical problems:

fol. 129

Quoniam autem omnis humana sciencia et doctrina ortum habet a sensu, et a prioribus causis quoque ad posteriora et causata procedit,

---

[1] *The Liber epistolaris of Richard of Bury*, ed. N. Denholm-Young, p. 14 n., citing P.R.O. Exchequer Accounts, 505/16, where the expenses of his imprisonment were assessed at 4s. 5½d. a day, beginning from 1 February 1276.

huius cause omnium prime, quoniam sub sensu non cadit, nullam scienciam uel certam doctrinam habuerunt, via sensus, racionis aut experimenti, quibus naturaliter utebantur. Quamuis enim de ipsa raciocinarentur quedam uera, ab effectibus posterioribus, et causatis, tamen nullatenus attigerunt misteria trinitatis, creacionis, redemcionis, et glorificacionis eterne. Que suis fidelibus ipse deus misericorditer reuelauit. Horum tamen periciores plusque sensati omnem humanam scienciam adaptarunt moribus informandis. Quoniam omnis sciencia manca quodammodo uidetur et inutilis, si non applicetur ad mores, ut ait tullius.

Having thus, to his own satisfaction, shown the inadequacy of the 'mundane particulares sciencie', as he terms them, Amaury goes on in the second chapter to a discussion of theology: 'De sufficiencia et principiis theologie'. Revelation, for Amaury, is an expression of God's compassion. And the divine knowledge God communicated in revelation in order to relieve human ignorance is only and wholly to be found in the Bible, the book of divine science: 'Hic liber diuine sciencie qui uulgariter biblia nominatur, in se continet scienciam uerissimam, que non fallit, completissimam, que omnia comprehendit, et uiuificam, que mortem excludit' (fol. 130). This science of God thus enshrined in the Bible is truly a demonstrative one: 'per discrecciones, supposiciones, et principia demonstratiue procedens' (ibid.). Beginning from the first (but now called 'per descripciones', not 'per discrecciones'), each of these ways of demonstration is now outlined in turn (e.g. 'Deus est prima causa omnium causatorum et omnium causa causarum . . . , Sapiencie xiiii capitulo; . . . Deus est qui est, id est, ens per se. Exodi iii capitulo'), covering the whole of theology from God, creation, and the Trinity, to the soul, sin, and the sacraments (fols. 129ᵛ–132).

The remaining eight chapters (fols. 132–136ᵛ) are given over to the 'seven walls' of theology ('Ueritas historiarum . . . Prophecia futurorum . . . Regula mandatorum . . . Figura sacramentorum . . . Informacio morum . . . Discreccio consiliorum . . . Spes futurorum'). The whole work ends with the colophon already cited above.

The second treatise, 'Distinctiones ewangeliorum' (fols. 137–141), is a mass of schematic divisions and scriptural references to document three headings which, he says, embrace the whole teaching of the Gospels: 'Primo, distinctiones ueritatis historice. Secundo, sermones domini et parabole. Tercio, questiones ewangelice' (fol. 137ᵛ). And it winds up with a splendidly devised schema to illustrate Christ's words in Matthew 5, 'Non ueni soluere legem sed adimplere', the basic division being, 'Impleuit corporaliter—Suppleuit spiritualiter—Finiuit temporaliter'. This schema occupies all of fol. 141.

Schemata, indeed, seem to have been Amaury's strong point. As he notes on fol. 131, when speaking of the place of imagination in the science of theology, he had already written a 'Figura et tractatus speculi et mundi' that very same year, and this included an 'imaginative schema' of the Trinity:

Et hoc quod de trinitate de qua in supposicionibus tangitur et minus forsitan ab aliquibus intelligitur ingenio racionis, ymaginabiliter declaraui et quasi sensibiliter in ymagine et figura in qua trinitatem personarum et coequalitatem ipsarum in substancie unitate depinxi, ymaginacione sensibili circulorum, corporum et colorum, et insuper trium dimensionum intelligibili racione, in figura et tractatu speculi celi et mundi . . . (fol. 131).

This 'three-dimensional' drawing was obviously a very elaborate affair, depicting everything from the 'orders of the heavenly spirits' (each distinguished from the other by the special insignia of office) to the fall of Lucifer. One wonders what impression this feat of imaginative theology made on his sister Eleanor, for whom it was composed, probably towards the end of the voyage from France, to alleviate her sadness at their mother's death; 'Que quidem simplicibus inspicienda composui in solacium sororis mee de transitu matris nostre' (ibid.).[1]

The most interesting and perhaps original part of Amaury's work in prison is, however, the third and the longest treatise, where, from fols. 142 to 211, he has a well-conceived concordance of biblical quotations relating to Christian behaviour. There are ninety-one chapters in all in this 'Tabula' (or 'Tabule'), and they are, as he explains in his 'De composicione, diuisione, et ordine tabularum' (fols. 213–214: Appendix A, lines 85–95), divided into ten main headings, five dealing with the good and with virtue,

---

[1] On fol. 131 he states that this work was composed 'ipso anno quo presens opusculum compilaui', i.e. 1276, but on fol. 214ʳᵃ he specifies that this was 'inmediate ante ingressum carceris'. If by 'prison' he means his present prison in Corfe Castle, then this puts the date of composition as late January 1276, while still at Bristol. But since he was also a prisoner at Bristol, the phrase could refer to a period before his capture, probably while at sea (though this would put the date in late 1275, around Christmas).

five with evil and vice (hence the alternative title, 'Arbor boni et mali', on fol. 214ra). For reasons given in the 'De composicione . . . tabularum', Amaury draws heavily on the Parables, Ecclesiastes, the Book of Wisdom, Ecclesiasticus, and the Psalms. The layout of the concordance is crisp and economical, with the subjects (*Deus, Fides, Mansuetudo*, etc.) and quotations neatly and clearly written in two columns.

.   .   .

If Amaury de Montfort was a splendid organizer of his materials, he was equally a careful and conscientious writer with a good sense of style and, as may be seen in some abundance in Appendix A, with an unflagging devotion to the cursus and its rhythmic endings, not to speak of the niceties of medieval punctuation. And what he devised and drafted with so much patience and professionalism was just as stylishly copied into his patchwork of quires 'manu mea' (fol. 214ra).

With the exception of the 'Confessio' (fol. 218 and Appendix B), which appears to be an unrevised draft marred by numerous cancellations and changes of direction, most of Amaury's autograph volume is probably a fair copy of rough drafts on odd scraps of parchment such as those which now serve as clamps or backings in some gatherings. Yet there are moments when Amaury seems to be composing directly on the spot. There are corrections, cancellations, afterthoughts, and, on occasion, revisions. The handwriting, however, is always firm and controlled and never fuzzy. Amaury wrote a steady notular hand which even in the 'Confessio', where it is minute and hurried, never poses any problems.

The great care that Amaury took, in spite of material difficulties, to produce a finished, legible text, was as much due to a certain ambition as to a desire to provide himself with a useful and usable instrument. True, as he reiterates, he was writing primarily for his own benefit, but there also glowed a hope that the work might be copied by others like himself who had little or no training in theology: '. . . nescio enim utrum hec noua sint uel antiqua, quoniam omnes scripture theologice preter textum biblie michi totaliter sunt ignote, sed causa memorie scripturarum incoans laborem, michi forsitan et aliis simplicibus theologiam aggredientibus profuturum' (fol. 214ra: Appendix A, lines 110–15).

But this was not all. At root the purpose was therapeutic, and the ambition morbid: 'Primo tamen et principaliter ut meipsum per scripturas instruam ad agonem et futura michi, humanitus que ignoro . . .' (ibid., lines 117–19). In most of the tormented pages in which these words occur towards the end of his volume, Amaury genuinely seems to have doubted the chances of his personal survival. By this time he had been eight months in prison, and in that August or September of 1276 the outlook seemed very bleak indeed: 'Utrum enim post hunc carcerem in quo ago presencialiter mensem octauum michi sit aliquid humanitus profuturum, nescio, deus scit' (ibid., lines 114–15). He and his sister had been detained on 'bare suspicion'. Both were being held without trial and without a chance to defend themselves. His frequent appeals for a hearing were ignored. Justice had fallen on bad days.

At one point, indeed, he was so convinced that his end was near that he composed a general confession in which he went through the commandments, the seven deadly sins, the corporal works of mercy, etc., accusing himself of everything from liturgical indifference to lasciviousness. He felt doomed; and this gave an edge of urgency to all his studying and writing: 'Laboro tamen instanter.' He had to make sure that something of him should survive and that his memory at least would not perish; this was why he placed his name at the beginning of each of his compositions: 'Tercio, ut si forte in hoc carcere faciam finem uite, saltem relinquam mei memoriam, hec duo opuscula in biblia et arborem sciencie boni et mali, que omnia scripsi in carcere manu mea, cum speculo celi et mundi quod inmediate ante ingressum carceris cum tractatu suo breuiter compilaui' (fol. 214ra: Appendix A, lines 119–23).

By the very end of these pages, however, the mood has passed. He straightens his shoulders and begins to hope again. Having prayed God to look after his sister and family, with whose fate he was warmly preoccupied ('nam pro ipsis concaluit cor meum intra me'), he emphatically professes his boundless and unqualified hope in God: 'Scio enim et indubitanter scio quod ipse exaudiet preces meas, et educet me de isto carcere, in corpore aut in anima, quod multo melius est . . . Ipse autem euellet de laqueo pedes meos qui est spes mea a iuuentute mea, et de uentre matris mee fuit protector meus, et erit in secula seculorum propter nomen suum' (fol. 214rb: Appendix A, lines 137–42).

· · ·

Amaury's hopes did not go unfulfilled, though some six years were to pass before he was finally set free. His cousin the king was taking no chances and would not hear of releasing him unconditionally and without the highest of guarantees.

Pope John XXI, who succeeded Hadrian V in September 1276, had a partial success when, as a result of a mandate of John's in January 1277,[1] Amaury was released into the custody of the bishops in January 1278 and was moved from Corfe to Sherborne in the same county of Dorset.[2]

The cessation of the war between Llywelyn of Wales and Edward in November 1277, and an appeal by Eleanor to Edward I in her brother's behalf just after her release and marriage to Llywelyn in October 1278,[3] saw no change in Amaury's condition. An offer by Pope Nicholas III that the papacy would hold itself responsible for Amaury's good behaviour were he allowed to depart England[4] met with Edward's favour, but the Pope died in August 1280 before negotiations had gone very far.[5] In the following year, however, a similar settlement was quickly reached under Pope Martin IV, and Amaury, who had been lodged since the previous November in the castle of the bishop of Winchester at Taunton, Somerset,[6] was finally set free on 23 April 1281, after a formal process in London at which he took an oath to depart the realm and never again return unless with papal permission. After his arrival in France, he repeated this oath before the papal representative at Arras on the following 6 May.[7]

Amaury never returned to England again, nor, so far as we know, did he ever take up again the theological writing which he had practised at Corfe Castle. The volume written so painstakingly there seems to have been left behind in Dorset, probably in the safe keeping of a monk of Cerne Abbas.

His only known literary effort afterwards is a will and last

---

[1] *C.P.L.* i. 452.

[2] *Calendar of Patent Rolls, 1272–1281*, p. 253.

[3] J. G. Edwards, *Calendar of Ancient Correspondence concerning Wales* (Cardiff, 1955), p. 76.

[4] *C.P.L.* i. 461: mandate of Nicholas to the English bishops, 17 February 1280.

[5] See the letter of Martin IV to Edward, 20 September 1281, *C.P.L.* i. 463; *in toto* in T. Rymer, *Foedera*, ii (London, 1705), 178–9.

[6] *Calendar of Patent Rolls, 1272–1281*, p. 403.

[7] See Rymer, *Foedera*, ii. 185–7, 192–4, and the documentation, with excellent notes, in F. M. Powicke and C. R. Cheney, *Councils and Synods with Other Documents relating to the English Church*, ii: *A.D. 1205–1313* (Oxford, 1964), pp. 822–3, 918–21, 977.

testament written in his own hand in November 1289 in the Dominican convent at Montargis, a little south of Paris, where his mother had died fourteen years before.

Among the many detailed bequests (e.g. his books and *instrumenta* to the Dominicans of Paris) made by Amaury, who describes himself as earl of Leicester and of Chester 'iure hereditario',[1] there is one unusual provision in which Amaury grants his hereditary rights in England to the Pope and the Cardinals, and, as well, places on them the responsibility both for the execution of the testament and for the restoration of the hereditary rights of the de Montforts in England:

Iura et acciones michi competentes in bonis hereditariis regni anglie, sancte romane ecclesie, summo pontifici et cardinalibus lego, eorum fidei tanquam dominis foedi capitalis committentes hereditatem restituere heredibus masculinis uel aliis patris mei . . . Horum autem execucionem pronus in terram committo humilitate deuota ipsius sancte romane ecclesie disposicione complendam tenore scripture presentis quam manu mea propria scripsi et sigilli mei karactere communiui . . .

Thirteen years later, presumably not very long after the death of Amaury,[2] the papacy in the person of Boniface VIII obtained a certified notarial copy of the will, which is still in the Vatican Archives.[3] How seriously the provisions of the document were taken in 1302 is not ascertainable at present, but there is no doubt that the papacy made a careful note of Amaury's donation to itself. For as late as the time of Urban V (1362–70), the 'favourable' part of the will was still being listed, with bureaucratic optimism, among debts owed by England to the papal treasury.[4]

---

[1] Amaury probably drew up the will as soon as he heard of the death of his elder brother Guy in a Sicilian prison. It has not been possible to document the statement in the early 14th-century *Flores Historiarum*, ed. H. R. Luard (R.S., 1890), iii. 67, that on Guy's death, 'Emericus, frater eius, clericus eminentis litteraturae, qui ultimus fuit de progenie Guenelonis [Simon de Montfort], factus est miles, abjecto habitu clericali.'

[2] The date of Amaury's death is at present unknown. It may have been shortly before 1302, the date of the papal copy of the will.

[3] AA. Arm. I–XVIII, 123, from which the quotation above is taken. It is not a flawless copy.

[4] Archivio Segreto Vaticano, Instrumenta Miscellanea 2592, fol. 22ᵛ (new fol. 23ᵛ): 'Item transumptum testamenti deffuncti domini Amalrici de Montfort

392   E cathena et carcere: *The Imprisonment of*

APPENDIX A

Oxford, Bodleian Library, MS. Auct. D. 4. 13, fols. 213ra–214rb

De composicione, diuisione, et ordine tabularum[1]

Traditus sum et non egrediebar. Oculi mei languerunt pre inopia.[2] Traditus quidem: etenim *homo pacis mee in quo speraui, qui edebat panes meos, magnificauit super me supplantacionem:*[3] tradens me fallaciter et nefande
5   *in manus querencium animam meam.*[4] Cuius tradicionis supplicium ab hiis quibus me tradidit iusto Dei iudicio reportauit, *proiectus in tenebras exteriores:*[5] *in lacu miserie, et in luto fecis.*[6] Qui autem sibi *mercedem iniquitatis*[7] iustissime exsoluerunt pro premio ad quod nefandis uisceribus hanelabat, me et meos sine causa iniustissime detruserunt in
10   carcerem et cathenam, insuper et sororem meam detinent contra iura omnia consuetudinesque regnorum, cum impio iniusto et nocente iustissime operantes zelo tradicionis admisse. Cum innocentibus uero ex causa suspicionis nude tam iniuste agentes ut in iuris iniuriam teneant ferro uinctos,[8] iuris instancia et defensionis copia interdictis. In quo
15   nullo accusante, nec criminis evidencia suadente, iniuste proceditur contra iura diuina, ecclesiastica et mundana. Innocentes autem dico non quidem coram deo, cum nec infans cuius est unius diei uita super terram sit absque peccato, teste scriptura:[9] set coram hominibus a crimine suspicionis ipsius. Nec mirum si iuste procedatur cum impio,
20   et iniuste cum iustis. Iusticia enim quamuis non tota simul per omnia obseruetur, ab omnibus tamen et singulis hominibus corde diligitur, ore laudatur et opere seruatur in parte. Quippe, sine qua nec hominum societas esse potest. Unde seneca, Iusticia est tantum bonum quod ab iniustissimis et nefandissimis latronibus obseruatur.[10] Aliter enim eorum
25   societas non constaret, nisi et spolia iuste diuiderent et suis ipsorum legibus inuiolabiliter tenerentur astricti. Ceterum, nomen iusticie totam

domini pape capellani, dicentis se iure hereditario comitatus Leycestrie et Cestrie palatinum senescallumque Anglie, in quo legavit ecclesie romane et summo pontifici omnes actiones et iura hereditaria in dictis bonis in regno Anglie existentibus sive competencia. Datum Parisius anno domini millesimo CCLXXXIX XII Kal. decembris de tempore domini G. pape X.' (The Pope at the time of the will was Nicholas IV not Gregory X, who was Pope from 1271 to 1276.)

[1] In this transcription of a passage that is a little contorted in places, Amaury's final periods, capitalization, and spelling have been preserved, but not his general punctuation. Since his prose is full of Scriptural quotations or phrases these have been identified wherever possible. Corrections, additions, and insertions are also noted.

[2] Ps. 87: 10. The word 'mei' is an insertion above the line.

[3] Ps. 40: 9–10.   [4] Ps. 34: 4.   [5] Matt. 8: 12.
[6] Ps. 39: 3.   [7] 2 Pet. 2: 13.   [8] Insertion above line.
[9] Cf. Gal. 3: 22.   [10] *Locum non inueni.*

Amaury de Montfort, 1276 393

legem diuinam et humanam simul complectitur in seipso, que [fol. 213rb] et ius naturale continent et eciam positiuum. Quorum quod naturale est non tantum homines uerum eciam animalia bruta sectantur, instinctu nature, quem heu hodie plures hominum imitantur quam 30 iudicium racionis. Iuris eciam positiui, diuini pariter et humani quod quisque sibi utile estimauerit: hoc heu hodie imitatur et seruat. Nec uoluntas legi subicitur siue iuri: sed uoluntati ius. Quandoque uerba iuris applicantur utcumque, sicque iuris uelamen in uerbis queritur, dum in factis plerumque iuris contrarium inuenitur. Cuius nomen 35 infame quia displicet et notatur ad placendum hominibus: nomen iuris et colorem accomodat sibi penitus aliena.

Icirco, *oculi mei languerunt pre inopia*,[1] iudicii scilicet siue iuris, cuius instancia seu prosecucio necdum michi impetrari, quamuis in forma iuris et in iure hoc iam frequenter fuerit postulatum. *Clamaui* autem ab 40 inicio huius tribulacionis et angustie *ad deum* altissimum, deum *qui benefecit mihi*,[2] et *exaudiuit uocem meam ab hiis qui appropinquant mihi*:[3] sic eorum corda demulcens, ut non *effunderent sanguinem innocentem*[4] quem quesierant effundendum, quinimmo ut mecum in carcere agerent graciose, curialiter, et benigne. 45

Clausus ergo in carcere et cathena, instanter cum fiducia petens a domino liberari, memini uerbi Iacobi dicentis, *Petitis et non accipitis eo quod male petatis*,[5] uel non recte, ut alibi inuenitur; illius eciam ewangelici, *Nolite petere agros* etcetera,[6] et post pauca, *primum querite regnum dei et iusticiam eius et hec omnia adicientur vobis*,[7] et tercium, *Nescitis* 50 *quid petatis*;[8] et sermonis christi ad patrem, *Non mea uoluntas set tua fiat*.[9] Ne igitur presumpcionis inmerite uel simplicitatis nimis indiscrete merito[10] [fol. 213va] culpandus inueniar petendo ad libitum uoluntatis humane, reuoluens in animo constanciam sare filie raguel et iudith et uerba ipsarum in tribulacionibus suis, flagella domini *quasi serui qui* 55 *corripimur ad emendacionem non ad perdicionem nostram*, credens firmiter *euenisse*,[11] ut uerbis iudith utar, ipsius agonem tribulacionis mee carceris et cathene domino deo omnipotenti tota fiducia precibus commendaui et disposicioni ipsius, sperans me aliquid accepturum ab eo qui *dat*

---

[1] Ps. 87: 10.   [2] Ps. 56: 3.   [3] Cf. Ps. 54: 19.
[4] Cf. Ps. 105: 38.   [5] Jas. 4: 3.   [6] Cf. Matt. 6: 25–7.
[7] Matt. 6: 33.   [8] Matt. 20: 22.   [9] Luke 22: 12.
[10] At the foot of fol. 213 there is a chronological jingle (after a false start: 'Annis ducentis'):

Annis quingentis decies iterumque ducentis
Unus defuerat: cum deus ortus erat.

Ab orbe condito usque ad romam conditam, anni iiii ccc lx.
Ab urbe condita usque ad natiuitatem christi, anni D cc xv.

The word 'urbe' has 'roma' written above it.
[11] Judith 8: 27.

60 *omnibus affluenter*[1] et non improperat pro iniuria calamitatis istius, qua
patior innocens ut predixi.

Hiis eciam animatus ad tribulacionis examen, destiti a peticionibus
cordis mei occasione predictorum, adherens precibus sancte matris
ecclesie, scilicet, horis canonicis, quibus dominum generaliter depreca-
65 tur, et oracioni dominice qua leuiora peccata soluuntur, qui utinam
dignus efficiar deuote exsoluere tam bene obsequium officii clericalis
atque id consequi, quod uerbis oracionis dominice ipse qui condidit
intellexit, et iniuste paciencium pro iusticia numero et meritis agregari,
pro, eo quod iniuste pacior vincula et carceres contra ecclesiasticas
70 libertates et sacrorum canonum instituta sacrilegis manibus laicorum.

Hiis igitur in corde firmatis, magna precum instancia textu biblie
michi uix concesso, legi continue in sacra pagina, cuius habueram a
puericia exercicium literale, et sic transacta quadragesima sacro pa-
schali tempore, breuem tractatum de principiis et partibus theologie
75 breuiter compilaui ad inuencionem facilem scripturarum, sciensque
quod *nemo mittens manum ad aratrum et respiciens retro aptus est regno
dei*[2] processi ad tabulas de moribus componendas, eo quod nec doctorum tabulas nec scripturam aliquam habere potui preter textum, tum
quia aliarum materiarum loca in predicto tractatu estimo satis [fol.
80 213vb] esse notata ad inuencionem facilem scripturarum. Quia uero de
moribus plures sunt materie de quibus mixtim agitur et confuse, ipsas
in tabulis ordinaui, illas potissime que tanguntur in parabolis salamonis,
eo quod datam sibi a domino prerogatiuam sapiencie scriptura testatur
et omnium librorum moralium hic plures materias continere uidetur.
85 Ordinantur autem modo subscripto, et denario numerantur. Primo
quidem ea que sunt a deo et de ipso faciunt mencionem expressam.
Secundo uita et boni mores ad uitam et mutuam hominum conuersaci-
onem. Tercio status hominum, iuuentutis, senectutis, et ceteri status.
Quarto fortitudo, iusticia, et mores alii, specialiter pertinentes ad
90 status. Quinto fama, et alia que sunt ad finem uite temporalis et eterne.
Deinde de contrariis predictorum. Primo quidem auersio a deo, et mala
consequencia auersionem inmediate. Secundo septem uicia principalia: superbia etcetera. Tercio status noxii, ut malum coniugium etcetera.
Quarto rixa cum uiciis consequentibus. Quinto miseria et cetera que
95 sunt ad finem mali temporalis et eterni.

Quamuis autem alia sint nomina bonorum et malorum morum, istis
tamen solis utitur salomon in parabolis. Et revera alia sunt hiis synonima,
et continentur in istis, ideoque hec in tabulis ordinaui. Et primo quidem
aggregaui uerba salomonis in parabolis, Ecclesiasten, et sapiencia
100 ipsius, propter prerogatiuam sapiencie quam pre cunctis hominibus a
domino meruit optinere. Quibus uerba ecclesiastici conuenienter ad-

---

[1] Jas. 1: 5.   [2] Luke 9: 26.

iunxi, quia et modum loquendi et materias sequitur salomonis. Secundo uerba psalmiste Dauid regis, qui magnitudine fidei firmissime ceteros antecessit, propter quod de ipso dictum est, *Inueni uirum secundum cor meum.*[1] Post hec autem concordancias aliorum, ut sicut hii in terris 105 prefulserunt regia dignitate et gracia scripturarum sic eciam merito proponantur in ordine tabularum. In aliis uero ordo temporum obseruatur.

Hec presumpsi scribere cum fiducia omnipotentis dei non causa alicuius nouitatis edende, nescio [fol. 214ra] enim utrum hec noua sint 110 uel antiqua, quoniam omnes scripture theologice preter textum biblie michi totaliter sunt ignote, set causa memorie scripturarum incoans laborem, michi forsitan et aliis simplicibus theologiam aggredientibus profuturum. Utrum enim post hunc carcerem in quo ago presencialiter mensem octauum michi sit aliquid humanitus[2] profuturum, *nescio, deus* 115 *scit.*[3] Nescio enim quamdiu subsistam, et si post modicum tollat me factor meus. Laboro tamen instanter. Primo tamen et principaliter ut meipsum per scripturas instruam ad agonem et futura michi, humanitus que ignoro. Secundo ut prosit aliis forsitan labor meus. Tercio ut si forte in hoc carcere faciam finem uite, saltem relinquam mei memoriam: 120 hec duo opuscula in biblia, et arborem sciencie boni et mali,[4] que omnia scripsi in carcere manu mea, cum speculo celi et mundi quod inmediate ante ingressum carceris cum tractatu suo breuiter compilaui. Propter quod ipsis tractatibus preposui in titulis nomen meum. Quarto quoniam, ut ait seneca, Nunquam[5] usque adeo interclusa sunt omnia ut 125 nulli accioni locus honeste sit.[6] Idcirco ceteris accionibus michi nunc penitus interclusis, hanc studii accionem exerceo diligenter, ad exercitacionem et solacium interioris hominis et exterioris.

Deus autem tocius pacience et solacii det sorori et familie mee idipsum *sapere* consolacionis et paciencie *in alterutrum, ut unanimes uno ore* 130 *glorificent deum.*[7] Nam pro ipsis *concaluit cor meum intra me et in meditacione mea exardescit ignis,*[8] angustie, scilicet, et doloris. Set consolatus sum uerbo[9] psalmiste dicentis, *Quoniam in me sperauit, liberabo eum. Clamauit ad me et ego exaudiam eum, cum ipso sum in tribulacione, eripiam eum et glorificabo eum.*[10] *Ego* enim *semper sperabo,*[11] et *memorabor iusticie* 135 *dei solius.*[12] *Expectans expectabo dominum* donec *intendat michi.*[13] [fol. 214rb] Scio enim et indubitanter *scio quod ipse exaudiet preces meas,*[14] et educet me de isto carcere, in corpore aut in anima, quod multo melius

---

[1] Cf. Ps. 88: 21; 1 Kings 11: 4.   [2] Inserted from margin.
[3] 2 Cor. 12: 3.   [4] The 'Tabulae', Amaury's third work at Corfe.
[5] 'Nusquam' expunged before 'Nunquam'.
[6] Seneca, *De tranquillitate animi* 4. 8.   [7] Rom. 15: 5.
[8] Ps. 38: 4.   [9] Corrected by expunction from 'verbis'.
[10] Ps. 90: 14–15.   [11] Ps. 70: 14.
[12] Ps. 70: 16.   [13] Ps. 39: 2.
[14] Judith 4: 12: 'Scitote quoniam exaudiet Deus preces vestras.'

396   E cathena et carcere: *The Imprisonment of*

est. Quoniam *innocens sanguis*[1] noster sine causa dampnatur. *Ipse* autem
140 *euellet de laqueo pedes*[2] nostros qui est *spes mea a iuuentute mea*, et *de
uentre matris mee* fuit *protector meus*,[3] et erit in secula seculorum *propter
nomen suum*.[4]

APPENDIX B

Oxford, Bodleian Library, MS. Auct. D. 4. 13, fol. 218 (see pl. XVII)
[Confessio Amalrici]

Confiteor tibi Domine pater celi et terre[5] tibique bone et benignissime
ihesu una cum sancto spiritu coram sanctis angelis tuis et omnibus sanctis[6]
quia in peccatis conceptus, natus et nutritus, et in peccatis post baptisma
5 usque ad hanc horam sum conuersatus. Confiteor eciam quia peccaui
nimis in superbia tam uisibili quam inuisibili et inmani gloria. In
extollencia tam oculorum quam uestium et omnium actuum meorum.
In inuidia. In odio. In auaricia tam honoris quam pecunie. In ira. In
tristicia. In accidia. In commessacionibus. In ebrietatibus. In fabulis
10 ociosis. In osculis et amplexionibus inmundis. In luxuria et omni
genere fornicacionis que et ipse feci et aliis faciendo consensi. In sacrile-
giis et periuriis. In furtis. In rapinis. In accipiendo corpus et sanguinem
domini indigne. In exhortacionibus et adulacionibus malignis. In sub-
trahendo elemosinas. In pauperibus exasperando. In hospitibus non
15 recipiendo. In pauperum despeccionibus.[7] In non uisitando infirmos et
carcere positos. In non sepeliendo mortuos. In non uestiendo pauperes.
In non pascendo esurientes. In non potando sicientes.[8] In sollempnitati-
bus sanctorum et dominicis diebus ac festis, debitum non impendendo
honorem nec sobrie nec caste in eis uiuendo. Consenciendo suadentibus
20 michi in malum, nocendo[9] pocius quam adiuuando me petentes, cla-
mores pauperum non libenter neque misericorditer audiendo. In pro-
pinquis meis ac prelatis detrahendo et blasphemando. Amicis meis et
benefactoribus meis fidem rectam non seruando, debita obsequia non
rependendo. In ecclesiam dei superbe intrando et in ea stando vel
25 sedendo et egrediendo et ociosis fabulis ac turpibus colloquiis in ea cum
aliis insistendo. Vasa sancta et ministerium sanctum polluto corde vel
manibus inmundis tangendo. Oracionem et psalmodiam atque officium
diuinum[10] negligenter in ecclesia dei faciendo et audiendo. In cogitaci-
onibus eciam pessimis. In meditacionibus peruersis. In suspicionibus

---

[1] Cf. Ps. 43: 21, etc.   [2] Ps. 24: 15.   [3] Ps. 70: 5–6.
[4] Ezek. 36: 22.   [5] Matt. 11: 25.   [6] 'tuis' expunged.
[7] 'In pauperibus, pauperum despiciendo' deleted before 'In pauperum despeccionibus'.
[8] For all the statements beginning 'In non . . .' see Matt. 25: 36–43 (corporal
works of mercy).   [9] Pen changes or is sharpened at this point.
[10] 'in ecclesia dei fac' deleted after 'diuinum'.

falsis. In iudiciis temerariis. In consensu malo. In consilio iniquo. In 30
concupiscencia carnali. In delitacione et pollucione inmunda. In uerbis
ociosis et superfluis, luxuriosis atque contumeliosis. In mendaciis et
falsitatibus. In iuramentis multimodis et diuersis. In detraccionibus
assiduis. In rixis. In discordiis seminandis. In irrisionibus et falsitatibus.[1] In transgressione propositi mei. In uisu, auditu, gustu, odoratu, 35
et tactu. In superflua et uana[2] et omnimodis boni omissionibus. In
inmunda cogitacione, locucione, uoluntate, et accione.

Quia ergo in hiis et in aliis omnibus peccatis quibuscumque humana
fragilitas contra deum creatorem suum aut cogitando aut operando
peccare potest, me peccasse et reum in conspectu dei super omnes 40
homines esse cognosco et confiteor. Ideo precor uos omnes sanctos dei
in quorum conspectu hec omnia confessus sum: ut testes michi sitis in
die iudicii contra diabolum hostem et inimicum humani generis, me
ex hiis omnibus confessum fuisse, quatinus *non gaudeat de me inimicus
meus*[3] et glorietur dicens me scelera mea tacuisse et non confessum fuisse, 45
verum sit *in celo gaudium* quod solet fieri *de peccatore* conuerso et
penitente.[4] Ipso prestante et adiuuante qui uiuit et regnat deus per
omnia secula seculorum.

[1] 'In transgressionibus' deleted after 'falsitatibus'.
[2] Blank space after 'uana'.
[3] Cf. Ps. 40: 12.   [4] Cf. Luke 15: 7.

VIII

The Constitution "Cum ex eo" of Boniface VIII

EDUCATION OF PAROCHIAL CLERGY

THE release of canons and other higher clergy from their benefices for purposes of study seems to have been an established custom by the end of the twelfth century.[1] From the same period onwards it was also not uncommon for individual bishops to grant a similar leave of absence to rectors and others who were engaged personally in the *cura animarum*. After the great pastoral reforms of the Fourth Lateran Council this practice in respect of rectors began to increase. By the middle of the thirteenth century it was largely taken for granted, although it varied in intensity from bishopric to bishopric.[2] It was not, however, until the pontificate of Pope Boniface VIII and the appearance of his constitution *Cum ex eo*, that the church as a whole realized at the highest level the possibilities of dispensation for study as a means of providing some educational facilities for the parochial clergy in general. It is with this constitution *Cum ex eo* that the present article is primarily concerned, and with its legislation for, and encouragement of, the release of rectors and vicars from their *cura animarum* for studies at universities. It does not propose to treat of the general subject of the presence of beneficed clergy in universities, nor of privileges granted to certain universities in virtue of which students could live off the fruits of their benefices for some or all of their years of study.[3] We shall therefore deal firstly with the background of the constitution *Cum ex eo*, then with the nature and limits of the legislation, finally with some of the effects which *Cum ex eo* had on the life of the church in the fourteenth, fifteenth and early sixteenth centuries, from the pontificate of Boniface VIII until the Council of Trent.[4]

1 See, for example, **X** [=Decretales Gregorii IX], 3.5,12, and the discussion in L. Thomassinus, *Vetus et nova disciplina circa beneficia et beneficiaria* (Venice, 1752), II, 616.

2 See J. R. H. Moorman, *Church Life in England in the Thirteenth Century* (Cambridge, 1946) 31, 96; M. Gibbs and J. Lang, *Bishops and Reform* (Oxford, 1934) 164.

3 On these privileges see F. Pegues, 'Ecclesiastical provisions for the support of students in the xiiith century,' *Church History* 26 (1957) 307-317.

4 The present article is an expanded version of a note communicated at the XIth International Congress of Historical Sciences, Stockholm 1960: see *Actes du Congrès* (Göteborg-Stockholm, 1962), 259.

264

I

It is well-known, of course, that there was ecclesiastical legislation on the education of candidates for the priesthood long before 1298, but it must be acknowledged that there was none which met the needs of the parochial clergy in general as specifically or as attractively as Boniface's constitution *Cum ex eo.*

In 1179, for example, the Third Lateran Council had attempted to provide for the elementary education of clerics, ordaining that a grammar master should be appointed in every cathedral,[5] but, if we may judge from remarks of the Fourth Lateran Council some thirty six years later, the measure must have met with little success. Strengthening the previous statute: quoniam in multis ecclesiis id minime observatur, this Council ordered that in addition to the master decreed by the earlier Council, metropolitan churches should also possess a theologian who would instruct priests and other clerics in the scriptures and prepare them for pastoral work.[6] Four years later Honorius III introduced a measure which further improved the educational facilities available to the clergy. In a letter of 1219 which was later incorporated into the *Compilatio Quinta* (a collection of Honorius's decrees) and into the *Decretales* (1234) commissioned by Gregory IX, Honorius ruled, among other things, that bishops and chapters should send some promising clerics (aliqui docibiles) to universities for the study of theology, and that these should enjoy the fruits of their benefices for five years while engaged in this study; this would help to offset a scarcity of teachers which some prelates might use as an excuse for their failure to observe the decree of IV Lateran.[7]

---

[5] Can. 18 (P. Labbe-G. Cossart, *Sacrosancta Concilia*, ed. N. Coleti, Venice, 1728-1733, X, 1518); X. 5.5,1.

[6] Can. 11 (Labbe-Cossart, *Concilia*, XIa, 164); X. 5.5,4.

[7] Super specula... Volumus et mandamus ut statutum, in concilio generali de magistris theologis per singulas metropoles statuendis inviolabiliter observetur, statuentes insuper de consilio fratrum nostrorum, ac districte praecipiendo mandantes, ut, quia super hoc propter raritatem magistrorum se possent forsan aliqui excusare, ab ecclesiarum praelatis et capitulis ad theologicae professionis studium aliqui docibiles destinentur, qui, cum docti fuerint, in Dei ecclesia velut splendor fulgeant firmamenti, ex quibus postmodum copia possit haberi doctorum qui velut stellae in perpetuas aeternitates mansuri ad iustitiam valeant plurimos erudire, quibus, si proprii proventus ecclesiastici non sufficiunt, praedicti necessaria subministrent. Docentes vero in theologica facultate, dum in scholis docuerint, et studentes in ipsa, integre per annos quinque, percipiant de licentia sedis apostolicae proventus praebendarum et beneficiorum suorum, non obstante aliqua alia consuetudine vel statuto, cum denario fraudari non debeant in vinea Domini operantes. Hoc autem inconcusse volumus

But once more the response was a long way from being ready or universal. Almost forty years afterwards St. Thomas would note in a polemical writing against William of Saint-Amour :

> propter litteratorum inopiam, nec adhuc per saeculares potuerit observari statutum Lateranensis Concilii, ut in singulis ecclesiis metropolitanis essent aliqui, qui theologiam docerent, quod tamen per religiosos, Dei gratia, cernimus multo latius impletum, quam etiam fuerit statutum[8].

The great canonist and Cardinal, Hostiensis, a year or two before his death in 1271, was even more blunt in his description of the indifference to the decree of IV Lateran and to Honorius's attempt to promote it :

> Sed quidquid velit, quidquid mandet, adhuc non observatur, unde et adhuc aut nullus aut rarus est fructus statuti ipsius et multorum aliorum... Non est culpa statuti, quod in se rationabile fuit et utile, sed culpa subditorum inobedientium, et statuentis non corrigentis, ac negligentiam praelatorum.[9]

Although these decrees of III and IV Lateran, and the decretal letter *Super specula* of Honorius III, are very important in the history of ecclesiastical education,[10] they were to a great extent limited to the

---

observari, firmiter disponentes, quod feriantur poena debita transgressores. (*Chartularium Universitatis Parisiensis*, ed. H. Denifle O.P. and E. Chatelain, I (Paris, 1889), 91; X. 5.5,5). This passage is from one of the three parts into which the decretal letter *Super specula* of 16 November 1219 was divided when the *Compilatio Quinta* was formed before 1226. The division was taken over by Raymund of Peñafort when compiling the *Decretales* issued by Gregory IX in 1234, as follows: X. 3.50,10 (Ne clerici vel monachi saecularibus negotiis se immisceant), the present X. 5.5,5 (De magistris, et ne aliquid exigatur pro licentia docendi), and X. 5.33,28 (De privilegiis et de excessibus privilegiatorum).

8 *Contra impugnantes Dei cultum et religionem*, ed. R. M. Spiazzi O. P., (Turin-Rome, 1954), n. 130, p. 31. St. Thomas is arguing the necessity for a learned religious order, specially set up to help out those engaged in the pastoral care: Eis qui procurant salutem animarum, necessarium est ut vita et scientia clareant: ex quibus non de facili possent tot inveniri qui singulis parochiis per universum mundum praeficerentur, cum etiam *propter litteratorum inopiam* (as above)... *quam etiam fuerit statutum*... Ergo saluberrime religio aliqua instituitur in qua sint homines litterati et studio vacantes ad iuvandum sacerdotes qui ad hoc minus sufficiunt.

9 *Lectura in quinque libros decretalium* (Venice, 1580), p. 30[ra]. The comment was, perhaps, too harsh. In some regions an attempt was being made at the particular time when Hostiensis was writing; for example, at the Council of Tarragona in 1266 it was ordered: quod in singulis ecclesiis cathedralibus nostrae provinciae, duae personae indoneae docibiles de gremio ecclesiae... eligantur, quae in theologia vel de iure canonico studeant... Quibus sufficienter edoctis... alii duo successive ad studium destinantur... (J. Tetada y Ramiro, *Colección des canones y de todos los concilios de la Iglesia de España y de America*, (Madrid, 1859-1863), VI, 53.

10 See P. Mandonnet O. P., 'La crise scolaire au début du XIIIe siècle et la fondation de l'ordre des Frères-Prêcheurs', *Revue d'histoire ecclésiastique* 15 (1914) 34-39 (reprinted in Mandonnet's *Saint Dominique*, ed. M. H. Vicaire and R. Ladner, Paris, 1938, II, 83-100).

provision of teachers in centres of education. The point of III Lateran was the setting aside of benefices for teachers of grammar in cathedral churches; that of IV Lateran was the same, with the addition of benefices for teachers of theology; that of *Super specula* was the maintenance of a supply of graduates who would man the cathedral chairs.[11] Priests engaged in the pastoral care would benefit only indirectly, in so far as the three decrees placed teachers of grammar or of theology at their disposal. *Super specula*, of course, differs from the two earlier constitutions in that it allowed those sent by bishops and chapters for theological studies to have the revenues from their benefices for five years, but it does not at all envisage *licentiae studendi* of which the generality of clerics engaged in the *cura animarum* could avail themselves while continuing to enjoy the fruits of their benefices.[11a] There is no doubt that many rectors were released for university studies in the period after 1219, and that these would enjoy the privilege of revenues for five years granted by *Super specula*, if they studied theology.[12] But whether they were released by bishops in compliance with Honorius' scheme to provide a supply of teachers of theology, or for studies in general, there was an obstacle to be overcome first which is not at all covered by *Super specula*. For rectors and those entrusted with a direct *cura animarum* were obliged by the Third Lateran Council to exercise their cure of souls *per se*.[12a] Therefore, when licences for study were granted to rectors, whether for theology or for any other branch of study, there had to be a justification of non-residence other than the constitution of Honorius III and that of IV Lateran, both of which decrees, in any case, probably were thinking in terms of the young men in the cathedral schools or on cathedral staffs, and not of those already committed to the *cura animarum*.

---

11 Cf. the *Glossa ordinaria* on the word "docibiles" of Honorius's letter: *docibiles*: id est habiles ad docendum, et isti a capitulis possunt eligi ut mittantur et postmodum doceant.

11a The impression given by some authors, however, is that *Super specula* was a blanket decree for all beneficed clergy and not just for those who were to function as teachers of theology in the metropolitan churches, for example, by A. L. Leach, *Educational Charters and Documents 598 to 1909* (Cambridge, 1911) 144-147; id., *The Schools of Medieval England* (Cambridge, 1915) 156-157.

12 The direct import of Honorius's words seems to be that only theological students sent to a university in accordance with *Super specula* would enjoy their revenues for five years, but in fact *studentes* were not restricted to this class, for, as Panormitanus (Nicholas de Tudeschis, 1386-1453) says: scholares sive sint missi sive non habent hoc privilegium per quinquennium (*Commentarium in quinque libros Decretalium* (Lyons, 1527), III, fol. 127ra).

12a X. 3.4,3.

As it happens, there was a way out of the decree of III Lateran on residence which was independent of, and indeed antedates, both IV Lateran and *Super specula*. This was to be found in a letter of Alexander III to the Archbishop of York a few years after the Third Lateran Council, which later was incorporated into the *Compilatio prima* (about 1192) and into the *Decretales* of Gregory IX, and thus gained a wider hearing. Answering a question about the recent Lateran decree on residence *per se,* Alexander wrote that clerics who had been installed in a church or a benefice to which a cure of souls was attached, legally could be removed if they were unwilling to reside there or to perform their duties in person: nisi forte de licentia suorum praelatorum, *vel studio litterarum,* vel pro aliis honestis causis, contigerit eos abesse.[13] From the tone of the letter, indeed, it seems that Alexander was not innovating when he countenanced absence on episcopal licence for the purpose of study, but was rather stating a practice which was in fact common, although not explicitly covered in the Lateran decree on residence.[14]

For almost a hundred years afterwards, bishops who granted licences for study had therefore an authoritative interpretation of the decree of III Lateran with which to rebut charges of transgressing the statute or of encouraging absenteeism from the *cura animarum.* In 1274, however, the situation changed. For when Gregory X published the decrees of II Lyons in that year, he included a post-conciliar constitution *Licet canon* which renewed the Lateran statute on residence and on ordination to the priesthood, and imposed a penalty of *ipso facto* deprivation for a failure to observe its conditions.[15] The only concession to non-residence

---

[13] Relatum est nobis ex parte tua, quod, cum in Lateranensi concilio statutum sit, ut personae tali ecclesia vel beneficium ecclesiasticum conferatur, quae residere in loco et curam eius per se valeat exercere, nonnulli ad ecclesias praesentati hoc se posse affirmant, sed efficere contradicunt. Ideo [nos] consulere voluisti, an propter hoc tales possis praesentatos repellere, vel institutos sublato appellationis obstaculo removere. Cum igitur verba accipienda sint cum effectu, tales, si praesentati fuerint, non debent admitti, et admissi, si instituti fuerint, licite poterunt amoveri; nisi forte de licentia suorum praelatorum, vel studio litterarum, vel pro aliis honestis causis, contigerit eos abesse (**X.** 3.4,4).

[14] See remarks of Thomassinus, *Vetus et nova disciplina,* II, 616.

[15] Licet canon, a felicis recordationis Alexandro Papa III praedecessore nostro editus, inter cetera statuerit, ut nullus regimen ecclesiae parochialis suscipiat, nisi xxv annum aetatis attigerit, ac scientia et moribus commendandus existat, quodque talis ad regimen assumptus huiusmodi, si monitus non fuerit praefixa a canonibus tempore in presbyterum ordinatus, a regiminis eiusdem amoveatur officio, et alii conferatur; quia tamen in observatione canonis memorati se multi exhibent negligentes, nos, periculosam illorum negligentiam volentes iuris executione suppleri, praesenti decreto statuimus, ut nullus ad

was that a bishop could grant a dispensation: ad tempus, prout causa rationabilis id exposcit.

In the next twenty five years some bishops would, no doubt, stretch "causa rationabilis" to cover licences of absence for study,[16] but in fact *Licet canon* made no explicit allowance for the prolonged absence that study would involve, nor did it make any reference whatsoever to Alexander's *declaratio* of III Lateran.   Indeed it was on this very point of study that the Gregorian constitution[16a] was subjected to some sharp criticism.   In attempting to stem absenteeism, the critics said, *Licet canon* in effect shut most of the parochial clergy off from all hope of education. The famous canonist Durandus the Elder, writing about 1291-2, said that it had killed an old and advantageous custom; a consequence of the

regimen parochialis ecclesiae assumatur, nisi sit idoneus moribus, scientia et aetate, decernentes, collationes de parochialibus ecclesiis, his, qui non attigerit xxv annum, de cetero faciendas viribus omnino carere.   Is etiam, qui ad huiusmodi regimen assumetur, ut gregis sibi crediti diligentius curam gerere possit, in parochiali ecclesia, cuius rector exstiterit, residere personaliter tenetur, et infra annum, a sibi commissi regiminis tempore numerandum, se faciat ad sacerdotium promovere.   Quod si infra idem tempus promotus non fuerit, ecclesia sibi commissa, nulla etiam praemissa monitione, sit praesentis constitutionis auctoritate privatus.   Super residentia vero (ut praemittitur) facienda, possit ordinarius gratiam dispensationis ad tempus facere, prout causa rationabilis id exposcit. (Labbe-Cossart, *Concilia*, XIV. 983; Sext, 1.6.14).

16 For example, by Archbishop Wickwane of York in 1280, 1281, 1282: *The Register of William Wickwane of York 1279-1285* (Surtees Society, York, 1907) 38-9, 84-5; and by Bishop Swinfield of Hereford in 1283, 1285, 1287: *Registrum Ricardi de Swinfield Episcopi Herefordensis 1283-1317*, ed. W. W. Capes (Canterbury and York Society, Oxford, 1915) 545.

16a Although the constitution *Licet canon* is generally regarded as an act of the second Council of Lyons, and was, of course, issued with conciliar authority, it is in fact a personal decree of Gregory X, being one of the four constitutions which Gregory added to, and published with, the decrees of the Council itself some five months after the Council had ended.   This is clearly pointed out by the canonist Durandus the Elder (Speculator) who was a secretary to Gregory at the Council and drew up some of its decrees (G. Durandus, *In sacrosanctum concilium Lugdunense commentarius*, ed. S. Maiolo (Fani, 1569), fol. iv).   But despite Finke's great work on the decrees of II Lyons (H. Finke, *Konzilienstudien zur Geschichte des 13. Jahrhunderts* (Münster-in W., 1891, 1-15), and that of E. Fournier on much the same ground: *Questions d'Histoire du Droit canonique* (Paris, 1936) 7-31, there is still a widespread impression that all the constitutions published by Gregory X on 1 Nov. 1274 are constitutions drawn up at the Council of Lyons itself (see S. Kuttner, 'Conciliar law in the making.   The Lyonese constitutions (1274) of Gregory X...', *Miscellanea Pio Paschini* (Rome, 1949), II, 39-81).   The credit of reasserting the true composition of the "Lyons" constitutions as they are found in Mansi, Labbe-Cossart, etc., is usually given to Finke, but the seventeenth and eighteenth centuries were not unaware of the distinction between "Lyons" and "Gregorian" constitutions.   For example, the Dominican savant Noël Alexandre was well aware of it in 1676-1686, when writing his *Historia Ecclesiastica* (ed. C. Roncaglia (Lucca, 1734), VIII, 427-432).

decree, he feared, would be that 'infra breve tempus pauci viri litterati invenientur.' [17]

Six or seven years later Boniface VIII leaves one with the impression that the misgiving was not confined to professional legal circles.[18] In his preamble to his constitution *Cum ex eo* in 1298, he states that *Licet canon* has had the effect of making many clerics reluctant to seek appointments to parochial churches. There were complaints, many of which had reached Boniface himself, that the obligations of permanent residence, and of ordination within a year of institution, gave the parochial clergy small prospect of improving their education, since, for most of them, an education was out of the question unless they had a benefice for their support while studying. Boniface's statement that complaints had reached him from many quarters is probably not an exaggeration. If only Durandus among the canonists seems to have taken a dislike to *Licet canon,* one official protest exists to suggest that dissatisfaction was perhaps as widespread as Boniface (and Durandus) give us to understand. Promulgating the Lyons' and Gregorian constitutions at the Council of Reading in 1279, Archbishop Pecham declared that a strict enforcement of the decree[19] would mean that the English parochial clergy could no longer be trained in philosophy and the arts, since few clerics were rich enough to study at a university without some endowment.[20] He therefore suggested that a letter should be sent to the

---

[17] Haec autem constitutio in plerisque provinciis in quibus pauca sunt beneficia sine cura perquam dura est et damnosa: nam olim episcopi in talibus dispensabant et cum hiis beneficiis multi proficiebant in scientia litterali, hodie vero, quia pauperes non habent unde proficiant, divites vero nollunt providere filiis ut statim presbiteri fiant, nisi remedium adhibeatur, infra brevi tempus pauci viri litterati invenientur... (*Commentarius, ed. cit.,* fol. 7ʳ). It is remarkable how well this summarizes the complaint of Pecham and the letter of the Council of Reading to which we are about to refer.

[18] Whether or not this was at all widespread in these circles cannot be stated definitely at the moment. The Bolognese canonist Garsias Hispanus in his apparatus on the Gregorian constitutions does not question *Licet canon* (Bodleian Library, Oxford, *MS Canon P.L.* 144), nor apparently do the commentaries on these constitutions described by E. Fournier, *Questions d'Histoire,* pp. 32-46, and in his *Nouvelles recherches sur les Curies, Chapitres et Universitaires de l'ancienne Eglise de France* (Arras, 1942) 222-240. The constitution seems, in fact, to have been rigidly enforced; see, for example, the directive of Pope Nicholas III in 1278: Item scribatur diocesanis quod canonicos et rectores ecclesiarum sibi subiectarum residere compellant in eis per subtractionem proventuum, nisi habeant indulgentiam vel domini Papae vel cardinalium obsequiis immorentur. (M. Tangl, *Die päpstlichen Kanzleiordnungen von 1200-1500* (Innsbruck, 1894), 77).

[19] Which Pecham, like Boniface VIII later, regarded simply as an act of the Council of Lyons.

[20] Cum iuniores annis et ordinibus quam sacerdotii constituti quamcumque perydonei ad

270

Pope requesting certain mitigations of *Licet canon*, both of the age limit and of the obligation of residence; all the bishops should endorse it, and the support of the King, barons and whole community of the realm should be canvassed.[21] However, although the letter, a remarkable document, was drafted, this was as far as the complaint was carried. As the cleric who copied it into a Salisbury register noted, it was never sent, 'quia clerus nolebat contribuere.' [22]

Although other representations of which we do not know at present

scienciam litterarum per hunc modum a beneficiis ecclesiasticis penitus excludantur; cum ecclesia anglicana parum prebendis habundat et pro maiori parte beneficia non habeat nisi quibus cura imminet [MS munet] animarum... cumque persone huiusmodi in numerositate plurima constitute quamcumque zelantes ad studium aliunde non habeant facultates quibus in studio sustententur, nec ad beneficia ecclesiastica optinenda habiles, recedunt a studio, qui, si doctrine vacarent, nobilissimi in ecclesia Dei per processum temporis efficerentur ministri quorum ministerio perpetuo per hunc modum defraudatur cotidie ecclesia anglicana... (Bodleian Library, Oxford, *MS Bodley* 794, fol. 180ʳ-180ᵛ). This passage appears in the *Acta* of the Council of Reading which are preserved in a few manuscripts; it is not printed in D. Wilkins, *Concilia Magnae Britanniae et Hiberniae* (London, 1737), II, 33-5. On the *Acta* see C. R. Cheney, 'Legislation of the Medieval English Church', *English Historical Review* 50 (1935) 407-8, and on the Council of Reading, D.L. Douie, *Archbishop Pecham* (Oxford, 1952) 95-105.

21 Ideo si vobis placet in communi scribere domino pape... parati sumus et nos scribendo et interpellando vobis assistere in hac parte; et credimus expedire eciam quod dominus rex a vobis interpellatus ut ipse et omnes comites et barones totaque communitas super ista materia summum pontificem communiter interpellent per solempnes nuncios communiter deputandos, per quos alleviacionem tanti gravaminis circa instituciones expectant et commendas: circa instituciones siquidem quod minor xxv annis ad beneficium curam animarum habens annexum possunt assumi cum aliquo moderamine per sedem apostolicam providendo, quodque is cui cura animarum committitur ad sacerdotium infra annum minime compellatur... (*MS Bodley* 794, fol. 181ʳ).

22 Salisbury Diocesan Registry, *Liber Evidentiarum* C, p. 321 (o.f., 148ʳ). The draft of this letter exists in one other known MS, the Register of Godfrey Giffard, bishop of Worcester (1268-1301), fol. 99 (Worcester Diocesan Registry). I owe a transcript of the Worcester copy, with collations from Liber Evidentiarum C, to the generosity of Miss Decima Douie. As the letter is rather long, the following extract must suffice here: Supplicatio domino pape ne rectores privarentur qui non sunt in primum annum in presbiterum ordinati... Circa instituciones pariter et commendas a tanto constitucionum rigore in ecclesia anglicana expediret recedere, nisi mandati vestri necessitas nos traheret et aliorum et in contrarium cohartaret, cum sit ibi beneficiorum paucitas sine cura multique precipue nobiles ab assecucione beneficiorum huiusmodi se propter statutorum duriciam abstinebunt, dumque ad beneficia huiusmodi assequenda viam sibi conspiciant esse preclusam, a doctrina litterarum se retrahent et efficiuntur inopes et multiplicabuntur latrones insignes, peribit pro parte maxima scientia litterarum, precipue iuris civilis, artium liberalium, philosophie naturalis, et etiam medicine, et in ecclesia Dei proculdubio subsequenter ydoneorum raritas ministrorum...

may have had a hearing at Rome,[23] the chief influence in shaping Boniface's decision to take some of the sting out of *Licet canon* clearly was that of Durandus the Elder, canonist and Bishop of Mende in the south of France. A friend of Boniface, whom he had known when both worked in the papal service, Durandus was persuaded out of retirement to take over the rectorship of the Romagna once again in the first year of Boniface's pontificate, shortly after the letter to the University of Bologna in which Boniface commissioned the compilation of a *Sextus Liber Decretalium.*[23a] With such an eminent canonist within reach, it is unlikely that Boniface went ahead with his own contributions to, or suggestions for, the new compilation, without now and then drawing on Durandus before the latter's death in Rome, 1 December 1296. Indeed, it is not impossible to think that Durandus's commentary on the Lyons and Gregorian constitutions may have been written during or shortly before this return to the Romagna,[24] perhaps even at the request of Boniface himself. At all events, Boniface must have had the canonist's comments on *Licet canon* before him when framing his emendations, for there are distinct echoes of his criticisms in Boniface's constitution *Cum ex eo* which appeared some eighteen months after Durandus's death. Promulgated in the *Liber Sextus* on 3 March 1298, this constitution is so important, and yet so neglected by historians, that we may repeat it here in full.

Cum ex eo quod felicis recordationis Gregorius Papa X praedecessor noster statuit in concilio Lugdunensi ut ad regimen parochialium ecclesiarum as-

---

[23] Perhaps there was one from the bishop of Langres, to whom Boniface wrote in October 1295 dispensing forty clerics who wished to study from the reception of sacred orders for five years: Tuis igitur supplicacionibus inclinati, ut cum quadraginta ex eisdem clericis qui sunt dociles et habeant animum ad studendum et ecclesiastica beneficia obtineant vel etiam obtinebunt, etiam si cura animarum eis immineat, dispensare valeas quod usque ad quinquennium sacros ordines suscipere minime teneantur, et ad id compelli non possint inviti, constitucione contraria non obstante, auctoritate presencium indulgemus, proviso quod interim huiusmodi beneficia debitis obsequiis non fraudentur, et animarum cura in eis si quae illis iminet nullatenus negligatur. Si vero ultra naturam huiusmodi cum aliquibus dispensare forte presumpseris, volumus quod dispensatio huiusmodi sit irrita et inanis, et quod tu ex nunc ipso facto excommunicacionis sentenciam incurras... (Archivio Segreto Vaticano, Reg. Vat. 47, fol. 123ᵛ-124ʳ).

[23a] On the friendship of Durandus and Boniface, see V. Le Clercq, 'G. Duranti,' *Histoire Littéraire de la France* 20 (1842), 421-422; and on the preparation of the Sext, A. Tardif, *Histoire des sources de droit canonique* (Paris, 1887) 207-212, S. Silvia, *Bonifazio VIII* (Rome, 1949) 290.

[24] Certainly after 1289-1291: see L. Falletti, 'Guillaume Durand', *Dictionnaire de droit canonique*, V, 1053.

sumpti se ad sacerdotium promoveri faciant infra annum a sibi commissi regiminis tempore connumerandum et personaliter resideant in eisdem, alioquin, si infra idem tempus promoti non fuerint, huiusmodi ecclesiis absque monitione alia sint privati, nonnullis ex tunc parochiales ecclesias recusantibus acceptare, legendi et proficiendi, cum eis facultates non suppetant, nec ab ecclesiarum praelatis de aliis beneficiis in plerisque mundi partibus interdum provideatur eisdem, opportunitas sit sublata in grande universalis ecclesiae, quae ad sui regimen viris literatis permaxime noscitur indigere, dispendium et iacturam : nos, super hoc multorum instantia excitati frequenter, volentes cupientibus in scientia proficere, ut fructum in Dei ecclesia suo tempore afferre valeant opportunum, utiliter providere, praesenti constitutione sancimus, ut episcopi eorumque superiores cum his, qui huiusmodi subiectas sibi ecclesias obtinent vel obtinuerint, in futurum dispensare possint libere, quod usque ad septennium literarum studio insistentes promoveri minime teneantur, nisi ad ordinem subdiaconatus dumtaxat, ad quem infra praedictum annum recipiendum, (ne, sicut a multis de Christi patrimonio sublimatis olim factum esse dignoscitur, a statu retrocedere valeant clericali) omnino adstringi volumus, et, nisi receperint, poena contenta in dicto concilio eo ipso percelli. Porro septennio praedicto durante iidem episcopi et superiores sollicite providere procurent, ut per bonos et sufficientes vicarios, ab eis in huiusmodi ecclesiis deputandos, animarum cura diligenter exerceatur, et deserviatur laudabiliter in divinis, quibus de ipsarum ecclesiarum proventibus necessaria congrue ministrentur. Elapso vero dicto septennio hi, cum quibus fuerit ut praemittitur, dispensatum, ad diaconatus et presbyteratus ordines infra annum se faciant promoveri, alioquin ex tunc dictam poenam, nisi iusta de causa id omiserint, ipso iure se noverint incursuros.[25]

II

In virtue of this constitution *Cum ex eo,* bishops were now at liberty to grant leave of absence for study to the parochial clergy, provided that these proceeded to the subdiaconate within a year of institution, and to the diaconate and priesthood within a year of the termination of the

---

[25] Sext, 1.6,34. The text given here is that of Friedberg in *CIC*, where the opening words are "Quum ex eo;" however, the constitution is always quoted in papal and episcopal registers as "Cum ex eo." — It has been noted above that the English bishops failed to send their letter of representation to the Pope. Yet it is quite possible that Pecham himself intervened personally with the Papacy (parati sumus et nos scribendo et interpellando vobis assistere in hac parte, he had assured the clergy at Reading), and that Boniface, some seventeen or eighteen years later, was aware of the English viewpoint on *Licet canon.* For although all of the mitigations suggested by Pecham and by the draft letter are not to be found in *Cum ex eo,* e.g., that the age for admission to the cure of souls be changed, yet Pecham's main contention, that those released for study need not become priests within a year of institution, is fully covered; indeed, as in the case of Durandus and *Cum ex eo,* the general approach of Boniface is much the same as that of Pecham and the Reading letter.

licence, and that suitable priests took over the running of their parishes while they were away at a university; in the meantime those absent for purposes of study were to have complete and juridical access to the revenues of their parishes, using them to pay for their studies and upkeep at the university, on condition that the substitutes received a fair and decent share of the parish revenues.

Cum ex eo was thus a considerable advance on *Licet canon;* indeed, as Joannes Monachus, the famous canonist and a cardinal in Boniface's curia, remarked, *Cum ex eo* not only modified *Licet canon* but also corrected it in part.[26] Unlike the Gregorian constitution, that of Boniface VIII did not ignore or overlook a practice which bishops before 1274 had rightly fostered on their own; rather it revived and encouraged it. Where the Gregorian constitution was unbending and at a remove from reality in its efforts to suppress absenteeism, *Cum ex eo* was all that Durandus, paraphrasing the *Decretum,* had demanded of a law in his comments on *Licet canon:* that in ordaining something that is necessary for, and beneficial to, the common good, one should also take the circumstances of place and time into account.[27] In legislating ruthlessly against absenteeism, *Licet canon* had in fact placed the common good in jeopardy; *Cum ex eo,* on the other hand, acknowledged that owing to the lack of educational facilities the Church had to countenance some form of non-residence if a supply of educated priests was to be maintained for parochial work. But there was no sacrifice of the principles and the spirit of *Licet canon,* nor of its harsh penalties for absenteeism pure and simple. In *Licet canon* Gregory had made two notable changes in the legislation of III Lateran on residence and ordination: according to III Lateran deprivation for non-residence could not take place without a warning, and for failure to be ordained priest within the specified time, only after judicial trial; Gregory, however, made deprivation *ipso facto* in both cases.[28] Now, while legislating with more realism than Gregory, Boniface VIII still retained his predecessor's approach to malignant absenteeism, making any transgression of the chief conditions in *Cum ex eo* result in deprivation *ipso facto.* Boniface in no way annulled *Licet canon* or turned a blind eye to absenteeism; rather he defined that absence for study was not only a 'reasonable cause'

---

26 *In Sextum Librum Decretalium Glossa Aurea* (Venice, 1585), p. 105ᵃ.

27 Debuit ergo lex loco et tempori esse conveniens, necessaria et utilis, et pro communi utilitate conscripta, ut iiii dist., c. erit (*Commentarius,* fol. 46ᵛ).

28 See H. J. Schroeder, O. P., *Disciplinary Decrees of the General Councils* (New York, 1937) 343.

for non-residence, but also one which was to be conceded liberally, without fear of conniving at absenteeism. A timely and realistic measure, *Cum ex eo* bears the marks of a pope who, stormy and intransigent as history tends to see him, was withal a shrewd canonist. No doubt the constitution was open to abuse,[29] but the three conditions upon which the validity of a licence rested, substitutes, subdiaconate and priesthood, were nicely-set traps for the insincere applicant. Placing his trust in the good-will of prelates, Boniface had seized an opportunity which *Licet canon* had overlooked, and no earlier papal constitution had considered, to exploit the universities in favour of the *cura animarum*.

To a large extent, of course, *Cum ex eo* appears to be merely an extension of Honorius III's *Super specula* to the parochial clergy. The terms are, indeed, to some extent the same, but in fact *Cum ex eo* has nothing to do with *Super specula* as such, nor did it replace or revise it.[29a] The rector or vicar who was released under *Cum ex eo* for studies at a university derived his privileges from that constitution directly and from that alone. If he enjoyed the revenues of his parish, this was in virtue of *Cum ex eo* and not by favour of any other papal constitution or of any privilege granted by papal decree to the university in question. On the other hand, a cleric released in accordance with *Super specula* could not as such benefit from any of the terms of *Cum ex eo*. Boniface's constitution was not designed to provide teachers of theology, or to cater to canons or other beneficed clergy; its purpose was to promote a literate parochial clergy directly, and its application was strictly confined to clerics who were destined for an ordinary and unencumbered *cura animarum*. In fact a dispensation *Cum ex eo*, on the ordinary authority of a diocesan bishop, could only be granted to a simple rector or vicar, that is, to a man of one living only; and that living had to have a *cura animarum*. From cases which reached the papal curia in the fifty years following Boniface's constitution, it seems clear that rectors or vicars

---

[29] Thus in April 1317 a licence for seven years' study was given to Adam Ayremin of York (*The Register of William Greenfield*, ed. W. A. Brown and A. H. Thompson (York, Surtees Society, 1931-40), V, 256), yet two years later we find him, now a Master, in the King's service in his native Yorkshire (*Calendar of the Close Rolls of the Reign of Edward II* (London 1894), III, 130. But even here it is possible that an ordinary papal dispensation for absence on royal service had been negotiated meanwhile.

[29a] A. F. Sokolich, *Canonical provisions for Universities and Colleges* (Washington, 1956) 25, misses the point of *Cum ex eo* when he writes, "when a period of seven years became necessary for encompassing the courses required for a doctorate, Boniface VIII granted to bishops the faculty of dispensing clerics from the law of residence for those years, and insisted on material support for such students."

who were not wedded directly and exclusively to a single cure of souls could not qualify for a *Cum ex eo* licence: pluralists,[30] for example, rectors of churches without a *cura animarum*,[31] rectors of churches canonically united,[32] rectors of churches with annexed parishes.[33] Likewise, if a rector already had a dispensation from some impediment, his release for study with a licence *Cum ex eo* was outside his bishop's jurisdiction. Normally a condition of personal residence was imposed on one who applied for a dispensation from an impediment in order to take on a *cura animarum;* and no one but the Pope or his delegate could mitigate that condition. For example, Reginald de Sancto Apostolo of the diocese of Exeter was dispensed by the Pope from illegitimacy, and then after institution to a living obtained a *Cum ex eo* licence from his bishop. Later, after his studies were completed, his attention was drawn to the fact that his licence had been illegal, since he had broken a condition of his dispensation from illegitimacy by residing outside his *cura animarum;* he was forced on that account to apply to Pope Clement V for habilitation in 1305.[34]

It seems clear, too, that *Cum ex eo* dispensations from residence were not to be granted to any and every 'simple' rector. The constitution, in fact, presumes that incumbents to whom licences were granted were not yet subdeacons. For it was designed to offer facilities for education to promising young men who might otherwise have been lost to the *cura animarum*. If the prospect of an education at the expense of a parish would make the parochial life more attractive, the obligation of

---

[30] Archivio Segreto Vaticano, Reg. Vat., 61, fol. 4ᵛ: Auch diocese; Reg. Vat., 59, fol. 17ᵛ: Lausanne diocese.

[31] Reg. Vat., 80, fol. 156ᵛ: Pisa.

[32] Reg. Vat., 57, fol. 237ʳ: Auch.

[33] Reg. Vat., 60, fol. 75ʳ: Agen.

[34] Reg. Vat. 52, fol. 16ᵛ (cf. *Calendar of Papal Letters*, II, 3); for a similar case from London see Reg. Vat. 60, fol. 241ʳ (*ibid.*, 116). The *Calendar of Papal Letters*, ed. W H. Bliss, etc. (London, 1894) and the *Calendar of Petitions to the Pope* I, (London, 1896), either through omission or a failure to appreciate the full import of a letter or a petition, sometimes misrepresent cases which deal with licences to study. For example, the *Calendar of Papal Letters*, II, 238 shows Pope John XXII giving a licence for 5 years' study on *Cum ex eo* terms to a rector of Maidstone, Kent (Reg. Vat. 77, fol. 44ʳ, n. 1134), but fails to note the next letter (n. 1135) in which the same rector emerges as a canon of Paris at the time of the licence, thus allowing us to understand why he should have had to have recourse to the Pope for his licence. There was, of course, nothing to prevent the Pope giving a *Cum ex eo* licence directly (see, for example, the case of a Rouen rector: qui est in diaconatus ordine constitutus, in Reg. Vat. 65, fol. 272ᵛ), but generally it will be found that rectors who apply to the Pope for their licences do so either because they have friends in the curia, or because they are not technically "simple" rectors.

taking the subdiaconate within a year, thus binding them to the clerical state, would put off all but the most sincere applicants;[34a] further, the condition of ordination to the priesthood within a year of the termination of their studies, would deter those who might hope to go on collecting degrees at the expense of their parish without incurring the disadvantages and responsibilities of the *cura animarum*.

In fact, *Cum ex eo* so obviously catered to the young and the uncommitted that bishops seem to have felt that they were not obliged to grant full *Cum ex eo* dispensations to rectors or vicars who were already subdeacons, deacons or priests. Thus, when a rector of the diocese of Lincoln was instituted to a living he did not obey *Licet canon* and become a priest within a year; instead, he took only the subdiaconate and then negotiated a licence *Cum ex eo* from his bishop, who, however, did not grant the usual permission not to proceed to further orders until the completion of his studies. As it happened, the rector ignored this restriction, continuing to the end of his studies as though he had a full *Cum ex eo* licence. What is interesting is that when the rector later sought permission from Pope Clement V to retain his benefice, his precise crime was not that he had failed to observe *Licet canon* after institution, but that he had not accepted his bishop's refusal to give him a full *Cum ex eo* licence ('et quod ad illos ordines recipiendos minime tenereris tibi dictus episcopus minime non concessit').[35]

As the origins and limitations of the constitution suggest, *Cum ex eo* was meant to attract young and fresh clerics who were not yet subdeacons to the ranks of the parochial clergy. It is, then, a mistake to think that full licences were granted readily, or at all, to rectors who were priests at institution or had exercised the *cura animarum* for some time. It is even more a mistake to imagine that rectors 'wearied with the tedium of medieval village life, doubtless saw in a so-called study-licence an opportunity for a pleasant stay in a university or cathedral city'.[36] This, as we shall see in detail later, is to misunderstand the nature and the applicability of the constitution. For normally rectors or vicars who were given *Cum ex eo* licences were not 'parish' priests, or priests in

---

[34a] As Boniface put it in *Cum ex eo*: ne, sicut a multis de Christi patrimonio sublimatis olim factum esse dignoscitur, a statu retrocedere valeant clericali.

[35] Reg. Vat. 54, fol. 28ʳ. The *Calendar* again gives an inadequate summary of the case: "licence to retain that church, he being in subdeacon's orders, and having received permission from John, bishop of Lincoln, to continue his studies for three years" (*Cal. Pap. Letters*, II, 23).

[36] C. J. Godfrey, 'Non-residence of parochial clergy in the fourteenth century,' *Church Quarterly Review*, 162 (1961) 436.

any capacity, at the time of the granting of a licence.   In fact, those for whom the constitution was designed were, by some sort of juridical fiction, rectors only in name.[37]   Nor were they really 'deserting' their parishes or 'having the best of both worlds'.   Since these '*Cum ex eo*' rectors were presumed by the constitution not to be subdeacons at the time of the granting of the licence, they could not, in any case, have engaged in the full *cura animarum* for some time.   In fact, since they did not have to become priests until a year after the end of their studies, they could be admitted to a living as early as the age of twenty one, a year, that is, before the canonical age for the subdiaconate, and some four years short of the age required for the priesthood.   Strictly speaking, a rector was supposed to be twenty five years of age at least at institution, according to III Lateran and *Licet canon,* but here again there was a legal fiction in the broader interests of the *cura animarum.*   The primary end of *Cum ex eo* (and of Pecham's proposals at Reading in 1279) was to provide opportunities of education for the parochial clergy *before* ordination to the priesthood and *before* they shouldered the full burden of the pastoral care; and this was to be achieved by allowing likely young clerics to be rectors juridically but not in practice so that their parishes could pay for their course of studies.   The admission of a young man of twenty one to a parish church on the understanding that he was to be released for studies did not really transgress *Licet canon,* nor did it nullify his institution.   Such a rector was, so to speak, canonically committed to, but dispensed *ipso iure* from, the exercise of the *cura animarum* until a course of studies had brought him up to the standard demanded by *Licet canon* of those to whom the *regimen animarum* was entrusted.   It is therefore very interesting to note how soon after institution *Cum ex eo* licences were granted.   More often than not, in the full spirit of Boniface's legislation, licences follow closely on the institution of clerics who are not yet subdeacons.[37a]

---

37 See the remarks of J. Absil, 'L'absentéisme du clergé paroissial au diocèse de Liège au xvᵉ s. et dans la première moitié du xvıᵉ s.,' *Revue d'histoire ecclésiastique,* 57 (1962) 41-2.

37a Joannes Andreae, in his gloss on the Sext, holds that when Boniface imposes a condition of ordination to the subdiaconate he is not thereby implying that clerics in minor orders are to be admitted to parish churches, but is rather thinking only of those who have had a dispensation from the law forbidding the institution to parish churches of clerics who are in minor orders. Here Joannes contradicts the more common opinion which held, as did the great canonists Joannes Monachus and Guido de Baysio, that after this constitution *Cum ex eo*: sine dispensatione de iure communi potest in minoribus constitutus eligi ad parochialem ecclesiam. (see *Liber Sextus, Decretalium Domini Bonifatii Papae Octavi suae integritati una cum Clementinis et Extravagantibus earumque glossis restitutus* (Venice, 1584),

VIII

A parish, then, was not really deprived of the services of a seasoned parish priest for periods up to seven years, if, as seems to be the general case, the ideal behind *Cum ex eo* was perceived by bishops who granted licences. Rather, in paying for the education of its absent 'rector', the parish was simply investing in its own future, and on terms which practically insured it against losses. As we shall see presently, the care with which those conditions were observed, and the extent to which licences *Cum ex eo* were granted, show clearly how appreciative bishops and clergy alike were of the purpose, timeliness and wisdom of Boniface's constitution. For Boniface, in fact, had proposed a solution to the problem of the education of the parochial clergy which would not be improved upon in practice until the Council of Trent some two and a half centuries later.[38]

III

Unlike the Trent legislation on seminaries, *Cum ex eo* does not specify what studies were to be followed, nor does it impose a condition that some at least of the licence should be spent in the study of canon law or theology. This, in fact, is probably the weakest point in the constitution, for one would have expected some mention of studies which would prepare rectors for the *cura animarum* as such, and for the priesthood. In this connection it is of interest to note that the letter drawn up under Pecham's guidance at Reading in 1279 was more concerned about a liberal education for those engaged in the pastoral care than about studies which would be of more direct benefit to the *cura animarum*. If *Licet canon* were not revised, it said : peribit pro parte maxima scientia litterarum, precipue iuris civilis, artium liberalium, philosophiae naturalis et etiam medicine, et in ecclesia Dei proculdubio erit subsequenter ydoneorum raritas ministrorum.[39]

The ideal thing, of course, would have been a combination of a study of the liberal arts and some sort of direct preparation for the priesthood, but Boniface, thinking perhaps to make the *cura animarum* more attractive, left those who enjoyed *Cum ex eo* licences free to make their own

col. 164, v. *subdiaconatus*). The common opinion is the one followed here. It seems to agree more with the preamble to Boniface's "declaratio" of *Licet canon*, and is certainly borne out by the practice of the bishops.

[38] It is therefore a little surprising not to find a mention of *Cum ex eo* in J. A. O'Donohue's *Tridentine Seminary Legislation; Its sources and its formation* (Louvain, 1957), which does discuss *Super specula* at pp. 13-14 and pp. 106-7.

[39] See n. 22, above.

choice of studies.   The type of cleric for which Boniface was legislating, and on whose behalf the Reading letter was written, was one who would have been lost to the *cura animarum* had there been no facilities for education at his disposal.   It could be presumed that he would not waste his time, and that at the end of his licence he would at least have some sort of formation and a general background.   At all events, the rector who had obtained a *Cum ex eo* licence would not be totally illiterate before ordination and before taking over the full *cura animarum*.

However, a *Cum ex eo* licence on the ordinary authority of a bishop did not immediately grant permission to study any and every subject, or indeed all of the subjects listed in the Reading letter, but only those which were not barred in any way by ecclesiastical law.   For example, if a rector wished to use a *Cum ex eo* licence for the study of civil law, he had first to have a papal dispensation, since Honorius III had forbidden any cleric who had a *personatus* or a *cura animarum* to frequent the civil law schools.[40]   Thus in 1313 Clement V was petitioned by the Archbishop of Bordeaux for faculties to dispense a rector for seven years' study of civil law;[41] in 1326 John XXII gave a three-year dispensation to a perpetual vicar;[42] while Benedict XII gave part of a year in 1338, and a full year in 1339, to a rector of the diocese of Cahors.[43]

When a licence was granted by a bishop for legitimate study,[43a] the maximum time allowed was seven years.   Any time over and above this period was outside the jurisdiction of the licensing bishop.   If a rector

---

[40] **X.** 3.50,10. The prohibition, which is part of the decretal letter *Super specula* of Honorius III, was designed to promote the study of theology: quia theologiae studium cupimus ampliari.   On this, and on the prohibition of the teaching and study of civil law at Paris in the same decretal, see S. Kuttner, 'Papst Honorius III und das Studium des Zivilrechts,' *Festschrift für Martin Wolff*, ed. F. M. Cammerer, etc. (Tübingen, 1952) 79-101.

[41] Reg. Vat. 60, fol. 163[r].

[42] Reg. Vat. 80,, fol. 243.

[43] Reg. Av. 85, fol. 414[r] (1338), Reg. Vat. 127, fol. 352[r] (1339).   For some other cases see Reg. Vat. 55, fol. 83[v] (Lichfield rector had seven years *Cum ex eo*; now he gets three more for civil law from Clement V); *ibid.*, fol. 29[r] (diocese of Braga); Reg. Vat. 60, fol. 163[r] (diocese of Bordeaux).

[43a] Joannes Andreae, in his gloss on the Sext, would include civil law as a legitimate subject: *Litterarum:* cum non distinguat, intelligo generaliter, sive in grammatica, sive in iure canonico, vel civili, vel scientia theologiae studeat (*Liber Sextus*, (Venice, 1584), col. 164).   He does not state whether the usual papal dispensation would have to be sought first.   Very few bishops appear to have acted on the assumption that "letters" or "scholastic disciplines" automatically included a dispensation to attend the civil law schools.

desired to continue his studies after those seven years were up, and to enjoy the privileges conferred by *Cum ex eo*, then he had to have recourse to the Pope. Thus the case of Ralph Ingham of Dean West in the diocese of Salisbury, who, by 1325, had exhausted a seven-year licence which he had from Bishop Mortival. Because he had developed an interest in civil law and now wished to study it more scientifically, he petitioned John XXII for an extension and was granted an extra two years with *Cum ex eo* privileges.[44] For the same reason a rector in the diocese of Lichfield successfully petitioned Clement V in 1308 for a three-year extension of a seven-year episcopal licence.[45] In all cases, however, where an extension of *Cum ex eo* was sought from the Pope, the petition had to be careful to state when the licence had ended, and whether all the conditions of *Cum ex eo* had been fulfilled. Thus when Master John de Sutton, rector of Tinford, Lincs., asked for and obtained a three-year extension, he noted that he had become a subdeacon within a year of the granting of the licence, as demanded by *Cum ex eo*, but that he had not yet proceeded to further orders after the end of his seven-year licence, since the year was not yet up within which he should have been ordained deacon and priest.[46]

[44] Reg. Vat. 80, fol. 27[r] (cf. *Cal. Pap. Letters*, II, 246).

[45] Reg. Vat. 55, fol. 83[v] (cf. *Cal. Pap. Letters*, II, 39). For some other examples of papal extensions of *Cum ex eo* licences granted "on the ordinary authority" of bishops, see, for John XXII's pontificate, Reg. Vat. 55, fol. 135[r] (five years extra to a rector of d. Rodez), 56, fol. 14[r] (seven years to rector of d. Agen), fol. 31[r] (three years to another rector of d. Agen), 59, fol. 122[r] (seven years to rector d. Auch), 60, fol. 248[r] (three years to rector of d. Cahors), etc. In Reg. Vat. 168, fol. 190[v], Master Walter de Wodhous, rector of Kippax, Yorks., asks for a seven-year extension, for civil law studies at Bologna, of a seven-years *Cum ex eo* licence, but is only granted three years by Pope Clement VI (1345); here again, the *Cal. Pap. Petitions* I, 98 renders the petition incompletely, while *Cal. Pap. Letters* renders the grace inadequately (III, 187); neither mentions that Walter has already had seven years from his bishop.

[46] ... episcopus Lincolniensis tecum cupienti in scientia proficere... iuxta constitucionem felicis recordacionis Bonifacii VIII predecessoris nostri super hoc editam, post cuius edicionem illam assequens te fecisti iuxta tenorem ipsius infra annum in subdiaconatum ordinari, per septennium litterarum studio licite insistere posses, cum auctoritate constitucionis huius dispensavit; tuque per idem septem prefato studio institisti, te non faciens quamquam huius sit elapsum sic septennium, cum nondum alius annus in constitucione prefata contentus effluxerit, ad ulteriores ordines promoveri. Quare, cum adhuc huiusmodi studio cupias sicut asseris immorari, fuit pro parte tua nobis humiliter supplicatum... (Reg. Vat. 54, fol. 96[r]; cf. *Cal. Pap. Letters*, I, 29). This request was made through Cardinal Thomas Jorz, O. P., whose kinsman Sutton was; as it happened, he did not devote himself to study during the three years' extra licence: see Reg. Vat. 59, fol. 140[v]-1[r]; *Cal. Pap. Letters*, II, 98. Another case comes from Rouen, where a rector states when applying for an extension that his seven-year licence has not yet ended; when Clement V gives him two years more, these are to begin: finito dicto septennio (Reg. Vat. 63, fol. 390[v]).

Apart from papal dispensations, the maximum absence of seven years allowed by *Cum ex eo* was with reference to the *cura animarum* as such and not to a particular living. A change of parish would not affect the issue and give a rector a fresh start,[46a] nor would a change of diocese. Rectors could not go around collecting licences, as Roger de Mortuomari found when he was forced to seek habilitation from John XXII in 1327 because he had enjoyed two maximum licences, one from the Bishop of Hereford when rector of Richard's Castle in that diocese, a second when he resigned that living at the end of the first licence and became rector of Staunton in the diocese of Ely.[47] But once a true and legitimate licence had been granted, it could not be withdrawn except for a very grave reason; and new bishops had to respect licences given by their predecessors.[48] Licences granted during a vacancy in a see are not common, but the *custos spiritualitatum* nevertheless had the power; we may instance a seven-year licence granted from York in 1317 during the vacancy on the death of Archbishop Greenfield.[49] But if a bishop were merely absent, then his vicar could neither dispense for studies nor withdraw a licence, unless the power had been delegated expressly by the bishop. Thus when Anthony Bek was away from Durham on one occasion, his vicar general took it upon himself to grant a seven-year licence; as a result the luckless rector later had to have recourse to Clement V for a dispensation to retain his living.[50]

[46a] Quid si pendente dispensatione mecum facta de isto septennio, assumor ad aliam parochialem ecclesiam sine fraude, numquid adhuc poterit in septennio mecum dispensari? Et satis videtur quod non, per hanc litteram, cum videatur tempus inspici ratione personae, et secundum hoc, et per ea quae dixi in principio glossae, videtur quod tempus istud incipiat a tempore dispensationis...: Joannes Andreae in v. *septennium* (*Liber Sextus*, Venice, 1584, col. 164).

[47] Reg. Vat. 85, fol. 246 (*Cal. Pap. Letters*, II, 261-2, but inaccurately rendered). Incidentally, Roger was only 14 years of age when he was given his first licence; he was just 22 (about the correct age for a first licence) when he received his second. Another interesting case of a change of diocese will be found in Reg. Vat. 162, fol. 84ʳ, in 1343.

[48] On this and other points connected with *Cum ex eo* see Oldradus de Ponte Laudensis, (ob. 1335), *Consilia seu Responsa et Quaestiones Aureae*, ed. Rainaldus Corso (Venice, 1685), fol. 104. See also the two *Cum ex eo* cases discussed in the early 14th century at Toulouse University in *Responsa Doctorum Tholosanorum*, ed. E. M. Meijers (Haarlem, 1938), pp. 112-114.

[49] *Reg. Greenfield*, V, p. 256; see the case discussed in the *Consilia* of Federico Petrucci of Siena, composed between 1334 and 1338: Quaestio est ista: an capitulum sede vacante possit cum rectore parochialis ecclesiae dispensare ut per septennium insistere valeat studio litterarum quin ad sacerdotium promoveri minime teneatur (*Consilia* (Venice, 1587), cons. 38).

[50] Reg. Vat. 58, fol. 237ᵛ: ...quidam eius vicarius generalis in dicta diocesi tecum ut insistens studio litteratum non tenereris inde ad septennium racione ipsius ecclesie nisi ad

If bishops and *sede vacante* vicars had to respect licences already in existence, they could, nevertheless, take steps to see that the conditions upon which the licence had been granted were being fulfilled. This was the duty as well as the right of any ordinary who gave a licence or countenanced one already granted. It is incorrect to think that 'bishops appear to have had no means of finding out whether the rector diligently pursued his studies or merely enjoyed a holiday.'[51] On occasion, indeed, university authorities were called upon to furnish testimonials to the quality and progress of a rector. When calumnious rumours were circulating about a certain rector whom Hamo of Hethe, bishop of Rochester, had released under *Cum ex eo* for studies at Oxford, two successive chancellors of the university, Henry Gower in 1325 and William Alberwik in 1326, gave testimony to Hethe that the rector in question had spent his time continuously and profitably in study.[52] In 1323, when Bishop Drokensford of Bath and Wells had heard that some licensed rectors were resorting to London instead of to places of study, he commissioned his official to examine all those who had been dispensed on the state of their studies, and to recall all licences which were found to have been abused.[53]

This episcopal watchfulness was necessary, not only in order to curtail abuses of *Cum ex eo* and of parish revenues, but also in order to protect

---

subdiaconatus tantum ordines promoveri, iuxta constitucionem felicis recordacionnis Bonifacii VIII predecessoris nostri super hoc editam, dispensavit, quamvis super hoc nullam specialem haberet ab eodem episcopo potestatem... (cf. *Cal. Pap. Letters*, II, 91, which misses the point of the letter). To add to the difficulty of his position the rector had only studied fitfully: cuius dispensacionis pretextu eidem studio non continuis, prout secundum constitucionem tenebaris eandem, sed interruptis temporibus institisti...

[51] E. H. Pearce, *Thomas de Cobham, Bishop of Worcester (1317-1327)* (London, 1923) 101.

[52] *Registrum Hamonis de Hethe Diocesis Roffensis 1319-1322*, ed. C. Johnson (Cant. and York Soc., 1948), 173/74, 177: Testimonium conversacionis et studii. Universis presentes litteras inspecturis, Henricus de Gower, cancellarius universitatis Oxoniensis, salutem in domino sempiternam. Noverit universitas vestra dominum Johannem de Westbrok, scolarem nostrum, rectorem ecclesie de Northcreye Roffensis diocesis, in universitate nostra debitis studenti temporibus commorando et literarum studio jugiter insistendo a festo purificacionis beate Marie anno domini millesimo tercentesimo vicesimo primo usque ad xiiij kalendas julii anno domini millesimo tercentesimo vicesimo tercio, se ita bene et laudabiliter habuisse quod testimonio laudabili merito debeat commendari, prout in magno parte per propriam noticiam ac eciam per... testes fidedignos, juratos, examinatos et ad hoc coram nobis judicialiter vocatos recepimus plenam fidem (pp. 173-4). The same testimony was repeated on 2 August 1325; ne insidiancium invidia vel calumpniancium ora maliciose captata status ejusdem alicui posset in dubium revocari (p. 174). On 17 July 1326 William de Alberick testified for the period 3 October 1325-17 July 1326 (p. 177).

[53] *The Register of John de Drokensforde, Bishop of Bath and Wells, 1320-1239*, ed. E. Hobhouse, (Somerset Record Society, 1887) 227.

the absent incumbent.   For if bishops were open to reprimand for granting licences recklessly or to the unworthy,[54] incumbents would lose their licences and would be held to have defrauded their parishes, when they in any way departed from the terms of their *Cum ex eo* licence.[54a] Besides, bishops had to be careful that the spirit as well as the letter of Boniface's constitution was preserved.   Writing just as the Black Death was beginning to take a grip on England, the Dominican moral theologian John Bromyard complained that many of the parochial clergy were frittering their licences away at the universities, making a mockery of Boniface's great constitution.   If they did not devote themselves manfully to their studies, then they were vitiating the purpose of the constitution.[55]   In his opinion there was no reason why they should remain

---

[54] See, for example, a letter drawn up by Benedict XII in 1337 in reproof of the bishop of Soissons (Reg. Vat. 124, fol. 210v). He had had a complaint from one of the bishop's archdeacons: quod tu rectoribus et capellanis curatis presertim in eius archidiaconatu Brie... minus etiam docilibus studiorum pretextu et aliter contra iura canonica de non residendo personaliter... licencias seu dispensaciones indiscretas et improvidas pro tua libitu concessisti et eas petentibus sine difficultate concedis... Benedict therefore ordered that: licencias seu dispensaciones huiusmodi... contra iura et sine racionabili causa concessas, indilate studeas effectualiter revocare, nullas alias deinceps licencias seu dispensaciones huiusmodi nisi in casibus a iure expressis aliquibus quomodolibet concessuras... Later, the letter was cassated.

[54a] For failure to become a subdeacon within a year of the granting of a licence, and a priest within a year of the termination of the period allowed, the express penalty in *Cum ex eo* was the *ipso facto* deprivation ordered by *Licet canon* for failure to become a priest within a year of institution. Boniface did not annul *Licet canon*. Rather he defined that, for purposes of study, the *Licet canon* obligation of ordination would only come into force after the termination of a licence. However, he replaced the obligation of ordination to the priesthood within a year of institution by the equally effective one of ordination to the subdiaconate.

[55] Et nota quod omnes predicte allegationes multum esse videntur contra illos cum quibus episcopi dispensant quod causa eruditionis scolas exercere poterunt per septennium vel per alium terminum infra septennium contentum: postquam ad ecclesias curam animarum habentes promoti fuerint antequam ad sacerdotium promoveantur, sicut patet libro sexto decretalium, titulo de electione, capitulo cum ex eo: nisi in scolis viriliter addiscent, quia illa est causa finalis quare eis licentia et privilegium de non residendo et ad ordines non promovendo datum est, sicut expresse patet ex illius capituli tenore, in quo prius ostendit quomodo ecclesia viris indiget literatis, et quod magnum damnum ex talium patitur defectu; deinde dat episcopis auctoritatem quod cum volentibus in scientia proficere dispensare poterunt: ut fructum in Dei ecclesia suo tempore afferre valeant opportunum. Ex quo patet quod profectus in scolis causa est quare papa cum eis dispensare voluit de non residentia; nec aliter eis talem dedit licentiam. Illa ergo causa cessante coram Deo iudicantur sine licentia... Licet ergo non ordinati coram mundo titulo dispensationis excusentur, si tamen viriliter non studuerint coram Deo excusati non sunt (*Summa praedicantium* (Paris, 1500), O. iv.17).

284

on at the universities until they had taken degrees.   Once they had
obtained a grasp of pastoral theology and the theology of the Incarnation,
they should return to their cure of souls and 'glorify God, setting a head-
line for their fellows by word and example.'[56] Again, the great and
liberal bishop of Salisbury, Simon of Ghent (1297-1315) was not always
happy about those who applied for licences; some clearly would not
derive much benefit from a course of studies.   On occasions when
he was unsure of the quality of an applicant, he simply granted a trial
licence; thus he released a rector who was already a priest for a short
term of study with the 'Magister scholarum' at Marlborough on the
understanding that he would be considered for a further dispensation
'si interim bene expediat et ad id (studium) se habilem reddat.'[57]   As
it is, this is not one of the happiest examples of Ghent's circumspection,
since in fact he seems to be a little at variance with *Cum ex eo*.   For
Boniface had clearly specified that the term of study should be spent at a
studium generale, which Marlborough was not.   Indeed, it is only on rare
occasions that one finds a licence being granted for study at a *studium
particulare* (the status, roughly, of Marlborough); and then only by the
Pope.[58] With his well-known zeal for the education of the clergy, Ghent's
application of *Cum ex eo* may have been at times more liberal than exact.

By and large Ghent's use of the faculties allowed him by *Cum ex eo*
was careful and conscientious, although on occasion he must have felt a
little overwhelmed by the eagerness of the parochial clergy.   If he was
brusque with Thomas of Lichfield, rector of Hinton Martell, who was
granted a licence of one year at Christmas 1301 with the proviso 'quod
de cetero ea de causa dominum non infestat,'[59] Ghent was over-cautious,

---

[56] Postquam in scolis didicerint de verbo incarnato: et gregis informatione ad breve
tempus audierint, redeant ad gregem suam, et Deum glorificent, fratres suos verbis et
exemplis confirmando. Nec expectent usque magistri fiant... (*ibid,* P. xiii.25).

[57] *Registrum Simonis de Gandavo Episcopi Saresberiensis 1297-1315,* ed. C. T. Flower and
M.C.B. Dawes (Canterbury and York Society, 1934), 849.

[58] See Reg. Vat. 57, fol. 117ʳ; and the comment of Joannes Andreae: Et habentes dispensationem propter studium, studere debent, non in castris vel villis, sed in studio generali,
ut supra de clericis non residentibus, tuae [X. 3.4,13], alias privilegium non habebunt,
ut ibi. (*Liber Sextus,* (Venice, 1584), col. 164, in v. *litterarum* of *Cum ex eo*). The usual
phrase in papal or episcopal licences is studio litterarum, ubi sollemniter vigeat, or simply
studium generale. On the differences between the various types of *studia* see Hastings
Rashdall, *The Universities of Europe in the Middle Ages,* ed. F. M. Powicke and A. B. Emden,
(Oxford, 1936), I, 6-17, with the later literature reviewed by S. Stelling-Michaud, *XIᵉ Congrès International des Sciences Historiques, Rapports,* (Stockholm, 1960), I, 99-100.

[59] *Reg. S. de Gandavo,* p. 850. In fact, Lichfield turned up again the following Christmas,
and wheedled another year out of Ghent (*ibid.,* p. 859).

perhaps, in the case of Alexander Newport, rector of Warfield near
Windsor, on the outskirts of the Salisbury diocese. Presented to
Warfield on 25 August 1305, Newport, then an acolyte, was instituted
to the rectory almost two months later, on 15 October 1305.[60] A few
days later, apparently, he left for studies at Oxford, for on 28 May 1306,
when he was ordained subdeacon, he was issued a *Cum ex eo* licence for
two years' study at Oxford, retrospective to the previous Feast of St. Luke
(18 October 1305), three days, that is, after the institution.[61] A week
after he had become a subdeacon, however, Newport managed to get
this licence increased by three years to a five-year licence, again dated
from the same Feast of St. Luke in 1305;[62] and when this licence was
nearing its term in October 1310, he exchanged it for a licence of six
years from the date of his institution to Warfield.[63] The total six years,
a period sufficient for a bachelor's degree at least, therefore came to an
end on 15 October 1311, by which date, however, Newport appears not
to have taken a degree since he applied for a further leave of absence.
Simon of Ghent, on the other hand, seems to have thought that Newport
should have taken his degree within the six years already granted, and that
there was not sufficient justification for a seventh year with *Cum ex eo*
privileges. Instead, perhaps because he did not wish to deprive Newport
of the crown of his studies, Ghent had recourse to Gregory X's constitution *Licet canon,* which allowed non-residence for a 'reasonable cause,'
and proceeded to allow Newport his extra year on *Licet canon* terms.[64]
But he still held that Newport should have completed his studies within
the original six-year licence, and that now he was technically bound to
become a deacon and a priest within the year after his *Cum ex eo* licence
ended. For we find that Newport, despite his additional *Licet canon*
licence, obtained letters dimissory for the diaconate on the day before
the Ember Saturday of Whitweek in the following May 1312,[65] and for
the priesthood in time for the Ember ordinations in September.[66] He

---

[60] *Ibid.,* p. 659.

[61] *Ibid.,* p. 875.

[62] *Ibid.,* p. 885.

[63] *Ibid.,* p. 896.

[64] *Ibid.,* p. 904. Ghent, in particular, on occasion made use of *Licet canon* rather than
Cum ex eo, especially where there was a question of releasing a rector who was already a
master or a priest (see *Reg.* pp. 905, 911). Sometimes, as in the case of Lavyngton, the
last year of study was on a *Licet canon* licence (see *Reg.* p. 913), so that the rector would
already be a priest by the time he returned to his parish at the end of his studies.

[65] *Ibid.,* p. 906 (19 May 1312).

[66] *Ibid.,* p. 908 (14 September 1312. The Autumn Ember days fell that year on 20, 22
and 23 September).

would thus have forestalled the anniversary (15 October 1312) of the end of his *Cum ex eo* licence by one month. Had he delayed his ordination to the priesthood until after that date, he would have lost his living *ipso facto*, and like a rector of Swindon in the same diocese in the previous year, would have had to seek papal habilitation before he could regain his rectory at Warfield.[67]

Ghent's refusal to grant the maximum licence immediately was not at all uncommon, for bishops were at liberty to grant the seven years as a whole, or to grant a part only, or to dole them out year by year; many, indeed, proceeded along lines similar to those suggested by a glossator of the Sext: 'imo commendabile est non a principio totum dare septennium ut experiatur si proficient, et tunc detur ulterius tempus: alias denegetur.'[68]   But whatever period was granted to a rector, it was valid only for the University or area specified by the bishop,[69] and it had to be spent continuously in study. Even an apparently innocent and unavoidable failure to maintain uninterrupted attendance at a university did not save a rector (or vicar) from legal penalties.   Thus when a rector of the diocese of Rodez had to interrupt a seven-year licence in order to accompany his bishop to the Council of Vienne, he was obliged to petition Clement V, asking that the time spent in going to and returning from Vienne would not be held against him.[70]   In the same way a Rouen rector had to seek habilitation because 'King's business' had forced him to desert his studies while enjoying a three-year licence.[71] Other breaches of *Cum ex eo* were not quite so innocent.   A rector of the diocese of Agen confessed in a petition to Clement that he had spent some of his licence 'following the episcopal curia of the bishop of Toulouse'; [72] and when Robert Pincebek, now a canon of Dublin, applied for habilitation in 1315, he stated that when rector of Erpingham

---

[67] Reg. Vat. 58, fol. 153ᵛ. The summary in *Cal. Pap. Letters*, II, 68, again misses the point of the letter.

[68] *Liber Sextus*, (Venice, 1584), col. 164, in v. *septennium* of *Cum ex eo*.

[69] Thus a rector of the diocese of Coventry and Lichfield had to seek habilitation from Clement V in 1308 because: insistendi infra regnum Anglie dumtaxat studio literarum tecum obtinuisti auctoritate ordinaria dispensari, tuque postmodum fere per quinquennium formam huius dispensacionis excedens extra regnum ipsum in regno Franciae institisti huiusmodi studio literarum... (Reg. Vat. 55, fol. 102ʳ; *Cal. Pap. Letters*, II, 41, but not accurately summarized).

[70] Reg. Vat. 59, fol. 180ʳ. The permission was, it seems, *viva voce*, for later the rector asked for letters to this effect; when Pope Clement gave them he increased the licence by a further five years.

[71] *Ibid.*, fol. 200ᵛ.

[72] *Ibid.*, fol. 132ᵛ.

in the diocese of Norwich, he had been granted a seven-year licence, more than two years of which had been spent in the *studium generale* of the Roman curia, but 'not quite in the spirit of *Cum ex eo*.'[73] Again, a rector of the diocese of Lincoln had to supplicate the same Pope because, among other things, 'nullum ex tali dispensatione commodum reportasti.'[74] Finally, in the register of Hamo of Hethe, bishop of Rochester, there is a striking memorandum after the record of institution (12.9.1332) of a rector: Non apparet de studio continuato... juxta dispensationem sibi factam a tempore institutionis usque ad festum Nativitatis Domini proximo sequens et postea, in anno domini MCCCXXXV, dum in universitate communiter legebatur.[75]

'Dum communiter legebatur' neatly defines what was meant by continuous study; vacation periods were not taken into account. Sometimes, however, a bishop might make his own conditions about the vacations, as when Simon of Ghent gave a licence to the rector of Chieveley, Berks., in 1307, with the proviso that 'he visited the parish in the Christmas vacation and resided there from the eve of Palm Sunday until the octave of Easter.'[76] If a rector was already a priest, and if, as in the case of Chieveley, the parish was not too far away from the university, then he could be expected to return to his parish sometime during Lent, when the annual obligation of confession in their parish church was being fulfilled by most of his parishioners. Thus Bishop Drokensford of Bath and Wells gave a licence to a priest-rector for one year's study at Oxford, 'ita quod tempore quadragesimali accedat ad ecclesiam suam pro cura sibi commissa visitanda.'[77]

During these licensed absences from the *cura animarum*, the parish would be cared for by the 'competent substitute' demanded by *Cum ex eo*. The responsibility for this 'vicar' rested with the bishop who granted the licence. There was not much point in allowing incumbents to depart their parishes in the hope that they would return better-equipped for the pastoral care, if, in the meantime, the parishes were to lie fallow. Ghent of Salisbury was most careful on this point. Granting a three-year licence to the rector of Blunsden St. Andrew in 1301, he

---

[73] ... in romana curia, ubi secundum alium dicti predecessoris constitucionem viget studium generale, iuris canonici studio duxeris insistendum, non tamen forsitan et prout predicte super hoc edite constituciones requirunt effectus eidem studio institisti (Reg. Vat. 59, fol. 115; the *Cal. Pap. Letters*, II, 97, does not include this in its summary).

[74] Reg. Vat. 54, fol. 2ᵛ (cf. *Cal. Pap. Letters*, II, 22).

[75] *Registrum*, p. 522.

[76] *Reg. S. de Gandavo*, p. 847.

[77] *Register of John Drokensforde*, p. 197.

only allowed the substitute when he had satisfied himself that he was up to the mark.[78]   A licence which he granted in 1312/13 was conditional on the provision of a substitute who would have to pass a test to see if he were 'pro cura inibi exercenda sufficiens.'[79]

Many of these substitutes were, no doubt, 'clerical hacks.'[80]   But where rectories and vicarages were already provided with an assistant priest, the incumbent simply handed the parish over to his second-in-command.   Thus when William of Pagula left his vicarage at Winkfield, Berks., for Oxford in 1314 or 1315, he was not faced with the difficulty of finding a steady substitute.   For when Bishop Ghent ordained a perpetual vicarage at Winkfield in 1310, he stipulated that the vicars should provide themselves, from their own resources, with an assistant priest who would fulfill the vicar's functions whenever necessary, and generally assist him.[81]   Of course, not all rectories or vicarages were as well-provided for as the vicarage at Winkfield; there the Dean and Chapter of Salisbury were committed to an annual payment of sixty marks a year, no mean sum when it is remembered that the minimum fixed by the Council of Oxford in 1222 was five marks a year, and that the majority of vicarages rarely paid much more than this.[82]   A man like William of Pagula could therefore afford to pay his assistant priest considerably more than these insecure clerics were usually vouchsafed,[83] and yet be comfortably secure while away at the university.   For with the set income from the Dean and Chapter, he was also entitled to a generous share of the general income of the parish.

When, on occasion, the revenues of a rectory or vicarage were found to be insufficient to cover expenses at a university and to pay for the required substitute, a papal dispensation to hold a second benefice could be sought.   Thus Michael de Estona of the diocese of Salisbury,

---

[78] Et dominus examinavit Iohannem de Norton, capellanum, et quia invenit eum sufficienter litteratum, ipsum admisit... (*Reg. S. de Gandavo*, p. 847).

[79] *Ibid.*, p. 913.

[80] C. J. Godfrey, 'Non-residence of the parochial clergy,' *Church Quarterly Review*, 162 (1961) 443-444.

[81] *Reg. S. de Gandavo*, pp. 512-513.

[82] See J. R. H. Moorman, *Church Life in England in the Thirteenth Century* (Cambridge, 1946), 45-6.

[83] Quinil of Exeter, for example, made four marks a year the minimum payment for assistant priests in his diocese in 1287 (Wilkins, *Concilia*, II, 147).   After *Cum ex eo* licences had become a common feature of ecclesiastical life, bishops generally gave a rector who obtained a licence the power to make his own arrangements with his assistant priest; originally the custom had been for the bishop to decide the salary: see *Liber Sextus*, (Venice, 1584), col. 162, reporting a comment of Dominicus de S. Geminiano (ob. 1436).

who already had a *Cum ex eo* licence from his bishop, was given permission by the Pope in 1305 to take another benefice while studying, because: dicte ecclesie de Erchesfonte [Urchfont, Wilts.] redditus et proventus sint adeo tenues et exiles quod ex eis decenter sustentari non potes.'[84] A year before this, the same Pope had given John Luttrell, rector of Holin, Yorks., a five-year licence during which he was to have the fruits of his rectory and one other benefice.[85]

Under a normal episcopal licence, however, the revenues of one parish only would be involved; and these were to be used primarily and directly for the expenses of an absence for study. A rector or a vicar could not do exactly as he wished with the fruits of his parish once he had obtained a licence, for the only title he had to these fruits while absent was *studio litterarum*. For example, he was not entitled thereby to farm them out, without first negotiating a dispensation from the law of the church on farming.[86] But if he made proper use of these revenues, and obeyed *Cum ex eo* to the letter, his rights to the fruits of his living could not be impeded in any way while he was absent; and whenever he experienced any difficulty in obtaining these revenues, he could appeal in all confidence for a papal mandate to ensure that they were not withheld from him or diverted to some other purpose,[87] knowing that access to parish revenues for purposes of study was an integral part of Boniface's scheme to provide educational facilities for those engaged in the *cura animarum*.

IV

The example given above of the revenues of the perpetual vicarage of Winkfield in the diocese of Salisbury, calls for further comment. For it presumes that perpetual vicars could be granted *Cum ex eo* licences in the same way as rectors. There is not, indeed, any record in Simon of Ghent's register of a licence to William of Pagula, the vicar of Winkfield, nor, in fact, of a licence granted to any perpetual vicar whatsoever.

---

84. Reg. Vat. 52, fol. 16ᵛ; *Cal. Pap. Letters*, II, 3.

85 Reg. Vat. 51, fol. 188ʳ; *Cal. Pap. Letters*, I, 616. In 1418 Martin V gave a *Cum ex eo* licence for seven years to the rector of Islip, Oxfordshire, with permission to take another benefice (Reg. Lat. 189, fol. 168ᵛ).

86 See the letter of John XXII to a rector of diocese of Cahors: quodque per idem quinquennium disciplinis scholasticis insistendo in loco ubi vigeat studium generale, fructus, redditus et proventus ecclesie ad firmam concedere, prout tibi videbitur expedire, libere valeas, generalis concilii et qualibet alia constitucione contraria non obstante (Reg. Vat. 65, fol. 128ᵛ-129ʳ).

87 See Reg. Vat. fol. 116ᵛ for a mandate of John XXII in 1331 to various ecclesiastics to see that a rector studying at Avignon received his revenues without further hindrance.

But we do know for certain that Pagula, the great pastoral manualist, was released for studies after his institution to Winkfield in 1314, for we find him engaged in writing his *Summa summarum* at Oxford in 1320/1321, while finishing his studies in the faculty of canon law.[88] Yet none of the legislation concerning clerical education and licences to study which we have considered to date, seems to take perpetual vicars into account.   Thus the Fourth Lateran Council in 1215/16 made no provision whatsoever for grants of absence for purposes of study to those vicars about whose standard of living it was otherwise so solicitous;[89] and the constitutions of the Legates Otto and Ottobono, that regulated the ordination and residence of vicars, are also silent on this point.   Perpetual vicars, indeed, were bound by the nature of their office to a more demanding residence than that imposed on a rector;[90] and they were bound by the Legatine constitutions to swear to reside continually in their vicarages.[91]   How then can we account for the fact that some English perpetual vicars such as William of Pagula seem to have been able to avail themselves of the facilities allowed to rectors by Boniface's constitution *Cum ex eo?*

As it stands, this constitution can hardly be said to envisage *licentiae studendi* for any clerics other than rectors.   In fact, the influential English canonist John Acton held that perpetual vicars could not be granted a *Cum ex eo* licence.   If he would allow any release of vicars from their very strict obligation of personal residence, this should be within the meaning of the clause 'prout causa ratonabilis id exposcit' of the constitution *Licei canon* of Pope Gregory X: a prolonged absence on Church or State business, or brief excursions for reasons of health, honest recreation or pilgrimage.[92]   Writing about 1334-36,[92a] and thus

---

[88] See L. Boyle, 'The *Oculus sacerdotis* and some other works of William of Pagula,' *Transactions of the Royal Historical Society*, 5th series, 5 (1955), 81-110; A. B. Emden, *A Biographical Register of the University of Oxford*, III, (Oxford, 1959), s.n. Paul, William de.

[89] X. 3.5,30.

[90] Licet vero Rectores Ecclesiarum ad hoc (in propriis personis ecclesiis deservire) obligantur... tamen fortius est astrictus Vicarius ad obsequium personale quam Rector (John Acton on Otto, *De institutione vicariorum*, vv. *Cum vicarii teneantur*: in William Lyndwood, *Provinciale... cui adiciuntur Constitutiones Legatinae D. Othonis et D. Othoboni... cum profundissimis notationibus Jo. de Athona* (Oxford, 1679), p. 28).

[91] Ad vicariam statuimus nullum de caetero fore admittendum nisi... qui... iuret ibi residentiam facere, ac faciat eam continue corporalem... (Otto, *ibid.*, pp. 24-27).

[92] On the constitution *Ad vicariam* of Otto, vv. *residentiam, continue, ibid.*, pp. 26-27.

[92a] According to F. W. Maitland, *Roman Canon Law in the Church of England* (London, 1898) 6-7, Acton's gloss on the Legatine Constitutions was written between 1333 and 1348, but from remarks in Acton's *Septuplum* (Gonville and Caius College, Cambridge, MS 182,

after the publication of the Clementines, Acton was obliged to take account of a very short but important enactment of Clement V at the Council of Vienne.   There, in the constitution *Quae de ecclesiis,* Clement had ordained that certain provisions in the laws which governed rectors were henceforth to be understood as applying to perpetual vicars also: Quae de ecclesiis, curam animarum habentibus, per receptionem aliarum similium amittendis, ac de ipsarum rectoribus promovendis ad sacerdotium, et de eorum aetate a iure statuta noscentur, in perpetuis ecclesiarum parochialium vicariis et asumptis ad eas volumus obser-vari.[93]   The question, therefore, which Acton had to answer was whether this could be interpreted to mean that perpetual vicars could now avail of Boniface's *Cum ex eo.*   The point had been passed over, or perhaps had not occurred to, the canonist Willelmus de Monte Lauduno, whose *Apparatus* on the Clementines had appeared in 1319, two years after these had been promulgated by John XXII;[94]   but it had been dealt with at some length seven years later by the influential canonist Joannes Andreae in a manner which caused Acton a little anxiety. Glossing the words 'ad sacerdotium' of the decree *Quae de ecclesiis,* the Bolognese canonist had held that this meant not only that bishops could give licences *Cum ex eo* to vicars for purposes of study, but also that they could dispense vicars from proceeding to the priesthood until the completion of their studies.[95]   For Acton, faced with Otto's constitution *Ad vicariam,* and with Ottobono's renewal of it in 1268, this was to ignore a situation in which a local statute imposed a greater obligation of residence on vicars than did the general law of the church.   In England, where an oath of residence had to be taken as the Legatine constitutions demanded, it was impossible to act on Andreae's reasoning, since the Legatine oath could not be lightly held, and, considering its origin, could only be dispensed by an authority of equal rank with, or higher than, that which had imposed the oath.[96]

Some of Acton's other arguments are decidedly weak,[97] but this seems to be one which no English bishop could circumvent, if he had not an

---

fol. 1ʳ), written in 1346 (*ibid.,* fol. 140ᵛ), it is possible to maintain that he wrote the gloss while regent-master at Oxford, and thus probably during the period Sept. 1334-Sept. 1336 when he had a two-year licence to study and became a doctor of both laws.   For the career of Acton see Emden, *Biographical Register,* I, (1957), *s. n.* Acton, John de.

[93] Clementines I.7, cap. un.

[94] Bodleian Library, *MS Bodley* 247, fol. 163ᵛ-164ᵛ.   Much of de Monte Lauduno's long passage on the "four types of vicars" has been taken over by Acton in the part of the gloss on the Legatine Constitutions which we are discussing.

[95] *Liber Sextus... una cum Clementinis* (Venice, 1584), col. 67.

[96] Acton on Otto's *Ad vicariam, ed. cit.,* pp. 26-7.

express power to dispense from the Legatine oath once it had been taken, or to dispense from it beforehand; normally a direct papal dispensation, or a delegation of the power to dispense was required.[98] Thus in March 1317 the bishop of Norwich was given power to dispense four perpetual vicars from their legatine oath of residence,[99] and in June 1363 Urban V permitted the bishop of Carlisle to dispense ten vicars, 'so that they may study and lecture in canon law for seven years at a university.'[1] Almost two years later, when replying to the complaint of Cambridge University that bishops were slow to grant licences *Cum ex eo* to rectors and perpetual vicars, the same Pope reminded the university than an episcopal licence for study only covered those incumbents (rectors) in whose institution no oath of residence was involved; where such an oath had been taken (perpetual vicars), a dispensation from the oath had to be sought before there was any question of granting a licence.[2] In fact, absence for study without papal

---

[97] For example, Acton seems to hold that *Quae de ecclesiis* was only meant to embrace *Licet canon* and not *Cum ex eo* in any sense, and, therefore, that no vicar whatsoever, whether bound by an oath of residence or not, could avail himself of *Cum ex eo*. He is here in complete disagreement with what was commonly held by canonists, and by the Papacy. Thus Petrus de Ancharano, glossing *Quae de ecclesiis* towards the end of the fourteenth century, can note without qualification that a perpetual vicar should proceed to the priesthood within a year of institution (*Licet canon*): nisi causa studiorum episcopus dispensaverit secum in septem annis, quod potest sicut cum principali rectore (from *Cum ex eo*): *Super Clementinis Lectura Aurea*, (Lyons, 1549), p. 59.

[98] Delegation to give licences for study were often included in a legate's appointment (Reg. Vat. 56, fol. 269ʳ: to Cardinal Arnold, 1309; Reg. Vat. 58, fol. 291ʳ: to a legate in Lombardy, 1311). Thus the legate Adrian gave a licence to study to a Durham perpetual vicar in May 1498, because: ratione dicte vicarie quam obtines et in qua residenciam facere teneris, huiusmodi desiderium tuum [studendi] adimplere non potest, *canonica dispensacione desuper non obtenta* (*Register of Bishop Richard Fox*, ed. M. P. Howden, (Surtees Society, 1932), 116-117; cf. 133).

[99] ... tibi dispensandi cum quatuor perpetuis vicariis parochialium ecclesiarum tue diocesis quod usque ad triennium disciplinis scolasticis in loco vel locis ubi studium generale vigeat insistento, sive tuis et ecclesie tue obsequiis immorando, in ecclesiis huiusmodi residere minime teneantur, constitucionibus legatorum qui in partibus illis fuisse dicuntur et quibuslibet aliis in contrarium editis nequaquam obstantibus, eciam si iuxta constituciones easdem de perpetua et personali residencia in dictis ecclesiis facienda... prestiterint iuramentum, plenam et liberam concedimus auctoritate presencium facultatem... (Reg. Vat. 65, fol. 170ᵛ: cf. *Cal. Pap. Letters*, II, 142; see also Reg. Vat. 56, fol. 89ʳ: *Cal. Pap. Letters*, II, 47).

[1] Reg. Suppl. 37, fol. 136: *Cal. Pap. Petitions*, I, 437.

[2] Urban does not state this explicitly, but it underlies a proviso in his reply: ... Salvo quod super residenciam iuramentum non intervenerit, et quod sui ordinarii in aliis ubi iuramentum non est super residenciam dispensaverit (Reg. Suppl. 43, fol. 12ʳ; see p. 300, below).

authorization was treated like any other breach of the oath of residence, as a vicar of the diocese of Hereford found in 1320 when Pope John agreed to absolve him for the perjury he had committed 'by daring to break the legatine oath, deserting your vicarage for studies at Oxford,' but would not allow him to retain his living.[3] Any instances there are of licences to perpetual vicars granted on the ordinary power of a bishop do not, in fact, come from England, but from dioceses on the continent, and, strangely, from Ireland. Although Ireland as well as the rest of the British Isles was bound by the Legatine constitutions,[4] a reasonably clear case to the contrary seems to be that of a perpetual vicar in the diocese of Lismore, who was ordered to resign his vicarage in 1373. For although he had had a seven-year licence to study 'on the ordinary authority' of his bishop, his dismissal was not due to this but to the fact that he had broken one of the conditions upon which a *Cum ex eo* licence was issued.[5]

---

[3] Ex tenore siquidem peticionis tue accepimus quod tu olim perpetuam vicariam parochialis ecclesie de Bromiard Hereforden' diocesis fuisti canonice assecutus, et licet tu secundum formam constitucionum bone memorie Ottonis et Ottobonis dudum apostolice sedis in Anglia legatorum iurasses in eadem perpetua vicaria residenciam facere personalem, tu tamen *post et contra huiusmodi iuramentum et constituciones temere veniens, te a predicta vicaria per biennium absentasti Oxonie in iure canonico studendo* ... eiusdem vicarie, quam per quatuor-decim annos vel circiter tenuisti, percipiendo redditus et proventus... Nos... tecum auctoritate predicta super periurio quod incurristi non residendo in ipsa vicaria prout ex religione iuramenti super hoc per te, ut prefertur, prestiti tenebaris, de speciali gracia dispensamus. Volumus autem quod vicariam ipsam ex nunc omnino dimittere tenearis... (Reg. Vat. 70, fol. 375ᵛ-376ʳ). The *Cal. Pap. Letters*, II, 197, surely misconstructs the Pope's phrase when it says that "while studying at Oxford he has not resided for fourteen years." Barrett, the vicar in question, had in fact obtained a seven-year *Cum ex eo* licence as a rector in 1301 (*Reg. Swinfield*, p. 545). If he became a perpetual vicar in 1306, that is fourteen years before his supplication in 1320, then what may have happened was that he continued on at Oxford for the two years which remained of his *Cum ex eo* licence (te a predicta vicaria per biennium absentasti Oxonie), but only adverted to his transgression of the legatine oath some 14 years later.

[4] In quibus locis habent locum constituciones Ottonis et Ottoboni? Dic quod in Anglia, Scocia, Hibernia et Wallia, ut in constitucione Ottoboni Mandata Dei in prohemio, par. Nos igitur (William of Pagula, *Summa summarum*, MS Bodley 293, fol. 23ʳ; cf. Acton on this paragraph of Ottobono, and on Otto, *Quoniam decet*, v. Angliae).

[5] ... Sane peticio pro parte tua nobis nuper exhibita continebat, quod cum olim tu perpetuam vicariam parochialis ecclesie de Colmell Lismoren. diocesis tunc vacantem, canonice tibi collatam fuisses pacifice assecutus, et in subdiaconatus ordine constitutus existeres, venerabilis frater noster Thomas episcopus Lismoren. tecum ut litterarum studio in loco ubi illud vigeret generale insistendo usque ad septennium ad superiores ordines te facere promoveri minime tenereris auctoritate ordinaria dispensavit. Cum autem, sicut eadem peticio subiungebat, tu huiusmodi durante septennio, deficientibus tibi expensis, a predicto studio recesseris et *in dicta vicaria per unum annum et tres menses vel circiter residenciam*

Whatever the situation may have been in Ireland, it may be assumed that English perpetual vicars would have had to seek a papal dispensation from the legatine oath before they could be given a *Cum ex eo* licence.[6] In the case of William of Pagula's release for studies from his perpetual vicarage at Winkfield, it is hardly likely that the problem of the applicability of the Clementine decree *Quae de ecclesiis* was known to Ghent, his bishop, at the time of Pagula's licence, since this decree would not be at all familiar to bishops in England until its promulgation by John XXII in October 1317,[7] two months after Ghent's death. However, apart from a papal dispensation from the legatine oath, there was, possibly, another way open to bishops in England. There is, for instance, a notable difference between the record of Pagula's admission to Winkfield and that of his successor, John Lavyngton, in 1332. Where Lavyngton is said to have been admitted 'de continue residendo iuxta constitucionem Ottoboni iuratus cum onere personaliter ministrandi,'[8] Pagula, in the words of Ghent's register, was admitted simply 'cum onere continue residendi et personaliter ministrandi.'[9] Although the formulae in which Ghent's register records admissions to vicarages are loosely worded and not always consistent,[10] the omission of any mention of an oath from the registration of Pagula's admission may not be entirely

---

feceris ad sacerdocium non promotus, licet postmodum, habitis expensis huiusmodi, reversus fueris ad studium memoratum, et ex tunc prefatam vicariam detinueris, prout adhuc detines, fructus percipiens ex eadem, dispensacione canonica super hoc non obtenta... Nos itaque... tuis in hac parte supplicacionibus inclinati, omnem inhabilitatis et infamie maculam... penitus abolemus. Volumus autem quod tu predictam vicariam ex nunc realiter et omnino dimittas... (Reg. Vat. 284, fol. 4ᵛ; cfr *Cal Pap. Letters*, IV, 185). For other examples of *Cum ex eo* licences to Irish perpetual vicars see, for instance, *The Register of John Swayne, Archbishop of Armagh, 1418-1439*, ed. D. A. Chart, (Belfast, 1935) 63: licence for seven years' study on 31 August 1427 to Philip Norreys on his admission to the perpetual vicarage of St. Nicholas, Dundalk.

6 See, for example, apart from cases already mentioned, dispensations for vicars: non obstantibus Ottonis et Ottoboni constitutionibus, in Innocent VII's pontificate (1404-1406) in Reg. Vat. 119, fol. 121ᵛ (Bath and Wells), 126ʳ (Lincoln), 127ᵛ (Bath and Wells), 141ʳ (York), 142ᵛ (Carlisle), 148ᵛ (York), etc.

7 John XXIII sent the Clementines to the University of Bologna on 25 October 1317 (*CIC*, II, 1131), and to Oxford at the same time (cf. Salisbury Cath. Library, MS 122, fol. 14ᵛ; Cambridge University Library, MS Ii.iii.7, fol. 102ᵛ), some six months, it may be noted, after the dispensation granted to the bishop of Norwich (above, p. 292). Ghent was not present at the Council of Vienne, where *Quae de ecclesiis* was first promulgated, having been excused by Clement V from attendance (E. Müller, *Das Konzil von Vienne* (Münster-in-W., 1934) 37).

8 Salisbury Diocesan Registry, MS *Reg. Wyvil*, II (2), fol. 19ʳ.

9 *Ibid.*, MS *Reg. S. de Gandavo*, fol. 132ᵛ.

10 Cf. *Reg. S. de Gandavo* (edition), pp. 559, 662, 825.

arbitrary.   Certainly a bishop could not remit the legatine oath in whole
or in part,[11] but he could, presumably, defer the taking of the oath for a
reasonable cause: in much the same way, therefore, as a rector with a
Cum ex eo licence was not bound to the *cura animarum* as such until he
had finished his studies, a perpetual vicar of promise conceivably could
be excused from the taking of the legatine oath until he had returned
from the university and had formally taken over the *cura animarum;* the
legal fiction would not be very different from that employed in the
grant of *Cum ex eo* licences to rectors, especially where there was, as at
Winkfield, a resident assistant priest who was used to the parish.   In
fact the wording of the legatine constitution does not state beyond all
doubt that the oath had to be taken before institution; certainly the
phrase 'statuimus nullum de caetero fore admittendum nisi... iuret ibi
residentiam facere' has not the force of 'nisi... iurasset' or of 'nisi... iuret
ante admissionem.'   On this point it is interesting to note that Acton,
commenting on the word 'admittendum' in the legatine constitution
quoted above, says rather mildly that 'it is fitting (expedit) that the oath
should be taken before admission';[12] he does not state that it was necessary for the validity of the admission that the oath should be taken on
the spot.

Since there is no record of a papal dispensation to Pagula, it therefore
seems possible to hold that Ghent, or any other bishop in a similar
situation, simply postponed the legatine oath, and thus avoided the need
of a papal dispensation or the danger of perjury.   At all events, the
question of the release of perpetual vicars for study was complicated in
England by the legatine oath.[13]   But where the residence of vicars was
not governed by any special legislation such as that of Otto and Otto-

---

11 See Acton on Otto, *Ad vicariam, ed. cit.,* p. 126, v. *faciat.*

12 *Ibid.,* v. *admittendum.*

13 It is interesting to note that an Oxford canonist, Thomas Walkyngton, writing about
1377, disagrees with Acton, and is of the opinion that bishops could dispense perpetual
vicars in England. Since the legatine constitutions were only *consilia,* the bishops could
choose to ignore them on occasion: Hoc non potest esse iuxta causam *cum ex eo* quod persona contra consilium superioris non licet inferiori dispensare. Sed ille constituciones
Ottoboni et Ottonis sunt consilium; ideo... Ex quibus concludo quod non obstante statuto
Ottoboni potest episcopus dispensare... (Canterbury, Dean and Chapter Library, MS C. 12,
fol. 97ᵛ-98ʳ).   William of Pagula, however, is unexpectedly silent on some of the points
discussed above. Thus, although he quotes *Quae de ecclesiis* with reference to the ordination
of vicars to the priesthood (*Summa summarum,* MS *Bodley* 293, fol. 49ʳ), and discusses *Cum
ex eo* licences and the release of rectors for study, he nowhere deals with perpetual
vicars and study, nor with the extent to which *Quae de ecclesiis* put vicars on an equal
footing with rectors. See also *Summa summarum* fol. 210ᵛ-211ʳ.

bono, there was no difficulty, after Clement's *Quae de ecclesiis*, in granting licences *Cum ex eo* as readily to vicars as to rectors. The perpetual vicar was, after all, as much committed to, and engaged in, the pastoral care as the rector; and, no less than the rector, would have need of, and derive benefit from, the facilities afforded by Boniface's scheme of allowing parishes to pay for the education of those clerics to whom they had been entrusted.

V

It goes without saying that Boniface's constitution was far from perfect and that his measure never really solved the abiding problem of *ignorantia sacerdotum*. Yet it cannot be denied that the promulgation of *Cum ex eo* in 1298 is a moment of considerable importance in the history of medieval education, if only because of the examples given above of the care with which the provisions of the constitution were observed. It is therefore surprising that the constitution *Cum ex eo* has merited little attention from historians. It rarely occurs in works on the history of the canon law or of education in the middle ages;[14] it is almost wholly absent from studies of the career and pontificate of Pope Boniface VIII.[15]

[14] For example, it does not receive any treatment in Hasting Rashdall's *History of the Universities*, in Leach's *Educational Charters*, in Lynn Thorndike's *University Records and Life in the Middle Ages* (New York, 1944), in Stelling-Michaud's fine summary of recent research on the history of the Universities ('L'Histoire des Universités au Moyen Age et à la Renaissance au cours des vingt-cinq dernières années,' *XIe Congrès International des Sciences Historiques, Rapports* (Stockholm, 1960), I, 97-143) or in P. Kibre, *Scholarly Privileges in the Middle Ages. The Rights, Privileges and Immunities of Scholars and Universities at Bologna, Padua, Paris, and Oxford* (London, 1961); and it only gets a passing mention in F. W. Oediger, *Über die Bildung der Geistlichen im späten Mittelalter* (Leiden-Köln, 1953), p. 59, n. 5, and in A. F. Sokolich, *Canonical provisions for Universities and Colleges* (Washington, 1956) 25. On the other hand, many editors of bishops' registers, and some historians of the Church in England in the fourteenth century, have remarked on the number of licences given by bishops, notably, Miss E. C. Carlyle, *The Office of an English Pishop in the first half of the Fourteenth Century* (Pennsylvania, 1903) 21; Miss Kathleen Edwards, 'Bishops and Learning in the Reign of Edward II,' *Church Quarterly Review*, 138 (1944), 79; and C. J. Godfrey, 'Non-residence of parochial clergy in the fourteenth century,' *ibid.*, 162 (1961), 433-446. A translation of a typical *Cum ex eo* licence (from Carlisle diocese, 1315) is given by C. J. Offler, *The Bishop's Register* (London, 1929) 136; there are also some notes on licences in I. J. Churchill, *Canterbury Administration* (London, 1933), I, 115-117, and in A. Hamilton Thompson, *The English Clergy* (Oxford, 1947) 103-104.

[15] For example, those of H. Finke, *Aus den Tagen Bonifaz VIII* (Münster-in-W., 1903), T.S.R. Boase, *Boniface VIII* (London, 1933), S. Silvia, *Bonifazio VIII* (Rome, 1949). A strong plea, in which *Cum ex eo* is mentioned briefly, for an evaluation of the full character of Boniface VIII has been made by G. Le Bras, 'Boniface VIII, Symphoniste et modérateur.' *Mélanges Louis Halphen*, (Paris, 1951) 383-384.

This reticence becomes all the more remarkable when one notes with what enthusiasm bishops responded to the constitution, and in what numbers the parochial clergy enjoyed licences *Cum ex eo*. Indeed, it is not an exaggeration to state that in contrast to the parochial clergy of the thirteenth century, those of the fourteenth century flocked to the universities. There were, of course, bishops of the stature of Grosseteste of Lincoln, Cantilupe of Hereford and Pecham of Canterbury in the thirteenth century, who were as acutely aware of the need for an educated clergy as the many bishops in England who granted *Cum ex eo* licences in the next century, but the real difference between the practice of the two centuries, with respect to university studies for the parochial clergy, may be attributed to the fact that after the appearance of Boniface's constitution there was now an official directive which bishops could follow with equanimity, secure in the knowledge that they were not conniving in any way at a form of non-residence which was not regularized beyond all reproach. Few, indeed, of the astonishingly large number of licences granted in England in the fourteenth century fail to include the significant phrase, 'secundum constitutionem domini Bonifatii octavi.' It is at once a key to, and a justification of, the bishops' toleration of 'absenteeism' from the pastoral care.

The number of licences granted by English bishops in the fifty years after the promulgation of *Cum ex eo* is indeed remarkable; if nothing else, it suggests that the desire to promote the education of the parochial clergy was stronger and more vital than in the days of the abortive attack on *Licet canon* at the Council of Reading in 1279. In the diocese of Winchester, for example, Henry Woodlock granted some 105 licences between 1305 and 1316; in that of Worcester almost 100 were granted by Walter Reynolds beween 1308 and 1313; in Exeter Bishop Stapledon gave over 400 licences between 1307 and 1326, and Bishop Brantyngham some 86 from 1370-1394.[16] And if Hamo Hethe of Rochester gave only 43 licences in a very long episcopate (1319-1357), Bishop Drokensford of Bath and Wells kept up a steady flow of rectors to the universities, issuing 15 licences in 1320, 17 in 1321, 19 in 1322, and 16 in 1323,[17] while in the ten years of Bishop Cobham's episcopate at Worcester (1317-1327), 93 licences for an absence of 1 year were given, 37 for two years, 11 for three years, 1 for five years, and 5 for the maximum licence.[18]

---

16 For these figures see Godfrey, *art. cit.*, pp. 434-435, etc.
17 See E. C. Lyle, *op. cit.*, p. 21.
18 E. H. Pearce, *Thomas de Cobham, Bishop of Worcester, 1317-1327* (London, 1923) 101-

The episcopate of Simon of Ghent, bishop of Salisbury (1297-1316) is, perhaps, the most striking and documented of all, and some of our best examples of the working of *Cum ex eo* have been taken from it in the pages above. He issued his first licence 'secundum formam novae constitutionis domini Bonifatii octavi' within six months of the promulgation of the constitution in the Sext, the forerunner, indeed, of the large number of 308 licences which he was to grant during the seventeen and a half years of his episcopate.[19] The majority of these were for periods varying from one to three years, a small portion running to the maximum seven years. As is only to be expected of a former Chancellor, the University of Oxford was the *studium* usually specified in these licences, with permission here and there for other *studia* in England (Cambridge, Marlborough, 'alibi in Anglia ubi viget studium generale'), and a few licences for study abroad at Paris or Orleans.

The extensive use made by bishops of the faculty to grant licences to study, and the interest that the constitution *Cum ex eo* evoked at all levels of ecclesiastical life, leave one with a distinct impression that Boniface's measure played a very important part in the life of the church from the beginning of the fourteenth century until the Council of Trent, both in England and in Europe.[19a] Indeed, the constitution was regarded so highly, and looked upon as so vital to the health of the *cura animarum,* that the Council of Constance made an explicit exception of *Cum ex eo* licences when it decreed a clean sweep of all dispensations at its third session 21 March 1418: 'Nos igitur, sacro approbante concilio, omnes dispensationes a quibuscumque pro Romanis pontifi-

---

105; *idem,* ed. *The Register of Thomas de Cobham,* (Worchestershire Hist. Soc., 1930) 250-263. Many more instances could be given from episcopal registers, but it must be remembered that the number of rectors released for studies generally is smaller than the number of licences issued, since many of these licences were extensions of previous licences.

[19] See K. Edwards, *art. cit.,* p. 79.

[19a] For England, the most impressive evidence, apart from certain episcopal registers, is to be found in Mr A. B. Emden's great *Biographical Register of the University of Oxford,* 3 vols. (Oxford, 1957-9), where large numbers of licences to study are recorded. For Europe in general the evidence at present is less plentiful, mainly because few episcopal registers are in print. Yet a good picture of the application of *Cum ex eo* in continental dioceses can be built up from cases that occur in papal registers. Thus the summary of a petition in a papal letter will often state that the petitioner has a licence *Cum ex eo* issued on "the ordinary authority" of, for example, the ordinary of Rodez (Reg. Vat. 55, fol. 135^r), Agen (56, fol. 14^r, 31^r; 59, fol. 132^v), Rouen (59, fol. 180^r), Cahors (*ibid.,* fol. 248r), Mende (58, fol. 147^r), Angoulême (*ibid.,* fol. 197^r), Lausanne (59, fol. 17^v), Utica (*ibid.,* fol. 182^v), Braga (60, fol. 180^r), Porto (*ibid.,* fol. 248^r), all from the pontificate of Clement V (1305-1314).

cibus se gerentibus concessas quibuscumque electis, confirmatis. seu provisis ad ecclesias, monasteria, prioratus conventuales, decanatus, archdiaconatus, et alia quaecumque beneficia, quibus certus ordo debitus est, vel annexus,... praeter illas quae secundum formam constitutionis Bonifacii VIII quae incipit Cum ex eo factae sunt, revocamus.' [20]

From a period some fifty years earlier there is an even more striking instance, which we may quote in full, of the place which Boniface's constitution had won for itself, when, in 1365, the Chancellor and Masters of Cambridge University went so far as to petition Pope Urban V to allow the university to grant, among other things, licences *Cum ex eo* to rectors and vicars whom bishops had refused; English bishops, the petition said, were proving 'inordinately difficult' about issuing *Cum ex eo* dispensations, thus unjustly hindering clerics with a cure of souls from proficiency in branches of learning which would be of benefit to themselves and to others:

> Supplicatur sanctitas vestra ex parte... cancellarii et doctorum et magistrorum regentium et non regentium universitatis nostre Cantebrigg' Elien. diocesis, quod cum locorum ordinarii suis rectoribus et curatis studere volentibus ad dandam licentias studendi in forma capituli Cum ex eo sepius se reddant ultra modum difficiles, propter quod curati ipsi ut in huiusmodi scientiis proficient, per quas sibi et aliis reddi possent multipliciter fructuosi, sunt indebite impediti ; quare, omnibus et singulis parochialium ecclesiarum rectoribus et perpetuis vicariis, ac aliis, beneficia quecumque etiam curata aut dignitates, personatus vel officia, cum cura vel sine, etiam in ecclesiis cathedralibus obtinentibus, in dicta universitate studere volentibus, etiam si in presbiteratus ordine fuerint constitui, iura canonica seu facultatem theologie, necnon et in subdiaconatus vel diaconatus ordine constituti, iura civilia ad triennium audire, legere et in eisdem studere ac fructus et cetera beneficiorum suorum interim integre recipere valeant, licentia ordinarii petita nec obtenta, quodque subdiaconi vel diaconi interim ad alios superiores ordines non teneantur promoveri, dignemini licentiam impertiri cum omnibus clausulis oportunis.

---

[20] H. von der Hardt, *Corpus Actorum et Decretorum Magni Concilii Constantiensis* (Frankfurt-Leipzig, 1699), IV, 1537; H. Finke, *Acta Concilii Constantiensis*, II, (Münster-in-W., 1923), 632-633. See also John Gerson, *Opera Omnia*, ed. L. E. du Pin, (Paris, 1727), III, 90 (*Regulae morales*, 68). The papal system of dispensation had deteriorated from the pontificate of Clement VI (1342-1352) onwards, and many rectors and vicars were given licences : vel studio litterarum vel in curia episcopali vel in uno ex beneficiis tuis, on terms similar to those regulating ordination in *Cum ex eo;* see, for example Reg. Vat. 159 (1343). By the end of the fourteenth century some papal licences for study were startlingly generous, giving licences "for life" to rectors and perpetual vicars: see, for example, Reg. Lat., 45, from the pontificate of Boniface IX. The only study-licences that the Council of Constance allowed to continue were simple *Cum ex eo* licences.

In the matter of *Cum ex eo* licences for the parochial clergy, Pope Urban gave the university little satisfaction, replying to their petition in a manner which in fact did not withdraw these licences from the control of the bishops, nor remove the obstacle of the legatine oath of residence sworn by perpetual vicars:

> Placet quod studentes omnes fructus beneficiorum suorum percipiant ad triennium. Item placet quod non teneantur promoveri infra dictum tempus habentes parochiales ecclesias, dummodo infra annum recipiant subdiaconatus ordinem. Salvo quod super residentiam iuramentum non intervenerit, et quod sui ordinarii, in aliis ubi iuramentum non est, super residentiam dispensaverint.[21]

Some two centuries later, in the middle period of the Council of Trent, we find that *Cum ex eo* is still a force, although reformers like Reginald Pole had misgivings about it, since so much depended on the goodwill of those who obtained licences and on the vigilance of bishops. At a national synod in London in 1556, Pole drew up some very severe legislation on residence, allowing, however, for absences 'prout causa rationabilis id exposcet' (*Licet canon*) and for those 'studiorum causa' (*Cum ex eo*). But he begged bishops to make sure that candidates for licences for study were of good quality, and that the leave of absence was really spent in study at a university.[22]

The legislation of the Council of Trent on residence (1547, 1563) and on the setting-up of seminaries (1563) did not do away immediately with licences *Cum ex eo*. For although the Congregation of the Council, the official interpreter of the Tridentine decrees, soon took exception to licences for study, it was forced to confess that non-residence in accordance with Boniface's constitution could be allowed on occasion, 'cum id non sit contra ius commune, nec contra concilium, sed solummodo

---

[21] *Reg. Supplicationum* 43 (formerly 41), fol. 12^r; cf. *Cal. Pap. Petitions*, I, 504.

[22] Eorum autem, quibus, studiorum gratia, ad certum tempus indultum sit, ne ad eos ordines promoveri teneantur, ad quos ratione beneficiorum quae obtinent promovendi essent, et ut absentes nihilominus fructus percipiant, quia plerique in nulla ex universitatibus, in quibus studium generale viget, sed in locis ubi nullus est studiorum usus atque exercitatio commorantur, et non pauci etiam in studiis generalibus degentes, quidvis potius aliud agunt, quam ut litteris operam dent: idcirco ne dolus et fraus hac in re cuiquam patrocinetur, omnibus locorum ordinariis mandamus, ut posthac, antequam ulli suae iurisdictionis huiusmodi indulta concedant, diligenter inquirant an is ad litterarum studia sit aptus, et an eae disciplinae, quibus operam se daturum profiteatur, tales sint, quae ei conveniant, et ecclesiae futurae sint utiles, et an temere vel in fraudem hanc licentiam petat... (*Reformatio Angliae ex Decretis Reginaldi Pole Cardinalis Sedis Apostolicae Legati* (Rome, 1562), 13).

contra decisionem congregationis.' [23]　By the mid-seventeenth century, however, the Congregation had succeeded in outlawing *Cum ex eo* licences; and the fact that *Cum ex eo* had outlived its time had impressed itself on most manuals of the pastoral care and of canon law.[24]　In 1661 Prosper Fagnanus, who was secretary of the Congregation of the Council and who in fact provides one of the best discussions of Boniface's constitution, would admit at the end that he had only been arguing 'disputationis causa,' when he had proved that *Cum ex eo* licences were not at variance with the Tridentine legislation on the residence of the parochial clergy.[25]

But it was the Tridentine legislation on seminaries which really outmoded *Cum ex eo* as a practical, and not wholly unsuccessful, means of providing some education for the parochial clergy, in the absence of anything more positive.　Where Boniface had proposed that each parish should directly sustain the educational expenses of the particular cleric to whose charge it was committed, Trent had now made the provision of an educated parish clergy a charge of a diocese as a whole; and where Boniface had merely encouraged a general education of not more than seven years' duration after institution to a parish and before ordination, Trent had imposed a course of ecclesiastical studies of much the same length, without which one could not be admitted to the priesthood,

---

23 See the decision of the Congregation on 12 July 1601 allowing a parish priest to finish his studies at Coimbra, in *Summa Apostolicarum Decisionum*, (Lyons, 1703), p. 328.　Earlier the Congregation had ruled that *Cum ex eo* licences could only be given to clerics under thirty years of age, and that: haec facultas solum habet locum in parochialibus ante Concilium Tridentinum obtentis, quia in obtentis post Concilium praedicta licentia non datur (*Decisiones et Declarationes Illustrissimorum Cardinalium Sacri Concilii Tridentini Interpretum*, ed. J. de Gallemart, (Douai, 1615), 147-8).　See also the "Declaratio quod gratiae de non residendo et percipiendo fructus ratione studii non valeant sine consensu ordinarii" of Pius IV on 24 November 1564, in *Canones et Decreta Concilii Tridentini*, ed. H. Lutius Calliensis, (Venice, 1566), appendix, Bb iv.

24 Quamvis olim potuerit parochus studiorum causa abesse per septennium ex consensu et licentia episcopi, ut deciditur in capitulo Cum ex eo, De electione, Libro Sexto, hodie tamen id non permittitur (A. Barbosa, *Pastoralis Sollicitudinis sive De officio et potestate Parochi* (Lyons, 1640), 77). See also *Collectanea Doctorum in Concilium Tridentinum* (Venice 1643), p. 176, n. 55; J. B. Possevinus, *De officio curati*, ed. A. Victorelli, (Venice, 1668), 14); S. d'Abreù, *Institutio Parochi*, (Venice, 1699), 71.

25 Caeterum haec disputationis gratia dicta sunt: nam proposito in S. Congregatione Concilii dubio infrascripto, videlicet, an ordinarius possit concedere licentiam parocho, qui parochialem post Concilium obtinuit, ut in publica universitate studiis sacrae Theologiae vel Canonum vacare possit?... Sanctissimus respondit non posse, jussitque Episcopos ab huiusmodi licentiae concessione abstinere (P. Fagnanus, *Commentaria in V. libros Decretalium* (Cologne, 1705), III, 87ᵇ, commenting on *Super specula*, X. 5.5,5: *De Magistris* and *Cum ex eo*).

302

much less to the *cura animarum*. There is, nevertheless, a continuity between Boniface and Trent that is more real than apparent. The emphases are different, but the fundamental idea is the same. In fact, the Tridentine seminary legislation improved on rather than rejected the solution of the problem of the education of the parochial clergy which had held the field from the promulgation of Boniface VIII's constitution *Cum ex eo* in 1298.

Angelicum, Rome, **and**
Pontifical Institute of Mediaeval Studies

IX

ASPECTS OF CLERICAL EDUCATION
IN FOURTEENTH-CENTURY ENGLAND

When we use the words "clerical education," just what do we mean? Do we mean "education as a cleric," or do we mean the "general education" which clerics had? If we mean "education as a cleric," then we should first ask the question, "Just what education was necessary for a cleric?" — in this case for the education of a parochial or "parish" priest in fourteenth-century England.

The answer is, precious little. As William of Pagula, a parochial priest himself, put it in his *Oculus sacerdotis* (1320-26) in a passage which was repeated by another English manualist, John de Burgh, in his *Pupilla oculi* about sixty years later:

> Ordinands are not to be examined too rigidly, but rather
> in a summary fashion and leniently. Too great a degree
> of perfection is not required as long as a reasonable
> literacy, a legitimate age and a good character are not
> wanting to the candidate. The good opinion in which a
> candidate publicly is held can be the equivalent of an
> examination; indeed it is clear from the *Decretum* (of
> Gratian) that local candidates for the priesthood are to
> be spared examination.[1]

Thomas Aquinas, some fifty or sixty years earlier than Pagula, was just as undemanding. Strictly speaking, he said, all that a candidate needs for promotion to orders is the knowledge which enables him to do what is proper to his order. It is not necessary to have an all-round knowledge of scripture. A priest as such should know how to administer the sacraments. A man destined for the *cura animarum* should, as well, "know those things which pertain to the teaching of faith and morals." Unlike a bishop, he does not have to have a command of difficult legal points (he can turn to his betters for these), but simply a knowledge of what his parishioners, by the law of the church, should believe and observe. He does not have to know "how to prove the things in which we believe and hope (these are invisible, anyway), but should know in general how to demonstrate the probability of faith and hope," a task, Aquinas concluded, "which does not demand any great learning."[2]

How and where the "sufficient learning" which Pagula and de Burgh mention was obtained, is not at all clear, especially in the case of rural aspirants to the priesthood and the pastoral care, but it seems likely that much of the "scientia" necessary for the pastoral care was picked up in towns and cities by attendance at a cathedral school or at the local theological schools of the Friars, and in rural areas by apprenticeship. The "good local reputation" of which Pagula speaks probably was sufficient of itself for the minor or preparatory orders. After that the candidate resorted to the local parish priest for instruction in the meaning and administration of the sacraments, particularly of the Eucharist. And if candidates had sufficient Latin, there were simple manuals to which they could turn for general information. The thirteenth century had left a fair legacy of these, not to speak of those which were produced in the fourteenth century itself. To mention only a few from thirteenth-century England, all of which survive in a goodly number of manuscripts, there were, in order of time, the *Summa* of Thomas Chabham, subdean of Salisbury (c. 1220), the "Qui bene praesunt" of Richard Wethersett (c. 1230), the *Templum Domini* (c. 1240) and other tractates of Robert Grosseteste, bishop of Lincoln, the *Summa iuniorum* of the Dominican Simon Hinton (c. 1250).[3] And if some or all of these proved too elaborate, there were always pamphlets such as the popular *Quinque verba*, a tract that usually takes up three or four folios in the twelve manuscripts I know of, and which lucidly, and in the least burdensome fashion possible, covers "all that should be believed, loved, observed, avoided, done."[4]

At the beginning of the fourteenth century, too, there was a scattering of university graduates in parishes to whom one could have turned for help or instruction. For although it has been well said by

Pantin and others that a university was not a seminary, the plain fact is that most of those who attended the universities of the thirteenth and fourteenth centuries ended up in a *cura animarum* of one sort or another, and were not unaware while at a university of the pastoral value of courses in theology and law at Oxford and Paris and elsewhere. In the Paris of the thirteenth century one certainly catches the pastoral interests of the audience in the theological schools from the questions put to the various masters at the periodical open sessions of the *Quodlibeta*.[5]

Many of these university men, when they took up residence later as rectors or vicars in parishes, kept up their learning, and were not unaware of their less fortunate fellows. One such, at least, was William of Pagula, vicar of Winkfield in Windsor Forest from 1314 to c. 1334. His *Oculus sacerdotis*, written just after he had returned to his parish from Oxford with a doctorate in canon law, was highly successful, and dominates the fourteenth century in England. College libraries, monasteries, priories, and various of the higher clergy possessed it. More importantly, it became part, so to speak, of the parish furniture in the period 1350-1450, when it was replaced by its "second edition," the *Pupilla oculi* of 1384.

The famous Mertonian and canon of Chichester, Simon Bredon (d. 1368) bequeathed his copy of the *Oculus* (which formerly had belonged to a vicar in Warwickshire) to William de Wakefield, vicar of Sevenoaks, Kent. Master Thomas de Laxham (d. 1382), rector of Feltwell, Norfolk, stipulated that his copy should be chained at the right-hand of the choir at Feltwell, where the vicar was wont to sit, "so that it may remain perpetually in the church for the common use of all the ministers of the church and of others." The church of Willingham, Cambridgeshire, owned an *Oculus* in 1369, while the church of Stanton All Saints, some miles away, had another. Over in Herefordshire, William Davy, rector of Kingsland, bequeathed his *Oculus* to that church in 1383. In 1385 John Bakyngton, rector of Harrow, Middlesex, left his "small book called the *Oculus sacerdotis*" to Stokenchurch, Wiltshire. At Emberton, Buckinghamshire, there is a brass of a priest in vestments with the inscription, "Pray for the soul of Master John Morden, once rector of this church, who during his lifetime gave a missal, an *Ordinale*, and a *Pars oculi* to his church." The church of St Martin in Ludgate, London, was provided with a copy of the *Oculus* by Roger Shirreve, clerk, in 1392, who also donated 17 shillings "in memory of the ten commandments and the seven deadly sins."[6]

*

Some of those who possessed copies of the *Oculus* were, like its author, William of Pagula, beneficiaries of a new opportunity for university education which had arisen just at the end of the thirteenth century. So if by "clerical education" one means a "general" clerical education rather than a basic one which all priests were expected to have before admission to the *cura animarum*, then the picture is a little brighter.

Until the end of the thirteenth century those who chose to join the ranks of the parish clergy had little chance of obtaining such a general education. There are, of course, instances of rectors being allowed to study at a university in the thirteenth century, but they are few and far between. The situation became particularly difficult after 1274, when the Second Council of Lyons imposed strict residence on rectors, and ordered that anyone admitted to a living as a rector should become a priest within a year of his institution. In 1298, however, Boniface VIII revolutionized the pastoral care by introducing a scheme whereby the parochial clergy could have access to a general education at universities before taking a *cura animarum* professionally. For reasons which I have suggested elsewhere, Boniface decided to mitigate the Lyons constitution and to inaugurate a system of episcopal licenses for study. In a constitution (known as *Cum ex eo* from its opening words) which he issued in his *Liber sextus decretalium* on 5 March 1298, Boniface gave bishops the power to grant leave of absence for study at a university to the parochial clergy for periods up to a maximum of seven years, but on certain conditions:

1. that those to whom licenses were granted should take on the order of subdiaconate within a year of their institution as rector;
2. that they should become deacons and priests within a year of the termination of the license;
3. that suitable priests should take over the running of their parishes while they were away at a university;

4. that these substitutes should be paid by those licensed for study
   out of the income of the parish (to which, of course, the licensed
   rector had full access, and out of which he supported himself at
   the university).[7]

It should be understood, however, that this licensing system was
not designed to allow rectors who were priests already to attend
university, though some such availed themselves of it. Rather, its
purpose was to attract young and promising clerics to parish work
who were not yet subdeacons (or, at least, who were not yet priests).
Normally, rectors who enjoyed *Cum ex eo* licenses were not "parish
priests," nor priests at all, when they were given licenses. Most were
simple clerics. John Wyclif, for example, who had a *Cum ex eo*
license (probably a full seven-year one) to study at Oxford from
1363-70, was not a priest at the time, and probably did not become a
priest until 1371, a year after his license terminated on 13 April
1370. William Waynflete, later bishop of Winchester (1447-86), was
only eighteen years of age when he became a rector by papal dispensation on 16 December 1410. Six years later, when he was 24, he was
given a three-year *Cum ex eo* license on 26 September 1416. He was
not yet a priest, and in fact did not become one until 1 June 1420,
towards the end of the year's grace which he had by the terms of
Cum ex eo after the end of his license on 25 September 1419.[8]

Although, by and large, those to whom licenses for study were
given were not yet priests, the purpose, all the same, of *Cum ex eo*
was not to educate these young men for the priesthood. All that
Boniface VIII says in his constitution was that the young men were
to pursue "scholastic disciplines." A general rather than a purely
clerical education was what he had in mind. The licensees were free
to study any legitimate subject. Some who already were Masters of
Arts could proceed to a higher faculty such as theology or canon law.
Those who had not, would just have enough time to earn a degree in
Arts if they were in possession of a full seven-year license. Those who
had only a one-year or two-year license, or anything less than a full
license, could pick and choose, depending on their needs. But whatever the term of the license, all licensees were expected to study
during that time and not simply browse around. Since, as the Dominican John Bromyard put it in his *Summa praedicantium* about

1348, "the final cause of *Cum ex eo* was to promote a literate clergy," those who had licenses "should study some theology for a while, and then, without waiting for a degree, return to their parishes and glorify God by confirming their parishioners in faith by word and example."[9] John Wyclif, himself a beneficiary of the system, speaks approvingly of *Cum ex eo* on several occasions, and says that "it is permissible for a rector to collect the seed of faith for a time outside of his parish in schools of theology so that he may sow in his parish when the time is ripe."[10]

Wyclif, of course, is probably referring to his own experience, since he had already spent some time in the Faculty of Arts at Oxford before he obtained a rectory and qualified for a *Cum ex eo* license, but the statute as such does not speak of theological studies. A general culture, whether theological or not, was the aim of *Cum ex eo* and not preparation for the priesthood. If the young rector was able to pick up some theology on the side while at the university, so much the better, but this was not ever mentioned by Boniface.

*

Statistics on the application of *Cum ex eo* in England are not hard to come by, but whether they are watertight or not is another matter. The magnificent series of bishops' registers for the fourteenth century, mostly unedited or uncalendared as yet, generally record these licenses, though not always by name. To rely solely on the published calendars of these registers is hazardous, however. Many editors, both past and present, do not make any distinction in their calendars between general licenses to study (to canons or arch-deacons or pluralists, for example) and *Cum ex eo* licenses (which, as a rule, applied only to simple rectors). Even those who are aware of the specific nature of *Cum ex eo* are often not conversant enough with the terms of the constitution to recognize and record it as such when it is not mentioned by name in the registers.

It is unwise, too, to base one's statistics solely on A. B. Emden's great biographical registers for Oxford and Cambridge. For although Mr. Emden bravely examined "all the surviving episcopal rolls and registers of England, Wales and Ireland, either in manuscript, or, where available, in printed texts, and sometimes both,"[11] he never refers to *Cum ex eo* by name in his entries, and simply uses the general term "license to study" without descrimination. Many of these licenses are, indeed, pure *Cum ex eo* licenses, but others, when one looks at Emden's source, are not. As well, Mr. Emden included in his registers only those licenses which specifically noted Oxford or Cambridge as the *studium generale* at which the license was to be held (unless he had some other evidence that it was to Oxford or Cambridge that the licensee went); consequently, there are many licenses to study in episcopal registers which do not find a place in the entries in Emden. Further, many of the printed sources used by Emden belong to a period when editors of episcopal registers or of calendars of these registers were unaware of the meaning of a *Cum ex eo* license and often classed it as a "leave of absence."

In a word, one will have to go behind Emden and the printed episcopal registers to the manuscript registers in order to have anything like accurate figures for the incidence of *Cum ex eo* licenses in fourteenth-century England.

All the same, the evidence as it stands in the printed registers and Emden is not unimpressive. For the two centuries between 1300 and 1500 Mr. Emden's *Biographical Register of the University of Oxford* carries some 14,000 entries, over 1000 of which concern rectors of parish churches who had a *Cum ex eo* license at one time or another, generally before ordination to the priesthood. Both in Emden and the printed registers the figures for the fourteenth century are high. This is particularly true for the period up to 1350. For example, bishop Simon Ghent of Salisbury granted some 303 licenses in nineteen years (1297-1315), Henry Woodlock of Winchester 105 between 1305 and 1316, Walter Stapledon of Exeter 175 from 1307-26, seven bishops of Worcester some 261 between them in the period 1308-49.[12]

The evidence for the second half of the century is not so striking, at least in the few registers published to date. Henry Wakefield of Worcester issued only 28 licenses in twenty years (1375-95), Sudbury of London two between 1362 and 1365, Langham of Canterbury eight for 1366-68. But, on the other hand, Wykeham of Winchester gave licenses to 43 rectors from 1367 to 1400, Brantyngham of Exeter to 86 (1370-94), Stafford of Exeter to 50 in five years (1395-1400), various bishops of Hereford to 63 from 1350-85. These figures probably do not represent anything like the full number of licenses in the second half of the fourteenth century. Just as the section containing the list of dispensations is now missing from the register of bishop Martival of Salisbury (1315-30), so the registers of the period 1350-1400 are often patently incomplete.

*

What of the effect of the *Cum ex eo* system of licenses on the clergy and, in particular, on the parochial clergy? There is no doubt that very many distinguished ecclesiastics in the fourteenth and fifteenth centuries owed their university experience and the beginnings of their careers as churchmen to a *Cum ex eo* license: John Acton and William Lyndwood, the celebrated canonists, for example, Walter Burley and Thomas Buckingham, the influential scholastics, Thomas Fastolf, an *auditor* in the Roman curia and later bishop of St. David's, William Waynflete, headmaster of Winchester and Eton, and, ultimately, bishop of Winchester. But although people such as these contributed in no small way to the *cura animarum* in general as administrators, canonists, theologians or bishops, the clergy who remained on in the parishes which had provided their *Cum ex eo* "scholarships" are more to the point. There were some, of course, who moved on with unseemly haste after a year or two to another or "better" parish, but generally I think it fair to state that many who had *Cum ex eo* licenses continued to serve the parish which had supported their studies for a considerable, or at least a reasonable, time after they had returned from the university. Ralph Ergum (not the bishop of Salisbury of the same name), whose first four years as rector of Greystoke, Cumberland, had been spent at Oxford from 1316-20, did not depart the parish for another living until 1357. Walter de Kelmescot, who as a simple cleric had a five-year license to Oxford from 1336-41, was still rector of Cheselbourne, Dorset, some forty years later. John Wychebury, who had licenses at various times between 1373 and 1381, and took a degree at Oxford in 1382, was rector of Whimple, Devon, from 1370 until his death in 1391.[13]

The shining example, of course, is William of Pagula. Instituted to the parish of Winkfield in Windsor Forest in 1314, when he was already a Master of Arts and a deacon, he took a doctorate in canon law at Oxford about 1320-21 at the end of a six- or seven-year *Cum ex eo* license, and then served Winkfield, his one and only benefice, until his death about 1334. In that short span of years he managed to put together three large and influential works of theology and law, the *Summa summarum*, the *Speculum praelatorum*, and *Oculus sacerdotis*, as well as two shorter treatises, the smaller of which, a sturdy defense of the rights of his parishioners against the depredations in Windsor Forest of Edward III and his retinue, exists in two redactions, one about 1330, the other about 1332.[14]

Others, shall we say, had more secular interests. John Gaddesden, who was a Master of Arts by 1307 and a Fellow of Merton College, became rector of Chipping Norton, Oxfordshire, in 1321, and then obtained licenses for five years' study at Oxford over the next seven years, probably to pursue his medical studies. A very eminent physician and the author of a *Rosa medicinae* (c. 1305-17), which is extant in many manuscripts and was printed at least four times, he is credited with at least eight medical treatises, and served from time to time as physician to the Black Prince, to Joanna, the second daughter of Edward III, and to Abingdon Abbey. One or two preferments came his way late in life, but he was still rector of Chipping Norton when he died in 1349. Again, William Merle, who was rector of Driby, Lincolnshire, from 1331 until his death c. 1347, had licenses to study at Oxford from 1335-41 and again in 1346. A Master of Arts by 1339, he kept records of weather at Oxford for the years 1337-44, and compiled at least three works, still extant, on weather topics.[15]

This last example may give the impression that *Cum ex eo* rectors pottered about Oxford or Cambridge during their licenses. Some did, of course, and were no great advertisement of the system: Gilbert Foxlee from Tormarton in Gloucestershire was killed in a brawl during the second year of his license in 1306; Elias de Walwayn, rector of Stoke Edith, Herefordshire, abducted a nun from Godstow nunnery near Oxford in 1342.[16]

There were, however, measures which many bishops took to ensure that rectors did not fritter away their licenses. An Oxford formulatory-book of 1316-22 contains a formula of attestation of the academic progress of a rector, with, in this case, a request by the university to his bishop for an extension of his two-year license to the maximum seven years.[17] Letters of testimony such as these seem, indeed, to have been a regular feature of the *Cum ex eo* system. When William Kaignes, who had a license from the bishop of Exeter from 1333-35, was accused of failing to become a priest within one year of the end of his license, he was able not only to produce his letters of institution as rector but also his *Cum ex eo* license and testimonial letters from Oxford to his studies there.[18] Again, when John de Lavenham was admitted by the bishop of Ely to the rectory of Wickham, Cambridgeshire, on 4 April 1339, it was on condition of studying at Oxford or Cambridge and submitting to yearly examination by the bishop, since he was too illiterate to be trusted with the direction of souls. In the next year, and again in 1343, he was granted short-term *Cum ex eo* licenses, but the bishop insisted on the latter occasion that Lavenham should take an oath that he would devote himself exclusively to his studies as soon as the next term began at the university, since he had failed miserably so far to do so.[19]

But for all the proven checks and balances, there are many today who on first encountering the phenomenon of *Cum ex eo* licenses, are aghast at what seems, at best, a form of licensed absenteeism, which, as one writer has said, "could easily result in the neglect of a church and its parishioners."[20] Some, moreover, are worried by the fact that after the return from the university and ordination to the priesthood, many *Cum ex eo* rectors, especially those who came back with a degree, were, like the medical rector of Chipping Norton above, often called upon to serve in administrative or other capacities outside their parishes, and were thus in danger of neglecting their parishioners and of further wasting the revenues of the parishes which had paid for their education. William of Pagula, for example, became penitentiary for the deanery of Reading in 1322, and served in 1326 as commissioner on a boundary dispute between two parishes in another diocese. John Mowbray, who was born in 1350 and died in 1389, and as rector of Ripley in Yorkshire was granted a five-year license to Oxford in 1370, returned to Oxford in 1379 as a member of the committee of twelve which the chancellor of Oxford had set up to examine the writings of Wyclif.

One must remember, however, that so far as the period of licensed study is concerned, the licensed rector, whether or not he was a priest (and ideally and generally he was not), had to provide a competent and certified substitute (often the assistant he had inherited from his predecessor) to look after the parish during his absence. As for absences after the rector had returned from the university, the assistant priest (and few parishes were without one) could step in again. John Wyclif, who in his usual fashion expected only the best of those engaged in the pastoral care, had a useful hint for rectors who, like himself, had had a university training and often had to answer calls upon their time outside their parishes. The best way to provide for the continuous spiritual nourishment of a parish, and to offset possible absences, was, he said, by training a suitable substitute to whom one could hand over the parish without a qualm of unease as occasions for absence arose.

And what of the general morality of using parish revenues to educate future priests, especially when many of them, after a token stay of gratitude on their return from their studies, moved on from the parishes which had supported them at a university to more attractive pastures? Not all who had *Cum ex eo* licenses abused the parishes in this way, but enough did to justify the query. There does not seem, however, to have been any contemporary criticism of *Cum ex eo* licenses on this score, perhaps because, as Wyclif states in the passage quoted above, "a doctor or any other rank of cleric may receive alms from his parish, not precisely as rector of that parish, but as someone who is working outside his particular cure of souls for the common good of the church."[21]

Wyclif, needless to say, was speaking of absences at parish expense on general church business, but the principle "ad utilitatem communem ecclesiae" cannot be overlooked in discussions of *Cum ex eo*. Licenses *Cum ex eo* may not always have directly benefited the parish that supplied the means for the general education of a given rector, but the church at large, and certainly the diocese to which the rector belonged, were not defrauded but rather enhanced. Parish revenues, if you wish, were not seen simply as parish revenues but as church revenues, as we may note in the case of William of Wykeham, who, as soon as he had his New College at Oxford under way as a place for the education of young clerics in the liberal arts, theology and law, sought and obtained in 1383 a papal license to appropriate two parish churches of which he was patron in his own diocese of Winchester, and to devote their revenues to his new foundation at Oxford.[22] The young men who lasted the course at New

College and became priests afterwards, as they were bound to do by statute, were not destined for these two parishes, nor, for that matter, for the diocese of Winchester as such. But the revenues of these parishes were seen, as I have suggested for *Cum ex eo*, as belonging to the diocese, if not the church, at large.

*

One final question: Was the *Cum ex eo* system of Boniface VIII really an attempt to raise the level of education of priests engaged in the cure of souls in parishes, or was it something far less idealistic? Commenting on an article of mine which outlined the legal trappings of *Cum ex eo* and for the first time suggested a place for the constitution in the history of clerical education in the Middle Ages, a recent writer has said that my "grand vision of a parish clergy educated at the universities is pure fantasy." All my evidence, he went on, "shows that the concern was to draw respected families into the clergy, and not to educate the local priest."[23]

One cannot deny that this is a point of view. For my part I can only repeat that the purpose of the constitution *Cum ex eo* and of licenses *Cum ex eo* was not "to educate the local priest" but to provide a supply, whether from respected families or not matters little, of educated "local" or parochial priests.

The real question, of course, is whether the quality of parish life was improved when parishes were stocked, as they were from the beginning of the fourteenth century, with priests who through *Cum ex eo* licenses had more than the basic, rudimentary clerical education. If one takes it as axiomatic that the parochial clergy of the Middle Ages was irretrievably illiterate, the answer will be an entrenched negative. But if one squarely faces the fact, the inescapable fact, that there was such a system as that of *Cum ex eo* licenses, and then allows that around ten per cent of those who demonstrably enjoyed such licenses may have been decent, sincere and dedicated, it seems reasonable to go further and conclude that some part of the conventional picture of clerical literacy in the Middle Ages — or at least in fourteenth-century England, the focus of the present paper — has to be modified, if only ever so little.

Pontifical Institute of Mediaeval Studies,
University of Toronto

NOTES

1. New College, Oxford, MS. 292, fol. 94r; *Pupilla oculi* (London, 1510), VII. 3.

2. *Summa theologiae, Supplementum*, 3. 2, ad 1; ad 2.

3. See in general Leonard E. Boyle, "Three English pastoral *summae*," *Studia Gratiana*, 11 (1967), 133-44.

4. British Library, London, MS. Harley 52, fols. 83r-84v, etc.

5. See Leonard E. Boyle, "The Quodlibets of St. Thomas and Pastoral Care," *The Thomist*, 38 (1974), 232-56.

6. Leonard E. Boyle, "The *Oculus sacerdotis* and Some Other Works of William of Pagula," *Transactions of the Royal Historical Society*, 5th series, 5 (1955), 81-110.

7. Leonard E. Boyle, "The Constitution *Cum ex eo* of Boniface VIII," *Mediaeval Studies*, 24 (1962), 263-302. The text of the constitution will be found there and in *Sextus liber decretalium*, 1. 6, 34, ed. Ae. Friedberg, *Corpus iuris canonici* (Leipzig, 1879-81), II, cols. 964-65.

8. A. B. Emden, *A Biographical Register of the University of Oxford to A.D. 1500* (Oxford, 1957), III, 2103, 2001 (abbreviated hereafter to Emden, BRUO and volume).

9. *Summa praedicantium* (Paris, 1500), O. iv. 17; P. xiii. 25.

10. *De veritate sacrae scripturae*, ed. R. Buddenseig, III (London, 1907), 39.

11. Emden, BRUO, I, xxxvii.

12. See Boyle, "The Constitution *Cum ex eo*," (as in n. 7); Roy M. Haines, "The Education of the English Clergy During the Later Middle Ages: Some Observations on the Operation of Pope Boniface VIII's Constitution *Cum ex eo*," *Canadian Journal of History*, 4 (1968), 1-22.

13. Emden, BRUO, I, 645; II, 1030; III, 2102.

14. See Leonard E. Boyle, "William of Pagula and the *Speculum Regis Edwardi III*," *Mediaeval Studies*, 32 (1970), 329-36.

15. Emden, BRUO, II, 739, 1264.

16. *Ibid.*, II, 720; III, 1977.

17. *Formularies which bear on the history of Oxford c. 1204-1420*, ed. H. E. Salter, W. A. Pantin, H. G. Richardson (Oxford, 1942), I, 10-11.

18. Dorothy M. Owen, *John Lydford's Book* (London, 1974), pp. 26-27.

19. A. B. Emden, *A Biographical Register of the University of Cambridge* (Cambridge, 1963), p. 356. J. W. Gray, "Canon Law in England: Some Reflections on the Stubbs-Maitland Controversy," *Studies in Church History*, 3 (London, 1966), 60, writes, "But although *cum ex eo* limited episcopal dispensation to a period of seven years and to *bona fide* students, it also contained a *nisi iusta de causa* escape-clause — and in England at any rate — bishops seem to have given this clause the widest possible interpretation." In point of fact the "escape-clause" does not refer to the term of the license but to the year's grace for ordination to the diaconate and the priesthood after the end of the license.

20. P. A. Bill, *The Warwickshire Parish Clergy in the later Middle Ages* (Oxford, 1967), p. 19; see also M. Bowker, "Non-residence in the Lincoln Diocese in the Early Sixteenth Century," *Journal of Ecclesiastical History*, 15 (1964), 45.

21. *De veritate sacrae scripturae,* III, 39.

22. *Wykeham's Register*, ed. T. F. Kirby (London, 1896-99), I, 140; II, 418.

23. Richard C. Trexler, *Synodal Law in Florence and Fiesole, 1306-1518* (Vatican City, 1971), p. 78, n. 1.

X

THE DATE OF THE *SUMMA PRAEDICANTIUM* OF JOHN BROMYARD

ANYONE who has read the two works of G. R. Owst on preaching in the middle ages[1] will be aware that one of his prime sources was the *Summa praedicantium* of John Bromyard, the fourteenth-century English Dominican. Owst, in fact, was rather awed by the work, admitting that it defied "any adequate analysis"[2] and that "to do justice to that great monument of Dominican preaching, the *Summa* of John Bromyard, in respect of its Complaint and Satire against the clergy, would require the space of a volume."[3] As Owst saw it, the *Summa* was a "colossal undertaking,"[4] and he variously described it as "a Latin sermon encyclopaedia"[5] and a "vast collection and storehouse of sermon-lore."[6]

All these epithets are, no doubt, justified, but in fact any description of Bromyard's *Summa* must begin from the author's own preface. For Bromyard, his *Summa* was simply an expansion of a previous work called the *Opus trivium*: "compilationem a me prius collectam in isto libello ad meam et aliorum utilitatem emendavi et augmentavi."[7] This *Opus trivium* (which, curiously, is described by Owst as "a shortened compendium, with extra sub-headings, of the *Summa pred.*")[8] was written some years before the *Summa*, and derived the name "trivium" from the fact that it is a threefold compilation of divine, canon and civil law: "Et dicitur trivium quia triplici distinctione utitur in quolibet vocabulo; etiam quia a tribus legibus divina, canonica et civili capit testimonium".[9] Generally the *Opus* is composed of short articles on subjects from *Abbas* to *Xtus*, and each entry is numbered for easy reference: thus *Abbas* is A.i, *Ab infantia* is. A.ii, *Absolutio* is A.iii . . . *Ordinatio* is O.viii . . . *Symonia* is S.xiii.

Although the *Opus* is a reasonably large work, Bromyard evidently felt that something more extensive was called for. If the *Summa praedicantium* that resulted is more than twice the size of the *Opus*, the basic layout is still much the same. Again the order followed is that of the alphabet (*Abiectio — Xtus*), and again the articles are numbered and subdivided: "compilationem a me prius collectam in isto libello . . . emendavi et augmentavi, ponendo certas materias sub determinatis litteris secundum ordinem alphabeti, per propria capitula distinguendo. Et quia frequenter contingit mittere de una littera et de uno capitulo ad

---

[1] G. R. Owst, *Preaching and Pulpit in Medieval England* (Cambridge, 1926); *Literature and Pulpit in Medieval England* (Cambridge, 1933), reissued in a "second revised edition" (Blackwell, Oxford, 1961), on which see L. E. Boyle in *Medium Aevum* XXXIII (1964) 227–230.

[2] *Preaching*, p. 303.

[3] *Literature*, p. 241.

[4] *Preaching*, p. 303.

[5] *Ibid.*, p. 279.

[6] *Literature*, p. 572.

[7] British Museum, MS. Royal 7 E IV, f. 10r, or in any printed edition, e.g., that of Paris, 1518, p. 1.

[8] *Preaching*, p. 68 n. 1.

[9] British Museum, MS. Royal 10 D X, f. lv, or in any printed edition, e.g., that of Lyons, 1500, p. 1.

aliud, propter similitudinem materiae de qua agitur in loco de quo mittitur, co-
tatur littera et capitulum ad quod mittitur et numerus algorismi extra in margine
sub quo quod quaeritur faciliter inveniatur."[10]

This cross-reference system is faithfully applied throughout the *Summa*, so
much so, indeed, that there is really no need when citing the *Summa* to refer to
pages of a printed edition or to cite the folia of a manuscript copy. For example,
the article *Operatio* is clearly noted in any manuscript or printed edition as O.iv,
the article *Scientia* as S.ii. Many of the articles are very, very long, but Bromyard
has countered this difficulty by a clever and quite consistent use of paragraph
numbers in the margins of each article. Thus, *Praedicatio* (P.xii) contains some
39 subsections and *Praelatio* (P.xiii) some 60, all of which are clearly noted in the
margins of the articles. As Bromyard himself states in his prologue, this system
of numeration allows the author to give numerous cross-references, and enables
the reader easily to follow them up. Bromyard, as it happens, is an unrepentant
addict of cross-references, moving his reader back and forth at will through the
Summa: if in P.xiii.25 there is a cross-reference to O.iiii.7, in O.iiii.7 there are
further references to F.iii.34 and M.ix.15.

The *Summa praedicantium* was, then, modelled upon as well as posterior to the
Opus trivium, but since we do not know the date of the *Opus* these facts are of
little use in dating the *Summa* itself. Of course, various attempts have been made
over the past century or so to date the *Summa*. Herbert and Owst were inclined
to date it in the 1380's, and Welter about 1360–1368, all of which suggestions
were only superseded in 1953 when Fr George Mifsud, while working on a dissertation on the sermons of Bishop Sheppey of Rochester, discovered that
Sheppey, who died in 1354, knew and cited the *Summa praedicantium*. Although
Fr Mifsud did not publish anything on the subject, his discovery has become
widely known through its incorporation into A. B. Emden's entry on Bromyard
in his *Biographical Register of the University of Oxford*.[11] The purpose of the present
article is to see if that pre-1354 date can be refined a little further.

At the outset, a date before 1352 is more likely than before 1354, since a copy
of the *Summa praedicantium* was among the books of Simon Bozoun, prior of
Norwich, who died in 1352.[12] This is borne out by the fact that Bromyard probably was dead by 1352, for there is evidence that Bromyard's place as penitentiary in the diocese of Hereford was filled in that year.[13] If the *terminus ante quem*

---

[10] MS. Royal 7 E IV, f. 10r.

[11] A. B. Emden, *A Biographical Register of the University of Oxford to A.D. 1500*, I (Oxford, 1957),
p. 278; J. A. Herbert, *Catalogue of Romances in the Department of Manuscripts of the British Museum*
(London 1910), III, pp. 450–2; J. T. Welter, *L'exemplum dans la littérature religieuse et didactique du
Moyen-Age* (Paris-Toulouse, 1927), pp. 330–1; G. R. Owst, *Literature*, pp. 224, 595, of original edition
(the reissue of 1961 substitutes the Mifsud date for the old one at p. 224 n. from Emden's *Biographical
Register*).

[12] H. C. Beeching, "The Library of the Cathedral Church of Norwich", in *Original Papers of the
Norfolk and Norwich Archeological Society* XXIX (1915) 72–3: "Summa predicantium, precio c. s.".
A facsimile of the inventory is in *New Palaeographical Society Facsimiles*, First Series, I (London,
1903–1912), n. 189 (plate 143).

[13] Emden, *Biographical Register* I, p. 278.

is thus reduced by at least two years to 1352, there are also factors that suggest that the *Summa* was nearing completion in the Summer of 1348 and that, in fact, it had been begun some twenty or more years earlier.

Bromyard had been licensed to hear confessions in the diocese of Hereford in early 1326, though he was actually absent from the Dominican house at Hereford when his fellow-penitentiary, Hugh Ledebury, was admitted to this office on 1 February 1326.[14] He may have begun the *Summa* a year or two after his return to Hereford and his assumption of a penitentiary's duties, for by 1330 he had reached the letter I of the *Summa*, as may be seen from the following interesting aside in I.xi. 3 (*Iudicium divinum*):

> Aliqui tamen certum computant tempus usque ad iudicium, allegantes prophetiam Danielis (12.12) qui dicit: 'Beatus qui expectat et pervenit ad dies milletrecentos triginta quinque.' Iudaeorum magistri hanc litteram exponunt de messia illorum per hunc modum: . . . diem pro anno exponentes. . . . Quod utrum verum sit et tempus illud ab incarnatione Christ computetur, quinquennii temporis expectatio ostendet, cum nunc annus currat millesimus trecentesimus tricesimus.[15]

The problem that remains is how soon after 1330 and before 1352 the *Summa* was completed. Again there are some useful indications in the *Summa*, though none as concrete as that which yields 1330. One such is to be found in a remark of Bromyard's in the article *Ordo clericalis* (O.vi.39):

> Magister Joannes de Monumuta episcopus Landavensis habuit responsum de curia romana per suum archidiaconum *qui adhuc vivit* et haec mihi retulit.

The archdeacon in question is M. Alexander of Monmouth. He became archdeacon of Llandaff in 1323, under bishop John of Monmouth, and was still alive in 1337,[16] the last date we have for him. Since Bromyard refers to the archdeacon as "still living," then it seems reasonable to suggest that *Ordo clericalis* may have been written sometime between 1330 and 1337 plus.

Happily we do not have to depend too much on this suggestion. For Bromyard (*Paupertas: P.iii.26*) makes some comments on clerical dress which in fact seem to place the *Paupertas* article definitely after 1346:

> Canonici etiam regulares *nuper* in actis et ordinationibus capituli sui stuatuerunt quod canonici tales cappas non portarent de burneto rugosas quales portant aliqui praedicatores.

A constitution on this point was issued at the general chapter of the Canons Regular of St. Augustine of the province of Canterbury and York at Leicester in 1346. Although it does not correspond exactly to that cited by Bromyard, it is near enough to suggest that it was precisely this constitution that Bromyard had in mind.[17]

---

[14] *Registra Ade de Orleton episcopi Herefordensis*, ed. A. T. Bannister (London, 1898), pp. 350–1.

[15] I owe this reference, which I missed when reading through the *Summa* some years ago, to Francis P. Donnelly. Mr Donnelly is preparing a doctoral dissertation on the character of the *Summa* for the University of Toronto.

[16] Emden, *Biographical Register*, iii (1959), p. 2197; John le Neve, *Fasti Ecclesiae Anglicanae, 1300–1541*, xi: *The Welsh Dioceses*, ed. B. Jones (London, 1965), pp. 21, 23.

[17] *Chapters of the Augustinian Canons*, ed. H. E. Salter (Oxford, 1922), p. 55: "Item quod canonici

536   *Date of* Summa praedicantium *of John Bromyard*

If this gives a date 1346×1352 for the completion of the *Summa* (*Paupertas —
Xtus*), the gap may now be narrowed a little further. Towards the end of the
Summa, Bromyard has a long and lugubrious article about the trials and tribula-
tions that have recently come upon the world. The article (T.v.: *Tribulatio*) opens
with the words of Psalm 118, *Tribulatio et angustia invenerunt me*, and then goes
on to state: "Et ideo ad tribulationem convertitur calamus scribentis" (T.v.1).
After a discussion of tribulations that come in the form of drought or rains,
Bromyard remarks, "Quid ergo mirabile *si modo sit pluviarum tempestas* quando
maior est luxuriae corruptio et malitiae cogitatio quam in diebus Noe . . . ?"
(T.v.3), "Quid ergo mirum est, *si modernis temporibus deus animalia occidat*
propter nostra peccata et possessiones et blada *pluvia destruat et tempesta-
tibus* . . . ?" (T.v.5).

Granted that we are in the period 1346 × 1352 for this part of the *Summa*,
then the mention of heavy rains strongly suggests that Bromyard was writing
Tribulatio in the summer of 1348 when, according to some chroniclers, England
was at the mercy of exceptional rains that endured from 22 June until Christmas.[18] Possibly these rains occasioned the animal mortality about which Bromyard was so very preoccupied: "Animalia in mortalitatem quam temporibus istis
specialiter vidimus de bobus maiorem quam antea factam audierimus vel le-
gerimus . . . " (T.v.20).

In such dire circumstances, Bromyard was of the opinion that bishops not
only should order the usual processions and prayers but also should make people
go to confession and communion "sicut in quadragesima" (T.v.14). But many,
he states, scoff at such measures, saying, " . . . propter parvam pluviam quid
timemus nos?". Instead, they lie on in bed without a care or adjourn to taverns,
"dum religiosi et pauci forte pauperes de populo et mediocres *ad processionem
pro aeris intemperie faciendam* et missas et letanias cantandum et sermonem dei
audiendum congregantur" (T.v.21).

Processions, litanies and masses were, indeed, the order of the day during that
summer of 1348, as the bad weather continued and rumours of the approaching
pestilence were confirmed.[19] On 25 July 1348 John Gynewell, bishop of Lincoln,

---

regulares dicti ordinis quicumque de cetero tunicis nimis strictis vel botonatis, capis, clocheis seu
rotundellis, et aliis quibuscumque vestibus aut capellis, serico aut sindone alterius coloris quam sit
ipsum indumentum sive capella apparatis seu botis rostratis, de cetero penitus non utantur".

[18] See R. Higden, *Polychronicon*, ed. J. R. Lumby, VIII (RS 41, London 1882), pp. 344–6: "Hoc
anno [1348] inundavit pluvia nimia a festo nativitatis sancti Johannis Baptistae usque Natalem
Domini proximo sequens, ita ut vix transivit dies quin plueret in die vel in nocte; sub quo temporis
decursu magna mortalitas hominum grassata est per orbem, maxime in curia et circa curiam Romanam Avinionensem et circa maritimas urbes Angliae et Hiberniae." Much the same information
about the rain ("magna pluviae inundatio") is in the *Chronicon Angliae ab anno Domini 1328 usque
ad annum 1388 auctore monacho quodam sancti Albani*, ed. E. M. Thompson (RS 64, London 1874),
p. 26. The rains seem to have preceded the plague by some months. Accounts of the arrival of the
plague in England are in Gasquet's *The Great Pestilence*, cited below; J. Saltmarsh, "Plague and
economic decline in England in the later Middle Ages," in *Cambridge Historical Journal* VII (1941–
1943) 23–41; and P. Ziegler, *The Black Death*, (London 1969).

[19] Opinions vary as to when exactly the plague came into England. Henry Knighton, who seems to

ordered processions, litanies and a mass for peace "et pro aeris serenitate".[20] Three days later archbishop de la Zouche of York also instituted processions, litanies and prayers, stating bluntly, "Quantae siquidem mortalitates, pestilentiae et aeris infectio in diversis mundi partibus et praesertim anglicanis *immineant his diebus*, non est, cum sit publicum, qui ignoret . . . ".[21] On 17 August the bishop of Bath and Wells followed suit, ordering processions "to beg God to protect the people from the pestilence which had come from the East to the neighbouring kingdom" (presumably France).[22]

Since Bromyard, living at Hereford, speaks only of heavy rains and of animal mortality and not of the great loss of human life which began in the autumn of 1348 and hit Hereford badly in early 1349, it seems likely that he was composing the article *Tribulatio* during those summer months of 1348, some eighteen years after he had written the *Iudicium* entry noted earlier.

Perhaps the *Summa* as a whole was complete by the end of that year. Not many articles (*Veritas — Xtus*: 13 in all) remained to be written after *Tribulatio*, the final words of which (from 2 Macc. 1) surely reflect the grim expectancy ("Non est qui ignoret", as de la Zouche put it) of the time at which Bromyard was writing: "Haec scripsimus vobis in tribulatione et impetu qui supervenerunt nobis in istis annis" (T.v.73).

PONTIFICAL INSTITUTE OF MEDIAEVAL STUDIES

---

be very well informed about the progress of the plague, places it in the autumn of 1348: "Eodem tempore eadem pestis invaluit in Anglia, incipiens in autumno in quibusdam locis et discurrens per patrias finivit eodem tempore anno sequenti", *Chronicon Henrici Knighton vel Cnitthon monachi Leycestrensis*, ed. J. R. Lumby, (RS 92, London, 1895), II, p. 59.

[20] A. H. Thompson, "Registers of John Gynewell, bishop of Lincoln, for the years 1347–1350", in *Archaeological Journal* LXVIII (1911) 309.

[21] H. Raine, *Historical Papers and Letters from the Northern Registers*, (RS 61, London, 1873), pp. 395–6.

[22] F. A. Gasquet, *The Great Pestilence (AD 1348–9), now commonly known as The Black Death*, (London, 1893), p. 71.

CANON LAW

XI

The Compilatio quinta and the registers of Honorius III

As is well known, the *Compilatio quinta* or *Honoriana* is a collection of decretal letters of Honorius III (1216-1227) which was put together by his order and promulgated towards the end of his pontificate. Some five or six years later the *Quinta* was the only source used by Raymond of Peñafort for the decretals of Honorius when, at the request of Gregory IX, he compiled the *Compilatio Gregoriana* or *Decretales Gregorii IX*.

Although the *Quinta* thus had a very short life as an authoritative collection, some 17 manuscripts of it from the thirteenth and fourteenth centuries are known to be extant.[1] It has been printed three times since the seventeenth century: by I. Ciron(ius) at Toulouse in 1645; by J. A. Riegger, with additions to the edition of Ciron, at Vienna in 1761; and by E. Friedberg at Leipzig in 1882, as part of his edition of the *Quinque compilationes antiquae* (pp. 151-186). The latter edition is generally thought to have supplanted the earlier editions, and, unless otherwise specified, is the one used here.[2]

In all, if one includes a statute *Hac edictali lege* of Frederick II which was broken up and placed under nine different headings, the *Quinta* contains 223 chapters or canons which are arranged in five books and 94 titles. Of these 223 chapters, 214 come from letters of Honorius III, but since three of the letters were so divided by the compiler that they form seven chapters in all, the actual number of letters of Honorius III in the Friedberg edition of the *Quinta* is 210, not 214.

The compiler of the *Quinta* must have been the Bolognese canonist Tancred, who in January 1226 became archdeacon of Bologna. The text of the *Quinta*

---

[1] Sixteen are listed by S. Kuttner, *Repertorium der Kanonistik* 383-4. A Lucerne manuscript (Zentralbibliothek P. Msc. 2 fol.) is described by S. Stelling-Michaud, *Catalogue des manuscrits juridiques . . . conservés en Suisse* (Geneva 1954) 34. See also Griesser, n. 12 *infra*, at pp. 438-9.

[2] Strictly speaking, Friedberg's *Quinque compilationes antiquae* prints only those parts of the *Compilationes* which were not incorporated into the *Decretales* of Gregory IX by Raymond of Peñafort. For the text of the incorporated parts (129 in the case of the *Quinta*), Friedberg's edition of the *Decretales Gregorii IX* (Leipzig 1879) has to be used. By and large Friedberg based his edition on that of Ciron: *Quinta compilatio epistolarum decretalium Honorii III Pont. Max. nunc recens e tribus veteribus manuscriptis in lucem data et notis illustrata* (Toulouse 1645). The edition of J. A. de Riegger (Vienna 1761) is really a reissue of that of Ciron, with additional material from a Vienna manuscript (now Nationalbibliothek, MS 2077).

10

as established by Ciron from three now-lost Albi manuscripts and as edited by Friedberg from Ciron's edition and some other manuscripts, carries a prefatory letter addressed to 'Magistro Tancredo, archidiacono Bononiensi'. This is not of itself proof of Tancred's authorship of the compilation, since the same covering letter, but addressed now to 'Magistro Marcoaldo et uniuersis scholaribus Padue commorantibus', is found prefacing copies of the *Quinta* in manuscripts at Vienna and Lucerne.[3]

There is, however, some evidence that puts the matter beyond reasonable doubt. A copy of an introductory lecture on the *Decretales* given by Joannes de Deo at Bologna shortly after 1245, states that 'transigus de Bononia archdiaconus composuit quintum librum'; as Kantorowicz, who first published the text, has shown, this 'transigus' can only be Tancred.[4] An anonymous introduction to the *Decretales* from 1243-1245, discovered by Stephan Kuttner, makes the same assertion, with some further details: 'Postmodum magister tangredus, tunc canonicus bononie et demum arcidiaconus, ad instantiam honorii pape compillauit alium librum: et uocatus fuit quintus liber . . .'.[5] Further, a colophon printed by Professor Kuttner from a copy of the *Quinta* in the British Museum, suggests that Tancred had completed his work by 2 May 1226: 'Anno domini MCCXXVI, die II intrante maio, liber iste compilatus erat'.[6] This may mean, as Professor Kuttner has taken it to mean, that the date in May 1226 is that of the promulgation of the *Quinta* and, therefore, of the covering letter to Tancred, but, on the other hand, the phrase 'compilatus erat' may denote simply the date on which Tancred finally completed the compilation and handed it over to Honorius.

Granted, then, that the compiler of the *Quinta* was Tancred, and that the compilation was completed by, if not actually on, 2 May 1226, there still remains the question of his sources. Because Ciron in his edition showed that most of the decretals present in the *Quinta* are preserved in the registers of letters of Honorius in the Vatican Archives, it has been taken for granted that Tancred used these registers at some point or other when making his compilation. But how or to what extent he used them has never been clearly stated.

---

[3] Vienna 2077, first utilized by Riegger in 1761, does not name Marcoaldus but says simply 'Magister M.' This was thought to be Magister M(artinus) until the discovery of the Lucerne manuscript showed (fol. 33r) that the name was Marcoaldus. [Magister Marcoaldus (Marcoardo Teutonico) appears in documents of 1226, 1232, 1236, cited by A. Gloria, *Monumenti della Università di Padova (1221-1318)* (Venice 1884; repr. Bologna 1972) 315. K. Pennington has found glosses of his on *Compilatio quarta*. ED.]

[4] H. Kantorowicz, 'Das Principium decretalium des Johannes de Deo', ZRG Kan. Abt. 12 (1922) 434-6.

[5] S. Kuttner, 'Johannes Teutonicus, das vierte Laterankonzil und die Compilatio quarta', *Miscellanea G. Mercati* V (Studi e Testi 125, Vatican City 1946) 633.

[6] *Repertorium* 383 and n. 2.

The present paper hopes to show that in fact these registers of Honorius were Tancred's exclusive source and, as well, that Friedberg's edition of the *Quinta* is open to improvement.

***

In the present classification of the Vatican Archives, the registers of letters of Honorius III run from RV 9 to RV 13. These five volumes of the *Registra Vaticana* (= RV) cover all eleven years of the pontificate of Honorius (18 July 1216-18 March 1227).[7] The first four embrace two years each, while RV 13 contains years nine and ten and the last eight months of the pontificate (11th year). There is nothing to suggest that the series is incomplete, in the sense that there are missing registers. But although the series contains some 6000 items, this is only a part of the total correspondence of Honorius. Many letters, in original or in copy, are in deposits all over Europe and yet are nowhere to be found in the registers. Clearly the registration of letters was as selective in the pontificate of Honorius as it had been in that of his predecessor, Innocent III.

One interesting feature of these registers is that a large number of letters is marked with a distinctive X. These X-marks generally occur in the outer margins of the registers. That they are medieval is suggested by the fact that many of the marks were cut in half when the volumes were rebound in the seventeenth century. That they are contemporary with the registers themselves is not irrefutably clear, but circumstantial evidence strongly hints that they are. There are, of course, other marks in the registers, particularly in RV 12 (7th and 8th years) where a series of crosses or daggers occurs opposite letters referring to the Military Orders and their territories, to the Order of Sempringham (e.g. three letters at fol. 24r-v), and to other topics. These crosses and daggers are, however later than our X-marks. They often accompany them (e.g. fos. 30v, 57v, 113r, 140v) or are superimposed upon them (e.g. fos. 130v, 153v, 163v).[8]

These X-marks first came to my attention when looking at the famous decretal *Super specula* in its setting in the registers (RV 10, fos. 142v-144r, n. 600). It is a long letter, and since it deals with three different topics, it was divided into three separate chapters in the *Compilatio quinta* and thence appears in three corresponding chapters in the *Decretales* (= X) of Gregory IX, thus: fos. 142v-

---

[7] There is an uneven calendar of these registers in P. Pressutti, *Regesta Honorii Papae III* (2 vols. Rome 1898, 1895). Many letters from the registers are printed by C. A. Horoy, *Honorii III Opera* (5 vols. Paris 1879-1883), and there are selected letters in G. H. Pertz and C. Rodenberg, MGH *Epistolae saeculi XIII a regestis Pontificum Romanorum selectae* 1 (Berlin 1883) 1-260.

[8] From time to time there is a note, 'Hoc cap. est Extra De . . . ', in a 17th-century hand, opposite letters which are to be found in the *Decretales* of Gregory IX. The identifications are not always accurate.

143r: *Quinta* 3.27 un. (= X 5.5.5); fol. 143r: 5.5.2 (= X 3.50.10); fos. 143v-144r: 5.12.8 (= X 5.33.28).[9]

In the register, the beginning of this letter *Super specula* (or *speculam*, as registered) is marked by an X in the left margin. This of itself would hardly be worthy of note, were it not for the fact that a smaller X occurs twice in the margin of the body of the letter, and precisely at the passages which became chapters 3.27 un. and 5.12.8 in the *Quinta*. The impression that these marks might have something to do with the preparation of the *Quinta* was confirmed by an examination of the two other letters which were broken up by Tancred for the *Quinta*: RV 9, fol. 12v, n. 44 = *Quinta* 3.10.2 and 3.25 un.; RV 13, fol. 77r, n. 16 = 1.6 un. and 5.5.3. For although these letters do not show any marks of subdivision, there is the same large, clear X opposite each of them in the registers, just as there is opposite *Super specula*.

Altogether, in fact, some 570 letters were found to have been marked with this X. These marked letters include all but six of the 210 letters of Honorius, as well as the statute of Frederick II (RV 11, fos. 95v-96r, n. 483), that comprise the *Compilatio quinta* as edited by Friedberg.[10] What is more, many registered letters which are curtailed or telescoped in the *Quinta* have a second (and sometimes a third) mark in the registers at the very passage which appears as a decretal in the *Quinta*, as in the case of the short decretal *Conquerente olim* (2.16.2). This decretal is to be found in a letter in RV 11, fos. 241r-242v, n. 396, which is duly marked with an X in the margin. A few lines from the beginning (fol. 241r) of the letter, however, the text as it is in the *Quinta* skips over all of fol. 241v, and only takes this long letter up again (and then only for a few sentences) at fol. 242r, precisely where there is a second X in the margin. Again, the decretal *Licet filius* (*Quinta* 2.12.2 = X 2.20.49) is found in a letter in RV 9, fos. 89v-90r, n. 341, which begins. 'Ortam dudum . . .'. This decretal, however, omits the opening of the letter, beginning instead with the words 'Licet filius' at the bottom of fol. 89v, and continuing on to fol. 90r, where it stops some six lines from the end of the letter. The limits of the decretal passage are marked with an X on these two pages.

Without belaboring the point, it seems reasonable to conclude that these X-marks represent a first stage in the preparation of the *Compilatio quinta*, when Tancred first went through the registers, quaternion by quaternion, marking any letter or passage that contained a point of law. Many letters were then marked

---

[9] On this decretal see S. Kuttner, 'Papst Honorius III. und das Studium des Zivilrechts', *Festschrift für Martin Wolff* (Tübingen 1951) 79-101; W. Ullmann, 'Honorius III and the prohibition of legal studies', *Juridical Review* 60 (1948) 177-86.

[10] The four decretals which have not yet been located in the registers are 5 Comp. 1.2.1 (= X 1.3.30; Pressutti 6286), 1.13.2 (Pressutti 6294), 2.13.2 (= X 2.21.10; Pressutti 6287), 5.11 un. (= X 5.32.3; Pressutti 6288). I have not given up hope of finding them. As we shall see, many decretals in the *Quinta* are not readily recognizable in the registers.

for copying in full, such as that in RV 9, fol. 13r, n. 50 (= *Quinta* 3.19 un.), where a note at the end says 'totum'. Others, particularly in the earlier registers, were divided or 'edited' on the spot; and where the copyist should begin, or begin and end, was indicated by some supplementary marks.

The second, definitive stage took place when all these 570 marked letters had been copied out and lay before Tancred in a block. They had then to be reduced to a coherent body and arranged into five books under headings established by previous compilations of decretals. Of the 570 letters, some 360 were in fact weeded out. Some were discarded because the point of law was unclear or was already covered by existing compilations. Others were plainly duplicates or made the same legal point. Thus, two letters on the same topic and to the same address (but in different years and volumes) are both marked with an X in RV 11, fol. 144r, n. 725, and in RV 12, fol. 210r, n. 276, but only the second is found in the *Quinta* (1.23.2). Another letter that occurs twice within a few folios is marked with an X on both occasions, but the second occurrence was rejected in favor of the first (RV 13, fol. 48r, n. 269 = *Quinta* 2.20.2 = X 2.30.9; RV 13, fol. 54r, n. 287).

The compilation as such, then, was not made directly from the registers but from copies of letters or passages that had been marked in the registers by Tancred. It is unlikely, indeed, that Tancred ever compared the finished product against the registers themselves. Otherwise, it is difficult to see how some of the inconsistencies in the *Quinta* could have escaped him. Either he trusted too much in the accuracy of his copies or, as I shall suggest later, he was pressed for time in the end. Contrary to his general practice, some decretals that begin in the middle of a letter are shorn of the incipits of the letters from which they derive and are, consequently, difficult to locate, e.g. *Quinta* 1.3.2, *Ad audientiam*, is part of a letter beginning, 'Cum ecclesia uestra . . . . Sane *ad audientiam* nostram . . . .' (RV 11, fol. 197v, n. 227); 1.23.2, *Procuratore monasterii Neuenbergensis*, is found in RV 12, fol. 210r, n. 276, with the opening, 'Questione inter Neuenbergense monasterium ex parte una . . . . Tandem R. *procuratore* ipsius *monasterii* . . . .'; 2.2.3, *Discretioni uestre mandamus*, is in RV 11, fol. 189r, n. 190, a part of a letter that begins, 'Iohannes de Cremona ciuis bononiensis . . . . Ideoque *discretioni uestre mandamus* . . .'.

There is one example, however, that shows more clearly than any other that Tancred did not have the registers before him when making his final redaction. In *Quinta* 5.19.2 (any edition and manuscript) and thence in X 5.40.30, the decretal *Ex parte uestra* bears the inscription, 'Idem Episcopo F. et P. Bertrandi' (to which some manuscripts add, 'archidiacono Cesaraugustan.'). Ciron however, using the registers of Honorius, correctly noted that the true inscription should be 'Abbati et conuentui monasterii S. Flore Aretine', but neither he nor Friedberg (who reports Cironius's note) offers any explanation of how the original address could have been replaced in the *Quinta* (and the *Decretales*) by a totally different one.

The X-marks in the registers help to solve the problem. The decretal *Ex parte uestra*, dealing with a dispute over a mill, is in RV 9, fos. 156v-157r, n. 648. It has the usual X in the margin, and is addressed to 'Abbati et conventui monasterii S. Flore Aretine'. No other X-marked letter occurs for some nine pages after this, and when it does (RV 9, fol. 160v, n. 667), it is a letter about the execution of the will of the King of Spain and is addressed to 'Episcopo F. et P. Bertrandi archidiacono Cesaraugustan.'

Now, although these two letters are separated from one another in the register by nine pages, they came immediately after one another when written out for Tancred by the copyist who followed Tancred's marks in the register. So what probably happened was that Tancred, when making his final choice of decretals from the copies before him, accepted the first of these now-juxtaposed letters and rejected the second, but accidentally replaced the heading of the first letter ('Abbati et conuentui' etc.) with that of the second ('Episcopo F. et P. Bertrandi' etc.).

If these X-marks prove to be of some importance for the history of the formation of the *Compilatio quinta*, they may also be of some consequence in establishing a definitive text of the compilation, not least because three decretals which Friedberg, for his own reasons, did not admit to his edition (*Cum olim* at *Quinta* 2.4.2; *Sapientia* at 3.20.2; *Id expectauimus* or *Expectauimus*[11] at 3.20.4), are marked with an X in the registers of Honorius and should be given a hearing. The decretal *Sapientia*, which Riegger printed from Vienna MS 2077 at *Quinta* 3.20.2, and which Friedberg relegated to a footnote, is particularly interesting in this respect and, as well, serves as some sort of test case of the credibility of the X-marks.

On the surface, the *Sapientia* of the Vienna MS does not seem worthy of credence, for although it is addressed to certain abbots ('Idem S. Remi. Remen. et de Macer. abbatibus'), the text of the decretal is an injunction to bishops, not at all to abbots. The recently discovered Lucerne MS of the *Quinta* (Zentralbibliothek P. Msc. 2 fol.) shows, however, that there were two decretals *Sapientia* side by side in some versions of the *Quinta*, one addressed to abbots ('sancti Remigii Remen. et de Mac. abbatibus'), the other to an archbishop and his bishops ('Remensi arciepiscopo et suis suffraganeis'), and that the single *Sapientia* of the Vienna (Riegger) MS was clearly a mistake of the scribe, who slipped by *homoioteleuton* from the inscription and opening words of the first *Sapientia* ('Item sancti Remigii Remen. et de Mac. abbatibus. Sapientia et cetera. Volumus et mandamus') into the text of the second ('*mandamus* quatinus').

With the help of the registers of Honorius and the X-marks, a good case, too, can be made that the two decretals *Sapientia* were taken straight from the registers and thus belonged to Tancred's original *Compilatio quinta*. As they

---

[11] *Id expectavimus* is probably a misprint in Riegger (p. 230) for *Expectavimus* of Vienna N.B. 2077, fol. 24va.

occur in RV 13, fos. 23r-24r, the *Sapientia* decretals are not separate entries. Rather they belong to one long entry which fills two and a half pages and consists of a 'main' letter (fos. 23r-24r), addressed to (Cistercian) abbots, and of a very brief 'In eodem modo' or 'follow-up' letter (fol. 24r) to the archbishop of Reims and his suffragans. The 'main' letter is dated 24 December 1225 (= Pressutti 5240) and the 'follow-up' letter, 20 December 1225 (= Pressutti 5233), which, of course, is the reverse of the true order of the letters, in which, presumably, the letter of 20 December was the 'main' letter. The texts of the two *Sapientia* decretals are located one after the other in the last twelve lines of this long entry (at the very end of fol. 24r), the first *Sapientia* coming from the last eight lines of the 'main' letter, the second from the four-line 'In eodem modo' that immediately follows.

As may be seen from the following table (where the square brackets in column two indicate what is omitted in the Vienna MS), the fact that the two decretals are visually and textually dependent on the reversed order of the 'main' and 'follow-up' letters in the register is enough to suggest that the decretals were made from the register and not from the originals of the letters. But there is more. For there is an X-mark on fol. 24r, the only one in fact in that long entry of two and a half pages; and it is found precisely at the point, twelve lines from the end, where the two decretals *Sapientia* begin:

RV 13, fos. 23r-24r, n. 128	Lucerne ZB P. Misc. 2 fol., fos. 54vb-55ra, at *Quinta* 3. 20. 2.
	R. *De statu monachorum et canonicorum regularium.*
Sancti Remigii Remen. et . . de Macheriis Atrebaten. dioc. abbatibus.	Idem sancti Remigii Remen. et de Mac. abbatibus.
Sapientia que ex ore prodit altissimi . . . *fol. 24ʳ (at X-mark in margin):*	Sapientia et cetera.
Volumus et mandamus ut huiusmodi capitulum in singulis regnis siue prouinciis, annis singulis celebretur, concessa eis qui ad presidendum annis futuris capitulis celebrandis fuerint ordinati, conuocandi abbates et priores predictos et cogendi rebelles, appellatione postposita, simili potestate, adicientes ut si uisitatores qui fuerint in eodem ordinati capitulo aliquos exemptos inuenerint deponendos, apostolice sedi non differant nuntiare, in ceteris iuxta formam sepedicti concilii processuri . . . et carmeli decorem . . . . Datum Lateran. viiii Kal. Ian. anno nono. [= Pressutti 5240].	Volumus et mandamus [ut capitulum quod precipitur in concilio generali in singulis regnis siue prouinciis, singulis annis celebretur concessa eis qui ad presidendum annis futuris capitulis celebrandis fuerint ordinati, conuocandi abbates et priores et cogendi rebelles potestate, adicientes ut si uisitatores qui fuerint ordinati in eodem capitulo aliquos exemptos inuenerint deponendos, apostolice sedi non differant nuntiare, in ceteris iuxta formam in generali concilio statutam processuri.
In eodem modo scriptum est Remen. archiepiscopo et suffraganeis eius usque decorem.	Idem Remensi arciepiscopo et suis suffraganeis. Sapientia que ex ore altissimi prodiit et infra.

Quocirca uniuersitati uestre per apostolica scripta mandamus quatinus rectores monasteriorum uestrarum diocesum quos uisitatores predicti uobis a suis locis denuntiauerint amouendos, singuli uestrum in sua diocesi, sublato cuiuslibet appellationis et contradictionis obstaculo, non differant amouere, alioquin poteritis non inmerito formidare quod uobis minus iurisdictionis relinquetur in eis quam habuistis hactenus et habetis. Datum Lateran. xiii Kal. Ian. anno nono [= Pressutti 5233].

Uniuersitati uestre mandamus] quatinus rectores monasteriorum uestre diocesis quos uisitatores predicti uobis a suis locis denuntiauerint amouendos, singuli uestrum in sua diocesi, sublato cuiuslibet contradictionis obstaculo, non differatis amouere, alioquin poteritis non inmerito formidare quod minus uobis iurisdictionis relinquetur quam habuistis actenus et habetis.

Given this clear dependence of the two *Sapientia* decretals in the Lucerne MS on the registered copies of the letters to the abbots and the bishops, it seems fair to conclude that these two decretals were part of Tancred's original *Compilatio quinta*. This conclusion, to which the X-marks in the registers have again contributed so much, is not without some strong external support. Within five years of the promulgation of the *Quinta* a Cistercian treatise of 1231[12] not only cites the two *Sapientia* decretals from the *Quinta* itself but also gives enough of their content to leave no doubt that these are the two decretals in question:

> Notandum quod scribitur in Quintis de statu monachorum et regularium capitulo Sapientia, quod uisitatores, qui fuerint ordinati in capitulo prouinciali, si quos exemptos inuenerint amouendos, apostolice sedi non differant nuntiare [= first *Sapientia*]. Item in eodem precipitur episcopis sub comminatione graui ut, si dicti uisitatores aliquos abbates sibi denuntiauerint amouendos, singuli eorum sublato cuiuslibet appellationi obstaculo non differant amouere [= second *Sapientia*].

***

Tancred became archdeacon of Bologna on 31 January 1226.[13] Because he was addressed as archdeacon by Honorius when the *Quinta* was promulgated, and because he is known to have pleaded a case in Rome in March 1226, Kantorowicz argued that Tancred had put the compilation together sometime during that year, and probably in the spring. This conjecture was confirmed by Professor Kuttner's discovery of the note already cited which states that the 'book' was 'compiled' on 2 May 1226.

The *Compilatio* itself, and the registers, too, support this dating. Now that with the help of the registers one is able to assign a precise date to almost all the letters in the *Quinta*, it turns out that the latest dated letter is 13 Dec. 1225

---

[12] B. Griesser, 'Eine juridische Instruction über das Vorgehen bei einer Klosterreform in päpstlichen Auftrag', ZRG Kan. Abt. 39 (1953) 436-42.

[13] The letter of appointment is not to be found in the registers of Honorius. It is printed from the original of the Bologna Metropolitan Archives in Sarti and Fattorini, *De claris Archigymnasii Bononiensis professoribus*, 2nd ed. II 266-7.

(RV 13, fol. 94r, n. 97 = *Quinta* 2.1.5 = X 2.1.22). As for the registers, the latest letter marked with an X is one of 30 Jan. 1226, in RV 13, fol. 108r, n. 169. The last X of all is on fol. 111r of the same volume. Some three pages later, at fol. 112v, there is a distinct break in the register, with a gap of almost a page and a half before the register resumes at fol. 113r. The remaining folios cover the last thirteen months of the pontificate of Honorius (RV 13, fos. 113r-174r).

One possible reason for the gap between fos. 112v and 113r is the fact that in the first week of February 1226 the papal court returned to Rome from Rieti, where it had been since the previous summer. The latest letter before the gap in the register is that of 3 Feb. 1226 (RV 13, fol. 109r-v, n. 179), and, like all the other letters in this part, it is dated from Rieti. The earliest letter after the gap is that of 11 Feb. (RV 13, fol. 114v, n. 212), and it is dated, like the other letters after the break, from the Lateran in Rome.

But another and more interesting reason for the break in RV 13 may be postulated, one that bears on the *Compilatio quinta* and on Tancred's role in its formation. It is at least curious that when the register resumes at fol. 113r, the entries in the register do not begin where they left off, with letters of February 1226, but with letters of April, thus: fol. 113r, n. 198 (5 Id. Apr.), n. 199 (4 Non. Apr.), n. 201 (Id. Apr.). A few letters from February do follow at this point (fol. 113r, n. 202: Id. Feb.; 114v, n. 212: 3 Id. Feb.), but they are accompanied by letters of April and March (in that order). After this, the registration picks up a stray letter of November 1225, but in the main it records letters from February, March and April (in that order), including at fol. 119v, n. 238, the letter of 20 Mar. 1226 that gives the papal decision on the case that Tancred had been pleading. Letters dated in May begin on fol. 123r (n. 257).

Now, allowing that the registration of the last batch of the Rieti letters (that is, up to 3 Feb. 1226) was not done on the spot at Rieti but rather after the return of the curia to Rome, the work of registering these Rieti letters was probably completed by early March. And if, as witnessed by the break in the register and the discrepancy of dates, no more registration was done for some time, then it may be suggested that this was not because the *scriptores* were negligent or had a holiday but because they had been seconded to Tancred for work on the *Quinta*.

It is not known when Tancred arrived in Rome to plead his case, but since the decision was issued on 20 March 1226, it may be presumed that Tancred had been in Rome for some weeks before this date. Perhaps while the case was in progress, Tancred may have put in some work on the registers in his spare time. The pace may have been a leisurely one at first, but it probably quickened as soon as the case was completed, with Tancred on the heels of the *scriptores* who were scrambling to finish the Rieti letters.

Copyists probably had been at work on the registers from the time that Tancred marked the first quaternion of RV 9 with a series of X-marks. But as soon as the Rieti letters had been registered, and Tancred had put in his last X on RV 13, fol. 111r, the small band of *scriptores* which was in charge of registration must have been diverted to work on the *Compilatio*. Otherwise, it is difficult to see how Tancred could have completed his work by 2 May 1226. And if, as Professor Kuttner has concluded, that day is the date of the promulgation of the *Quinta*, then Tancred and his assistants must have worked very hard indeed. There were at least 570 letters to be copied out. When these had been sorted, reduced to a manageable number and edited, a fair copy (or copies) of the finished product had to be made for the consideration of Honorius. And when the compilation had been given final approval, copies had to be made again for despatch to various legal centres, such as those to Tancred himself and Bologna, and to Marcoaldus and the university of Padua.

Then, and only then, would the *scriptores* have been able to return to their normal duties as *registratores*. And they began not with letters from the beginning of February where they had left off, but with those which were more recent and were, so to speak, lying on the top of the pile, those of mid-April 1226.

**

At all events, Tancred's search for decretal letters in the registers of Honorius III ended with the last of the Rieti letters of early February 1226, while the latest letter selected from the 570 or more which he had marked with an X up to that date belongs to December 1225. The letters of Honorius for the last thirteen months of his pontificate find no place in the *Quinta*, nor for that matter, since Raymond of Peñafort did not venture beyond the *Quinta*, in the *Decretales* of Gregory IX.

This raises a number of questions, none of them entirely new. First of all, do the *Decretales* of Gregory IX really represent the total, not to speak of the cream, of papal decretals between, say, Alexander III and Gregory IX? Obviously the answer is negative. In the present case of Honorius, which is all I am concerned with here, the last thirteen months of his pontificate are not represented in any collection of decretals. Besides, Tancred seems not to have gone outside the registers of Honorius for any other decretals. Yet it is a well-attested fact that the registers of Honorius contain only a portion of his known correspondence.

A second, and less rhetorical question, therefore, is what was the relation of decretal letters to the registration of papal letters? It is a commonplace that only selected letters, and not any and every letter, went into the registers of the popes of the thirteenth century. For the pontificate of Honorius, to take him as an example, some 400 original letters are extant in archives and libraries outside of the Vatican Archives, but only some 80 of these are to be found in the registers.[14] What the basis of selection was for these and other papal registers is far

---

[14] F. Bock, 'Originale und Registereinträge zur Zeit Honorius III.', in *Bullettino dell'Archivio paleografico italiano*, n.s. 2-3 (1956-7) pt. 1, 101-16.

My best thanks to Professor Stephan Kuttner for much helpful criticism in preparing this article. The above article was written in December 1974 for a Festschrift in honor of Giulio

from clear. But given that Tancred and the authors of some earlier compilations drew almost exclusively on what they found in the registers of papal letters, it is fair to assume that one of the purposes of the registers was to maintain a record of the decretal letters of the papacy.

If so, then a third question comes to mind: Who decided precisely what decretal letters went into the registers? In each pontificate there must have been someone who had the specific task of earmarking certain letters of legal import for copying into the registers against the day when some lawyer or scholar or compiler would need to draw on them.

In fine, what ultimately became 'Decretal law' in compilations such as Tancred's was entirely dependent upon that initial process of selection. And since Raymond of Peñafort seems not to have done much original research, what went into the definitive and exclusive *Decretales* of Gregory IX was of necessity confined to what Tancred and other compilers had found in registers which of their nature were far from embracing the totality of papal decretals.

Pontifical Institute of Mediaeval Studies,
Toronto.

Battelli to be published under the editorship of A. Pratesi by the Edizioni di Storia e Letteratura in Rome. In January 1979, when most of the articles, including the present one, were in page proof, the Festschrift was abandoned. When the present article was put together it was without any knowledge of Paulius Rabikauskas, '"Auditor litterarum contradictarum" et commissions de juges délégués sous le pontificat d'Honorius III', BEC 132 (1974) 213-44, who, in passing, remarks on the X-marks in the registers of Honorius, and notes : 'Il semble que ce signe ait été tracé par celui qui a eu la charge de choisir les textes à extraire en vue de la préparation de la *Compilatio Vᵃ*. Comme le même signe se trouve également en regard de lettres qui par la suite ne sont pas entrées dans la *Compilatio Vᵃ*, il doit se référer à la phase préparatoire et non à l'exécution de la compilation' (p. 217; cf. also p. 219).

[For the 'extravagantes' *Cum olim, Sapientia, Expectavimus,* see now K. Pennington, appendix to 'The French recension of Compilatio tertia', BMCL 5 (1975) 67-9. Ed.]

The Date of the Commentary of William Duranti on the Constitutions of the Second Council of Lyons

Between the promulgation in November 1274 of the constitutions of the Second Council of Lyons (May-July 1274) and the appearance of the *Liber Sextus* in 1298, at least seven commentaries on the constitutions were published, one of which, that of Garsias Hispanus in 1282, came to be accepted as the *Glossa ordinaria*.[1]

The first of these, the anonymous *Hoc dicit quod spiritus sanctus* saw the light within ten months of the promulgation of the Lyons' constitutions (certainly before 4 September 1275), and possibly originated in the papal curia.[2] A second is the work of Joannes Anguissola of Cesena, and was finished sometime before the end of 1275.[3] A third appeared in 1277 (a little after February of that year) from the pen of Boatinus of Mantua, a professor at Padua.[4] A fourth, that of Franciscus de Albano of Vercelli, was written in the Faculty of Law at Avignon at much the same time in 1277 (probably before 28 March).[5] The fifth, *Si qui erant excommunicati*, is anonymous, and possibly was written at Naples before the end of 1279.[6] A sixth, that of the Bolognese professor Garsias Hispanus, almost certainly was written in 1282, as some manuscripts attest.[7] The last known commentary, perhaps some ten years later, is that of Willelmus Duranti Senior, the author of the influential *Repertorium iuris*, *Speculum iudiciale* and *Rationale divinorum officiorum*, who was bishop of Mende in the south of France from 1286 to 1296.[8]

By any measure, Duranti is the most engaging of the commentators. Like Franciscus de Albano, Duranti was present at the Council, but unlike Franciscus and the other commentators I have read, Duranti is not afraid to criticize some

---

[1] See in general, E. Fournier, *Questions d'histoire du droit canonique* (Paris 1936), 7-31, reprinted in *Nouvelles recherches sur les curies, chapitres et universités de l'ancienne église de France* (Arras 1942) 221-40; M. Bertram, 'Zur wissenschaftlichen Bearbeitung der Konstitutionen Gregors X.', QF 53 (1973) 459-67.

[2] Fournier 9-12, Bertram 462.

[3] Schulte, *Geschichte* II 134-6. [4] Bertram 463.

[5] Fournier 12-31. [6] Bertram 460-1.

[7] S. Kuttner, 'Decretalistica', ZRG Kan. Abt. 26 (1937) 459 n. 1; Bertram 460 n. 6. Bertram gives some MSS which give the date 1282, to which may be added British Library (fomerly British Museum) Royal 9 C 1.

[8] See L. Falletti, 'Guillaume Durand', DDC 5 (1953) 1014-74, at 1053-5; Bertram 464-5. This is the only commentary to have been printed: *In sacrosanctum Lugdun. conc. sub Gregorio X Guilelmi Duranti cognomento Speculatoris commentarius, ed.* S. Maiolo (Fano 1569).

of the constitutions and to go beyond the letter of the constitutions on occasion. Duranti, of course, was in a better position to speak his mind than Franciscus or the others. At the time he was writing his commentary he was bishop of Mende and, as well, had two editions of impressive works of canon law to his credit, the *Repertorium* (a first edition of which appeared before 1271; the second before 1279) and the *Speculum iudiciale* (the first version of which may be dated to 1271-76, the second to 1287-91). Besides, he had spent most of his life either working in the papal curia or acting for it in various parts of Italy and France. Under Clement IV (1265-68) he had become an *Auditor generalis causarum*. From 1277-87 he had served the papacy in various capacities, notably as rector of the Patrimony of St. Peter. Above all else, he had been present at the Council of Lyons itself as a member of the curia and had had the ear of Gregory X both before and during the Council.[9]

It has become a commonplace to describe Duranti as one of the draftsmen, if not the principal draftsman, of the decrees of that Council,[10] but in the light of, among other things, what he has to say about the wording of some of them, this is very unlikely. The passage which has given rise to this commonplace occurs in his prologue to the commentary on the constitutions, where he says that he was present at the Council, 'et aliquas de infrascriptis constitutionibus procuravimus'. If we many judge, however, from another passage in which the word also appears, 'procuravimus' probably means nothing more than that Duranti had engaged in lobbying of one kind or another at the Council. Noting in his comment on the constitution *Statutum* (const. 21) that many prelates had tried during the Council to persuade Gregory to repeal a constitution of Clement IV on benefices that fell vacant *in curia*, Duranti confesses that he himself had worked hard towards that same end (*efficaciter procuravi*), but had failed to move Gregory, who simply modified Clement's constitution ever so slightly and then had it approved by the Council as the present constitution *Statutum*.[11]

For all his admitted failure here, Duranti probably was a formidable lobbyist who had, as his preface claims, quite a lot of success in rallying support for some constitutions at the Council, as in the case of *Quamvis* (const. 8), of which he makes a modest boast: 'Iuste ergo motus, hanc constitutionem promulgari . . . procuravi'. Even in the indifferent edition of 1569 from a defective manuscript, Duranti comes through in his commentary as a man who was rather sure of himself and not at all in awe of anyone. On at least two occasions he conveys his dissatisfaction with the wording of certain constitutions, as when in his com-

---

[9] The best biography is that of Falletti in DDC 5, but the long study of V. Le Clercq in *Histoire littéraire de la France* 20 (1842) 411-97, is still valuable.

[10] E. g. Falletti 1020; A. Franchi, *Il Concilio di Lione (1274)* (Rome 1965) 25.

[11] *Ed. cit.* 74r (20-1): 'praelati in concilio lugdunensi instantissime petierunt illam per dominum Gregorium revocari, et ego ipse etiam hoc efficaciter procuravi. Papa vero non revocavit sed eam modificavit, prout hic patet. Quae modificatio si bene consideretur verbalis est potius quam realis'.

mentary on *Hoc consultissimo* (const. 22), he suggests that the opening paragraph would read more easily if a whole phrase were dropped.[12]

He is particularly severe on the constitution *Exigit* (const. 24), claiming that it did not really catch what Gregory had in mind. As he had often heard from the pope, the plain purpose of the measure was to punish visitators who accepted procurations from places they in fact had never visited. But the present constitution, he says, muddles things up—a drawback which Duranti overcomes by reworking the central part of the constitution:[13]

const. 24: COD 303	Duranti, *ed. cit.* 83 (6)
. . ., statuentes ut universi et singuli qui, ob procurationem sibi ratione visitationis debitam, exigere pecuniam vel etiam a volente recipere, aut alias constitutionem ipsam, recipiendo munera sive visitationis officio non impenso procurationem in victualibus aut aliquid aliud, procurationis occasione, violare praesumpserint, duplum eius quod receperint, ecclesiae a qua id receptum fuerit, infra mensem reddere teneantur;. . . .	. . ., statuentes ut universi et singuli qui, visitationis officio non impenso, ob procurationem sibi ratione visitationis debitam, id est quae sibi debetur si visitarent, praesumpserint exigere vel etiam a volente recipere pecuniam aut alias constitutionem ipsam violare, recipiendo munera sive procurationem in victualibus aut aliquid aliud procurationis occasione, duplum eius quod receperint, ecclesiae a qua id receptum fuerit, infra mensem reddere teneantur;. . . .

From another point of view he is just as critical of one of the most celebrated and resented of the constitutions—one of the three, in fact, which were drawn

---

[12] *Ed. cit.* 76r (13-15): '*Non concedendo*: quasi dicat: Licet prohibeamus fieri submissionem, subiectionem et suppositionem sine consensu capituli et sine licentia sedis apostolicae, constituendo vel recognoscendo, etc., prout infra sequitur, non tamen prohibemus bona ipsa vel iura in emphiteusim dari seu alias alienari in forma et casibus a iure permissis. Et hunc intellectum evidenter probat illa adversativa coniunctio "sed" posita in principio clausulae sequentis. Sic ergo ordina litteram: post verbum illud "speciale" iunge verba infraposita "constituendo vel recognoscendo, etc.", et coniunctio illa "sed" superflua est. . ., posita enim est ut respondeat illi dictioni "non" supra positae'. The text is indeed somewhat awkward in this constitution 22: 'Hoc consultissimo prohibemus edicto, universos et singulos praelatos ecclesias sibi commissas, bona immobilia seu iura ipsarum, laicis submittere, subicere seu supponere, absque capituli sui consensu et sedis apostolicae licentia speciali, [non concedendo bona ipsa vel iura in emphitheosim seu alias alienando in forma et casibus a iure permissis, sed] constituendo vel recognoscendo seu profitendo ab illis . . .': COD 303. Duranti's instruction to jump from 'speciali' to 'constituendo' is here represented by the square brackets.

[13] The text in the second column follows Duranti's recasting of the clauses, *ed. cit.* 83 (6): '*Statuentes.*. . . Et haec fuit mens domini papae prout saepe ab ipso audivi, licet littera ista confuse loquatur. . . . Et secundum hanc litteram ordinabis: "Statuentes ut universi et singuli qui" [iungas] "visitationis officio non impenso", redeas supra, "ob procurationem sibi ratione visitationis debitam, id est quae sibi debetur si visitarent, praesumpserint exigere, vel etiam a volente recipere pecuniam aut alias constitutionem ipsam violare, recipiendo munera sive procurationem in victualibus, aut aliquid aliud procurationis occasione, duplum, etc.". Et verba illa "procurationis occasione" superfluunt, quia supra praemissa sunt'.

up after the Council and had not been debated there.[14] This was the constitution *Licet canon* which, while renewing the decree of the Third Lateran Council in 1179 that enjoined ordination to the priesthood within a year and residence *per se* on rectors and others entrusted with a *cura animarum*, had imposed a penalty of deprivation *ipso facto* for a failure to observe these conditions. Duranti agreed that this was a very effective measure for stemming absenteeism from the *cura animarum* but it had, in his opinion, a disastrous side-effect in that it effectively shut off most of the parochial clergy from all hope of education through, for example, a leave of absence for study. In many provinces in which there were few benefices without a *cura animarum*, the constitution *Licet canon* was, he felt, 'perquam dura . . . et damnosa'. In those areas, at least, it put an end to an old and well-tried custom whereby bishops could dispense rectors and others from residence for periods of study. If no remedy of this constitution were forthcoming, he feared that within a short time the *cura animarum* would be devoid of literate priests. To be worthy of the name, he drily remarked, citing a number of legal authorities, a law should be suitable, necessary and useful both for the time and the place, and should serve the common good.[15]

If Duranti thought that Gregory's post-conciliar constitution *Licet canon* fell somewhat short of that ideal, he was also of the opinion that some successors of Gregory were far from prudent when they decided to suspend the conciliar constitution *Ubi periculum* (const. 2), on the election of popes in conclave.

This constitution, so sorely needed after the shambles of the three-year vacancy before the election of Gregory himself in 1271, was welcomed by the anonymous commentary of 1275, written while Gregory was still alive and before *Ubi periculum* had been put to the test.[16] The year after that, as Franciscus de Albano informs us in his commentary, the constitution was successfully observed at the elections of the short-lived Innocent V and Hadrian V. Although Hadrian, who lived for only five weeks after his election, drew up a bull revoking *Ubi periculum* (his one official act as pope, it appears), he died before he could publish it, so the constitution, as Franciscus de Albano points out, was observed

---

[14] See S. Kuttner, 'Conciliar Law in the Making: The Lyonese Constitutions (1274) of Gregory X . . .', *Miscellanea Pio Paschini* (Rome 1949) II 39-81.

[15] *Ed. cit.* 46v (35): 'Haec autem constitutio in pierisque provinciis, in quibus pauca sunt beneficia sine cura, perquam dura est et damnosa. Nam olim episcopi in talibus dispensabant, et cum hiis beneficiis multi proficiebant in scientia litterali. Hodie vero, quia pauperes non habent unde proficiant, divites vero nollunt providere filiis, ut statim presbiteri fiant, nisi remedium adhibeatur, infra breve tempus pauci viri litterati invenientur. Debuit ergo lex loco et tempori esse conveniens, necessaria et utilis, et pro communi utilitate conscripta, ut iv. D. c. erit'. For the possible effect of this criticism on the decision of Boniface VIII to modify *Licet canon*, see L. E. Boyle, 'The Constitution *Cum ex eo* of Pope Boniface VIII', *Mediaeval Studies* 24 (1962) 267-72. There is nothing to indicate that Duranti's rewording of *Exigit* or of *Hoc consultissimo* had any similar impact on Boniface when he was preparing the *Liber Sextus*.

[16] Saint-Omer, Bibl. mun. 518, fol. 42ra-3va, listing 'octo specialia' in the constitution.

once more at the election of John XXI in September 1276. As we know from Franciscus and other sources, it was in fact John who took up the unfinished work of Hadrian, suspending *Ubi periculum* definitively some three weeks after his election because (or so Franciscus de Albano assures us) 'at his own and previous elections many cardinals had failed in health and had died on account of the strict life they had had to lead during the conclaves'.

For all that he knew that *Ubi periculum* was prorogued, Franciscus de Albano, writing a few months later, comments at length on it, possibly because he was unsure just how definitive the suspension was. Among other things, Franciscus comments on the usefulness of the constitution (it keeps the cardinals away from distractions and expedites the process of election) and makes the interesting suggestion that a turntable of the kind used in monasteries of cloistered nuns could be employed to pass food discreetly into the conclave.[17] Other commentators, however, do not bother to comment on *Ubi periculum*. Some six years after the suspension, Garsias Hispanus was willing to grant that 'the decretal' was 'holy and useful', but excused himself from writing about it further on the ground that it was spendthrift to take up space with a gloss on something which had been revoked.[18]

In much the same terms, William Duranti makes the same point a decade or so after Garsias. Yet, after several other echoes of Garsias and an explicit statement that he is not going to gloss *Ubi periculum*, Duranti proceeds to give a long lecture on papal elections which does not fall far short of a commentary on the suspended constitution.[19] This unexpected 'lecture', coupled with the obvious regret of Duranti at the suspension of *Ubi periculum*, deserves more attention that it has hitherto received for its position on papal elections. For the purposes of the present note, however, what is important is that certain remarks of Duranti suggest a date for the commentary on 2 Lyons as a whole that is somewhat more precise than that of L. Falletti, the author of the most informed biography of Duranti, who dated the commentary vaguely 'after 1287-91' (after, that is, the second edition of the *Speculum iudiciale*, which it quotes).

To Duranti, *Ubi periculum* was a 'salutary provision'. Although he knew full well that popes had plenitude of power by which to revoke what had been solemnly decided by a Council, he hoped that God would forgive the pope who

---

[17] Saint-Omer, Bibl. mun. 446, fol. 124rb-129va. A summary of these folios is in Fournier *Questions* 21-7, *Nouvelles recherches* 233-7.

[18] Bodleian Library, Oxford, MS Can. Pat. Lat. 144, fol. 14rb: '*Ubi periculum.* Hec decretalis sancta et utilis toti mundo suspensa fuit per Adrianum et postea per Iohannem penitus revocata quoad coactionem cardinalium, et eius revocatio sub bulla redacta, et ideo non est necesse ut legatur vel glossetur. Ad quid enim glossa eius membranas occuparet, xix D. Si Romanorum, ex quo revocata est? Continentur tamen in ea multa bona notabilia quae quilibet per seipsum elicere poterit, et utile erit videre. Licet enim ius antiquatum sit, tamen eius memoria utilis est vii. D. Fuerunt. Gar.'

[19] *Ed. cit.* 5r-11r.

44

had revoked *Ubi periculum*. He found it hard, indeed, to understand how a constitution which had been promulgated 'tam solemni concilio approbante' could have been revoked without the consent of a universal or at least of a particular council. There is no point, he goes on, in asking a Council to approve of and to consent to something if it can be done away with as *Ubi periculum* was without benefit of Council.[20]

One by one Duranti considers at some length the main problems that had beset papal elections (how long, for example, should cardinals be allowed for arrival at the place of election), and shows how many of these problems were adequately covered in the rejected constitution *Ubi periculum*, and how necessary that constitution was after the troubles of the long vacancy before the election of Gregory X.

From the repeated praise of the provisions of *Ubi periculum* and from other indications, it is not impossible that Duranti was really pleading a case and was in fact writing his commentary during another long vacancy, that which lasted from 4 April 1292, when Nicholas IV died, to 5 July 1294, when Celestine V was elected. On the death of Nicholas, the small college of cardinals, twelve in all, had begun the election process in Rome after an interval of ten days. Later, however, the college split into two factions, one at Rome, the other (and larger) at Rieti. Both factions eventually were united in October 1293 at Perugia where, finally, the unlikely Pietro Morrone became Celestine V on 5 July 1294.[21] Three months later this same Celestine reinstated *Ubi periculum* once for all, and four years after that Boniface VIII incorporated it into his *Liber Sextus* (1.6.3) together with all but one of the constitutions of Lyons.

By the time of the vacancy Duranti was in residence in his diocese of Mende. Like the rest of Europe, he probably looked with a certain helplessness and not a little distaste on the petty intrigues, procrastination and general disarray of the college of cardinals in those two years. This is possibly the reason why Duranti, unlike some earlier commentators to whom the constitution was at most a pious memory, could not pass over *Ubi periculum*. He was fully aware that it had been prorogued, and he observed the form by announcing that he did not propose to gloss it, but he showed how disturbed he was at the state of the Church

---

[20] *Ed. cit.* 6r (11): 'Sed quid si duae partes nullo modo consentiunt? Respondeo. Invocetur brachium saeculare . . . et ponantur in conclavi. . . . Sic enim quandoque est, et praesens constitutio super hoc satis salubriter providebat. Quae cum tam solemni concilio approbante fuerat promulgata, mirum est quomodo absque universalis saltim particularis requisitione concilii fuerit revocata, ff. De reg. iuris. l. Nil tam naturale. . . . Frustra siquidem concilii approbatio et assensus requiritur si sic sine concilio quod tam solemniter agitur, revocetur. Sed tamen potuit de plenitudine potestatis, secundum quam potest papa super omne concilium quidquid placet. . . . Indulgeat ei deus qui causam praebuit revocandi . . .'.

[21] See H. K. Mann, *The Lives of the Popes* 17 (London 1931) 254-65; R. Brentano, *Rome before Avignon* (New York 1974) 141-3.

by making twelve points at length about papal elections in which *Ubi periculum* was held up as a model time and again.

Curiously, although any pope could have lifted the suspension of *Ubi periculum*, Duranti makes no suggestion, as he does in the case of *Licet canon*, that the situation should be remedied. It is as though he were writing when there was no pope to hand and none in the offing, and when the cardinals, who could do nothing about the suspension anyway during a vacancy, were entirely on their own and, in the absence of something as sane as *Ubi periculum*, at sixes and sevens.

This, I feel sure, is what lies behind Duranti's cryptic remark about the cardinals at the beginning of his discussion of papal elections: 'Although the lord cardinals may play around with the forms of election as much as they wish, I shall here set out what the doctors have taught, and what I myself hold, about the election of a pope'.[22] It is no less plausible that he is advocating a remedy of the shilly-shallying of the cardinals at Perugia between October 1293 and July 1294 when he later makes the point: 'It is therefore a useful thing, and the present constitution [*Ubi periculum*] makes ample provision for such a measure, that the cardinals should be placed under lock and key and deprived of all delicacies until they are agreed on a candidate, as I myself saw done at Viterbo after the death of Clement IV'.[23]

From what follows it seems clear that what Duranti is speaking about here is not a regular conclave as set out in *Ubi periculum*, which made provision for the control of the conclave by the local townspeople of the place of election, but rather about a conclave which is forced on the college of cardinals by the laity and then is conducted along the lines laid down in *Ubi periculum*. From his reference to Viterbo, it seems further clear that what Duranti is actually proposing is a repetition of the celebrated forced election there in 1270-71, when the townspeople in despair of a result otherwise, shut the cardinals up (though possibly with the agreement of some of them), and at one point took the roof off the place of election.

Duranti, of course, was aware that he was on treacherous ground in advocating such a measure. He admitted at once, with a string of legal references, that those who forcibly put cardinals under lock and key were thereby excommunicate.

---

[22] *Ed. cit.* 5r (2): 'Verum licet civile ius destruatur, ratio tamen eius durat, ut ff. de capit. minut. l. Eas, et i.D.c. Consuetudo . . ., ideo aliqua circa huius materiae notitiam disputabo. Et licet domini cardinales formas pro suo velle varient, tamen quod super hoc a doctoribus traditum est, et quod super hoc sentio, reservabo'.

[23] *Ed. cit.* 6v (14-15): 'Utile est igitur quod in uno conclavi ponatur, ut supra, vers. prox., et eis cibaria saltim delicata donec concordaverint subtrahantur, sicut factum vidimus Viterbii post obitum domini Clementis papae IV, arg. C.v.q.v.c. Non omnis, et C.xxiii. q.iv.c. Nimium, super quo satis praesens constitutio providebat. Arg. tamen contra lxxxvi.D.c. Pasce. Sed solve per ff. De reg. iuris, l. Quod quis ex culpa, et C. xxxiii. q. iv. c. Displicet'. (This passage continues in n. 24).

But he was sure (and he pulled out an even longer string of authorities to prove it) that a very good case could be made for lay intervention. For one thing, the canons state that those who could be the ruin of many should firmly be taken in hand by the secular powers (citing D.17 c.4). For another, anyone who abuses the power entrusted to him deserves to lose that privilege (C.11 q.3 c.63). Again, sins are punished by God not only through judges but also through the people (C.23 q.5 c.21). Further, when ecclesiastical power breaks down, jurisdiction within the church falls to the laity (C.23 q.5 c.20), as it also does when clerics are causing a schism (*ibid.* c. 43), or when some through ambition want to be pope (D.79 c.9). Moreover, the assent and vote of princes are required in the election of a pope (C.7 q.1 c.5). Finally, although it is indeed true that there are canons which legislate for the excommunication of nobles who intervene in the election of a pope, all that these canons say in fact is that such nobles are *to be* excommunicated, not that they *are* excommunicate. In reality these nobles are not so much interfering with an election as making it possible to take place. Anyway, Duranti states by way of conclusion of this comment, it does not really matter what the law on the point is. For it is the easiest thing in the world for a pope elected by means of such a forced conclave to absolve from any excommunication those who had taken the step of locking the cardinals up.[24]

It is difficult to imagine that such a passage on papal elections was written in the abstract. It is a little too pointed.

Given, then, that Duranti's commentary on the Lyons' constitutions is definitely after 1287-91, the date of the *Speculum iudiciale*, it seems possible to conclude, in the light of the above, that it was written during the vacancy of

---

[24] Ed. cit. 6v-7r (16-18): 'Sed nonne ponentes eos et custodientes in conclavi et consentientes eis sunt excommunicati? Videtur quod sic, ut De sent. exc. c. Nuper et c. quarto, nam laicorum violentia est in electione romani pontificis removenda, ut praedicta constitutione Innocentii Quia frequenter, et electus populari seu militari tumultu non apostolicus sed apostaticus est dicendus, ut lxxxix. D. c. Si quis pecunia.

Arg. contra De sent. exc. c. Veniens et c. Voluntate, xxiii. q. v, c. Prodest interdum et c. De occidendis. Debent enim hii qui plurimorum perditio esse possunt per saeculares comprimi potestates, xvii. D. c. Nec licuit, in fine, xi. q. i. c. Petimus, quia privilegium meretur amittere qui permissa sibi abutitur potestate, xi. q. iii. c. Privilegium, et supra titulo proximo c. ii. Et Deus punit peccata non solum per iudices verum etiam per populos, xxiii. q. v. c. Remittuntur, et § seq. Item laici habent iurisdictionem intra ecclesiam cum potestas ecclesiastica deficit, ut xxiii. D. q. v. c. Principes, et cum clerici schisma faciunt, ut in predicto c. De Liguribus, et cum aliqui per ambitionem papatum habere volunt, ut lxxix. D. c. Si quis pecunia. Et suffragium et assensus principum in electione papae est requirendus, ut vii. q. i, c. Factus est, et xxiii. D. c. i. vers. Quapropter, [et] supra, vers. Sed quid fiet. Et in electione summi pontificis cum nullus sit superior aliqua sunt specialiter observanda, ut in const. Licet, § fin. Item primates nobiles impedientes electionem papae anathematizandi sunt, non dicit anathematizati, ut lxxix. D. c. Si quis ex sacerdotibus. Isti autem non impediunt sed promovent eam. Verumtamen quicquid sit de iure, romani pontifices taliter electi de facili et libenter tales ab excommunicatione absolvunt'.

1292-4, if not in the period October 1293 to July 1294, when the cardinals at Perugia were proving exasperatingly slow to come to a decision.[25]

Pontifical Institute of Mediaeval Studies,
   Toronto.

---

[25] Although Falletti DDC 5.1071-2 adverts to some of these passages on *Ubi periculum,* he does not go beyond the following statement: 'L'autorité du concile est confrontée à celle du pape à propos du conclave . . . . Durant, pour qui ce règlement [*Ubi periculum*] avait été établi *salubriter,* s'étonne qu'il n'y ait point eu de concile contraire. Mais le pape l'a pu faire de par sa puissance entière qui prévaut sur tout concile. Encore n'est-ce point sans responsabilité: *Indulgeat ei Deus.* . . . Dès lors, la mise des cardinaux en conclave, en tant que fait, pourrait paraître de la part des laïques une *violentia in electione,* possible d'exco- munication. Durant y voit au contraire une légitime manifestation du bras séculier et des peuples eux-mêmes, en cas de défaillance de la puissance ecclésiastique. Cet argument même paraît que l'*assensus principum in electione papae requirendus est (ibid.,* n. 14-16, p. 6)'.

XIII

THE *DE REGNO* AND THE TWO POWERS

IN a well-known article of 1958,[1] the late Fr I. T. Eschmann, O.P.,
discussed the two main texts in the writings of St Thomas which deal
with the relations between the 'spiritual' and 'temporal' powers. The
first (*S*) is at the end of Book Two of the *Scriptum super sententiis*.[2] The
second (*R*) is in Book One, c. 14 of the *opusculum De regno ad regem Cipri*,
also called, though less correctly, *De regimine principum*.[3] In Fr Eschmann's opinion, 'The two texts do not present an identity of views nor
such a similarity as could easily be synthesized. Rather they are contradictory' (177); 'Texts *S* and *R* are contradictory in doctrine as well as
method. They also originate in differing and conflicting schools of
thought' (182).

For Eschmann (and he shows this at some length), the *Scriptum* 'recalls
to mind the dualistic thesis of some 12th and 13th century canonists'
(183). The roots of this thesis lie in a letter of pope Gelasius in 494 to

---

1 I. T. Eschmann, 'St. Thomas Aquinas on the Two Powers', in *Mediaeval Studies* 20 (1958) 177-
205. In the present essay page-references to this article are given in brackets immediately after
citations from Eschmann.

2 2 D 44, q. 2 a. 3, *expositio textus: S. Thomae Aquinatis Scriptum super sententiis*, II, ed. P. Mandonnet
(Paris, 1929), pp. 1135-6.

3 This writing, which is attributed to St Thomas by the earliest catalogues of his works, is incomplete and seems to belong to the years 1265-1267. It is generally agreed that the *De regno* in its
incomplete form consisted of 21 chapters, ending at Book Two c. 4 as found in modern editions; the
remainder is probably the work of Ptolomy of Lucca (ob. 1327). The 'Vulgate' text of the work,
which Eschmann uses, is that in various editions of the *Opera omnia* of St Thomas, e.g., Roman
edition, I, pp. 160v-168v; Parma edition, XVI, pp. 225-291; Vivès edition, XXVII, pp. 336-412. The
same 'Vulgate' text is also to be found in P. Mandonnet, *Opuscula omnia S. Thomae* (Paris, 1927), I,
pp. 312-487; J. Mathis, *S. Thomae Aquinatis De Regimine Principum et De Regimine Judaeorum politica
opuscula duo* (Turin, 1948). A fresh, but interim, edition is in *S. Thomae Aquinatis Opuscula Omnia necnon Minora*, ed. J. Perrier, I (Paris, 1949), pp. 221-267. An English translation, with valuable introduction, notes, and textual appendices, is to be found in G. B. Phelan and I. T. Eschmann, *St.
Thomas Aquinas On Kingship to the King of Cyprus* (Toronto, 1949).

The text followed in this essay is the 'Vulgate' text used by Eschmann in his article. The Perrier
edition, which uses four Paris MSS., numbers the chapters differently to that of the 'Vulgate'
edition. Thus I c. 14 of the 'Vulgate' is I c. 15 in Perrier.

Reprinted by permission of the publishers,
Pontifical Institute of Mediaeval Studies, Toronto, © *1974.*

the emperor Anastasius,[4] an extract from which was celebrated in the middle ages as the canon *Duo quippe sunt potestates* in the *Decretum* of Gratian (D96 c10).[5] Broadly speaking, and as described by Fr Eschmann, advocates of the dualistic thesis held that 'spiritual and secular powers are not derivative but original *imperia*. They are like first causes, each autonomous in its own order, the spiritual power in the things belonging to the salvation of souls, the political power in things concerning the civil good' (178). If, in a given case, e.g., the popes of the time of St Thomas, the two powers are found in one person, they still remain 'formally distinct' though 'materially united'. 'Not one but two specifically different competences and jurisdictions are attributed to the pope' in such circumstances, and 'these two are not reduced one to the other' (178-9).

The *De regno,* on the other hand, 'contradicts' the *Scriptum* 'exactly at this point', since it holds, according to Eschmann, that 'the pope has one power only: the spiritual power', which, of its nature, 'includes secular power' (179). In a word, the *De regno,* contrary to the *Scriptum,* 'brings about a formal *reductio ad unum* by formally subsuming secular power under spiritual power, especially the papal power' (ibid.). For the *Scriptum,* 'the pope as pope, i.e. as spiritual sovereign and head of the Church, has no political power whatsoever' (ibid.). For the *De regno,* however, 'supreme political power is given him by reason of his spiritual primacy' (180).

Fr Eschmann, then, sees the *De regno* as a prime example of 'theological Gregorianism', the fundamental principle of which, in Fr Eschmann's words, 'is that both *potestas sacerdotalis* and *potestas saecularis* are found within the one church, which therefore emerges as the one super-comprehensive society' (192). It is, moreover, the only work of St Thomas in which there is 'any trace of that curious theology of the Primacy which includes secular power in its essence and appeals to a certain christological materialism for its support' (189). Having compared the *De regno* text on the two powers with that of the *Scriptum,* Eschmann is inevitably persuaded to question the very authenticity of the *De regno* as a work of St Thomas, because of 'the presence, in works of an author of the stature of St Thomas, of two texts belonging to different worlds' (195).

*

* *

4   *Epistolae Romanorum Pontificum,* ed. A. Thiel, I (Braunsberg, 1868), pp. 349-58.
5   *Corpus iuris canonici,* ed. A Friedberg (Leipzig, 1879-1881), I, cols. 340-1.

Now, in all of this Eschmann confines himself to c. 14 of Book One of
De regno. He does not use any other chapter, nor does he situate that
chapter in relation to the chapters that precede or follow it. Further, he
presents the *Scriptum* and *De regno* passages as though they were speaking
of precisely the same subject. Yet, unlike the *Scriptum,* where the
problem is one of conflicting obediences (spiritual and secular), the
subject of c. 14 of *De regno* is the precise limits of secular or royal
power. Spiritual or papal power is discussed only in order to establish
these limits and to highlight the 'intrinsic end' of secular power or
kingship.

In c. 12 of *De regno* the author had outlined the office of kings, ending
with the striking statement, 'Hoc igitur officium rex se suscepisse
cognoscat, *ut sit in regno sicut in corpore anima et sicut Deus in mundo'*.[6] In c.
13 he explains just what he meant by that statement, saying that a king
is like God in that he 'creates', 'produces', 'provides', 'governs'. Does
this mean, the author then asks, that, like God, the king has complete
power over his kingdom and, in particular, over any and every end of
his kingdom? Not at all, he explains in c. 14 (the crucial chapter). For
although it is true that 'ad omnes reges pertinet gubernatio et a guber-
nationis regimine regis nomen accipitur' (c. 13), this only applies to the
'intrinsic end' of the kingdom.

For the kingdom also has an 'extrinsic end': 'Sed est quoddam bonum
extrinsecum homini quamdiu mortaliter vivit, scilicet ultima beatitudo
quae in fruitione Dei expectatur post mortem'.[7] This 'ultima beatitudo'
belongs to Christ. The king's rule does not embrace that 'divine
kingdom'. For the office of bringing man to the 'ultima beatitudo' or
final end is not confided to kings or princes (that would be to confuse
the intrinsic and extrinsic ends of society, the spiritual with the temporal) but rather to the priests, the representatives of Christ. In particular this office is entrusted to the Roman Pontiff in as much as he is,
by the authority of Christ, the supreme ruler of the kingdom of Christ
and the supreme earthly guardian of the final end of man. Where the
ministry of this kingdom of Christ is concerned, even the kings of
Christian peoples are subject to the pope as to Christ, and must obey his
rule:

> Huius ergo regni [Christi] ministerium, ut a terrenis spiritualia essent
> distincta, non terrenis regibus sed sacerdotibus est commissum, et
> praecipue summo sacerdoti, successori Petri, Christi vicario, romano pon-
> tifici, cui omnes reges populi christiani oportet esse subditos sicut ipsi
> Domino Iesu Christo.[8]

---

6 Ed. Perrier, par. 40. Chapters 12-15 in the Vulgate edition are cc. 13-16 in that of Perrier.
7 Perrier, par. 44, reads 'extrinsecum' where the 'Vulgate' and other editions read 'extraneum'.
8 Perrier, par. 46, reads, probably correctly, 'Huiusmodi' for 'Huius'.

In Fr Eschmann's view, this passage in the *De regno* gives 'supreme political power' to the pope 'precisely by reason of his spiritual primacy' (180). It is difficult to see how the text can bear this interpretation. For the passage above never suggests that popes have political power, whether direct or indirect, much less that 'secular power is subsumed under spiritual power, especially the papal power' (179). Moreover, it is already clear from c. 13, which Eschmann does not cite, that temporal well-being (the intrinsic end of a kingdom) is the preserve of the ruler (secular power) and of no one else. The point that is made directly in c. 14 of the *De regno,* and precisely in the text above, is that spiritual power, the 'divine kingdom', does not belong to kings but to priests: '*Huius* ergo regni ministerium ...'. If the kings of Christendom are said by *De regno* to be subject to the pope as to Christ, this is only in terms of the spiritual regimen committed by Christ to the priesthood and, in particular, to the pope. Kings and princes have to obey the pope and be guided by him whenever there is question of the relationship of the intrinsic end which they control to the extrinsic end, salvation, which is not under their control.

A philosophical justification of this conclusion is advanced by the author of *De regno* immediately after the passage ('Huius ergo regni ministerium ... sicut ipsi Domino Iesu Christo') quoted above:

> Sic enim ei ad quem finis ultimi cura pertinet subdi debent illi ad quos pertinet cura antecedentium finium, et eius imperio dirigi.[9]

For Fr Eschmann, this 'brings about a formal *reductio ad unum* by formally subsuming secular power under spiritual power' (179). He strongly objects to the principle, as he also does forcefully (197) to another statement of the same principle in the preceding paragraph of *De regno*:

> Semper enim invenitur ille ad quem pertinet ultimus finis imperare operantibus ea quae ad ultimum finem ordinantur; sicut gubernator ad quem pertinet navigationem disponere imperat ei qui navem constituit qualem navem navigationi aptam facere debeat ...[10]

According to Fr Eschmann, the author's practical conclusion from this principle and the shipbuilding example is that 'all kings in Christendom must obey the pope' — a conclusion which, Eschmann says, 'begs the question, for the captain has no authority over the shipbuilder in the

---

9 Perrier, par. 46, has a slightly different word-order for the opening phrase: 'Sic enim ei ad quem ultimi finis pertinet cura'.

10 Perrier, par. 45, reads 'ea quae in finem ordinantur ultimum' instead of 'ea quae ad ultimum finem ordinantur'.

sense of what St Thomas would call the *ordo praelationis*, in virtue of which obligation and subjection is constituted' (197).

The only difficulty is that the 'practical conclusion' is Fr Eschmann's, not that of the author of the *De regno*. For the *De regno* does not conclude from the principle invoked that the shipbuilder (king) is 'obliged and subject to' the captain (pope) in an *ordo praelationis,* as though his whóle existence sprang from and was 'subsumed under' the authority of the captain. The shipbuilder is subject to the captain precisely in as much as the ship be builds (*finis antecedens*) must be fit for sailing (*finis ultimus*). This in no way makes him dependent upon the captain for his very existence ('reductio ad unum'), no more than it implies that the captain builds ships or 'makes' shipbuilders. Like the captain, the spiritual power (the pope), and no other power, has charge of the final end of man, salvation. Like the shipbuilder, the secular power (kings) has to obey the spiritual power in all that involves that final end. But this leaves kings in complete charge of the well-being of their own kingdoms (antecedent end).

Contrary to what Fr Eschmann proposes, there is nothing of 'Theological Gregorianism' here. Rather there is the simple, unadorned Gelasian 'dualism' which Fr Eschmann finds so clearly in the *Scriptum*. A king, the *De regno* holds, rules over his kingdom as a priest (pope) rules over the kingdom of God; but he is subject to the priest (pope) whenever there is question of the 'dominium et regimen quod administratur per sacerdotis officium' (c. 15), that is, the salvation of souls, the end or good that is extrinsic to that of the secular power. As pope Gelasius put it in his famous letter to the emperor Anastasius in 494:

> Duo quippe sunt, imperator auguste, quibus principaliter mundus hic regitur: auctoritas sacrata pontificum et regalis potestas. In quibus tanto gravius est pondus sacerdotum quanto etiam pro ipsis regibus hominum in divino reddituri sunt examine rationem.
>
> Nosti [etenim, fili clementissime, quod licet praesideas humano generi dignitate, rerum tamen praesulibus divinarum devotus *colla submittis* atque ab eis causas tuae salutis expectas inque sumendis coelestibus sacramentis eisque ut competit disponendis, *subdi te debere cognoscis* religionis ordini *potius quam praeesse,*] itaque inter haec *ex illorum te pendere iudicio* non illos ad tuam velle redigi voluntatem.[11]

If further proof were needed of just how Gelasian the *De regno* is, then

---

11 This is the first part of par. 2 of the letter of Gelasius as edited by Thiel, *op. cit.,* pp. 350-1. The version in Gratian, D96 c10, has the opening sentences, 'Duo quippe sunt ... examine rationem', but then jumps ('Et post pauca') from 'Nosti' to 'itaque inter haec ex illorum te pendere iudicio non illos ad tuam velle redigi voluntatem'. The remainder of the text in Gratian is not that of Gelasius but of Gregory VII.

one can turn to the beginning of the next chapter (c. 15) of the *De regno* and to a passage which Eschmann never quotes. There it is stated clearly, and in the best dualistic tradition, that the spiritual and temporal powers are distinct juridical entities:

> Si igitur, ut dictum est, qui de ultimo fine curam habet *praesse debet* his qui curam habent de ordinatis ad finem et eos *dirigere suo imperio*, manifestum ex dictis fit quod *rex* sicut dominio et regimini quod administratur per sacerdotis officium subdi debet, ita *praeesse debet omnibus humanis officiis et ea imperio sui regiminis ordinare*.[12]

In a word, kings rule as directly over their own kingdoms as priests over the kingdom of God. The two powers, spiritual and temporal, are so in command of their own separate spheres that the same terminology is applied in each case in the *De regno*. If the spiritual power 'praeesse debet' and is entitled to 'dirigere suo imperio', so also the secular power 'praeesse debet' and has the right to 'imperio sui regiminis ordinare'.

Again the principle invoked twice in c. 14 is present in c. 15: 'qui de ultimo fine curam habet praeesse debet his qui curam habent de ordinatis ad finem et eos dirigere suo imperio'. This principle, which Eschmann called 'the cornerstone of the construction' of c. 14, is depicted by Eschmann (182) as formally denoting that the ends of the spiritual and secular powers 'are subordinated *per se*'. Later (197), arguing that the conclusion drawn by *De regno* 'begs the question', he approves of Bellarmine's insight when he 'discreetly suggested that the general notion of *architektonike*, taken from Eth. I, 1894a 10, be replaced by the more specific *politike* of Eth. I, 1094a 27'. For Eschmann, convinced as he was that the *De regno* was using the architectonic principle to bolster an hierocratic argument, 'The all too general idea of an architectonic art will not carry the argument one step ahead ... The Aristotelian polis must first be transformed into the *respublica christiana*, then Aristotelian principles will be applicable. St. Bellarmine has shown with refreshing clarity and vigour how an hierocratic argument should be constructed so as to be at least formally correct' (197-8).[13]

---

12   For 'rex sicut dominio et regimini ... subdi debet', Perrier, par. 48, reads 'rex, sicut Domino, regimini ... subdi debet'. For other readings (e.g. 'rex sicut divino regimini') see Phelan and Eschmann, *Kingship*, p. 88.

13   R. Bellarmine, *De summo pontifice* 5.7, in *Bellarmini Opera omnia*, I (Naples 1856), p. 532 b: 'Prima ratio eiusmodi est. Potestas civilis subjecta est potestati spirituali, quando utraque pars est ejusdem reipublicae christianae; ergo potest princeps spiritualis imperare principibus temporalibus, et disponere de temporalibus rebus ad bonum spirituale: omnis enim superior imperare potest inferiori suo'. While not questioning Eschmann's version of Bellarmine, I must point out that most of the Bellarmine argument here, if it depends in any way on *De regno*, does not reflect *De regno* I.14 but rather Book Three. See next note.

The plain fact is, however, that Bellarmine simply *had* to change from *architectonice* to *politike* so as to turn what the *De regno* I. 14 had to say into a 'hierocratic argument'. For (as Bellarmine seems to have recognized), *De regno* I. 14 is anything but hierocratic. If it were, and if the Aristotelian principle invoked in cc. 14 and 15 were meant to prove an absolute subordination of the secular to the spiritual power, then it is curious that the conclusion from that principle in c. 15 is that the secular power is an independent juridical entity.

In fine, the 'all too general idea of an architectonic art' was used deliberately by the author of the *De regno* for the very good reason that he was not advancing an hierocratic argument. Had he resorted, as Bellarmine did, to the *politike* notion, then of necessity he would have arrived at a conclusion which he did not hold and which, I may venture to suggest, Bellarmine saw that he did not hold and therefore changed, brilliantly perhaps, to suit his own 'hierocratic' purpose.[14]

*
* *

If Bellarmine, unlike Eschmann, saw the real, untheocratic thrust of the architectonic argument as deployed by the *De regno,* so also did John of Paris, that celebrated proponent of dualism at the beginning of the fourteenth century.

Eschmann mentions John of Paris once or twice, but apparently without realizing just how much of cc. 14 and 15 of the *De regno* was taken over by John in his *De potestate regia et papali* (1302-1303).[15] Commenting on the principle invoked by the *De regno,* 'Semper enim invenitur ille ad quem pertinet ultimus finis imperare operantibus ea

---

14 It is surely significant (though Eschmann does not mention it) that when Bellarmine cites *De regno* I.14 and the architectonic argument there, all that he is able to conclude is that the passage teaches a simple dualism: 'Sic igitur loquitur Lib. I. c. 14: Huius ergo regni ... et eius imperio dirigi. *Haec ille. Qui clarissime distinguit regna terrena, quae habent pro fine pacem temporalem, a regno spirituali Christi et eius vicarii, quod pro fine habet vitam aeternam' (De summo pontifice,* 5.5: *ed. cit.,* p. 530a). To support his own moderately theocratic position, Bellarmine turns at once, after this unexceptionable comment, to Book Three of *De regno,* the work, probably, of the ultra-theocrat Ptolomy of Lucca. Citing *De regno* III, cc. 13 and 15, Bellarmine comments: 'Haec ille; quibus verbis significat Christum habuisse quidem dominium temporale totius mundi, sed indirecte; directe autem solum dominium spirituale'. He then goes on to discuss III. c. 19, and to mitigate an ultra-theocratic statement there and in III. c. 10.

15 This work has had two recent editions: J. Leclercq, *Jean de Paris et l'ecclésiologie du XIIIᵉ siècle* (Paris, 1942), pp. 168-260, and F. Bleienstein, *Johannes Quidort von Paris Über königliche und päpstliche Gewalt. Textkritische Edition mit deutschen Uebersetzung* (Stuttgart, 1969), pp. 67-352. There is an English translation by J. Watt, *John of Paris on Royal and Papal Power* (Toronto, 1971). A section in Leclercq's introduction gives most but not all of the borrowings from the *De regno* in John of Paris (pp. 35-6). Bleienstein does not note any borrowings, nor does Watt.

244

quae ad ultimum finem ordinantur', Eschmann notes (182) that 'imperare' has 'a jurisdictional sense'. Then in a long footnote to 'imperare' (181 n. 18) he states that John of Paris simply suppressed 'the embarrassing authority' of the *De regno* 'on this point', for on 'p. 178.30 of Leclercq's edition' of John of Paris 'a long quotation of *De regno* I.14 is suddenly cut short' just before before the architectonic principle is introduced.

Now it is true that John of Paris breaks off his quotation from the *De regno* I. 14 in c. 2 of the *De potestate* just before the phrase, 'Semper enim invenitur ille ...', which precedes the example of the captain and the shipbuilder. But Eschmann nowhere notes that John of Paris explicitly returns later in c. 5 to that very same 'embarrassing authority':

> Ex praedictis patet de facili quid sit prius dignitate regnum vel sacerdotium ... Et ideo dicimus potestatem sacerdotalem maiorem esse potestate regali et ipsam praecellere dignitate, quia *hoc semper reperimus quod illud ad quod pertinet ultimus finis perfectius est et melius et dirigat illud ad quod pertinet inferior finis.*[16] [*De regno* I.14: 'Semper enim invenitur ille ad quem pertinet ultimus finis imperare operantibus ea quae ad ultimum finem ordinantur'].

Although John of Paris does not reproduce the *De regno* text word for word, it does seem clear that he had the passage in question before him, and has taken over from there the architectonic principle which Eschmann implies he avoided.

It must be admitted, however, that the 'imperare' of *De regno,* which according to Eschmann has a jurisdictional sense, has been replaced by John of Paris with the seemingly milder 'dirigere'. But, in fact, John of Paris is simply following the usage of the *De regno* itself, and for reasons which we shall see later. It is true that the *De regno* uses 'imperare' in the example of the captain and the shipbuilder from which the above quotation ('Semper enim invenitur ...') comes, but when it cites the same principle a few sentences later in relation to the spiritual power and the pope, it uses 'imperio dirigi' instead: 'Sic enim ei ad quem finis ultimi cura pertinet subdi debent illi ad quos pertinet cura antecedentium finium, et eius imperio dirigi'. Again, when in c. 15 the *De regno* speaks of the independent spheres of spiritual and secular power, 'praeesse' and 'imperio dirigere' are used in place of 'imperare' — and, significantly, in respect of both powers: 'Si igitur, ut dictum est, qui de ultimo fine curam habet, *praeesse debet* his qui curam habet de ordinatis ad finem et eos *dirigere suo imperio,* manifestum ex dictis fit quod *rex,* sicut dominio et regimini quod administratur per sacerdotis officium subdi debet, ita *praeesse debet* omnibus humanis officiis *et ea imperio sui regiminis ordinare*'.

---

16 *De potestate,* c. V: ed. Leclercq, p. 183; ed. Bleienstein, p. 87.

John of Paris, then, by using 'dirigere' instead of 'imperare', is following the terminology employed by the *De regno* itself. Far from rejecting the architectonic principle and its application, as anyone who has read Fr Eschmann might expect of a forthright proponent of the 'dualistic' system, John of Paris accepts it, and indeed uses it to show, as the *De regno* does, that in the spiritual order, where the relationship is that of final end to 'inferior' end, the spiritual power is not only over and above but also directs ('dirigit') the secular power.

As it happens (and this, again, is a point that Fr Eschmann overlooks), it is John of Paris himself who states very clearly what is meant by 'imperare' and 'imperio eius dirigi' and who provides an answer to Fr Eschmann's blank assertion that 'imperare' has a 'jurisdictional sense'. For among the many hierocratic arguments that John of Paris lists ('Nunc videndum est quibus innitantur fundamentis qui dicunt sacerdotes et praecipue papam habere potestatem primariam et ipsam a summo pontifice derivare ad principem'),[17] there is one that arrives at a hierocratic conclusion exactly in the same way that Fr Eschmann draws a hierocratic conclusion from the architectonic argument of the *De regno*:

> [23] Item idem arguunt ex ordine finium. In artibus enim ordinatis ars ad quem pertinet ultimus et principalis finis *imperat* aliis artibus ad quas pertinent fines secundarii. Sed saecularis potestas intendit bonum multitudinis quod est vivere secundum virtutem ad quod pervenire potest virtute naturae et eis quae huic adminiculantur. Potestas autem spiritualis intendit bonum multitudinis supernaturale, scilicet aeternam beatitudinem et in ipsum *dirigit*. Finis autem supernaturalis potior est et principalior quolibet alio fine. Ergo spiritualis potestas quae ministris ecclesiae collata est *superior est* non solum dignitate sed etiam causalitate *saeculari* et *ei praecipit* qualiter debeat operari.[18]

Of course, as was pointed out above, the *De regno* never arrives at a hierocratic conclusion such as this. Again, it was also pointed out above that the architectonic argument, which Eschmann (rightly) felt was too 'limping' to support the hierocratic position with which he credited the *De regno,* was deliberately employed precisely because the author of the *De regno* was *not* establishing a hierocratic thesis. Now John of Paris, who himself had used the architectonic argument earlier, shows in his reply to the hierocratic argument above just how the 'ordo finium' is to be understood, and how one cannot jump from the architectonic principle to a hierocratic conclusion:

---

17   *Ibid.*, c. XI: ed. Leclercq, p. 201; ed. Bleienstein, p. 118.
18   *Ibid.*, c. IX: ed. Leclercq, p. 204; ed. Bleienstein, p. 121. For 'et *eis* quae huic adminiculantur' Bleienstein reads 'et *ea* quae huic adminiculantur'.

Quod vero dicitur vigesimo tertio de ordine finium, respondeo: multipliciter deficit. Primo, quia ars ad quam pertinet superior finis *movet et imperat* artem ad quam pertinet finis inferior *non quidem simpliciter* sed quantum ei competit ad necessitatem ultimi sui finis, et hoc aliqualiter est concessum superius in proposito. Amplius, deficit quia ars illa superior *non semper necessario imperat inferiori movendo per modum auctoritatis et instituendo eam, sed solum ei imperat per modum dirigentis* ...[19]

This, I submit, is sufficient to modify Fr Eschmann's unqualified assertion that 'The word *imperare* [in the *De regno* passage] must be understood in the jurisdictional sense is evident from the text and context where the univocally jurisdictional words: *subdi, esse subjectum, subjacere, obedire, servire, famulari,* are frequently and emphatically used' (182). Certainly it does not bear out his further assertion (181 n. 18) that 'imperare' in the *De regno* passage 'has been so understood [i.e. in a jurisdictional sense] by all ancient commentators'. John of Paris, at least, saw a distinction between 'imperare per modum auctoritatis' and 'imperare per modum dirigentis'.[20]

*

* *

The teaching of the *De regno,* therefore, is not 'Theological Gregorianism' but that of undoubted dualists such as John of Paris (who, indeed, may well have been combating those who, like Fr Eschmann, interpreted the work as hierocratic, or who were adapting it, as Bellarmine would later do, for hierocratic purposes). Further, the *De regno* is no more at variance with the dualistic teaching of the *Scriptum super sententiis* of St Thomas than it is out of harmony with the ('univocally jurisdictional'?) language of that font of dualism, the Gelasian letter, with its 'subdi debere' and, rather startlingly, 'colla submitti'.

What, then, of the *De regno* as an authentic or non-authentic work of St Thomas? In some brilliant pages (195-6 especially), Fr Eschmann advanced the opinion that the *De regno* occasioned 'mistrust', chiefly because *De regno* I.14 'belonged to a different world' than that of the

19 *Ibid.,* c. XI: ed. Leclercq, pp. 226-7; ed. Bleienstein, p. 159.

20 It may be noted that in c. 15, when delineating the spheres of the two powers, the *De regno* speaks of the superior (spiritual) power as being in a position to 'dirigere suo imperio' when there is question of the final end of man; and it then goes on to say that the secular power has a similar right to 'imperio sui regiminis ordinare' with respect own, human end. Eschmann does not cite the passage, but had he cited it he would have had to explain why his 'jurisdictional sense' of *imperare* (here 'dirigere, ordinare. suo imperio') is not as applicable to the secular *imperium* as he claims it is to the spiritual *imperium*.

Scriptum. And in concluding his article (204) he entered a resonant plea for the rejection of the *De regno*: 'On the foregoing pages St. Thomas' legacy in the matter of the two powers, its native integrality, its substance and meaning, has been put on trial. The defence submits the plea that the testimony of the *De regno* be rejected, this witness not being reliable'.

The present essay has suggested, on the other hand, that the *De regno* text is as 'dualistic' as the rest of St Thomas' 'legacy on the two powers', and it has called John of Paris, an unimpeachable dualist, to witness for the very passage upon which the case for the 'defence' rested. If it now respectfully submits that the defence's plea be denied forthwith, it also expresses the deepest regret (not unmingled with relief) that Fr Eschmann's massive scholarship is no longer with us to sweep the submission fraternally aside.

Pontifical Institute of Mediaeval Studies.

XIV

THE CURRICULUM OF THE FACULTY
OF CANON LAW AT OXFORD IN THE
FIRST HALF OF THE FOURTEENTH
CENTURY

FOR the student of the history of the canon law in medieval England one of the least satisfying features of the *Statuta Antiqua* of the University of Oxford is the somewhat fragmentary nature of the sections on the faculty of canon law. Of course one can always arrive at an overall picture of the general requirements for degrees in canon law from the fourteenth to the sixteenth century, as Hastings Rashdall has done in his great *Medieval Universities*[1] and Strickland Gibson in his introduction to his fine edition of the Oxford Statutes,[2] but there always remains a danger that this picture may not be wholly verifiable at any given moment within those two centuries. If, for example, one has to decide what the course of studies in canon law would have been at Oxford between the years 1320 and 1340, it will be found that the summaries of Rashdall and Strickland Gibson do not always agree with one another, and that they often require modification, particularly where the texts used in the faculty are concerned. Thus, although it is perfectly correct to state that a bachelor who wished to incept as a doctor 'must have given one lecture for each regent doctor, have opposed in the schools, have responded to the questions of the regents of the faculty, and have lectured cursorily (*extraordinarie*) on one or two causes (or *De symonia*, or *De consecratione* or *De poenitentia*)',[3] this is to leave out of account the part played by the Sext and the Clementines in the curriculum of the faculty from the first quarter of the fourteenth century onwards.

The purpose, therefore, of the present essay is to see with what success one can trace a student's course from the statutes at any given period, the years chosen being the first forty or fifty of the fourteenth century, when the Sext and the Clementines were first

---

[1] Hastings Rashdall, *The Universities of Europe in the Middle Ages*, ed. F. M. Powicke and A. B. Emden, Oxford, 1936, iii. 157.

[2] *Statuta Antiqua Universitatis Oxoniensis*, ed. Strickland Gibson, Oxford, 1931, introd., pp. cvii–cix.　　　　　　[3] Ibid., pp. cvii–cviii.

making their impact felt at Oxford. We shall consider at some length the qualifications required for the licentiate and doctorate in canon law, adding some notes on the baccalaureate, the period of regency, and the texts used in the schools. Unfortunately the statutes of the University do not give very much direct information about the faculty of canon law at Oxford in the period we have chosen, but what they contain may reasonably be supplemented from what is known about legal studies during those years at Bologna (statutes of 1317)[1] and at other universities, particularly that of Padua (statutes of 1331).[2] For Oxford there are four important statutes; since we shall have to refer to them time and again, it may be helpful to set them out fully here, in the order in which they occur in the printed statutes:[3]

A. Qualifications for lecturing *quasi-ordinarie* on the Decretals:

Forma decretalium. Ut in lectura decretalium expedicius procedatur, auctoritate tocius universitatis est concorditer ordinatum quod liber decretalium quasi ordinarie eo tempore matutino legatur, quo ordinarie solent legere iurium civilium professores. Qui autem sic voluerint legere decretales infra annum quasi ordinarie, hora non mutata, eas perlegere iuramento prestito tenebuntur. Ad huiusmodi lecturam nullus admittatur omnino nisi iura civilia per quinquennium, bis decretales, decreta per biennium se iuret audisse. Ac omnia volumina utriusque iuris apparitata cum glosis se iuret habere; tenebitur insuper prius cursorie legisse secundum librum decretalium sive quintum. . . . Ut autem magistris secundum sui status exigenciam debita reverencia deferatur, doctores decretorum, qui Oxonie seu Cantebrigie docuerunt, super audicione legum decretalium et decretorum seu lectura secundi vel quinti decretalium, et magistri legum super iurium civilium audicione, ut premissum est, nullatenus iurare cogantur. (*Stat. Ant.*, pp. 45, l. 20–46, l. 19.)

B. (*a*) Decree ordering Sext to be taught *ordinarie* and *extraordinarie*:

Item, de lectura decretalium statutum est quod sextus liber decretalium legatur ordinarie a legente decretales eadem hora, et quod certi

[1] H. Denifle, 'Die Statuten der Juristen-Universität Bologna vom J. 1317–1347, und deren Verhältniss zu jenen Paduas, Perugias, Florenz', *Archiv f. Literatur- und Kirchen-Geschichte des MA.* 4 (1887), 196–397.

[2] Id., 'Die Statuten der Juristen-Universität Padua vom Jahre 1331', ibid. 6 (1892), 310–560.

[3] Strickland Gibson dates A, B, C, as pre-1350, but they are rather pre-1333, since statute D (14 Dec. 1333) is clearly a revision of the legislation in A, B, C, on ordinary and extraordinary lectures and on the course for the doctorate. See p. 151, n. 2, below.

tituli, extracti secundum disposicionem magistrorum ad hoc deputatorum, extraordinarie legantur. (*Stat. Ant.*, p. 46, ll. 20–24.)

(*b*) Qualifications for lecturing *extraordinarie* on Sext and Decretals:

Ad lecturam vero extraordinariam alicuius libri decretalium nullus de cetero admittatur, nisi iura civilia saltim per triennium, et decreta per biennium, ac decretales complete se iuret audisse. Doctoribus tamen decretorum et legum, ut predictum est, reverencia semper salva. (*Stat. Ant.*, p. 46, ll. 25–30.)

C. Qualifications for inception as a Doctor in Canon Law:

(*a*) For Bachelors who were Doctors in Civil Law:

De modo incipiendi in decretis. Qui incepturi sunt in decretis, prius vices omnium magistrorum in eadem facultate ordinarie legencium supleant in legendo, et per omnes scolas publice opponant, et questionibus magistrorum respondeant, semel ad minus in scolis singulis, et duas causas vel tres, vel tractatum *De symonia*, vel *De consecracione*, vel *De penitencia*, legant extraordinarie. Quod si premissa laudabiliter compleverint, . . . licenciari poterunt. (*Stat. Ant.*, p. 47, ll. 5–15).

(*b*) For Bachelors who were not Doctors in Civil Law:

Incepturi in decretis, si prius in iure civili non rexerint, iura civilia ad minus per triennium, Bibliam, quatenus legitur in studio, per biennium, decreta per triennium, ac decretales integraliter se iurent audisse; necnon et antequam ad incipiendum presententur saltem unum librum decretalium legisse tenentur. Item, prius vices omnium magistrorum in decretis ordinarie legencium supleant in legendo. (*Stat. Ant.*, p. 47, ll. 17–23.)

D. Statute of 14 Dec. 1333 setting up a course of ordinary and extra-ordinary lectures on Decretals, Sext, and Clementines, to be covered every two years by Doctors and Bachelors:

Cum caveatur de statuto quod legens ordinarie decretales, eas una cum sexto libro decretalium quasi ordinarie infra annum, iuramento prestito, perlegere teneatur, ac constitucionibus Clementinis universitas uti debeat in iudiciis et scolis, et plerumque nichil de sexto nec de Clementinis legitur et nichilominus multum omittitur de antiquis, ut universitati legentibus pariter et audientibus salubriter succuratur, statutum est quod legens ordinarie decretales sub pena centum solidorum obligetur, quod per se et extra ordinarium suum complebit lecturam inferius annotatam, videlicet quod uno anno per se et extra ordinarium suum legat primum, quartum et quintum libros decretalium antiquarum una cum constitucionibus Clementinis, et quod ille, qui secundo anno lecturus fuerit, sub pena eadem obligetur ad lecturam sexti libri, ac secundi et tertii antiquarum, ita quod lectura antiquarum, sexti et Clementinarum per biennium, modo quo premittitur, compleatur; nec duobus annis continuis legatur aliqua porcio predictarum, sed vicissim, ut in codice et digestis. Item, statutum est quod lectura sexti libri sufficiat pro forma legentis tanquam lectura cuiuscumque alterius libri decretalium antiquarum. (*Stat. Ant.*, pp. 132, l. 22–133, l. 9.)

(i) *The licence to lecture*

As far as one can make out from these Oxford statutes and from corresponding statutes in continental universities, the licence to lecture ('admissio ad lecturam extraordinariam alicuius libri Decretalium', as it is described in statute B(*b*) above) did not involve a formal examination.[1] It was given to a scholar as soon as he was in a position to satisfy the rector or the chancellor of the University, or the principal of the faculty of canon law, that he was qualified to lecture. In effect this probably did not entail anything more than an interview,[2] at least for the candidate who was already a doctor in civil law. For the aspirant who did not possess this degree the important requirement was an oath that he had heard a set number of lectures on civil and canon law.

What that course of studies was at Oxford is not immediately clear from the statutes; and the issue is further complicated by the fact that the qualifications given by Strickland Gibson are at variance with those listed by Rashdall. As it happens, Strickland Gibson is completely correct when he states that the course 'ad lecturam extraordinariam' (the licentiate) was 'civil law for three years, the Decretum for two years, and the Decretals complete'.[3] However, if we are to uphold him against Rashdall, we must examine with attention the passage which he is summarizing and, if possible, find other evidence. As it stands, the statute on which he is relying (B(*b*)) does not immediately yield his conclusion. For one thing the general statement of qualifications 'ad lecturam extraordinariam alicuius libri decretalium' arises out of, and appears to go with, the decree immediately preceding (B(*a*)), namely, that the Sext was to be lectured on *extraordinarie* as well as *ordinarie*.[4] For

---

[1] Cf. Bologna (*Archiv*, iv. 325–7), Padua (ibid. vi. 412–13).

[2] See B. Kurtscheid, 'De utriusque iuris studio saeculo XIII', *Acta Congressus Iuridici Internationalis Romae 1934*, ii (Rome, 1935), 315–16.

[3] *Stat. Ant.*, p. cvii.

[4] 'Item, de lectura decretalium statutum est quod sextus liber decretalium

another, when these qualifications for extraordinary lecturing have been set out in B(*b*), the oath required before admission is stated not to be universally binding: 'Doctoribus tamen decretorum et legum, ut predictum est, reverencia semper salva.'[1] Now the reference back here is to quasi-ordinary lectures (A), with which we shall deal presently, and in fact to the exemption in that statute of doctors from the oath required of bachelors;[2] the import of the statute B(*b*) is therefore much wider than Strickland Gibson gives us to understand, since (i) doctors in civil or canon law are envisaged for the extraordinary teaching which Strickland Gibson took to be simply the licentiate, (ii) the oath to the qualifications was obligatory only when there was question of admitting students to extraordinary teaching who were not doctors in either law.

The problem now is to decide to what class of non-doctor student do these qualifications refer, and to what type of extraordinary lecturing; more precisely, we have to decide (*a*) whether the qualifications are special qualifications for students who already had a general licence to teach *extraordinarie*, that is, for students who were already *licentiati*, (*b*) whether they are simply the basic qualifications for any type of extraordinary teaching, (*c*) whether they are, as well, the qualifications for extraordinary teaching as such, that is, for the licentiate. Incidentally the nature of statute B becomes clearer, and the shape of the canon law curriculum more definite.

Strickland Gibson has taken the statute in the third sense (*c*), but, as we have noted, without adverting to the fact that the statute includes doctors as well as non-doctors. More importantly, he has failed to note that the list of qualifications for extraordinary lecturing is occasioned by the decree (B(*a*)) that introduced

---

legatur ordinarie a legente decretales eadem hora, et quod certi tituli, extracti secundum disposicionem magistrorum ad hoc deputatorum, extraordinarie legantur': B(*a*) (*Stat. Ant.*, p. 47, ll. 20–24).

[1] 'Ad lecturam vero extraordinariam alicuius libri decretalium nullus de cetero admittatur, nisi iura civilia saltim per triennium, et decreta per biennium, ac decretales complete se iuret audisse. Doctoribus tamen decretorum et legum, ut predictum est, reverencia semper salva': B(*b*) (*Stat. Ant.*, p. 47, ll. 25–30).

[2] 'Ut autem magistris secundum sui status exigenciam debita reverencia deferatur, doctores decretorum, qui Oxonie seu Cantebrigie docuerunt, super audicione legum decretalium et decretorum seu lectura secundi vel quinti decretalium, et magistri legum super iurium civilium audicione, ut premissum est, nullatenus iurare cogantur': A (*Stat. Ant.*, p. 46, ll. 14–19).

extraordinary lectures on the Sext. For although the statute on the qualifications (B(*b*)) is more general than that on the Sext (B(*a*)) in so far as the opening phrase is 'ad lecturam alicuius libri decretalium', it must have been drawn up originally with direct reference to the extraordinary lectures on the Sext. If it is simply a statement of the terms of admission to the licentiate as such (extraordinary teaching as such), then there would be no question of exempting doctors of canon law from the oath demanded of applicants for extraordinary lectures who were not doctors of civil or canon law. A doctor of canon law 'of Oxford or Cambridge' would hardly have to be taken into account·if this statute as such simply governs admission to the licentiate in canon law at Oxford. The two decrees (B(*a*) and B(*b*)) are clearly correlative; in fact, they are but two parts of the one decree. In the first part a scheme was enacted whereby the professors' burden of lecturing *ordinarie* on the Decretals and Sext was to be shared with doctors and non-doctors of either law who would take over parts of the Sext in extraordinary lectures. In the second part the qualifications for such extraordinary lectures were set out, with a distinction between doctors and non-doctors. The introduction of 'special' extraordinary lectures on the Sext (B(*a*)) was thus made the occasion of a definition of the terms of admission to any type of extraordinary teaching (B(*b*)), including the licentiate. The immediate end of the statute (special lectures on the Sext open to doctors and non-doctors) is indicated by the exemption of doctors in either law; its general applicability by the opening words of the second part, 'ad lecturam vero extraordinariam alicuius libri decretalium'. In time, however, this second part came to be regarded as primarily a statute on admission to extraordinary teaching as such, that is, to the licentiate. For although the rubric, *Forma legencium decretales extraordinarie*, is not in the earliest manuscript of the statutes, rubrics and notes in other manuscripts are quite explicit, thus: 'ista brevis clausula sequens precise legatur (admittendo) ad lecturam extraordinariam decretalium'; 'statutum legatur et nullum aliud (in) admissione bachilariorum iuris canonici'.[1] However, the clause about the exemption of doctors of either law

---

[1] *Stat. Ant.*, p. 46, note to line 25. See also gravamen of faculty of canon law in 1397: 'Inter cetera dictae universitatis statuta cavetur quod nullus ad lecturam extraordinariam decretalium in ipsa universitate debeat admitti nisi iura civilia per triennium . . . [et] decretales se iuret complete audivisse.' (D. Wilkins, *Concilia*, iii. 228.) See also p. 144, n. 2, below.

reveals the original and wider setting of the decree, for the oath to the qualifications for admission to the licentiate in canon law naturally affected non-doctors in civil law alone.

The qualifications for extraordinary lectures on the Sext in statute B are thus, as Strickland Gibson assumed, those for the licentiate course as well. This conclusion is put beyond all doubt when we compare these qualifications (to which, as we noted, non-doctors in civil law would have to swear before the licentiate) with those in the oath sworn before the doctorate by this same class of non-doctor in civil law. With respect to attendance at lectures in civil and canon law the qualifications are exactly the same, with one exception:

Oath of non-doctors in civil law before

extraordinary teaching (B(*b*))	the Doctorate (C(*b*))
1. Iura civilia saltim per triennium.	Iura civilia ad minus per triennium.
2. Decreta per *biennium*.	Decreta per *triennium*.
3. Decretales complete.	Decretales integraliter.

Given that the courses in the two oaths are almost identical, it seems reasonable to conclude that the second oath is retrospective to the beginning of the course for the doctorate of a student who was not a doctor in civil law, and that, in fact, the matter in common to the two oaths is the course for the licentiate. The additional year of the Decretum would be made up, no doubt, in the interval between the licentiate and doctorate which we shall describe presently. Bachelors who were not doctors in civil law were thus required before the doctorate to repeat the oath sworn at the licentiate, but with the addition of an extra year of the Decretum. If there is no mention whatsoever of this course of lectures in civil and canon law in the qualifications for the doctorate demanded on oath of a candidate who was already a doctor in civil law, this is precisely because he had been granted an exemption from the oath to that course before his admission to the licentiate. As we shall see later, the student with a doctorate in civil law was more privileged all through his canonical studies than the student who did not possess it. The latter was barely tolerated, and was never allowed to forget that he had come in by the back door.

If Strickland Gibson is thus proved to be in the main correct about the course for the licentiate, Hastings Rashdall on the contrary appears to rely on the wrong statute when he states that for the licentiate (which he calls the Bachelor of Degrees) five years' study of civil law were required, and 'to have heard the Decretals twice and the Decretum for two years'.[1] For the statute in question (A) has nothing to do with the course for the licentiate as such. It is concerned rather with teachers who are to help out the ordinary professors by giving quasi-ordinary lectures: 'ut in lectura decretalium expedicius procedatur, auctoritate tocius universitatis est concorditer ordinatum quod liber decretalium quasi ordinarie eo tempore matutino legatur, quo ordinarie solent legere iurium civilium professores.' The qualifications demanded of those proposing themselves for this quasi-ordinary teaching could not possibly have been possessed by a student of canon law before admission to the licentiate: 'ad *huiusmodi* lecturam nullus admittatur omnino nisi iura civilia per quinquennium, bis decretales, decreta per biennium se iuret audisse . . .; tenebitur insuper prius cursorie legisse secundum librum decretalium sive quintum.' Doctors of civil or of canon law are exempted from this oath; those upon whom the oath is binding are clearly *licentiati* who are already well on their way to the doctorate, for cursory lectures (extraordinary) on the Decretals are stipulated. Therefore, although the qualifications listed in this statute on quasi-ordinary lectures include part of the course of studies for the licence to teach *extraordinarie* or cursorily, there are clearly elements that are post-licentiate. Since this is the case it is not surprising to find that Rashdall found this statute (A) 'impossible to adjust' with the course set out in the oath taken before the doctorate by candidates who were not doctors in civil law (C(*b*)).[2] For the qualifications listed there should not be adjusted with those for quasi-ordinary lectures, although they may profitably be compared, but rather, as we have seen, with those set out in the statute on admission to extraordinary teaching (B(*b*)). Rashdall, however, seems to have been unaware of this latter statute.

Summing up, we may therefore state that, for admission to extraordinary teaching (the licentiate) in the early part of the fourteenth century, the course required at Oxford was three years of civil law,[3] two years of the Decretum, and a complete study of

---

[1] *Universities*, iii. 157.   [2] Ibid., p. 157, n. 3.

[3] An appeal was made against these three years of civil law in 1397, 'cum viri religiosi, et qui in ordine sacerdotum sunt constituti, adeo existunt multipliciter

the Decretals;[1] that students who were already doctors of civil law were excused from taking an oath to this course; that the oath was obligatory for all other students, even for those who were already bachelors in civil law; and, finally, that students in this latter class were bound to present an extra year of the Decretum after the licentiate in order to qualify for admission to the doctorate. What the general qualifications were for the doctorate we shall see presently.

(ii) *The course for the doctorate*

In the interval between the granting of the licence to teach cursorily or *extraordinarie* and the inception as a doctor, the title of Bachelor was conferred on the *licentiatus*. At some universities this took place shortly after the licentiate, in others at a point nearer to inception. At Montpellier (1349) the time between the baccalaureate and the doctorate was as much as five years, but at Bologna (for civil law) it was one year, and at Padua (for canon law) it was even less.[2] At Oxford the period seems to have fluctuated. Sometimes it is four or five years, but on one occasion (a century later than the years under consideration here, it is true) a law student took his baccalaureate on the very day he incepted as a doctor.[3] But although Rashdall and Strickland Gibson make no distinction between the licentiate and the baccalaureate, it seems that normally the two were not simultaneous or equivalent, and that in fact the *licentiatus* would not qualify for the title of bachelor until he had given a certain number of cursory lectures,

impediti' (Wilkins, *Concilia*, iii. 228), presumably on account of the decree *Super specula* of Honorius III in 1219, which, among other things, prohibited the study of civil law to priests, regulars, and beneficed clerks (see Rashdall, *Universities*, i. 322, and the fine essay by S. Kuttner, 'Papst Honorius III. und das Studium des Zivilrechts', in *Festschrift für Martin Wolff*, Tübingen, 1952, pp. 79–101). But nothing was done on behalf of this class of scholar until 1438, when the University allowed 'quod sacerdotes qui ad leges civiles transire non possunt compleant 7 annos in iure canonico ante gradum bacallariatus . . . antiquo statuto penes omnes alios in suo robore permansuro' (*Stat. Ant.*, p. 259, ll. 1–7).

[1] See one of the gravamina of 1397: 'Nunquid iste terminus "complete" debet ita stricte intelligi scilicet pro quolibet verbo cujusque capituli libri decretalium . . . vel in quantum humana fragilitas patitur . . .' (Wilkins, *Concilia*, iii. 228).

[2] See Kurtscheid, art. cit., p. 329.

[3] See the unpublished B.Litt. dissertation of K. R. N. Wykeham-George, O.P., *English Canonists in the Late Middle Ages*, Oxford, 1937, p. 245.

or, perhaps, had given a formal repetition of some canon.[1] While the title of bachelor may have been a nominal requirement for inception as a doctor (this may well explain the case of the student who took his baccalaureate and incepted as a doctor on the same day), it was the licence to lecture *extraordinarie* or *cursorie* that really mattered. For it was the number of cursory lectures that a *licentiatus* had given after he had obtained his licentiate, and, to a lesser extent, the number of ordinary lectures that he had given for each regent doctor, that formally qualified him for admission to the doctorate. For the sake of convenience, however, we shall ignore the distinction for the remainder of this paper, referring simply to the student between the licentiate and the doctorate as 'bachelor'.[2]

The course for the doctorate depended, as we have noted above, on whether or not the bachelor was already a doctor in civil law. But apart from that extra year of the Decretum mentioned above there were other differences, as may readily be seen from the following comparison of the statute governing the inception of bachelors in general with the terms of the oath sworn before inception by bachelors who were not doctors in civil law:

All bachelors before inception (statute C(*a*))	Non-doctors in civil law (statute C(*b*))
Qui incepturi sunt in decretis,	Incepturi in decretis, si prius in iure civili non rexerint,
(*a*) prius vices omnium magistrorum in eadem facultate ordinarie legencium supleant in legendo	prius vices omnium magistrorum in decretis ordinarie legencium supleant in legendo

---

[1] Kurtscheid, art. cit., pp. 329–30.

[2] The term 'licentiate' does not occur in the statutes we have been discussing. That used generally is 'admissio ad lecturam extraordinariam', although a late rubric speaks of 'admissio bachilariorum' (*Stat. Ant.*, p. 46, and note to l. 25) and a statute of 1438 gives 'bacallariatus' (ibid., p. 259, ll. 4–5). Our use of the term here is justified by the usage of the civil law faculty (see ibid., p. 43, l. 11: 'nullus licenciam optineat legendi aliquid *cursorie*') and from a gravamen of 1397 that shows that the term 'licentiatus' was not unknown in the University in respect of cursory or extraordinary lectures: 'Item, dicto universitatis statuto continetur quod *licentiatus* ad lecturam de qua prefertur (extraordinariam), nullus admittatur nisi decretales se iuret "complete" audivisse . . .' (Wilkins, *Concilia*, iii. 228).

(b) et per omnes scolas publice opponant, et questionibus magistrorum respondeant, semel ad minus in scolis singulis,

(c) et duas causas vel tres, vel tractatum *De symonia*, vel *De consecratione*, vel *De penitentia*, legant extraordinarie.[1]

necnon et antequam ad incipiendum presententur saltem unum librum decretalium legisse tenentur.

iura civilia ad minus per triennium,

Bibliam quatenus legitur in studio, per biennium,

decreta per triennium, ac decretales integraliter se iurent audisse.

From this comparison it is clear that for the bachelor who was not a doctor in civil law the course for the doctorate was much more exacting than that of the bachelor who already had the civil law degree. In contrast to the latter the non-doctor was obliged to take an oath to the specified course before admittance to the doctorate. Part of that oath is, as we have seen, retrospective to the course for the licentiate, but the non-doctor was further obliged to present (or make up) two years of the Bible and an extra year's study of the Decretum. Doctors of civil law, on the other hand, were not bound to attend lectures on civil and canon law after the licentiate. Their obligations were confined to the more specific acts of a bachelor: to stand in as ordinary lecturer for each regent doctor in turn, to give a set of cursory lectures on parts of the Decretum, and to take part in the *quaestiones disputatae* of each of the doctors of the faculty. The non-doctors had these formal duties of a bachelor in common with the doctors, but with the addition of a series of cursory lectures on one book of the Decretals.

The desirable thing, of course, was that all students for the

---

[1] In this and in many other statutes of the canon law faculty the phrasing is modelled on that of the corresponding statutes of the civil law faculty, thus: 'Qui in iure civili sunt incepturi, (a) primo vices omnium magistrorum in eadem facultate ordinarie legencium supleant in legendo, (b) et per omnes scolas decretistarum in questionibus opponant et respondeant saltem semel, (c) et unum volumen legale legant cursorie, et *Libellum institucionum* vel *Corpus auctenticorum* vel tres libros extraordinarios *Codicis*' (*Stat. Ant.*, p. 44, ll. 15-21).

doctorate in canon law should possess a doctorate in civil law. If the non-doctor was to be admitted it was only at a price. His position was, in fact, as unenviable as that of a non-master of arts in the faculties of theology or civil law,[1] and his course was accordingly longer than that of the doctor. Hence, too, the somewhat material obligations imposed on him, and the insistence on an oath at each milestone on the way to the doctorate.

(iii) *Quasi-ordinary teaching*

Apart from this essential course of ordinary and extraordinary lectures common to all aspirants to the doctorate, there was, in the early part of the fourteenth century, an optional course of lectures open to all bachelors. This was a set of 'quasi-ordinary' lectures. As we have seen earlier, the University was forced to institute this quasi-ordinary type of lecture in order to expedite the ordinary lectures of the doctors on the Decretals. But although doctors of canon law would be more suitable to take the place of the ordinary professors, the doctors of the faculty, provision was also made for bachelors. However, the qualifications were such that only bachelors who were well advanced in their studies for the doctorate could possibly qualify, as the following comparison between the course for the licentiate and that given for quasi-ordinary lectures may suggest:

Licentiate (statute B(*b*))	Quasi-ordinary lectures (statute A)
Ad lecturam vero extraordinariam alicuius libri decretalium nullus de cetero admittatur, nisi	Ad huiusmodi lecturam nullus admittatur omnino nisi
(*a*) iura civilia saltim per triennium,	iura civilia per quinquennium,

---

[1] For the faculty of theology see *Stat. Ant.*, p. 48, ll. 15–31, and p. 49, ll. 10–14, and for that of civil law, ibid., p. 43, ll. 10–19. The latter statute goes on to state why the master of arts is more acceptable than the non-master: 'Statutum est ut nullus licenciam optineat legendi aliquid cursorie in iure civili nisi iura civilia saltim per quadriennium, si prius in artibus rexerit, se iuret audisse. Magistros enim arcium, tum propter etatis maturitatem, tum propter ingeniorum perspicuitatem, tum propter subtile in artibus exercicium, verisimile est in talibus ceterorum comparacione felici duplomate posse uti. Qui autem prius in artibus non rexerunt, antequam licenciam optineant sic legendi, iurare tenentur se audisse iura civilia per sex annos.' Much the same deference was shown to a doctor in civil law when he entered the faculty of canon law.

(*b*) et decreta per biennium,

(*c*) ac decretales complete

se iuret audivisse.

decreta per biennium,

bis decretales,

se iuret audisse . . . ,

tenebitur insuper prius cursorie legisse secundum librum decretalium vel quintum.

An oath to these qualifications as a whole was obligatory only on the bachelor who was not a doctor of civil law, but 'doctores decretorum, qui Oxonie seu Cantabrigie docuerunt', were only excused from swearing 'super audicione legum decretalium et decretorum seu lectura secundi vel quinti decretalium', and doctors in civil law 'super iurium civilium audicione'.[1] The University was obviously hard pressed for lecturers to help out the doctors, but the conditions imposed were none the less stringent. Clearly only the very exceptional bachelor, whether a doctor of civil law or not, would qualify for admittance to these quasi-ordinary lectures. The non-doctor would have had to complete his cursory lectures on the decretals before he could be considered. Few bachelors would have had time to attend a complete set of lectures on the Decretals between the licentiate and the doctorate. The provisions, therefore, of this statute on quasi-ordinary lectures can no more be taken as an indication of the course for the doctorate than they can be presumed to give the qualifications for the licentiate. But they are of value, all the same, in that they suggest what a bachelor could do or could study, outside the normal curriculum, in the years before the doctorate.

(iv) *Extraordinary teaching*

The most important requirement, then, for any bachelor presenting himself for inception, was to have lectured cursorily or *extraordinarie*, and to have completed a certain amount of ordinary teaching.

The distinction between 'ordinary' and 'extraordinary' lecturing was based mainly on time and matter.[2] Doctors usually gave their lectures in the morning period (at Oxford after Prime, according

[1] *Stat. Ant.*, p. 46, ll. 14–19. See p. 139, n. 2, above.
[2] J. F. Schulte, *Geschichte der Quellen und Literatur des canonischen Rechts*, Stuttgart, 1875–80, ii. 456; Rashdall, *Universities*, i. 216–17.

to a pre-1380 statute),[1] and on the important parts of the course: these were the ordinary lectures. The extraordinary lectures took place in the afternoon, and were given either by bachelors acting formally as bachelors, in which case they were known as cursory lectures, or by doctors and bachelors who had been called on to give lectures supplementing the ordinary lectures of the doctors.[2] On the other hand the category known as quasi-ordinary lectures, for which specially qualified bachelors and certain doctors were engaged, took place in the morning time at the same hour as the lectures of the professors of the civil law faculty.[3]

The matter, too, was divided into ordinary and extraordinary, according to the texts used, but this division does not exactly coincide with that of the lectures. For although an ordinary lecture was normally on an ordinary text, the extraordinary lecture could be on an ordinary as well as on an extraordinary text.[4] Thus although the Sext was declared to be an ordinary book at Oxford some time before 1333, certain portions of it were lectured on *extraordinarie* by bachelors or by doctors.[5]

As the statutes survive for Oxford certain changes in the ordinary and extraordinary books in use in the faculty of canon law may be discerned in the period with which we are dealing here. Where originally the Decretum was the ordinary text, by the beginning of the fourteenth century it seems to have dropped to the position of an extraordinary book, since to qualify for the licence to incept as a doctor the bachelor had to lecture *extraordinarie* on portions of the *Decretum*.[6] But although the Decretals had by now taken the place of the Decretum as the ordinary text, not all of the matter could be covered in ordinary lectures. For, as we have seen, certain bachelors and doctors had to be engaged by the University to help out the ordinary by giving quasi-ordinary lectures on the Decretals in the morning period.[7] Sometime before 1333, however, the Decretals achieved full ordinary status in fact, the Sext of Boniface

[1] See *Stat. Ant.*, p. 175, ll. 19–21: 'Item, statutum est quod nullus in facultate arcium leccioni ordinarie alterius facultatis quam sue intersit, nisi forte talem leccionem post primam, sicut in decretis, legi contigerit . . . .'

[2] For example, the 'extraordinary' lectures on the Sext in statute B.

[3] 'Liber decretalium quasi ordinarie eo tempore matutino legatur, quo ordinarie solent legere iurium civilium professores': statute A (*Stat. Ant.*, p. 45, ll. 22–24).

[4] Rashdall, *Universities*, i. 217.   [5] Statute B (*Stat. Ant.*, p. 46, ll. 22–30).

[6] Statute C(*a*) (ibid., p. 47, ll. 5–11).   [7] Statute A (ibid., pp. 45–46).

VIII now taking over the quasi-ordinary role previously assigned to parts of the Decretals. This at least is what seems to be implied in the preamble to a statute (D) of that year: 'Cum caveatur de statuto quod legens ordinarie decretales, eas uno cum sexto libro decretalium quasi ordinarie, infra annum iuramento prestito perlegere teneatur . . . .'[1] This statute, however, appears at first sight to be at variance with an earlier statute (B(a)) in which the Sext was ordered to be read *ordinarie*. The divergence between the two statutes may possibly be explained as follows. In the period between the appearance of the first statute and the formulation of the second a situation had arisen similar to that which had caused quasi-ordinary lectures on the Decretals to be introduced. It was found, perhaps, that the Sext could not conveniently be covered in ordinary and extraordinary lectures, so, following the course adopted earlier for the Decretals, the University resorted to quasi-ordinary lectures in the morning, enlisting the help of doctors of canon law or of unusually qualified bachelors. Thus, by the time the 1333 statute was enacted the Sext was being read *quasi-ordinarie*.

(v) *Ordinary teaching*

The other qualification for the doctorate common to all bachelors was an ordinary lecture for each doctor lecturing in the faculty. The number of occasions on which the bachelor would take over in this way from the regent doctors varied from year to year, depending on the number of regent doctors in residence. At Orleans between 1290 and 1310 there were only 9 or 10 regents in contrast to 30 at Padua in 1331.[2] For Oxford the number would probably be slight, since it seems clear that only a small proportion of students in the law schools remained to the end of the full course.[3]

Ordinary and extraordinary lectures then, were the primary qualifications for all bachelors. If some of the bachelors were

---

[1] Statute D (ibid., p. 132, ll. 22–25).

[2] See Kurtscheid, art. cit., pp. 316–17.

[3] Cf. G. Barraclough, 'Praxis Beneficiorum', *Zeitschrift d. Savigny-Stiftung f. Rechtsgeschichte*, 58 (*Kan. Abt.* 27, 1938), 97; E. F. Jacob, 'Notanda quaedam de iure canonico inter Anglos praesertim inter Oxonienses Saec. xv', *Acta Congressus Iuridici Internationalis Romae 1934*, ii, Rome, 1935, 474. The statute on depositions (see p. 153, n. 1, below) in the canon law faculty clearly allows for less than four regent doctors ('in eadem facultate actualiter legencium').

admitted to quasi-ordinary lectures on the Decretals (A) or the Sext (D), or to extraordinary lectures on the Sext (B), no doubt they could supplicate for a grace to present these lectures in place of the statutory ordinary and cursory lectures, but officially this exceptional lecturing does not seem to have been taken into account among the requirements for inception before 1333. Then, on 14 December 1333, a statute (D) was introduced which throws an interesting light on the faculty of canon law.

All ordinary professors, the statute begins, are bound to take an oath that the Decretals have been read *ordinarie* and the Sext *quasi-ordinarie* in the course of each year. Now this heavy programme has been further taxed by the arrival of the Clementines, an important collection of decretals 'which the University should make use of in legal decisions and in the schools'. Indeed the course was so crowded that not only were the Clementines not getting due attention but the Sext itself and portions of the 'older decretals' were being omitted altogether.

To remedy this situation the University resorted to a practice of the faculty of civil law. The Decretals, Sext, and Clementines would be covered in a two-year cycle as the Codex and Digest were in the civil law schools, the matter being divided between regent doctors and bachelors. In the first year of the cycle the lectures would be on the first, fourth, and fifth books of the Decretals, together with the Clementines. In the second year the course would be the whole of the Sext and the second and third books of the Decretals. Under a penalty of five pounds each regent doctor was now obliged by statute to see that he and his bachelor covered the complete course of the particular year of the cycle with which his year of regency coincided. Thus if the regents of one year were bound to the first year of the cycle, those of the following year were bound to the second. There was to be no overlapping.[1]

---

[1] 'Cum caveatur de statuto quod legens ordinarie decretales, eas una cum sexto libro decretalium quasi ordinarie infra annum, iuramento prestito, perlegere teneatur, ac constitucionibus Clementinis universitas uti debeat in iudiciis et scolis, et plerumque nichil de sexto nec de Clementinis legitur et nichilominus multum omittitur de antiquis, ut universitati legentibus pariter et audientibus salubriter succuratur, statutum est quod legens ordinarie decretales sub pena centum solidorum obligetur, quod per se et extra ordinarium suum complebit lecturam inferius annotatam, videlicet quod uno anno per se et extra ordinarium suum legat primum, quartum et quintum libros decretalium antiquarum una cum constitucionibus Clementinis, et quod ille, qui secundo

In any year of this two-year cycle the main burden of the teaching would naturally fall on the doctor, the bachelor taking care *cursorie* of a book or more of the Decretals and of the less exacting parts of the Sext. The Clementines, however, were probably the preserve of the doctor, for there is no mention of them when the statute goes on to allow that if a bachelor lectured on the Sext, then this could be accepted 'pro forma legentis tanquam lectura cuiuscumque alterius libri decretalium antiquarum'.[1] This means in effect that from 1334 onwards any bachelor who lectured on the Sext was thereby excused from the obligation incumbent on all bachelors to lecture cursorily on parts of Gratian's Decretum and on non-doctors of civil law to lecture on a book of the Decretals in addition. There is not, however, any mention of quasi-ordinary lectures in this statute, so it is possible that the category had outlived its usefulness, now that the Decretals and Sext had been spread more conveniently over a two-year course.[2]

anno lecturus fuerit, sub pena eadem obligetur ad lecturam sexti libri, ac secundi et tertii antiquarum, ita quod lectura antiquarum, sexti et Clementinarum per biennium, modo quo premittitur, compleatur; nec duobus annis continuis legatur aliqua porcio predictarum, sed vicissim, ut in codice et digestis' (*Stat. Ant.*, pp. 132, l. 22–133, l. 6).

[1] Ibid., p. 133, ll. 7–9. It is clear from this provision, and especially from the words 'pro forma legentis', that the words 'extra ordinarium suum' in the statute above refer to the bachelors in canon law, that is to those who gave the extra-ordinary or cursory lectures. Strickland Gibson appears to be mistaken when he treats 'extra ordinarium' as two words: 'Under a penalty of 100s. any one 'legens ordinarie decretales' had to lecture ('per se et extra ordinarium suum') in the first year on . . . and in the second year on . . .' (Introd. to *Stat. Ant.*, p. cviii, n. 3). Further, he appears to take it for granted that a two-year regency is indicated here, in accordance with a statute which he gives as pre-1350: 'quilibet incipiens in iure canonico arctetur ad lecturam biennalem . . .' (*Stat. Ant.*, p. 47, ll. 24–27). The whole point of the 1333 decree, however, is the institution of a two-year cycle; it does not necessarily suggest a two-year regency. Indeed, from the opening phrases ('Cum caveatur *de statuto* quod legens ordinarie decretales, eas . . . *infra annum*, iuramento prestito, perlegere teneatur, . . .'), and from the wording of the phrases on the cycle ('legens ordinarie . . . uno anno . . ., ille, qui secundo anno lecturus fuerit . . .') it is possible to maintain that the statute on the two-year regency had been abrogated long before 1333 and that the statute in question here is that which reduced the regency from two years to one and is given by Strickland Gibson as pre-1380: 'Item, statutum est quod incipiens in decretis de cetero non teneatur nisi ad lecturam *annalem* . . . antiquo statuto super lectura biennali . . . non obstante' (*Stat. Ant.*, p. 178, ll. 18–22). Both statutes on the regency would therefore be pre-1333, not pre-1350 and pre-1380. The 1333 statute is making sure that the two-year cycle will be maintained, allowing precisely for the fact that the regent doctors of one year will not be those of the year following.

[2] It seems clear that the statute on quasi-ordinary lectures (A) was introduced

Besides cursory and ordinary lectures on the various texts of canon law there were other obligations to fulfil during the period between the licentiate and doctorate. Thus a bachelor had to object and respond at public *quaestiones disputatae*, once at least for each doctor; he was not, however, allowed to hold a public disputation himself.[1] The procedure in these disputations was much the same as that in the better-known disputations of the theological schools, although they took place much less frequently.[2] While for the doctor the disputation was a supreme moment in which to pronounce definitively on some point, for the bachelor it was a necessary exercise that appears to have been as unpopular in the canon law faculty as the disputation was rare.[3] Once he had put his objections or had replied to those of a fellow-bachelor he stepped down and the doctor took over. As these *quaestiones disputatae* survive some of the objections are the only traces of a bachelor's part that remain; the definitive exposition and the

at the same time as and because of the statute setting the Sext up as an ordinary book (B). The ensuing problem of maintaining a heavy morning course of ordinary lectures on both Decretals and Sext was solved by the introduction of quasi-ordinary lectures on the Decretals in the morning at the time of the civil law lectures, and extraordinary lectures on portions of the Sext in the afternoon. By and large this arrangement lasted until the statute of 1333, with the exception that quasi-ordinary lectures on the Sext were also set up. Statutes A and B are therefore pre-1333 and not as Strickland Gibson dates them, pre-1350. So also is C, for the 1333 decree allows cursory lectures on the Sext to be presented by bachelors in place of the cursory lectures on the 'old decretals' ordained by C.

[1] See *Archiv*, vi. 475 (Padua). An Oxford statute of 1376 forbids bachelors to accept money for formal responsions (*Stat. Ant.*, p. 169, ll. 12–25).

[2] See M. Grabmann, 'H. Kantorowicz und meine Geschichte der scholastischen Methode', *Zeitschrift d. Savigny-Stiftung*, 43 (*Kan. Abt.* 12, 1932), 545.

[3] 'Raro nimis disputant', according to a pre-1350 statute (*Stat. Ant.*, p. 59, l. 25). *Responsiones* in both civil and canon law faculties appear to have caused some contention. Thus a Royal Commission had to be appointed in 1375 'occasione quorundam statutorum formam et responsiones bacalariorum iuris civilis et canonici ad questiones per doctores decretorum et legum disputandas, concernentium, noviter editorum' (Wilkins, *Concilia*, iii. 107). The commission found against the bachelors: '. . . Item, statutum est quod, cum bacalarius iuris canonici ante eius incepcionem in iure canonico singulis doctoribus in facultate decretorum teneatur respondere, requisitus a doctore decretorum, qui tenetur disputare, ut sibi respondeat . . . et respondere recusaverit, . . . quod nec annus ille nec aliquis actus scolasticus eiusdem anni infra universitatem Oxonie eodem anno sibi cedat pro forma' (*Stat. Ant.*, pp. 168, l. 39–169, l. 12). Strickland Gibson possibly interprets this statute as though there was a shortage of bachelors (ibid., p. cviii, n. 3). This is not the point, although on occasion doctors experienced difficulty in persuading bachelors to fulfil their statutory obligation of 'responding at the *quaestio disputata* of each doctor of the faculty'.

answers to the objections are, as a rule, the doctor's. The bachelor's own turn to be the central figure in a *quaestio* came only at the first public act that he performed after the licence to incept as a doctor had been granted by the chancellor of the University.

(vi) *The licence to incept*

Whether or not an examination preceded this licence to incept is not at all clear, for the statutes of the faculty of canon law at Oxford in the fourteenth century confine themselves to the following general statement which, in fact, is as bare as that on the inception in the faculty of civil law:

> Qui incepturi sunt in decretis, prius vices omnium magistrorum in eadem facultate ordinarie legencium supleant in legendo. . . . Quod si premissa laudabiliter compleverint, et ceteris condicionibus vite, quas de theologis premisimus, fuerint decorati, ad deposicionem magistrorum in eadem facultate actualiter legencium, si quatuor vel plures fuerint, licenciari poterunt. Quod si pauciores fuerint iuris civilis professores ad eorum deposicionem requirantur.[1]

Rashdall has noted that in contrast to continental universities there is no express evidence for Oxford of the existence of examinations in the literary sense of the word in any faculty; nor can we be certain, he says, that the masters 'had any other means of judging of the candidate's knowledge and capacity than had been afforded by his performances in the various disputations required for the degree'. Of course Rashdall is speaking primarily of the faculty of arts, but he has no doubt that 'in the superior faculties' the masters had no opportunities of judgement other than the disputations.[2] This, however, is possibly not wholly true of the faculty of canon law, or, for that matter, of that of civil law. For one thing, disputations were rare in the faculty of canon law and, as we have suggested earlier, only directly concerned bachelors who possessed

---

[1] *Stat. Ant.*, p. 47, ll. 5–7, 11–16. This echoes the civil law provision: 'Qui in iure civili sunt incepturi, primo vices omnium magistrorum in eadem facultate ordinarie legencium supleant in legendo . . .; quod si premissa laudabiliter compleverint, et moribus, ut de theologis est premissum, fuerint decorati, ad deposicionem magistrorum in eadem facultate actualiter legencium, si quatuor vel plures legentes fuerint, licenciari poterunt: quod si pauciores fuerint, doctores in decretis ad eorum deposicionem requirantur' (*Stat. Ant.* p. 44, ll. 15–17; 23–28).

[2] *Universities*, iii. 141–2.

doctorates in civil law. For another, the cursory and ordinary lectures of bachelors would afford many opportunities of forming that judgement of a man's ability which was required for the solemn deposition before the chancellor.

On the other hand, as Rashdall has well put it, 'due weight must be allowed to the intrinsic improbability of the total absence . . . of examinations such as certainly existed everywhere outside England'.[1] It is in fact difficult to imagine that a doctor in civil law who was co-opted for the depositions on a bachelor in canon law, or vice versa, would be content in all conscience to take an oath to that bachelor's ability if he had not had practical proof of this, perhaps indeed in the manner practised on the Continent. At Bologna, for example, there was a private examination which was a real test of competence. On the morning of this examination a ceremony took place which, it has been said, was customary in all universities.[2] This was the *assignatio punctorum*. Two doctors selected from the doctors of the faculty decided on the matter for examination by opening the Decretum and Decretals once each at random. If the matter lighted upon was thought to be unsuitable, then the doctors could go through the two folios before or after the random opening (this varied from university to university) until a more fitting passage was located. The candidate was now invited to comment on these texts, being given a few hours in which to prepare himself. Later in the day he delivered his exposition of the themes before the doctors of the faculty, and then was subjected to objections (but not more than three) from each of the doctors, beginning with the juniors. After this the votes of the doctors present were taken by ballot and the candidate's fate decided by the majority. The successful candidate was then admitted to the public examination which made him a full doctor.

The deposition *De moribus et scientia* required by the Oxford statutes appears not to have been obligatory at Bologna, and was in fact imported from Paris.[3] In the faculty of canon law at Oxford four doctors at least were necessary for the act of deposition; and if there were less than this number available in the faculty, doctors

---

[1] *Universities*, iii. p. 144.

[2] See Kurtscheid, art. cit., pp. 323–4; Rashdall, op. cit. i. 224–30; Denifle, *Archiv*, iii. 329–38.

[3] See A. G. Little and F. Pelster, *Oxford Theology and Theologians* (O.H.S., XCVI, 1934), pp. 42–43.

from the faculty of civil law were called in to form the quorum.[1] This 'board' of regent doctors testified to the morals and learning of the candidate to the chancellor, the University proctors being present to record the doctors' judgements.[2] All present were bound to secrecy,[3] and the formula of deposition laid down for all faculties was as follows: 'Domine cancellarie, presento vobis istum bachilarium talis facultatis ad incipiendum in tali facultate, quem scio ydoneum tam in scientia quam in moribus, ad incipiendum in eadem facultate, in fide prestita universitati.'[4] For doctors of civil law on a canon law 'board', however, the formula was a little different: 'Scio talem esse etc. in fide prestita, quatinus rectum sciendi iudicium ad meam permittitur facultatem', the change being due to the fact that civil law was 'inferior' to canon law. On the other hand doctors of canon law on a civil law 'board' were allowed to use 'Scio' without qualification, since 'in cunctis scientiis superior de inferiore poterit et debeat iudicare'.[5]

On these depositions the admission or rejection of a candidate for the doctorate depended. The percentage of votes required for promotion in the faculty of canon or civil law is not stated in the statutes, but it is possible that the unanimous vote demanded in the faculty of theology held good here also.[6] At all events a candidate who obtained a favourable vote was presented with the licence to incept by the chancellor, solemnly promising to observe the statutes, privileges, and customs of the University, to keep the peace,[7] and to incept within a year. Should he neglect to fulfil this last promise he automatically lost his licence and had to present himself afresh, the whole process of deposition being repeated.[8]

[1] 'Quod si pauciores fuerint iuris civilis professores ad eorum deposicionem requirantur', *Stat. Ant.*, p. 47, ll. 15–16.

[2] Ibid., pp. 28, l. 28–29, l. 6: 'De licencia et repulsa presentati cuiuscumque facultatis.'

[3] Ibid., p. 31, ll. 10–16: 'De secretis celandis in deposicionibus quorumcumque.' Nor could the doctors reveal their depositions to the bachelor either before or after the act of deposition (ibid., p. 31, ll. 29–32).

[4] Ibid., p. 29, ll. 13–20: 'De modo presentandi bachelarios (cuiuscumque facultatis).'

[5] Ibid., pp. 30, l. 26–31, l. 7: 'Qualiter magistri cuiuscumque facultatis debent deponere pro bachilariis alterius facultatis.'

[6] Ibid., p. 225, ll. 3–7. This statute is dated 1413–15 but the opening phrase is 'Ex statuto etiam et ex consuetudine universitatis'.

[7] Ibid., p. 177, ll. 20–35: 'Statutum de iuramento illorum qui licenciandi sunt ad lecturam ordinariam decretalium' (pre-1380). See also the statutes of pre-1350 (p. 19, ll. 3–20) and 16 Oct. 1327 (pp. 130–31).

[8] Ibid., p. 29, ll. 7–12: '. . . nullus . . . licencietur in aliqua facultate nisi

In the middle of the fourteenth century, indeed, the numbers failing to incept within the prescribed year appear to have been considerable, for in a statute given by Strickland Gibson as pre-1380 the University was compelled to impose some stiff fines on dilatory inceptors, the fines for the faculties of theology, canon law, and civil law being appreciably higher than those for other faculties.[1]

(vii) *Inception*

Following the practice at Paris the inception was made up of two distinct parts, the *vesperiae* and the *inceptio* proper.[2] The former could be held on any day on which there were lectures in the faculty of arts; the latter was limited to days set aside for disputations, or at least to days on which there were only cursory lectures in the faculty of arts.[3] The time of day at which these exercises took place depended on the custom prevalent in the different faculties, but in general *vesperiae* were held in the afternoon and the inception proper in the morning period. Invitations to the *inceptio* were presented in person to the regents of his faculty by the newly-licenced inceptor himself, but those to the *vesperiae* were issued through the bedel of the faculty by the doctor who would preside there. If an affluent inceptor was moved to give a pre-inception feast in his lodgings, he was obliged to invite the masters present to his inception.[4]

There are no detailed rules laid down in the statutes for the *vesperiae* and *inceptio* of inceptors in canon law, but we may assume that the general statutes governing both these stages were observed in the faculty of canon law.[5] At both *inceptio* and *vesperiae* the principal act was a disputation, but with certain differences. The questions to be disputed at the *vesperiae*, for instance, were published not by the inceptor himself but by the presiding doctor, who in fact announced these in congregation some time before the

promiserit se fideliter proponere hic incipere infra annum. Quod si forte non contingat illum incipere infra annum, iterum licencietur per deposicionem magistrorum modo debito et statuto' (pre-1350).

[1] *Stat. Ant.* pp. 174–5 (pre-1380).
[2] See Little and Pelster, op. cit., pp. 42–53.
[3] *Stat. Ant.*, p. 36, ll. 30–36: 'Quibus diebus licet tenere vesperias in quacumque facultate.'
[4] Ibid., pp. 36, l. 36–37, l. 7.
[5] Thus in the statute on inception: 'Licet autem hec incepturi in artibus, medicina, iure civili et canonico soleant observare . . .' (ibid., p. 38, ll. 11–12).

appointed day.[1] Again, at the *vesperiae* the respondent was the inceptor, objections being put by the doctors in order of seniority,[2] but at the inception proper the respondents were the doctors, beginning from the most recently qualified, the inceptor now taking over the role of opponent.[3] The inceptor thus proved his ability not only to defend a given thesis, but also to take it to pieces. We know very little, however, about the exact procedure at the 'defence' or *vesperiae*, but, allowing for the reversal of roles, we may suppose that the *vesperiae* disputation proceeded along much the same lines as that at the *inceptio*. There the inceptor, standing the while,[4] first introduced the theme of the disputation and then proceeded to demolish it with a series of objections. The turn of the respondents came next. Standing, the junior doctor proposed solutions to these objections, which the inceptor then proceeded to rebut as succinctly as possible. This method of objection, solution, and counter-objection continued until, after some or all of the doctors had objected, the presiding doctor (the 'doctor creans') announced that the assembly was satisfied.[5] The whole proceedings then closed towards midday with a public promise on the part of the new doctor to observe the customs of the University.[6]

(viii) *Regency*

Following their inception, doctors in canon law at Oxford in the early years of the fourteenth century were obliged to lecture

---

[1] Ibid., pp. 37, l. 29–38, l. 2.   [2] See ibid., p. 37, ll. 19–20.

[3] Ibid., p. 37, ll. 13–16.

[4] 'Item, statutum est quod incipiens in iure canonico debeat stare in incepcione sua disputando. Item, idem de sibi respondente' (ibid., p. 48, ll. 3–5; pre-1350).

[5] 'Incepturi quidem suas legant in principio lectiones, deinde questiones, quas disputare voluerint, proponentes magistris opponant, ac iidem magistri respondeant qui in eadem facultate in precedentibus incepcionibus ultimo inceperunt; ita videlicet, quod qui incipiendo posteriores fuere fiant respondendo priores. Si vero contingat omnes, qui prius inceperunt, incipientibus respondisse, tunc prius respondeant seniores. Licet autem hec incepturi in artibus, medicina, iure civili et canonico soleant observare, incepturis tamen in sacra scriptura . . .' (ibid., p. 38, ll. 3–12). See also the early-sixteenth-century description of procedure at inceptions in the faculties of civil and canon law printed by Strickland Gibson, *Stat. Ant.*, p. 625.

[6] 'Item, regentes incepcionibus magistrorum rite requisiti . . ., ibidem, saltim usque ad horam nonam pulsatam, moram facere, ubi etiam incipientes fidem, vel, si sint theologi, sacramentum de conservandis consuetudinibus publice dare debent' (ibid., p. 57, ll. 5–10). After 1334 there was also an oath not to teach or study at Stamford (ibid., p. 20, ll. 15–17).

ordinarie for two years, during which they were known as regent doctors. Sometime before 1333, however, the period of regency was reduced to one year.[1] The time was counted from the beginning of the next scholastic year, even for those doctors who had incepted in the middle of the previous year. Thus any doctor who incepted in Hilary or Trinity Term could not begin his regency until the following Michaelmas.[2] The academic year itself was divided into three terms, the first running from 10 October to 17 December, the second from 14 January until the Vigil of Palm Sunday, the third from the Wednesday after Low Sunday until just before 7 July, for the University in general, and until 1 August for the faculty of civil law, and, possibly, for that of canon law also.[3]

During the period of his regency a doctor at Oxford was entitled to receive at least forty shillings from those of his students who could afford a fee. In return he and a bachelor or *extraordinarius* covered the whole of the statutory course of canon law in ordinary and cursory lectures, but the bachelor (at least in Bologna) was not entitled to any fee.[4] The stipend was generally collected from each of the students by the doctor, who, if the stipend was not a fixed one (as at Oxford), negotiated a contract with the students as to the total amount that they would subscribe between them. But where, as at Bologna in the fourteenth century, there were 'state-paid' professors, or professors occupying endowed chairs, these collections were not permitted, although in fact this prohibition was often ignored where the salary or endowment was too slender. At Oxford, however, all *legentes ordinarie*, without any exception, appear to have had the right to a steady salary from their students.[5]

The books lectured on *ordinarie* by a regent before the appearance of the 1333 statute were the five books of the Decretals and part of the Sext.[6] The Clementines had been promulgated and sent

---

[1] See p. 151, n. 1, above.

[2] '. . . quilibet incipiens in iure canonico arctetur ad lecturam biennalem, excepto anno in quo incipit, etiam si post Natale incipiat' (*Stat. Ant.*, p. 47, ll. 11–16; cf. p. 178, ll. 18–22).

[3] See Strickland Gibson, introd. to *Stat. Ant.*, pp. lxxx–lxxxi.

[4] *Archiv*, iii. 326. On salaries in general at universities see Rashdall, *Universities*, i. 208–12; Gaines Post, 'Masters' salaries and Student-fees in Medieval Universities', *Speculum*, 7 (1932), 181–98.

[5] 'Legens ordinarie decretales percipiat de singulis auditoribus suis potentibus, pro salario suo, ad minus quadraginta solidos' (*Stat. Ant.*, p. 47, ll. 1–4). This statute is again pre-1333.   [6] Ibid., pp. 45–46.

to Oxford in late 1317,[1] but as we may see from the 1333 statute
they were not received as anything approaching an ordinary book
until the latter date, mainly because the course was too crowded.
This does not mean, however, that doctors were unaware of the
importance of the new collection, or that the exceptional regent
did not attempt to include the Clementines in his course before he
was forced to do so by the 1333 decree. William of Pagula, for
example, was composing his *Summa Summarum* at Oxford between
1319 and 1321, during his regency, and every page of his work
shows a remarkable familiarity with the Clementines, then very
new indeed to Oxford.[2]

After 1333 the books lectured on by a regent depended on what
year of the two-year cycle coincided with his regency. If it was the
first then he and his bachelor had to lecture on the first, fourth, and
fifth books of the Decretals, together with the Clementines; if it
was the second then the course was the second and third books of
the Decretals and the whole of the Sext. Here as in all other statutes
on ordinary lectures the regent himself was held responsible personally for the course laid down by the statute of 1333, including
that part that he had confided to the bachelor. It was the regent,
not the bachelor, who was required to swear to the completed
course.[3]

It is interesting to note, however, that although the 1333 statute
brings the faculty of canon law up to date with canonical legislation,
it makes no mention of any of the decrees of John XXII, twenty of
which had been published as a collection eight years earlier by
Zenzelinus de Cassanis. This is not too surprising. For in fact
John XXII's *Extravagantes* (as they were to be known later) did
not achieve scholastic status anywhere for a long time after 1325,
since as a collection they lacked the authority of papal promulgation that the Decretals, the Sext, and the Clementines enjoyed.[4]
But some at least of Pope John's constitutions were public knowledge at Oxford before 1333. For in November 1324, some eight
months after he had ordered certain of his decrees to be read at

[1] 1 November 1317: see copies of Clementines in Salisbury Cathedral
Library (MS. 122, fol. 14ᵛ), Cambridge University Library (MS. Ii.iii.7, fol.
102ᵛ), &c.
[2] See L. Boyle, 'The *Oculus Sacerdotis* of William of Pagula', *Trans. Royal
Hist. Soc.*, ser. 5, 5 (1955), 105, &c.
[3] See p. 150, n. 1, and p. 151, n. 1 above.
[4] See A. M. Stickler, *Historia Iuris Canonici*, i (Turin, 1950), pp. 270-2.

Paris University, John sent a similar mandate to Oxford with respect to three decrees, *Ad conditorem, Cum inter nonnullos*, and *Quia quorumdam*, all of which concerned the question of the absolute poverty of Christ and his Apostles, and involved the Franciscans almost exclusively.[1]

During the period of regency there were other acts besides lecturing that played an important part in the newly-licenced doctor's life as a teacher, particularly *repetitiones* and *quaestiones disputatae*. These two acts differed considerably, the former being less formidable than the latter. Where the *quaestio*, which regents at Oxford were supposed to hold at the end of each term,[2] was a lengthy affair involving a respondent and perhaps several opponents, the *repetitio* had more the nature of an excursus, opposition being allowed only on rare occasions. As the great Bolognese lawyer Odofredus says in his prologue to the *Digestum vetus*, the purpose of the *repetitio* was to underline some famous or knotty point.[3] Thus we may see from a *repetitio* of a canon from the Sext given at Oxford in 1311 by John Stratford, the future archbishop of Canterbury, that the act did not consist of much more than a straightforward exposition of the points made by a canon. The canon in this case was *Commissa*, and Stratford simply divides it into five parts, briefly expounding each part in turn;[4] the same method may be further observed in two *repetitiones* given respectively by Stephen Kettlesbury and Thomas Plumstoke, who were

---

[1] Arch. Segr. Vaticano, Reg. Vat. 113, fol. 124ᵛ (Paris), fol. 120ʳ (Oxford). See *Cal. Pap. Lett.* ii. 472.

[2] 'Statutum est quod doctor iuris decretorum singulis terminis primi anni integri sui regiminis semel disputare teneatur' (*Stat. Ant.*, p. 178, ll. 12–13). This statute is given by Strickland Gibson as pre-1380, but since it clearly envisages a two-year regency we may now date it pre-1333 (see p. 151, n. 1, above). Disputations, however, were so few and far between in the faculty of canon law that regents were allowed to go ahead with disputations arranged for a day on which the funeral of a doctor occurred, 'quia raro nimis disputant' (ibid., p. 59, ll. 21–25).

[3] See Kurtscheid, art. cit., p. 321, and Rashdall, *Universities*, i. 218–19. On the difference between a *repetitio* and a similarly-named exercise in other schools see ibid., i. 249.

[4] British Museum, MS. Royal 11D.VI, fol. 2ʳ. This appears to be the very *repetitio* to which the celebrated canonist John Acton (*Constitutiones Legatinae*, ed. Oxford, 1679, p. 129) refers when he quotes 'Venerabilem Patrem Dominum Johannem de Stratford Doctorem meum, nuper Wintoniensem Episcopum, jam vero Cantuariensem, in sua repetione [*sic*] dictae Decretalis, commissa, lib. 6'. Indeed, it was this reference to Stratford that enabled F. W. Maitland (*Roman Canon Law in the Church of England*, London, 1898, pp. 6–7) to assign a date after 1333 to Acton's commentary on the Legatine constitutions.

regents in the law schools at Oxford about 1318. The difference between a *repetitio* and a *quaestio disputata* is clearly to be seen in two *quaestiones* which follow in the same manuscript on the *repetitiones* of Kettlesbury and Plumstoke. Both *quaestiones* were held by Benedict Paston, and one of them is dated 1318. In contrast to the *repetitiones*, a bachelor or *responsalis* now plays a part. The subject is given first, then the objections of the bachelor ('Baccalaureus tenet quod . . .' or 'Responsalis tenet contra . . .'), and finally the replies of the regent doctor ('Doctor tenet quod . . .').[1]

For a period some fifty or sixty years later a fine set of *reportata* survives from the canon law schools at Oxford, which includes not only very complete *repetitiones* but also some of the ordinary lectures of nineteen doctors.[2] These lectures, however, do not reveal any great originality, any more than do the lengthy *reportoria* of Thomas Walkyngton[3] or Thomas Chillenden[4] which belong to this same late period of the fourteenth century. The general idea was to take a decretal phrase by phrase, giving a synopsis of what the great commentators had written, thus: 'Summatur sic per Iohannem . . . per Willelmum . . . per Archidiaconum . . . .' A copy of the Decretals used by a doctor in the schools at Oxford (possibly by Thomas Walkyngton) also survives, with many marginal and interlinear notes.[5] Most of these notes are copied simply from established foreign commentaries, the only concession to native authorities being a quotation from William of Pagula's

---

[1] MS. Royal 11D.vi, fol. 1ʳ⁻ᵛ. It is just possible that these notes from the Oxford schools, including the *repetitio* of Stratford in the previous note, may be the work of John Acton. They occur on flyleaves of a manuscript of the Digest, on a folio on which the name 'Johannes' is scribbled. Acton probably studied at both Oxford and Cambridge, taking his doctorate at the latter: see A. B. Emden, *B.R.U.O.* i. 11–12.

[2] These lectures (MS. Royal 9E.viii, fols. 27ʳ–197) have been studied by K. R. N. Wykeham-George, O.P., in an unpublished B.Litt. dissertation, 'English Canonists in the Late Middle Ages', Oxford, 1937.

[3] MS. Canterbury, Dean & Chapter Library, C.12, fols. 80ʳ–152ʳ. The MS. was written in 1377 'post magistrum Thomam de Walkynton doctorem decretorum' (fol. 80ʳ). On Thomas, who is one of the doctors whose lectures are reported in MS. Royal 9E.viii, see *B.R.U.O.* iii. 1964–5 (*Walkyngton, Thomas de*).

[4] On Decretals (Oxford, All Souls Coll., MS. 53), Sext (Hereford Cath. MS.P.8.3; British Museum, Royal 11C.ii) and Clementines (Oxford, All Souls Coll. MS. 53; Hereford Cath. P.8.3). On Chillenden see *B.R.U.O.* i. 415–16.

[5] British Museum, MS. Royal 9F.ii. Walkyngton's name occurs on fol. 206ᵛ.

162

Summa Summarum.[1] Without going deeper into this question at present, it may be said that by and large the Oxford canonists of the fourteenth century were content to repeat or summarize the writings of continental authors, although a few of them did try their hand at authorship.

No doubt the long course of studies which we have attempted to set out here produced a competent body of professional canonists, but the fact remains that all too few seem to have made an academic mark, even in their own country.

[1] British Museum, MS. Royal 9F.II, fol. 142ᵛ.

XV

THE 'SUMMA SUMMARUM'
AND SOME OTHER ENGLISH WORKS OF CANON LAW

I

In contrast to the late twelfth and early thirteenth centuries,[1] English writers in the field of canon law are few in the fourteenth century. Indeed the general opinion seems to be that the only canonist of note between William of Drogheda (d. 1239) and William Lyndwood (d. 1446) is John Acton, the famous fourteenth-century glossator of the Legatine Constitutions.[2]

Yet, although outstanding canonists were indeed wanting in fourteenth-century England, the study of canon law more than held its own at Oxford and Cambridge. Many clerics, no doubt, pursued the study of law in a hope of ultimate preferment, but interest in the subject was still vigorous if practical. Bishop Bateman of Norwich, a former and respected auditor of the papal cur a at Avignon, founded a college at Cambridge in 1350 'ad cultus divini ac scientiae canonicae et civilis universitatisque Cantabrigiae augmentum,' stocking it with a good selection of legal source-books;[3] and in 1346 Bishop Hethe of Rochester gave a fine set of books (*Decretum, Decretales, Sext and Clementines*, Raymund of Pennafort's *Summa de casibus* and Richard Wetheringsett's *Summa* 'Qui bene praesunt') to the penitentiaries of his cathedral church who, for lack of books, were 'handling cases rather wildly.' [4]

A practical regard for canon law was not, however, confined to the bishops of the fourteenth century. The professional lawyers, that much-maligned class which John Bromyard, the Dominican moralist, and many other writers,

---

[1] On this period see S. Kuttner and E Rathbone, 'Anglo-Norman Canonists of the Twelfth Century: An Introductory Study,' *Traditio* 7 (1949-1951) 279-358; C. Duggan, *Twelfth-Century Decretal Collections and their Importance in English History* (London 1963).

[2] Sec F.W. Maitland, *Roman Canon Law in the Church of England* (London 1898) Chap. 1; H.W.C. Davis, 'The Canon Law in England,' ZRG Kan. Abt. 34 (1914) 349-350, reprinted in J. R. Weaver and A. L. Poole, *H.W.C. Davis, A Memoir* (London 1933) 123-43; W. Holdsworth, *Sources and Literature of English Law* (Oxford 1925) 229; W. Ullmann, 'Canonistics in England,' *Studia Gratiana* 2 (1954) 521-28.

[3] G. E. Corrie, 'A Catalogue of the Books Given to Trinity Hall, Cambridge, by the Founder,' *Communications of the Cambridge Antiquarian Society* 2 (1864) 73-8; see also J. R. L. Highfield, 'The English Hierarchy in the Reign of Edward III,' *Trans. Royal Hist. Soc.*[5] 6 (1956) 126-30.

[4] *The Register of Hamo of Hethe* ed. C. Johnson (Canterbury and York Society; Oxford 1948) 673.

416

held responsible for most of the prevalent non-residence,[5] were not unconscientious in their calling. They seldom were without the materials of their profession,[6] and generally they studied these with diligence. Thus on the margins of a *Sext* owned by Richard Vaughan, a lawyer of the mid-fourteenth century, we may note the care which some canonists took to perfect their legal knowledge and to keep it up to date. Vaughan had occasion to visit Avignon in 1339 and 1346 as a proctor of Edward III. While there, he made the most of an opportunity of studying the methods of the curia, taking notes of judgements pronounced by papal auditors, by 'Dominus Oldradus' (de Ponte Laudensis) or by 'Dominus Willelmus de Norwyco' (William Bateman), for example. He duly used these notes to gloss his *Sext*, placing his signature ('R') after each note so as to distinguish these personal notes from glosses which he or previous owners of his copy of the *Sext* had culled from various commentators;[7] 'the following is the practice in the papal curia,' he notes on occasion, 'I myself was present when the point was debated.'[8]

But although the English law schools produced an abundance of good and diligent canonists in the fourteenth century, they fathered very few writers on canon law. Indeed, apart from Acton's gloss on the Legatine Constitutions and William of Pagula's *Summa summarum* (anonymously), it is seldom that an English canonical writing of the fourteenth century appears in a catalogue of a medieval library.[9] If writings of any other canonists survive, they are

---

[5] See John Bromyard, *Summa Praedicantium* (Paris 1518) P. xiii. 24.

[6] See, for example, the remarkable library of John Newton, treasurer of York (d. 1414) in *Testamenta Eboracensia* (Surtees Society; York 1836-1902) I 370, and the solicitude of William Swan, an English proctor at the papal curia, for his books and quaternions in a letter of 1410 (E. F. Jacob, 'To and from the Court of Rome in the Fifteenth Century,' *Studies Presented to Mildred K. Pope* [Manchester 1939] 175).

[7] New College, Oxford, MS 207, fols. 17ᵛ, 39ʳ, etc. The Sext (fols. 2ʳ-90ʳ), with the gloss of Joannes Monachus, is only one of several items in this manuscript; it is heavily annotated in several hands of different periods. It seems clear that this was Richard Vaughan's Sext and that the whole MS belonged to him. For one thing there is a fourteenth-century *cautio* at the end of the MS, 'E(s)t Ricardi Wachan'; for another, the papal auditors quoted in the notes signed 'R' all belong to the first half of the fourteenth century. As we noted above, Vaughan was King's proctor at Avignon in 1339 and 1346, so the notes probably were made during Vaughan's first soujourn at Avignon, since William Bateman was still there (see, for example, fol. 78ʳ: 'secundum dominum Willelmum de Norwyco. R'); by the time Vaughan revisited Avignon in 1346, Bateman was Bishop of Norwich. For Vaughan's career see A. B. Emden, *A Biographical Register of the University of Oxford* (Oxford 1957-59) III 1942.

[8] E.g., fols. 3ʳ, 11ʳ, 16ʳ . . . 81ᵛ, etc.

[9] See the catalogue of books in the newly-founded All Souls College, Oxford, in E. F. Jacob, 'Two Lives of Archbishop Chichele with an Appendix Containing an Early Book-list of All Souls College, Oxford,' *Bulletin of John Rylands Library* 16 (1932) 469-81, and Pro-

generally in the category of scholastic exercises. There are a few fragmentary *quaestiones* and *repetitiones* from the schools at Oxford about 1318;[10] from Cambridge there is a fine *quaestio* which was debated between John Acton and Walter Elveden about 1330;[11] from the canon law schools at Oxford in the second half of the fourteenth century there is a great series of *lecturae* and *repetitiones* of some nineteen regent-doctors.[12] Two *reportoria*, or legal summaries, of two Oxford doctors, Thomas Walkyngton and Thomas Chillenden, also survive from the second half of the century, but like the *quaestiones* and *repetitiones* noted above they are rarely anything more than resumés of continental commentaries.[13] There will, of course, be some local color — Walkyngton gives a fictitious case in which the Abbey of Osney at Oxford occurs[14] — and there are remarks on the application of particular decretals in England,[15] but on the whole a personal approach is lacking. Yet the standing of these men as teachers must have been high. Walkyngton's *Reportorium* was copied 'post magistrum T. Walkyngton' by an Oxford student in 1377;[16] that of

---

fessor Jacob's remarks on the same catalogue in 'Notanda quaedam de iure canonico inter Anglos praesertim inter Oxonienses saec. xv,' *Acta Congressus Iuridici Internationalis Romae 1934* II (Rome 1935) 477: ' . . . Anglicanum nihil, nisi quidam liber vocatus Chellyngdon super decretis.'

[10] See further L. Boyle, 'The Curriculum of the Faculty of Canon Law at Oxford in the First Half of the Fourteenth Century,' *Oxford Studies Presented to D. A. Callus* (Oxford 1964) 135-162.

[11] Cambridge, Gonville and Caius College, MS 483 fol. 275r.

[12] British Museum, MS Royal 9. E. VIII; these have been studied in an unpublished B. Litt. thesis by the late K. R. N. Wykeham-George, O.P., *English Canonists in the Late Middle Ages* (Oxford 1937). A similar set of *lecturae* and *repetitiones* from the civil law schools of the same period is in New College, Oxford, MS 179 fols. 1-124.

[13] See, for example, the opening section of Walkyngton's *Reportorium* of the Clementines: 'Sequitur prohemium Clementinarum et reportorium post mag. Thomam de Walkyngton doctorem decretorum anno millesimo cccLxxvii. Paulus (de Liazariis) dicit hic in prohemio quod hec compilacio non continetur sub nomine libri; concordant alii doctores. Ulterius Paulus: conclusio: quilibet suis terminis debet contentari; adde de sepulturis, c. 1 et ibi Hostiensis. — EPISCOPUS. Paulus: variis modis vocatur Papa. . . . JOHANNES. Gesselinus: Raciones quare nomen pape mutatur. . . . (Canterbury, Dean and Chapter Library MS C. 12 fol. 80r; the commentary here is on the Bull by which John XXII promulgated the Clementines in 1317).

[14] *MS cit.* fol. 82r.

[15] See Chillenden on the Sext (New College, Oxford, MS 204 fols. 4r-216v) and on the Clementines (*ibid.* fols. 218v-404v), for example: 'Quero quid sit pene extrahencium aliquem ab ecclesia . . . . Willelmus (de Monte Lauduno) hic in glossa dicit quod talis ultimo supplicio punietur; sed in Anglia est excommunicatus, ut notatur in consticucione que incipit Ad tutelam' (fol. 389r; Walkyngton, *MS cit.* fol. 147v, makes much the same point).

[16] See n. 13.

Chillenden on the *Sext* and the *Clementinus* survives in a number of manuscripts, one of which was written for a college library.[17]

II

The legacy of legal writings from the fourteenth century would be very
slight indeed were it not for two canonists who would be outstanding in any
generation. John Acton, a professional canonist, has left us his magnificent
commentary on the constitutions of the Legates Otto and Ottobuono; William
of Pagula, parish priest of Winkfield in the Forest of Windsor, has given us his
Summa summarum and *Speculum praelatorum*, not to mention his *Oculus
sacerdotis* and *Speculum religiosorum*.

Acton probably began his commentary during his regency at Cambridge
about 1334, setting himself the stiff task of making a coherent gloss on every
important word in the Legatine Constitutions. But he was in no way daunted.
He was, as he himself confessed some twelve years later, full of self-confidence.
He had just taken a doctor's degree in both laws, and now 'lecturing, disputing,
writing my gloss on the Legatine Constitutions, speaking with all the assurance
of a man with a professorial chair at his back,' he was, it seems, not wholly
above vanity and self-seeking.[18] This, of course, is Acton writing a treatise
on the seven deadly sins. If we may judge from his glosses on the constitutions,
he is being a little severe on his younger self. His writing betrays no arrogance,
and it is singularly level-headed. It was to be valued highly by canonists in
the next two centuries.[19]

Although Acton's contemporary William of Pagula (William Poul or Paul),[20]

---

[17] MSS: New College, Oxford, 204; All Souls 53 (Decretals and Clementines: possibly
this is the 'Chellyngdon super decretis' which was at All Souls shortly after its foundation;
see n. 9 above); Hereford Cathedral Library P. VIII. 3; Trinity Hall, Cambridge, 7; Gonville
and Caius College 308; British Museum Royal 11 C II. For Chillenden's career see Emden,
Biographical Register I 415-6; for that of Walkyngton *ibid.* III 1964-5.

[18] *Septuplum*, Gonville and Caius College, Cambridge, MS 182 fol. 1v; University Coll., Oxford, MS 71 fol. 16v. The *Septuplum* was written in 1346 (Caius Coll. MS fol. 140v) and from
these remarks of Acton's I am inclined to think that his commentary on the Legatine Constitutions was written (at Cambridge?) during his regency. Since the commentary is definitely after 1333 (see Maitland, *Roman Canon Law* 6-7) and Acton was a 'doctor utriusque iuris'
by September 1335 (Emden, *Biographical Register* I 11-12), then a date about 1334 may be
assigned to the Legatine commentary.

[19] See, for example, T. Walkyngton, *Reportorium* (Canterbury, Dean and Chapter Library,
MS C. 12, fol. 98v); and quotations in a *Tractatus de materiis decretorum* (Oxford, Corpus
Christi College, MS 145, fols. 99r, etc) and in a fine dictionary of canon law (Cambridge, Gon-
ville and Caius College, MS 36 fols. 1r-71r, *passim*).

[20] He was a native of Paull (Pagula) in Yorkshire and was perpetual vicar of Winkfield,

also was composing elaborate treatises during his regency (at Oxford, 1319-1321), we do not know whether he, too, was an 'intonans cathedraliter,' to use Acton's phrase. Certainly he was as industrious as Acton was to be some fifteen years later. He had been released for studies at Oxford from his parish at Winkfield in Windsor Forest in 1314, and now, some five or six years later, he already had some three or four works of canon law and pastoral theology in hand. By 1319/20, indeed, he had composed parts of his *Oculus sacerdotis* and *Speculum praelatorum*, both works of pastoral theology.[21] Then he set himself a heavier task than Acton was to attempt in his legatine commentary: Pagula proposed, as he informs us in the prologue to the *Summa summarum*, to provide every 'literate cleric' from curates to lawyers with a compendium of canon law and pastoral theology in which an answer would be found to any and every question.[22] *Summae*, in his opinion, fell into four classes. First of all, there were the *reportoria* in which questions were answered simply by a reference to a relevant legal source: the *Reportorium* of William Durandus the Elder, one of the most celebrated treatises of the Middle Ages, fell into this class. Then were *summae* for unlettered priests in which questions were answered as simply as possible, with little or no display of legal knowledge: a typical example of this was the *Summa* 'Qui bene praesunt' (of Richard Wetheringsett), written in the first half of the thirteenth century. A further type of manual considered all the aspects of a problem before proposing a solution: under this heading there came the *Summa copiosa* of Hostiensis, and the *summae* of Raymund of Pennafort, Geoffrey of Trani, and Bernard of Compostella (Iunior). The final type of *summa* was a *Summa*

Berkshire, from 1314 to 1332. Properly he should be called William POUL: this is how he signs himself in the one document in which he himself gives his full name, a letter to his bishop (Mortival of Salisbury) in 1326 (*Registrum Ade de Orleton, Episcopi Herefordensis*, ed. A. T. Bannister [Canterbury and York Society; 1908] 348-9); a document of the previous year also describes him as William 'de Poul' (Salisbury, Muniments of the Dean and Chapter 4.E.2,6). In the episcopal registers of Mortival's predecessor he is always described as Willelmus de Pagula, On William see L. Boyle, 'The *Oculus sacerdotis* and Some Other Works of William of Pagula,' *Trans. R. Hist. Soc.*[5] 5 (1955) 81-110; W. A. Pantin, *The English Church in the XIVth Century*, (Cambridge 1955) 195-202; Emden, *Biographical Register* III 1536-7 s.n. Paul.

[21] Altogether, between 1319 and 1331, Pagula wrote five works, some of them after he had returned from Oxford to his Berkshire vicarage: *Summa summarum* (1319-1322), *Speculum praelatorum, Speculum religiosorum, Dextera pars* and *Sinistra pars* of the *Oculus sacerdotis* (1319-1322), *Pars Oculi* of *Oculus* (1327-8), an *Epistola ad Regem Edwardum (Tertium)* (1330-1331).

[22] Bodleian Library, Oxford, MS Bodley 293 fol. 1ʳ: 'Incipit speculum compendii et reportorium iuris canonici per quod quilibet litteratus quascumque materias et quaestiones iuris canonici cuiuscumque ponderis faciliter poterit invenire. . . . '. For the complete prologue see Appendix I, below.

420

summarum, a summa, that is, which took over all that was best in, and characteristic of, these other manuals. This, Pagula held, was the most useful type
of all. For in it 'a question is proposed and then is answered at once, the
exact source of the question and the answer being given without fail.' His
own Summa summarum was, he claimed, a prime example; it was made for
ready reference. Any cleric, whether in the papal curia or in a rural chapter,
would have no difficulty in locating a reliable answer to any urgent problem,
with abundant references. If he is not satisfied, and has time at his disposal,
he can easily check and ponder these references.[23]

Pagula's Summa summarum is therefore by no means an original work.
Rather it is, in his paraphrase of the prologue to the Codex, 'a collection of
thorny problems' of canon law, made for the simple purpose of arming priests
against ignorance. It is utterly unlike Acton's gloss on the Legatine Constitutions, or Lyndwood's commentary on the provincial statutes of England a
century later. Pagula does not take a word or a phrase and then bring a
wealth of legal learning to bear on it: he answers questions with words which
rarely are his own. To ensure the success of his work he has effaced himself
completely. He was 'only a compiler'; he was not breaking new ground.
For that reason he withheld his name; the important thing was 'not who
had compiled the Summa but what the Summa contained.'[24] It is a tribute
to his planning of the work, and to his superb control of sources, that this

---

[23] MS cit. fol. 250ʳ: 'Sed hec tercia summa (summarum) inter ceteras est utilior et expe-
dicior, quia in curia romana et in curia archiepiscoporum et aliorum magnatuum et in con-
sistoriis diversis et eciam capitulis ruralibus multi occurrunt casus diversi et dubii; ut
quando proponitur casus dubius, statim ad illud dubium ab aliquo respondetur dicendo
veritatem sic esse vel non esse et alligat decretum seu decretalem, glosam seu doctorem. . . . '
This discussion of different types of summae takes up the whole of the last chapter of the
Summa summarum (5.69: De regulis magistralibus).

[24] 'Noli eciam, lector pie, de actore seu pocius compilatore huius summe sicut nec de
calamo quo scripta est inquirere curiose, sed attende ea que in ea scribuntur, quia non
sunt mea dicta sed aliorum, prout in hac summa poteris ad plenum videre. . . . Tu ergo
lector ora pro collectore et diligenter suscipe quesita cum alieno labore et gaude de inventis sine labore. Nomen autem collectoris exprimere nolo ne colleccio vilescerit cognito collectore' (MS cit., fol. 1ᵛ). Despite this assertion he does in fact give away his name at one
point — and the fact he is lecturing at Oxford while writing the Summa: 'Sed quid si per
alia eciam rescripto contenta constat de persona mea, ut impetrat contra me W. doctorem
iure canonico legentem Oxon. . . . ' (MS cit. fol. 25ʳ; Pembroke Coll. Cambridge, MS 201
fol. 32ᵛ; Lucca, Library of Cathedral Chapter, MS 303 fol. 28ᵛ; and all other MSS). Only
one copy of the 13 known MSS is ascribed, that of Christ's College, Cambridge, 2: 'hoc opus
compositum fuit per dominum Willelmum de Pabula' (fol. 269ʳ). Of the 56 known MSS
of the Oculus sacerdotis only that of Hatfield House, Herts., is ascribed to Pagula (MS 290
fol. 80ʳ).

bleakly-named *Summa summarum* had a success in England which is second
only to that enjoyed by Acton's *Glossa*.[25]

III

Following Raymund of Pennafort's distribution of the collection of Decretals which Gregory IX sponsored in 1234, William of Pagula divides his
Summa summarum into five books, arranging his material under the heads
of *iudex, iudicium, clerus, connubia, crimen*; and, with the exception of one,
he also takes over all of Raymund's 185 rubrics or chapter headings. But he
felt that these rubrics did not adequately cover all that he wished to include
in the *Summa*; that they limited the scope of his work. To these 185 rubrics
(which form 182 chapters of the *Summa*[26]), Pagula therefore added 75 rubrics
of his own choice, thus giving the *Summa* 257 chapters in all. In this departure
from the set tradition of the Decretal rubrics, as in the general layout of the
whole work, Pagula's model was the great *Reportorium* of William Durandus
the Elder. By and large Durandus had followed Raymund's order, but he
had composed rubrics of his own whenever he had to deal with subjects which
did not fall readily under the rubrics of the Decretals. Thus in the fifth book
of the *Reportorium* Durandus proposes many new rubrics, for example, after
the Decretal rubrics *De poenis* (X. 5.37) and *De sententia excommunicationis
et interdicti* (X. 5.39).[27] At these points in the fifth book of the *Summa summarum* Pagula also inserts rubrics 'of my own composition' (*Summa* 5.44-48;
50-59; 61-66), most of which are in fact borrowed from or modeled upon Durandus.

Durandus is indeed the inspiration of Pagula's methodology here and in all
his other works. Even that formula in the *Speculum praelatorum* and the
Oculus sacerdotis ('Quae autem hic desunt quaere in *Summa summarum*')
which helped some years ago to establish that all of these works are from the
pen of William of Pagula, also derives from the *Reportorium*. For it is the
phrase with which Durandus invariably refers readers of the *Reportorium* to
his earlier *Speculum iudiciale*: 'Quae autem hic desunt: vide in nostro Speculo
iudiciali.'[28] But unlike Durandus, who is not at all shy of personal asides and
references, Pagula never refers to these other works as 'ours', apart, that is,

---

[25] See Appendix IV below for a summary table of the circulation and influence of the work.

[26] See Appendix I below for a discussion of the relationship between Decretal rubrics
and those of the *Summa*.

[27] *Reportorium* (Frankfurt 1592) 63-5.

[28] *Ibid.* 2, 3. In his prologue Pagula also leans on that of Durandus: see Appendix I,
lines 19-27.

422

from a happy lapse in the *Summa summarum* which proves beyond all conjecture that the author of the *Summa* is also the author of the *Speculum
praelatorum* and the *Oculus sacerdotis.*[29]

But although a sub-title of the *Summa summarum* is *Reportorium iuris
canonici*, the *Reportorium* of Durandus and the *Summa* of Pagula differ considerably. As Pagula himself has pointed out, the volume of Durandus does
nothing more than arrange a whole series of questions under different heads,
without any attempt to expound or to solve the questions; references to the
Decretum or the *Decretales* are the only answers given. In as much as Pagula
has taken over most of these questions and legal references, the *Reportorium*
and the *Summa summarum* have a great deal in common; and the priest who
wrote a marginal note on the Exeter Cathedral copy of the *Summa* was justified
to that extent at least when he stated rather caustically that 'any one who
possesses a copy of this *Summa* has no need of the *Reportorium* of Durandus,
for it is all here.'[30] There, however, the equality ends. Pagula ranges far
beyond the confines of the *Reportorium*. The *Summa* is not an index of canon
law; rather it is an encyclopedia. Expanding the references in the *Reportorium*
and giving the relevant legal passages in full, Pagula also reaches out to later
legal texts (*Sext* and *Clementines*) as well as to Hostiensis, Durandus' own
Speculum iudiciale, Joannes Andreae, Willelmus de Monte Lauduno, Joannes
Monachus, and a host of other authorities. Besides, Pagula also includes
related texts from local English ecclesiastical legislation. Indeed, there is
hardly a point of legatine or provincial legislation which has been overlooked

---

[29] 'De huius misse exposicione . . . tractavi ad plenum in modica summa sacramentali
que vocatur Sinistra pars oculi sacerdotis eodem titulo. Sed plenius de hoc tractabo in
Speculo prelatorum in quarta particula prime partis. . . . ' (MSS Bodleian Libr., Laud Misc.
624 fol. 108^v; Exeter Coll. 19 fol. 182^v; Cambridge, Christ's College 2 fol. 109^v; Pembroke
College MS 201 fol. 189^r); the nine other MSS, however, abbreviate the passage and speak
impersonally: 'De hac materia tractatur ad plenum in quadam nova summa que vocatur
Speculum prelatorum' (e. g. Bodley 293 fol. 144^v; Magdalen Coll., Oxford, lat. 134 fol.
172^v; British Museum Royal 10. D. X fol. 174^v; Edinburgh Univ. Libr. 136 fol. 157^r; Durham
Cath. Library C.II.13 fol. 143^r; Worcester Cath. Libr. F. 131 fol. 213^r; Lucca, Libr. of Cath.
Chapter 303 fol. 163^v). In two of the four MSS which carry the personal passage there is
an addition which suggests strongly that Pagula had the *Summa* and *Speculum* in hand at
the same moment: 'De officiis autem divinis singulis horis canonicis faciendis et significa-
cionibus eorumdem *tractabitur* ibidem in rubrica proxima precedenti per totum. *Que omnia
nondum adhuc plene complevi*; in quibus et in aliis nos adiuvet omnipotens Deus' (Laud.
Misc. 624 fol. 108^v; Pembroke Coll. Cambridge 201 fol. 189^r).

[30] 'Nota que continentur. Et hanc summam habens, Reportorium W. Durandi non
indiget, quia totum illud in hac continetur' (MS Bodley 293, fol. 1rb). On the use of the
word 'Reportorium' instead of 'Summa' see N. R. Ker, 'Patrick Young's Catalogue of
the Manuscripts of Lichfield Cathedral,' *Medieval and Renaissance Studies* 2 (1950) 162,
164.

and is not correlated to the general law of the Church. As in the *Oculus sacer-dotis*, particular attention is given to excommunications peculiar to England: for example, Pagula includes the substance of *Magna Carta* and the *Carta de Foresta* and of the excommunication sentence of 1253; texts which are also to be found in the *Oculus* and the *Speculum praelatorum*.[31]

The greatest difference, however, between the *Reportorium* of Durandus and the *Summa* of Pagula lies in the theological content of the latter. Here again there is a balance of canon law and theology, which is so marked in the *Oculus sacerdotis*. Once more, as in the *Oculus* and the *Speculum praelatorum*, the unacknowledged source of Pagula's impressive theological learning is the great *Summa confessorum* of the Dominican John of Freiburg. Written in 1297/8, this *Summa confessorum* set out to bring Raymund of Pennafort's *Summa de casibus* up to date, filling it out from the theology of the principal Dominican theologians who had written since Raymund had published a revised edition of his *Summa* in 1234, and from the writings of a later generation of canonists, such as Hostiensis and William Durandus. Pagula, writing some twenty years later, was perfectly familiar with this *Summa confessorum*; in fact there is scarcely a reference to the great theologians Albert the Great, Thomas Aquinas and Peter of Tarentaise, or to many of the famous canonists, which does not come directly from the work of John of Freiburg.[32] Yet

---

[31] Thus: a) Magna Carta: *Oculus* (New College MS 292 fols. 21vb-23ra); *Summa* (MS Bodley 293 fols. 235ra-vb); *Speculum* (Merton College MS 217 fols. 165va-166rb).

   b) Carta de Foresta: *Oculus* fols. 23rb-24ra; *Summa* fols. 235vb-236rb; *Speculum* fols. 166va-167ra.

   c) Sentence of 1253: *Oculus* fol 24r; *Summa* fol. 236r; *Speculum* fol. 167r.

[32] Thus at the end of *De testibus* (*Summa summarum* 2.26; MS Bodley 293 fol. 83): 'Quot numerus testium requiratur? Dic quod duo testes ad minus sunt necessarii . . . secundum Host. et Gauf. eodem titulo (= *Summa confessorum* 2.5, 158). Quare requiritur maior numerus testium contra episcopos et superiores quam contra alios simplices homines? Dic quod triplex est racio . . . secundum Thomam in Summa (= *Summa confessorum* 2.5, 180). Quid si testis producatur super re de qua non est omnino certus? Dic secundum Thomam in Summa. . . . (= *Summa confessorum* 2.5, 183). An liceat homini testimonium facere de hiis que ei in secreto commissa sunt? Dic quod (potest) . . . ex precepto superioris, secundum Thomam in Summa (= *Summa confessorum* 2.5, 185).' The examples could be multiplied indefinitely. See especially Bk 3, c. 48, *De celebracione missarum* (*MS cit.* fol. 140v) where the Quodlibets of St. Thomas, a prime source of the *Summa confessorum*, are quoted from John of Freiburg's work without any acknowledgment when discussing the obligation of prebendaries etc. to perform certain liturgical offices, for example: 'An clericus prebendatus in duabus ecclesiis in die quo diversum est officium in ecclesia debeat dicere utrumque officium vel unius ecclesie officium dicere debet? Dic quod duobus obligatur scilicet Deo . . . et ecclesie . . . secundum Thomam in quadam questione de quolibet (= *Summa confessorum* 1.7, 19). . . . An clericus prebendatus in scolis existens tenetur dicere officium mortuorum? . . . . Dicendum . . . secundum Thomam in quadam questione de quolibet' (= *Summa confessorum* 1.7, 21).

424

curiously, Pagula never once acknowledges the *Summa confessorum* as his source in any of his works. Perhaps, like some of his contemporaries,[33] and some medieval (and modern) library catalogues, he was under the impression that the *Summa confessorum* was a work of Raymund of Pennafort, whom he quotes time and again.[34]

At all events the *Summa summarum* is a striking, if unexpected, amalgam of theology and canon law, of general legislation and local discipline. It is, indeed, almost a perfect work of reference. As may be verified in the Index transcribed at the end of this paper, there is hardly a subject that has been overlooked, from the election of a pope to the hearing of confessions. The backward parish priest as well as the learned ecclesiastic could derive benefit from it. If there are chapters on Kings and Princes (1.11) and on Councils and Synods (1.15), there are also some fine chapters 'De corpore et sanguine Christi' (3.49) and 'De peccatoribus et eorum peccatis' (5.42). And if the executor would find a magnificent chapter on his office and obligations (3.11), and the official of the Court of Arches a chapter in which the 'unwritten customs' of the Court are set out in question and answer form (1.21, etc.),[35] others might be more interested in chapters on impediments to promotion (5.44), the laws affecting mendicants (3.41) and nuns (3.42), the interpretation of rescripts (1.20), or in the excellent chapters which deal with the intricacies of the jurisdiction of confessors (5.50-66).

Thus, despite all Pagula's protestations, his *Summa summarum* was, in its way, original. At least it was something which no English canonist had ac-

---

[33] Thus the *Regimen animarum* (1343): 'Compilavi enim hoc opusculum ex quibusdam libris, videlicet, Summa summarum, Raymundi Summa confessorum. . . . ' (Bodleian Library, MS Hatton 11 fol. 4ʳ).

[34] Pagula states explicitly in the prologue to the *Summa summarum* that he is making use of the '*summae* of Raymund, Geoffrey and Compostellanus' (see Appendix I, below), yet in fact any passages in which Raymund's name appears come not from the *Summa de casibus* of Raymund himself but from John of Freiburg. In the prologue itself Pagula has copied one whole passage from John of Freiburg's prologue to his *Summa confessorum*.

[35] 'Que sunt consuetudines et observancie non scripte apud Archus Lond. in appellacionibus tuitoriis?' (1.21: *De consuetudine*; MS Bodley 293 fol. 30ʳ); 'Qui est modus procedendi in curia de Arcubus in contemptibus tam contra suffraganeos quam extraneos?' (2.19; fol. 75ᵛ); 'Que est forma iuramenti clericorum et examinatorum curie de Arcubus?' (2.7; fol. 84ʳ); see also fols. 68ʳ, 83ʳ, etc. The great compilation *Omne bonum* (see n. 78 below) in the British Museum appears to take its text of the 'unwritten customs' from the *Summa summarum*. Straight texts of these customs (i.e. not in the question and answer form used by Pagula) are to be found in MSS Bodl. Libr. Ashmole 1146 fols. 111ᵛ-115ᵛ; Queen's Coll. Oxford, 53 fols. 392ᵛ-3ʳ; Canterbury, Dean and Chapter Library, D.8 fols. 53ʳ-68ᵛ; see also Corpus Christi Coll. Oxford, MS 72 fols. 68ᵛ-71, where there is a treatise which appears to illustrate these customs from real cases. A study of these customs is now being prepared by Fr. Donald Logan of St. John's Seminary, Brighton, Mass.

complished, whether before or after Pagula. William of Drogheda, John Acton, William Lyndwood, to take the three great names of the period between the publication of the Decretals (1234) and the Reformation, come nowhere near Pagula's material achievement. William of Drogheda's interests were confined to a section of canon law, to procedure in particular; John Acton displayed a considerable knowledge of law in glossing the Legatine constitutions; William Lyndwood followed in Acton's footsteps when he composed his commentary between 1422 and 1430 on the main provincial constitutions of England.[36] Pagula, however, embraced the whole field of general Church law and local English legislation in his *Summa summarum*. He may not exhibit a convincing degree of personal thought, but where Lyndwood, Acton, and William of Drogheda kept within well-defined limits, Pagula wisely or unwisely attempted to be encyclopedic, giving as his justification the needs of impecunious clerics ('ad profectum et utilitatem pauperum clericorum'), the interests of the *regimen animarum* ('valde ignominosum est clericis ad hoc regimen vocatis causam ipsius regiminis penitus ignorare'), and the advancement of learning in the Church as a whole ('Et hoc feci pro rudibus et penitus ignorantibus ius canonicum, et potissime pro prelatis et sacerdotibus, cum ignorantia iuris canonici sit eis inter ceteros magis periculosa').[37]

IV

Pagula's hope that his work would reach the poorer clergy hardly allows for the fact that the lengthy *Summa*, even in its cheapest form, would be far beyond the reach of most normal clerical purses of the fourteenth and fifteenth centuries;[38] in fact there is little or no evidence that the *Summa* circulated

---

[36] On Lyndwood see C. R. Cheney, 'Wiliam Lyndwood's *Provinciale*,' *The Jurist* 21 (1961) 405-34.

[37] Prologue (Appendix I, below).

[38] The extant copies of the *Summa* run to over 250 large folios, all with double columns, containing perhaps 350,000 words. In an inventory of 1369 in which the *Óculus* (perhaps only *Pars oculi*) and the *Summa* occur side by side, the former is valued at 6s. 8d while the latter costs twelve times as much (A. F. Leach, *Visitations and Memorials of Southwell Minster* [London 1891] 198). The Queen's College, Oxford, commissioned a relatively inexpensive copy in 1366-7: 'parchment was bought for iiid, perhaps twice; xxd was paid pro scriptura, and xiid 'lymnatori'; vs. viiid was paid 'pro reparacione eiusdem libri videlicet pro ligacione et cooperatura' (J. R. Magrath, *The Queen's College, Oxford* [Oxford 1921] I 78). About 1330-40 Henry Fowke of Worcester Cathedral Priory paid 50s., and about 1344-52 Simon Bozoun of Norwich Priory 40s., for their copies (see nn. 54, 57), while the copy bought by Magdalen College from an Oxford stationer in 1457 cost 33s.4d (MS Lat. 134, endleaf); by 1508, however, a copy in the library of Martin Collins, treasurer of

much among the lower clergy or that it found its way into more than a few parish churches. At other and more monied and professional levels, however, Pagula's *Summa* won a place for itself which, if it does not even distantly resemble the resounding and popular success of his *Oculus* sacerdotis, is nonetheless impressive. A cursory search in library catalogues, wills, and inventories provides evidence of at least 70 copies in circulation in England in the two centuries between the composition of the *Summa* and the break with Rome. So far as is known at present, thirteen of these manuscripts still survive, all of which are written with care and a few at some expense; many of the others were no doubt destroyed in the sixteenth century, or were used by bookbinders as pastedowns, or, perhaps, like the gatherings now in Leicester Museum, as handy folders in which to file accounts.[39]

The majority of the extant copies and of those others of which there is record belonged to monastic, cathedral or college libraries, but there must have been many other copies in less public domains, such as those possessed before 1369 by Lewis Charlton, bishop of Hereford,[40] and by Ralph Erghom of Bath and Wells before 1396,[41] or by a Dean of Chichester (before 1383),[42] a notary public who willed his copy in 1395 to Archbishop Arundel of York,[43] a canon in 1396 and a subtreasurer of York in 1432,[44] and by priests at Monmouth in Wales (before 1393)[45] and Sall in Norfolk (before 1417).[46]

The presence of the *Summa* in libraries is more marked, especially in those of religious houses. If it appears only fitfully in libraries of collegiate churches (St. George's, Windsor, 1410; St. William's, York, 1485; a chained copy in the Lady Chapel of All Saints, Derby before 1525),[47] it was available (and sometimes consulted) in Benedictine and other monastic centres all over Eng-

---

York Minster, was valued, with the *Speculum* and *Reportorium* of Durandus, at xiid (*Testamenta Eboracensia*, Surtees Society; 1836-1902) IV 280.

[39] See appendix III for a list of extant MSS.

[40] Lambeth Palace Library, Reg. Whittlesey (Cant.) fol. 102ʳ.

[41] F. W. Weaver, 'Somerset Medieval Wills — 2', *Somerset Record Society* 17 (1903) 29.

[42] Lambeth Palace Library, Reg. Courtenay (Cant.) fol. 203ʳ.

[43] *Testamenta Eboracensia* III 1.

[44] *Ibid.* I 207; III 91.

[45] *Registrum Johannis Trefnant Episcopi Herefordensis* (Canterbury and York Society; 1916) 100-1.

[46] H. Harrod, 'Extracts from Early Wills in Norwich Registers,' *Norfolk and Norwich Archeological Society* 4 (1900) 317-8.

[47] *Inventories of St George's Chapel, Windsor*, ed. M. F. Bond (London 1904) 104; *Testamenta Eboracensia* III 117n. (bequest of John Danby of York Minster to College of St. William); J. C. Cox and W. H. St. John Hope, *Chronicles of the Collegiate Church of All Saints, Derby* (Derby 1881) 175-7; see also E. A. Savage, *Old English Libraries* (London 1903) 130-1.

XV

land. There were, for example, two copies at Hulne,[48] and one at Lindis-farne[49] in 1397; and of the three copies at Durham in that year one was sent to Oxford in 1409 by John Wessington for the use of Durham monks studying there.[50] Prior Wessington himself was not unfamiliar with the contents of the *Summa*, for he copied into a personal notebook part of Book 3, c. 56 on the Lenten fast,[51] a passage which also occurs in yet another Durham manu-script.[52] At Peterborough, Prior Adam Boothby owned a copy some time before his death in 1338,[53] and at Norwich Cathedral Priory there was a copy among the books of Prior Simon Bozoun who died in 1352.[54] Early copies, too, were in the libraries of the Ipswich Franciscans, perhaps as early as 1332-35,[55] St Augustine's, Canterbury (1334-43)[56] and Worcester Cathedral (about 1330-40).[57] The copy which occurs in charges brought against an Abbot of Eynsham, Oxfordshire, during a visitation of 1363/66,[58] possibly was in the monastery for some time previously, while the two copies of the *Summa* at Glastonbury Abbey (together with Pagula's *Oculus* and an ascribed *Epistola ad Regem Edwardum*) could have been acquired any time between 1341 and 1374;[59] likewise the copy possessed by the Austin Friars of York in 1372 and

---

[48] *Catalogi veteres ecclesie Dunelmensis* ed. J. Raine (Surtees Soc.; 1838) 47, 130, 134.

[49] J. Raine, *The History and Antiquities of North Durham* (Surtees Soc.; 1852) 93.

[50] *Catalogi veteres* 41.

[51] British Museum, MS Lansdowne 397 fol. 7r: 'Nota in Summa summarum libro tercio tit. 56: Quare ieiunamus quadragesimam? . . . . '

[52] Durham Cathedral Library, MS B. IV. 41 fol. 97v: 'Nota in Summa summarum lib. 3 tit. 56, de observacione. . . . '

[53] M. R. James, 'Lists of Manuscripts formerly in Peterborough Abbey Library,' *Suppl. Transactions of Bibliographical Society* 5 (1926) 25.

[54] See the list of his books printed from B. Museum, MS Royal 14.C.XIII in Giraldus Cambrensis, *Opera omnia* (Rolls ser.; London 1861-91) V xxxix n., and the facsimile in New Palaeographical Society *Facsimiles* new ser. I 143. The copy cost, or was valued at, 40s.

[55] 'A Medieval Manuscript of Ipswich Interest,' *Ipswich Library Journal* 46 (1939) 14-17. The copy was given by Fr. Laurence Bretoun, Lector of the Oxford Franciscan Convent between 1332 and 1335. On Bretoun see Emden, *Biographical Register* I 261.

[56] According to a late 15th-century catalogue there were then two copies in the library (M. R. James, *Ancient Libraries of Canterbury and Dover* [Cambridge 1903] 404 nn. 1810, 1811), but in fact one of these (n. 1810) had belonged to Abbot Thomas Poucyn, who was a D. D. by 1334 and had died in 1343 (See Emden, *op. cit.* III 1508).

[57] The *Summa* at present in the library of the Cathedral (MS F. 131) was bought for 50s. by the monk Henry Fowke about 1330-40 (MS flyleaf).

[58] W. A. Pantin, *Documents Illustrating the Activities of the General and Provincial Chapters of the English Black Monks 1215-1540* (Camden ser.; 1931-37) III 47.

[59] Trinity College, Cambridge, MS 711 p. 246 nn. 39, 40: a list of books acquired by Abbot Walter de Monyton (1341-74); the *Epistola* is actually noted as 'Magistri Willelmi Paul' (see n. 20 above).

the two copies of the Benedictines of Dover Priory in 1389[60] — or for that matter the two copies each in St. Mary's Abbey, Leicester,[61] and Exeter Cathedral[62] at the end of the fifteenth century — probably were not fresh acquisitions at the time their presence was recorded in the catalogues that have survived to us.

In university and legal circles, too, the *Summa* was known and respected. If John Acton appears not to have known the work when writing his commentary on the Legatine Constitutions about 1334, he showed some twelve years later in his *Septuplum* that he was by then well aware of the special value of the *Summa* when he referred his readers to it for excommunications coming from English provincial legislation.[63] About the same time Walter Elveden, Acton's fellow disputant in the *quaestio* noted above and an indefatigable compiler of indexes,[64] used the *Summa* to gloss parts of his copy of a *Tabula iuris*.[65] Some thirty years later (this time at Oxford) we find the *Summa* keeping company with Joannes Andreae, Willelmus de Monte Lauduno and many other canonists in a series of marginal glosses on a copy of the Decretals which belonged to or was annotated by Thomas Walkington.[66] The *Summa* was used also to gloss a *Liber Decretalium* which belonged to M. Nicholas Elys, notary public, a late fourteenth-century vicar of St. Audeon's,

---

[60] M. R. James, 'The Catalogue of the Library of the Augustinians of York,' *Fasciculus Iohanni Willis Clark dicatus* (Cambridge 1909) 63; *Ancient Libraries* 427, 476.

[61] *Id.* 'Catalogue of the Library of Leicester Abbey,' *Transactions of Leicestershire Archeological Society* 19 (1936-7) 400.

[62] G. Oliver, *Lives of the Bishops of Exeter* (Exeter 1861) 367, 369; one of the two copies, the present MS Bodley 293, was written in mid-14th century.

[63] 'Sunt et alii casus qui per constituciones provinciales diversimmode puniuntur, de quibus tractatur in Summa summarum, libro v, tit. lv, versus finem' (Gonville and Caius Coll., Cambridge, MS 282 fol. 136r). See also fol. 129r: 'De aliis autem casibus quibus solus Papa dispensat, vide . . . Summa summarum, libro v, tit. de dispensacionibus' (= *Summa* 5.49).

[64] For example, Gonville and Caius MS 242: an index to the *Speculum iudiciale* of William Durandus; Cambridge, Peterhouse, MS 42 and British Museum MS Royal 9. E. II: a *Tabula Sexti*.

[65] Gonville and Caius Coll. MS 36, fol. 71v, where what I take to be Elveden's hand has copied the passage from the *Summa summarum* about the four types of *summae* (see at n. 23 above) at the end of a *Tabula iuris*. In the gloss on the *Tabula* (fols. 1r-71v) the notes from the *Summa summarum* are not acknowledged as such, but they have been noticed on fols. 4r (= *Summa* 1.37), 6r (= 3.52) 12r (= 1.21) and 38r (= 2.8-9). The borrowings on fols. 6r and 12r are interesting in that they quote St. Thomas and Peter of Tarentaise from the *Summa summarum*, which in turn had copied these authors from John of Freiburg's *Summa confessorum*.

[66] British Museum, MS Royal 9. F. II fol. 142v: 'Nota de diversis intencionibus renunciacionum. . . . Eger abstinet quia non potest comedere vel propter medicinam. . . . Hec in Summa summarum' (= *Summa* 3.56). Walkington's name appears on fols. 200v and 206v.

Gloucester;[67] more piquantly, it provided a gloss on one occasion of a passage in Pagula's own *Oculus*.[68] Again, in 1415-16 Robert Heete of Woodstock, a New College canonist, used both the *Summa summarum* and *Speculum praelatorum* of Pagula in a lecture at Oxford on the Clementines. Thus to the question, 'Qualiter et quando debeat missam celebrare?' Heete answers: 'De istis materiis plenius notatur in Summa summarum'; and shortly afterwards he pays a tribute to the *Summa*, bracketing it with Hostiensis: 'Hostiensis in Summa in 4º titulo, et quando; et bene in Summa summarum.'[69]

There were, of course, copies in some Oxford Colleges by this time. A copy of the *Summa* was written for Queen's College in 1366/7;[70] the one which Heete would have seen at New College was probably that donated by the founder William of Wykeham about 1382.[71] At Cambridge, Michael Causton gave a copy to Pembroke College before 1396, possibly the present MS 201;[72] and it may be suggested that the *Summa sententiarum* which occurs among the law books at King's Hall (Trinity College) in 1386 is really the *Summa summarum*.[73] In the fifteenth century a copy was purchased for Magdalen College, Oxford, in 1457;[74] at Cambridge there was a copy in Queen's College before 1472, and copies occur as *cautiones* in 1484-5 and 1489.[75] Outside of these college and canonical circles the *Summa* appears from time to time in pastoral and other miscellanies.[76] Thus together with Pagula's *Oculus* and John of Freiburg's *Summa confessorum* it is one of the acknowledged sources

---

[67] Cambridge Univ. Library, MS Ee. v. 4 fols. 42ᵛ etc.

[68] Balliol College, Oxford, MS 83 fols. 34ᵛ-5ʳ. The passage is from the *Summa* 3.48 (*De celebracione missarum*).

[69] New College, Oxford, MS 192 fols. 101ᵛ, 102ʳ. Heete's 'Reportorium super primo libro Decretalium' occurs on fols. 9ʳ-82ᵛ. At fol. 100ʳ Pagula's *Speculum praelatorum* is also quoted. On Heete see Emden, *Biographical Register* II 901-2.

[70] F. R. Magrath, *The Queen's College* I 78n; see n. 38 above.

[71] With the *Speculum praelatorum*: A. F. Leach, 'Wykeham's Books at New College,' *Oxford Historical Society Collectanea* III (Oxford 1896) 237.

[72] See M. R. James, *A Catalogue of the Manuscripts of Pembroke College, Cambridge* (Cambridge 1905) xiv.

[73] C. E. Sayle, 'King's Hall Library,' *Cambridge Antiquarian Society Communications* 24 (1923) 58.

[74] See Appendix III(a) below.

[75] W. G. Searle, 'Catalogue of the Library of Queen's College in 1472,' *Cambridge Antiquarian Society Communications* 2 (1864) 180; *Grace Book A of the University of Cambridge* ed. S M. Leathes (Cambridge 1897) 195; *Grace Book B* ed. M. Bateson (Cambridge 1903) 15.

[76] For example, MS Bodley 784, a miscellany which contains various notes from the *Oculus* (fols. 71ᵛ, 75ᵛ, etc) and a large section from the *Summa* (fols. 108ʳ-124ᵛ): 'Hic incipiunt quedam notabilia extracta de quodam libro qui vocatur Summa summarum. . . . Expliciunt quedam notabilia extracta de Summa summarum.'

430

of the well-known pastoral manual *Regimen animarum* in 1343;[77] and there are some thirty-five rather lengthy borrowings from it, mostly explicit, in the massive *Omne bonum* compiled between 1330 and 1350 by Jacobus Anglicus, who perhaps is echoing the prologue to the *Summa* when he conceals his full name 'ne videlicet intuentibus istum librum et compilatoris huius nomen vilescerit idem liber.'[78]

The theological as well as the legal content of the *Summa* probably attracted many of its devotees. Yet it is a little surprising to find that the earliest use of the *Summa* of which we know at present occurs in the work of a professional theologian, the great Carmelite doctor John Baconthorpe, whose Postill on St. Matthew may be dated to 1336-1337 and *Quaestiones canonicae* on the 4th book of the Sentences to about 1344.[79] Some of Baconthorpe's acquaintance with the canonists derives from the *Summa*, generally with due acknowledgment ('ille qui fecit Summam summarum'; 'hoc habes in Summa summarum'). What is perhaps more intriguing is the fact that although Baconthorpe possessed John of Freiburg's *Summa confessorum*, he often copied passages from the *Summa summarum* which Pagula had in fact lifted from the *Summa confessorum*. On occasion, indeed, he prefers to quote St. Thomas from the *Summa summarum* rather than from St. Thomas himself, or, for that matter, from the *Summa confessorum*, which had supplied Pagula with his quotations. Thus when he writes, 'In Summa summarum et Summa confessorum habes multos casus expressos necessitatis excusantes (a ieiunio) . . . Primo quid de laborantibus in vineis. . . . Respondetur ibidem (i.e. Summa summarum). . . . Sic tenet Thomas in secunda secundae q. 174, art. iv,' the wording of the passage from St. Thomas is that of the *Summa summarum*. Yet Baconthorpe clearly had the *Summa confessorum* of John of Freiburg open at the same time. For where Pagula's treatment of fasting ends simply 'secundum Thomam in Summa,'[80] Baconthorpe proceeds to give a more precise reference to St. Thomas, taking it straight from the *Summa confessorum*.[81] Of course this does not mean that Baconthorpe knew St. Thomas

---

[77] 'Compilavi enim hoc opusculum ex quibusdam libris, videlicet, Summa summarum, Raymundi Summa confessorum' (Bodleian Library, MS Hatton 11 fol. 4ʳ). The first 23 chapters of the first part of the *Regimen* (fols. 4ʳ-55ᵛ) are made up of selections from the *Summa summarum* and the *Summa confessorum*.

[78] See part 2 (1340-50) of the *Omne bonum* (B. Museum, MS Royal 6. E. VII fols. 54ʳ-55ᵛ; 60ᵛ-62ᵛ; 118ᵛ-120ʳ; 131ᵛ-132ᵛ, etc.). In part I (1330-1340) the *Summa* is given as one of the sources of the work (fol. 18ᵛ). On the *Omne bonum* and Jacobus Anglicus see A. Gwynn, 'The Sermon-Diary of Richard Fitzralph,' *Proc. Royal Irish Acad.* 44 (1937-8) sect. C., 15-16.

[79] B. Smalley, 'John Baconthorpe's Postill on St Matthew,' *Medieval and Renaissance Studies* 4 (1958) 99-110, 119, 143.

[80] *Summa*, MS Bodley 293 fol. 149ᵛ.

[81] Baconthorpe, Commentary on 4 *Sent.* 20.2, 2 (ed. Cremona 1616 II 446). The same

only at second hand. If he preferred on occasion to quote St. Thomas from the *Summa summarum* and *Summa confessorum* rather than from St. Thomas himself, this probably was because these secondary sources conveniently placed the moral doctrine of St. Thomas in the legal setting with which Baconthorpe was concerned in these passages.

By and large, then, the *Summa summarum* appears to have made an impression at all levels of ecclesiastical life in England in the fourteenth and fifteenth centuries.[82] Outside of England the *Summa* seems not to have had any influence or circulation apart from two quotations in the *Manuale confessorum* of John Nider, the famous fifteenth-century Dominican moralist.[83] To my knowledge there was not a demand for the *Summa* on the continent at any time; nor was there a copy of the *Summa* in the library of the Dominican convent at Basle[84] either before or after Nider composed his *Manuale* there. However, since Nider was Prior of the Basle Dominicans and was composing his *Manuale* during the time of the Council of Basle,[85] it may be suggested that Nider owes his unexpected acquaintance with the *Summa summarum* to one or other of the English delegates to the Council, some of whom certainly took books with them from England for reference purposes. The Bishop of Glasgow had borrowed some books from Aberdeen Cathedral before leaving for the Council;[86] and a certain M. Robertus de Anglia, possibly Fitzhugh, bishop of London, donated one of his books (a copy of the Decretals) to the Carthusians while at Basle.[87] At least one of the English delegation was the owner of a copy of the *Summa summarum*. Just before he left England in late 1432 for Basle, the then Bishop of Worcester Thomas Polton made

---

passage, together with other passages from Pagula and the *Summa summarum*, is also to be found in the *Postilla in Mattheum*, Trinity College, Cambridge, MS 348, fols. 120[v] etc; Miss Smalley has dealt fully with these borrowings in the article cited in n. 79.

[82] See Appendix IV, below, for a summary table of circulation.

[83] *Manuale confessorum* (Bodl. Library, MS Laud Misc. 296 fols. 85[r]-127[r]; ed. Paris 1477): '(Septimus casus principalis excommunicationis): contra illos cleros qui sponte et scienter participant cum excommunicatis recipiendo in divinis oficiis; et in eodem adit Summa summarum: Extra de sentencia excommunicationis, Significavit' (MS fol. 89[r], ed. 7[v]; see also MS fol. 90[r], ed. 8[v], 9[r]), verified in the *Summa* (MS Bodley 293 fol. 233[vb]): '(Excommunicati sunt) communicantes scienter et sponte et eodem crimine cum excommunicato a Papa, et (qui) ipsum in officio recipit: Extra de sententia excommunicationis, c. Significavit.'

[84] See P. Schmidt, 'Die Bibliothek des ehemaligen Dominikanerklosters in Basel,' *Basler Zeitschrift* 18 (1919) 183-254.

[85] Nider died in 1438. The latest date quoted in the *Manuale* is the 12th session of the Council (1434).

[86] *Ecclesiae Cathedralis Aberdonensis Regesta* (Edinburgh 1845) II 129.

[87] S. Stelling-Michaud, *Catalogue des manuscrits juridiques de la fin du* XIIe *au* XIVe *siècle conservés en Suisse* (Geneva 1954) 13, 25.

432

detailed arrangements in his will for the disposal of his *Summa*: after his death it was to be chained in the choir or some other suitable place in the priory church of St. Margaret at Marlborough, there to remain in perpetuity.[88] Perhaps the reason why he mentioned it so specifically was because he intended to take it with him to the council; certainly it would have been of great use to him since in fact it covered the whole corpus of canon law with the exception of the legislation of John XXII. If he did take it with him, then it may be presumed that it reverted to St. Margaret's after his death in 1433 at the Council and that it did not go to enrich the library of the Dominicans or the Carthusians of Basle.[89] Possibly, then, it was some copy of the *Summa summarum* such as that owned by Polton that came briefly into John Nider's hands during the Council while he was writing his *Manuale*.

V

Of William of Pagula's five works the companion volume to the *Summa summarum* is clearly the *Speculum praelatorum*, a collection of devotional, pastoral and homiletic material which survives incompletely in one manuscript.[90] Conceived on a very large scale, the *Speculum* attempted in Books 1 and 2 to cover most of the matter of the *Oculus sacerdotis* and the *Summa summarum*, devoting Book 3 to sermon *themata*.

The link with the tripartite *Oculus* (*Pars Oculi*, *Dextera pars*, *Sinistra pars*) is unmistakable. Thus the greater part of the *Dextera pars* is repeated in the *Speculum*, as may be seen from the following table:

Dextera pars (New College, Oxford, MS 292)	*Speculum praelatorum* (Merton College, Oxford, MS 217)
fols. 35ra-41rb	142ra-146rb
41rb-48ra	148va-153va . . . ut notatur infra in 3a parte s.v. peccatum; 3rd Part: *Peccatum*
48ra-48vb	154va . . . ut notatur infra in 3a parte s.v. iactantia

---

[88] 'Similiter lego unum librum qui vocatur Summa summarum precii vi marcarum . . . cum cathena ferrea in choro ecclesie ipsius prioratus aut in alio loco magis ad hoc apto perpetuo ligandum et inibi sub pena anathematis perpetuo remansurum, et scribatur in primo folio nomen conferentis et causa' (*The Register of Henry Chichele*, ed. E. F. Jacob [Oxford 1938] II 487).

[89] See Stelling-Michaud, *op. cit.* 11-14 for various books donated by conciliar Fathers to these religious houses.

[90] Merton College, Oxford, MS 217. The late F. M. Powicke, *The Medieval Books of Merton College* (Oxford 1930) 238-40, was the first to describe this manuscript and to suggest its possible connection with a *Speculum praelatorum* ascribed by Pits, etc. to William of Pagula.

48rb-49ra	3rd Part: *Iactantia*
49ra-51vb	154va-155rb
51vb-61v	155rb-160r

Likewise most of the sacramental part of the *Oculus*, the *Sinistra pars*, occurs word for word in the *Speculum*:

	Sinistra Pars	Speculum
Baptism	66v-70r	30v-33r
Confirmation	70r-70v	33r-33v
Penance	71r-76v	33v-37r
Eucharist	76v-90r	37v-55v
E. Unction	90r-92v	55v-58v
Order [91]	92v-96v	58r-62r
Matrimony	96v-107v	62r-71r

The close relationship of the *Speculum* to the *Summa summarum* is no less obvious. There are many references to the *Summa*,[92] and chapters often end with a phrase which Pagula also uses in his *Oculus*: 'Quae hic desunt vide in *Summa summarum*, libro . . . titulo . . . '[93]

However, the impression that one gets from these first two books of the *Speculum* is that Pagula had attempted too much in setting about the composition of a work which would be both *Summa summarum* and *Oculus sacerdotis*. He seems to have been aware of this himself, for on two occasions he merely lists the numbers and titles of blocks of chapters which his index had promised,[94] referring the reader in the case of each chapter to the corresponding chapter in the *Summa summarum*.[95] In general, indeed, the features which have been noted of the *Summa* and the *Oculus* are present again in these two books of the *Speculum*: a rigorous attention to detail, a remarkable ability

---

[91] In the *Dextera pars* and in the first part of the *Speculum*, where the emphasis was on preaching the sacraments rather than on the theory of the sacraments, Order was only listed, 'Quia istud sacramentum non pertinet ad laicos de hoc sacramento nichil hic tango' (*Oculus*, New Coll. MS 252 fol. 44v; *Speculum*, Merton Coll. MS 217 fol. 151r).

[92] For example, 'Item dicit Raymundus . . . ut notatur in nova Summa summarum in IIIo libro in titulo de celebracione Misse, paragrapho celebrabuntur' (*MS cit.* fol. 53vb; verified in *Summa*, MS Bodley 293 fol. 139ra); 'De hac materia dic ut notatur in Summa summarum libro Vo titulo LIXo' (fol. 100vb), etc.

[93] Thus: Book I: end of c. 4 (fol. 34va), c. 5 (fol. 39va), c. 6 (fol. 41vb); Book II: c. 16 (fol. 131ra), c. 29 (fol. 167va), c. 44 (fol. 172ra), etc.

[94] See fol. 80rb: 'Tituli huius (secundae) partis.'

[95] Book II cc. 21-28 (*MS cit.* fol. 166r), 31-40 (fol. 170v). A few examples of Pagula's summary disposal of these chapters will suffice: 'Titulus XXI. Pro quibus peccatis debet presbyter mittere peccatorem ad curiam romanam pro absolucione habenda. Quere in Summa summarum libro Vo, titulo LIIIIo . . . . Titulus XXVII. De sequestrationibus. Quere in Summa summarum libro IIo, titulo XXIIo . . . Titulus XL. De arbitris. Quere in Summa summarum libro Io titulo ultimo.'

434

to manipulate the sources of canon law, a strong sense of the place of the legislation of the Church in England, and that balance of law and theology which
is due to Pagula's discerning use of the *Summa confessorum* of John of Freiburg. Perhaps the only difference between these two books of the *Speculum*
and the *Summa* or *Oculus* is that Pagula has taken over almost the whole
of the *Stimulus amoris* of James of Milan in the *Speculum*. The greater part
of the *Stimulus* occupies the second part of the second chapter of Book 1,[96]
while the section on predestination appears in the middle of the first chapter,[97]
which otherwise is composed of extracts from the popular *Summa veritatis
theologicae* of Hugh of Strasbourg.

The third part of the *Speculum* is in many ways the most rewarding section
of the work. Here Pagula has introduced material which has not already
been used in the *Summa* and *Oculus*. The result is a great, coherent body of
sermon material which has scarcely a rival among English sermon manuals.
For each Sunday and every possible liturgical occasion Pagula gives three
or four sermon outlines, following these with four or five, and sometimes as
many as seven or eight, sermon *themata*. Then, in case any preacher should
find this material too slight, Pagula provides also a fine dictionary of quotations
from the Fathers, with many cross-references to the second book of the *Speculum*.[98]

VI

Although the *Speculum* as a whole is probably Pagula's greatest pastoral
work, it was completely outshadowed by the *Summa* and the *Oculus*; it is
extant in only one manuscript, and it is rarely that one comes across a reference
to it.[99] It was not, however, an unmitigated failure, for in fact two offshoots
from it were to command some attention in the fourteenth and fifteenth

---

[96] *MS cit.* fols. 11r-30v: 'De contemplacione. . . . Hec sumuntur ex summa que vocatur
Stimulus amoris.' See C. Kirchberger, ed. Walter Hilton, *The Goad of Love* (London 1952)
18-19 n.3, who discusses the relationship of Pagula's text of the *Stimulus* with Hilton's translation and with the English manuscript tradition.

[97] Fols. 5r-v.

[98] Fols. 180r-248r (sermon themes), 248r-441r (Dictionary, *Aperire-Zelus*): 'Incipit tercia
pars huius summe in qua tractatur de predicacionibus verbi divini et auctoritatibus sanctorum patrum et aliorum doctorum per quas quicunque literaturam intelligens poterit
faciliter subditis suis predicare.'

[99] William of Wykeham gave a copy to New College about 1382 (n. 71, above); Robert
Heete, the New College canonist, quotes it once in a lecture of 1415 (New College MS 192
fol. 100r); there is also a reference to it in a pastoral miscellany in MS Bodley 54 fol. 88r:
'Que hic desunt quere in Speculo prelatorum super verbo invidia.'

centuries. The first of these, a chapter on the duties of archdeacons ('Archidiaconus oculus episcopi appellatur'), is extant in some five manuscripts;[100] the second is the important *Speculum religiosorum*, a compendium of moral and disciplinary matter for non-mendicant religious. In its excellent outline of the general and provincial laws affecting monks, the *Speculum religiosorum* is a forerunner of the legal tracts *De religiosis* which are a common feature of the post-Tridentine Church.

The second of the two books of which the *Speculum religiosorum* is composed leans heavily on the parts of the *Stimulus amoris* of James of Milan which Pagula had incorporated into the *Speculum praelatorum*.[101] The central chapters (7, 8, 9) of the first book come word for word from Book 2, c.4 of the *Speculum praelatorum*, on non-mendicant religious, as may readily be seen from the following summary comparison:

Speculum praelatorum (MS Merton College 217, fol. 90^{va-b})	*Speculum religiosorum* (MS Gray's Inn 11, fol. 25^r)
De Abbatibus et Prioribus et aliis religiosis non mendicantibus.	De abbatibus et prioribus et religiosis.
Abbas vel prior seu alius presidens desiderans se et conventum suum servire Deo, fideliter et devote debet scire canones et regulas sanctorum patrum et constituciones provinciales ad eos et eorum ordinem precipue pertinentes et eas tenetur observare et aliis subditis facere custodiri . . . xxv. Q. 1, c. Nulli fas, et c. Violatores . . . etc.	Abbas vel prior seu alius presidens desiderans se et conventum suum servire deo, fideliter et devote debet scire canones et regulas sanctorum patrum et constituciones provinciales ad eos et eorum ordinem precipue pertinentes et eas tenetur observare et aliis subditis facere custodiri . . . xxv. Q.1, c. Nulli fas, et c. Violatores etc
Ne autem ignorancia canonum regularum ac constitucionum predictarum ab earum observancia quemcumque religiosum possit avertere, omnes canones et regule ac constituciones tangentes non mendicantes hic faciliter exponuntur, et ubi et de quibus locis assumuntur *in hoc titulo* breviter inseruntur.	Ne autem ignorancia canonum regularum ac constitucionum predictarum ab earum observancia quemcumque religiosum possit avertere, omnes canones et regule ac constituciones tangentes non mendicantes hic faciliter exponuntur, et ubi et de quibus locis assumuntur *in hac summa* breviter inseruntur.
Abbas debet esse cautus in regimine, humilis castus et misericors ac divina precepta verbis et exemplis ostendens: xviii. Q.2, c. Si quis abbas	Abbas debet esse cautus in regimine, humilis castus et misericors ac divina precepta verbis et exemplis ostendens: xviii. Q.2, c. Si quis abbas . . . .

---

[100] Balliol College, Oxford, MS 158, fols. 171^r-5^v; Peterhouse, Cambridge, MS 84, fols. 178^r-182^v; Cambridge Univ. Library, Gg. vi. 21, fols. 162^r-167^r; British Museum, MSS Royal 6. E. VI fols. 132^v-4^v (part of *Omne bonum*; see n. 78, above), Harl. 220 fols. 59^r-64^r. The chapter in the *Speculum* is Merton College MS 217 fols. 130^v-131^r.

[101] *Speculum religiosorum*, MS Gray's Inn Library 11, fols. 101^r-165^r (= *Speculum praelatorum*, MS cit. fols. 11^r-30^v).

436

With the exception of one short section of the *Speculum religiosorum*[102] these two works continue line for line together until the end of this chapter of the *Speculum praelatorum* and of chapter 9 of the *Speculum religiosorum* is reached. There the *Speculum religiosorum* leaves legal matters affecting religious and returns in a chapter entitled 'De religioso mortuo mundo' to the moral considerations with which the work began. But even in some of the 'moral' chapters of the *Speculum religiosorum* the influence of the *Speculum praelatorum* may be noticed, especially in the nine chapters which follow the three 'legal' chapters. In these chapters (Bk. 1, cc. 10-18; fols. 54 -65) and in one other chapter (ibid. c.2; fols. 5 -9) the author, obviously following references given at the end of the chapter of the *Speculum praelatorum* from which he has been borrowing the 'legal' material, makes good use of sections of the third (the homiletic) part of the *Speculum praelatorum*:

Speculum praelatorum (Pt. 2, end of c.4: MS Merton Coll. 217, 96ᵛ)	*Speculum religiosorum* (Bk. 1, end of c.9: MS Gray's Inn 11, 54ʳ-65ʳ; 5ʳ-9ʳ)
. . . sicut patet in beato antonio et beato benedicto secundum Thomam in Summa. Religiosus verus debet esse mortuus mundo, etc. ut notatur infra in 3ᵃ parte super verbo 'religioso', paragrapho ultima.	. . . sicut patet in beato antonio et beato benedicto secundum Thomam in Summa. c.10: De religioso mortuo mundo.
Religiosus vel alius murmurans de cibo vel potu deficit in principio belli spiritualis, etc. ut notatur infra super verbo 'murmura' par. 'homo'.	c.11: De religoso murmurante.
Religiosi sapienter faciunt qui mundum relinquunt, etc. ut notatur infra in 3ᵃ parte super verbo 'mundus', par. 'relinquendus est mundus'.	c.12: De mundo relinquendo.
Item religiosus debet esse mitis et humilis ut notatur in 3ᵃ parte super verbo 'humilitas'.	c.13: De humilitate.
Item religiosus non debet esse verbosus ut notatur in 3ᵃ parte super verbo 'loquacitas'.	c.14: De religioso verboso.
Religiosus non debet esse gulosus nec ebriosus ut notatur infra in 3ᵃ parte super verbo 'ebrietas'.	c.15: De religioso guloso (et) ebrioso.
Religiosus debet tenere silencium, ut notatur infra in 3ᵃ parte super verbo 'silencium'.	c.16: De silencio religiosi.
Religiosus debet esse in solitudine, ut notatur super verbo 'solitudo' paragrapho 'in solitudine'.	c.17: De solitudine religiosi.

---

[102] MS Gray's Inn 11 fols. 32ʳ-37ʳ, which nevertheless appears to depend on the third part of the *Speculum praelatorum*. The *Speculum religiosorum* never quotes the S. praela-

Religiosus debet esse pacificus, ut notatur infra in 3ª parte super verbo 'paciencia'.	c.18: De paciencia.
Religiosus debet esse obediens prelato suo, et ad faciliter obediendum multa valere possunt, ut notatur infra in 3ª parte super verbo 'obediencia'.	c.2: De obediencia (fols. 5ʳ-9ʳ).

Five copies of this *Speculum religiosorum* survive, and there is extant a version of it in five other manuscripts. If thus it had some success, this was largely due to the fact that it set out in an ordered fashion in its central or legal chapters all the monastic legislation of the Church and of legatine and provincial synods. On that account it is not surprising to find that it appealed to the Benedictines, from whose monastery in Durham the majority of the manuscripts come. In fact it accompanies five of the eight collections of monastic legislation which were made at Durham in the middle ages;[103] for although the *Speculum religiosorum* in its original form accompanies only one of these collections, the treatise *Abbas vel prior*, which is found with four of the others and has been thought to be a work of Uthred of Boldon,[104] is in fact a rearrangement of the *Speculum*,[105] opening with the three chapters of the *Speculum* on monastic legislation (7, 8, 9) and then continuing with selections from other parts of Pagula's work.

Of course the *Speculum religiosorum* itself is almost as derivative as the *Abbas vel prior*, and oné could argue therefore that it is not necessarily a work of William of Pagula himself. Yet there seems to be no good reason to doubt his authorship, any more than there is to question his authorship of the *Dextera pars* and *Sinistra pars* of the *Oculus sacerdotis*, both of which, in as much as they occur textually in the *Speculum praelatorum*, also could be described as derivative. For, in fact, when the Benedictine bibliographer Boston of Bury at the beginning of the fifteenth century listed the *Oculus sacerdotis*, the *Summa summarum*, the *Speculum praelatorum*, and the Letter to Edward III as works of William of Pagula, vicar of Winkfield in the Forest of Windsor, he also gave the *Speculum religiosorum*, noting indeed the incipit

---

torum by name, but it does refer on one occasion to the *Oculus sacerdotis*: 'De ceteris peccatis mortalibus et de remediis contra illa quere in summa que vocatur *Oculus sacerdotis*' (Gray's Inn, MS 11 fol. 96ʳ; B. Museum, MS Royal 8. C. II fol. 39ʳ; MS Egerton 746 fol. 84ʳ which adds 'scilicet in dextera parte').

[103] For a description of these collections see the introduction of W. A. Pantin to his *Chapters of the English Black Monks* (Camden series, London 1933) II viii-xvii.

[104] W. A. Pantin, 'Two Treatises of Uthred of Boldon on the Religious Life,' *Studies in Medieval History Presented to F. M. Powicke* (Oxford 1948) 365. Possibly Uthred was responsible for arranging the material.

[105] See Appendix IIIc for manuscripts of the *Speculum* and the *Abbas vel prior*.

('Accipite') and the closing words ('passionem Christi') which have now made possible its identification.[106]

However, of these five works of Pagula the *Summa summarum* is that which above all entitles him to be considered a great writer in the field of canon law. From that point of view the influential *Oculus sacerdotis*, the over-ambitious *Speculum praelatorum* and the highly valuable *Speculum religiosorum* are secondary works. But whether we single out the *Summa summarum* or take all of Pagula's considerable output as a whole, the severely legal and theological with the popular and practical, there can hardly be any doubt that the Vicar of Winkfield was a man of more than ordinary industry, if not of uncommon ability.

Pontifical Institute of Mediaeval Studies,
Toronto;
Pontifical University of St. Thomas,
Rome.

Appendix I

THE PROLOGUE TO THE 'SUMMA SUMMARUM'

The prologue to the *Summa summarum* differs little from the prologue to the *Speculum praelatorum* and the prologues to the three parts of the *Oculus sacerdotis*. Here, as in these other works of William of Pagula, the burden is the duty of priests, of whatever walk of life, to acquire familiarity with the doctrine and discipline of the Church and to abhor ignorance; and, once again, the exposition of this introductory theme is a web of legal quotations, explicit and implicit. Part of the prologue contains a very fine index of chapter rubrics in which Pagula has followed the order and number of the books of the Decretals of Gregory IX, and, for the most part, the rubrics also. But, as he explains in the prologue, he has also from time to time inserted rubrics of his own making, and has distinguished these from Decretal rubrics by placing a letter of the alphabet after each of his own rubrics.

Altogether the *Summa summarum* contains 257 chapters, the rubrics of 182 of which come from the Decretals. In fact, however, only one of the 185 rubrics in the Decretals has not been taken over by Pagula. For although only 182 separate rubrics from the Decretals appear in the Index, Pagula has on two occasions taken two rubrics together to form one rubric in the *Summa*. Of the remaining 75 rubrics composed by Pagula himself two appear in the Index without the letter of the alphabet which Pagula had promised. The MSS which have been examined are perhaps at fault, for on two occasions MS Bodley 293, our basic manuscript here, is innocent of letters of the alphabet which are in fact in other manuscripts. The 75 rubrics which are, according to our count,

---

[106] Boston of Bury *apud* T. Tanner, *Bibliotheca Britannico-Hibernica* (London 1748) xl.

THE 'SUMMA SUMMARUM'   439

definitely of Pagula's making, exclude one (*Summa*, 1.14) which the Bodley
MS and other MSS claim as a 'Pagula' rubric; this is suspect in that it is really
a version of a Decretal rubric. But this seeming inaccuracy, and a failure to
provide all the promised letters of the alphabet for rubrics which did not come
from the Decretals, is possibly not the fault of Pagula but of the MSS which
have thus far been examined.

The distribution of the rubrics, as set out in the present transcription from
MS Bodley 293, may be summed up as follows:

Rubrics in *Summa summarum*		Rubrics in the Decretals	Rubrics from Decretals in *S. summarum*	Personal Rubrics claimed	in fact
Bk. 1	67	43	43	25	24[3]
2	40	30	30	10	10
3	61	50	50	11	11
4	20	21	20[1]	—	—
5	69	41	39[2]	28	30[4]
	257	185	182	74	75
			182		182[5]
	257				257

The prologue and text are edited here from MS Bodley 293 (= B), with
collations from Pembroke College, Cambridge, MS 201 (= P), British Museum,
MS Royal 10 D. X (= R), Bodleian Library, Oxford, MS Laud Misc. 624 (= L),
and Lucca, Biblioteca Capitolare, MS 303 (= Lu). The first apparatus embraces
variants from PRL and Lucca, and also notes differences between the rubrics
as they are listed in the index and as they occur in the text itself; rubrics in the
index are noted as Kalendar (= Kl) while those in the body of the text are
designated Textual (= Tx). The second apparatus contains legal and other
references cited explicitly or implicitly by Pagula. Scriptural references are not
included since the scriptural quotations come directly from Gratian's *Decretum*
and do not reflect any industry on Pagula's part.

⁎⁎*

[1] X. 4.10 is missing from the *Summa*.

[2] But in fact all 41 rubrics of X. 5 are in the *Summa*, since X. 5.7 and X. 5.8, and X. 5.34
and X. 5.35, have become *Summa* 5.10 and 5.39, respectively.

[3] *Summa* 1.14, although claimed as 'personal' in the MSS, has to be rejected, since in
part the rubric is clearly X. 1.2.

[4] Two 'Pagula' rubrics are unclaimed in Book 5: 5.30 and 5.42.

[5] In the index as transcribed below I have indicated Decretal rubrics thus: (X. 1.2).

440

MS Bodley 293,
fols 1ʳ-2ᵛ

INCIPIT SPECULUM IURIS CANONICI ET REPORTORIUM ET VOCATUR SUMMA
SUMMARUM. RUBRICA.

Ad honorem et laudem nominis Ihesu Christi quod quando recolo debeo
capud inclinare seu flectere genua saltim cordis, ut extra. de immunitate
5 ecclesiarum c. Decet, libro viᵒ et de con. d. i. c. Apostolica, et ad honorem
beatissime Marie semper virginis gloriose et omnium sanctorum, ac eciam
ad profectum et utilitatem prelatorum, religiosorum et omnium clericorum.
Incipit speculum compendii et reportorium iuris canonici per quod quilibet
litteratus quascumque materias et questiones iuris canonici cuiuscumque
10 ponderis faciliter poterit invenire, et breviter eisdem materiis et questionibus respondere que continentur in textu et glosis decretorum et decretalium,
una cum sexto libro et tribus glosis eiusdem et constitucionibus pape Clementis Quinti, et eciam in summis Innocencii, Hostiensis, Compostolani,
Raymundi, Gaufredi, et quorumcumque famosorum in ecclesia doctorum
15 sacre theologie, prout cuilibet lectori huius summe plenius apparebit, ac
eciam in constitucionibus legatorum, Octonis, Octoboni, et in constitucionibus provincialibus, videlicet Oxonie, Radinge et Lameth, Pecham, et
. Bonifacii, et statutis curie de Arcubus Londiniarum.
Quidquid igitur in prato spinoso iuris tanquam lato et diffuso sparsim
20 seritur quasi in unum manipulum ex diversis spicis collectum breviter hic
collegi, ut accedat quod legitur C. de veteri iure enucleando l. i. ultra medium,
ibi, 'in tali prato spinosum,' et quicquid alibi diffuse queritur in hac summa
breviter invenitur: xxxvii. di. § hinc eciam, ibi, 'quicquid alibi queritur,'
et hic momentanea inspeccio tribuit quod in priori tempore vix post qua-
25 driennium contingebat: Instit. in prohemio § Cumque, ibi, 'et quod in
priori tempore,' ut sic a me et aliis simplicibus possint dubia lata et obscura
et diffusa alibi hic sub compendio faciliter inveniri.
Et quia regimen animarum est ars arcium, sciencia scienciarum, cum
anime hominum sint preciores omnibus aliis rebus et corporibus, ut extra.
30 de eta. et qual. ord. c. Cum sit ars, et extra. de penit. et remis. c. Cum
infirmitas, in fine, xii. q. i. c. Precipimus, valde ignominosum est clericis
ad hoc regimen vocatis causam ipsius regiminis penitus ignorare, sicut turpe
est advocato ignorare ius in quo versatur, ut ff. de origine iur. l. ii. Igitur
sciencia iuris canonici sacerdotibus et potissime curatis est semper necessaria
35 iuxta illud Malachie, 'labia sacerdotis custodiunt scienciam et legem requi-

---

1-2 *Rubrica deest* P   6 Ma (*del.*) Marie B   8 repertorii LLu   21 enuclien-
tur B   24 tibuit B   27 inveniri] reperiri PRLLu   34 semper] perquam PLLu,
om. R

3-5 *nominis — libro VIᵒ*: cf. Sext. 3.23.2   5 De cons. D.1 c.68   19-27: ex prologo Will. Durantis in *Breviarium* sive *Reportorium*   21-2 Cod. 1.17.1.9
23 D.37 dict. p.c.7 §6   25-6 Inst. proem. §3   28 *regimen — arcium*: cf. X.1.14.14
28-9 *cum anime — corporibus*: cf. X.5.38.13   30-1 X. cc. cit.; C.12 q.1 c.24
32-3 cf. Dig. 1.2.2.43   35-7 *Malachie — ex iniuncto*: D.43 c. 1; C.11 q.1 c.41; X.5.7.12

runt,' scilicet subditi, 'ex ore eius': xliii. d. c. Sit rector; xi. q. i. Sacerdotibus, et extra. de heret. c. Cum ex iniuncto, et non sufficit prelatis
bona conversacio et morum honestas nisi addatur sciencia doctrine: xxxvi.
d. § Ecce, in fine. Nec possunt sacerdotes qui docendi officium in populo
40 Dei susceperunt propter iuris ignoranciam excusari, set pocius accusari,
cum secundum apostolum Paulum, sacerdotes legere sacras scripturas am-
monentur et scire debent sacras scripturas et canones, et quod omne opus
eorum in predicacione et doctrina consistat atque edificent cunctos tam
fidei sciencia quam operum disciplina. Nulli igitur sacerdotum liceat igno-
45 rare canones nec quicquam facere quod patrum regulis poterit obviare, ut
xxxviii. d. c. i. ii. et iii. et c. Nulli sacerdotum, et extra. de constitucionibus
c. i.
    Unde discretus querendus est sacerdos sciens solvere et ligare: de pe.
d. i. quem penitet, et de pe. d. vi. Placuit; extra. de pe. et remis. c. Omnis
50 et c. ultimum, et extra. de symonia, Ex diligenti. Et caveat sibi iudex
spiritualis ut non careat munere sciencie. Oportet enim ut sciat discernere
quicquid debet iudicare quia iudiciaria potestas hoc postulat ut quod debet
iudicare discernat: de pe. d. vi. c. i, circa medium. Et cum per ignoranciam
cecati aliis ducatum prestare ceperint in foveam ambo cadunt. Unde ver-
55 sus,
            si cecus secum conatur ducere cecum
        in foveam ductor primo cadit inde secutor,
et in psalmo dicitur, 'obscurentur oculi eorum ne videant et dorsum eorum
semper in curva'; cum enim obscurentur illi qui preeunt ad ferenda onera
60 peccatorum, facile sequentes inclinantur. Laborare igitur debent prelati
et sacerdotes ut ignoranciam a se quasi quamdam pestem abiciant. Unde
secundum Augustinum ignorans ignorabitur, quod de illis intelligendum est
qui addiscere poterant et ad hoc operam non dederunt: xxxvii. d. § ult.
[1rb] et xxxviii. d. Que ipsis; de pe. d. vi. c. i. in principio, et extra. de
65 renunc. c. Post translacionem. Item, cum ignorancia scripturarum est
ignorancia Christi: xxxviii. d. Si iuxta, elaborandum est itaque sacerdotibus
ut ab eis omni modo ignorancia propulsetur iuxta illud apostoli Pauli ad
Timotheum, 'attende leccioni et exhortacioni et semper permane in hiis':
xxxviii. d. c. i, xliiii. d. Multis, ne mereantur illud propheticum audire,
70 'tu scienciam repulisti et ego te repellam ne sacerdocio fungaris michi':

---

36 Sit] sic B   49 de pe. ²] d. vi. *male add.* B   52 expostulat PLLu   60 igi-
tur] ergo RLLu, *om.* P

37-9 *non sufficit — in fine*: D.36 dict. p.c.2 §12   39-44 *qui docendi — disciplina*:
cf. D.38 c.1   44-5 *Nulli — obviare*: D.38 c.4   45-7 D.38 cc. 1-4; X.1.2.1
48-9 De poen. D.1 c.88, D.6 c.3   49-50 X.5.38.12, 16; 5.3.17   50-3 *caveat — medium*: De poen. D.6 c.1 §3   53-4 *cum per — cadunt*: D.37 dict. p.c.15   58-61 *ibid.*
61-3 *Unde — § ult.*: cf. *ibid.* fin. et c.16   62 *secundum Augustinum*: potius 1 Cor. 14.38
64-5 D.38 c.5; De poen. D.6 c.1 pr.; X.1.9.11 §2   65-6 *ignorantia — Si iuxta*: cf. D.38 c. 9
67-9 *apostoli — Multis* : D.38 c.1 ; D.44 c.5   70-2 *tu scientiam — Pro defectu*: D.38
c.6; X.1.9.10 §4

442

xxxviii. d. Omnes, in fine, et extra. de renunc. c. Nisi cum pridem § Pro
defectu, et pro defectu sciencie potest quis a beneficio removeri, ut extra.
de eta. et qual. ord. c. penult. et ult.

Scire igitur debent iura canonica et maxime ea que in iure canonico preci-
75 piuntur cum illa sint necessaria observanda, quia quod precipitur imperatur
et quod imperatur necesse est fieri. Si non fiat, penam habent, et quisquis
preceptis canonicis non obtemperat reus est, et sic, debitor pene: xiiii. q. i.
Quod precipitur et c. Quisquis. Item, hii qui mandata apostolorum postponunt
non solum rei set extorres Dei fiunt: que non solum nobis cavenda set omni-
80 bus predicanda sunt: xii. q. i. Dilectissimis. Item, si decreta romanorum
pontificum non habeant de neglectu atque incuria sunt arguendi: si vero
habeant et non observent de temeritate sunt arguendi et increpandi: xx.
d. Si decreta.

Ne quis igitur de cetero ignorancia iuris canonici valeat honeste accusari,
85 hanc summam composui quam breviter et levius potui secundum modicam
scienciam mihi a Deo ministratam qui unicuique propria dividit prout
vult: i. q. i. Cum multe; de con. d. iiii. Cum tantum. Et hoc feci pro rudibus et penitus ignorantibus ius canonicum, et potissime pro prelatis et
sacerdotibus, cum ignorancia iuris canonici sit eis inter ceteros magis peri-
90 culosa: xxxviii. d. § i. et c. i. et c. Si in laicis, hoc humiliter ab eis pro labore
requirens ut cum ad dignissimum sacramentum corporis Christi accesserint,
inter ceteros peccatores mei memoriam habere dignentur seu aliter prout
eis placuerit pro me orent, quia qui pro aliis orat pro seipso laborat: iii. q. i.
Nulli; de pen. d. i. De cotidianis; i. q. i. Ipsi sacerdotes; xxxvi. d. Si quis
95 vult. Hanc eciam summam feci ad profectum et utilitatem pauperum
clericorum, ut si forte copiam librorum non habuerint hic collecta sub compendio multa de hiis inveniant que requirunt: et ea sicut scripta sunt ab
aliis, nec conprobando nec inprobando reliqui, quia de mea propria sentencia nichil posui in presenti summa set tantum aliorum famosorum in ecclesia
100 doctorum sentencias referens, et ut plurimum eciam ipsorum verba ponens,
et librorum ac summarum et eciam scriptorum de quibus assumpta sunt
nomina et loca assignans, relator sum minimus non inventor.

Hoc quoque sciendum est quod ubi aliqua materia seu questio incipit
et plures sequantur questiones semper intelliguntur illius decreti seu decre-
105 talis et constitucionis vel glose et doctorum qui proximo secuntur ibidem.
Et si quam diversitatem vel eciam contrarietatem determinacionum seu

---

78 quisque B   84 valeant B   85 breviter] brevius PRLLu   98 conprobando]
probando PRL   ad 99-102 nota marg. dext.: Nota que continentur.   Et hanc summam
habens, Reportorium W. Durandi non indiget, quia totum illud in hac continetur

---

72-3 X.1.14.14, 15   75-6 quod precipitur — habent: C.14 q.1 c.3 §2   76-7 quisquis
— pene : ibid. pr.   77-8 ibid. §2 et pr.   78-80 hii qui — Dilectissimis : C.12 q.1
c. 2 §5 fin.   80-3 si decreta — decreta: D.20 c.2   86-7 unicuique — tantum: C.1
q.1 c.38; De cons. D.4 c.47   89-90 ignorantia — periculosa : cf. D.38 pr.   90 ibid.
et cc. 1, 3   93-5 C.3 q.1 c.5; De poen. D.3 c.20; C.1 q.1 c.91; D.36 c.3   95-102 ex
prologo Iohannis Friburgensis in Libellum questionum casualium, i.e. ex prologo primo in
Summam confessorum

dictorum circa eandem materiam in questionibus diversis inveneris, intellige illa esse diversorum doctorum dicta et interdum quodlibet illorum secundum diversitatem circumstanciarum et casuum posse racionabilius
110 observari.

Noli eciam, lector piè, de actore seu pocius compilatore huius summe sicut nec de calamo quo scripta est inquirere curiose, set attende ea que in ea scribuntur, quia non sunt mea dicta sed aliorum prout in hac summa poteris ad plenum videre, nec est multum considerandum quis dicat set
115 pocius quid dicatur: ix. d. Ego et c. Noli.

Noli eciam, lector benigne, aut propter inpericiam conpilantis aut propter rusticitatem sermonis aut forte propter inconsequenciam ordinis ea que hic ad instruccionem fidelium simplicium utiliter colliguntur ante plenam inspeccionem indignando respuere, set prius si placet animo pa-
120 cienti cuncta diligenter inspiciendo revolve. Post hoc vero prout tue insederit racioni aut recipe aut contempne, ne, si forte ante contempseris, videaris magis ex odio quam ex recto iudicio reprobare, quemadmodum dicit Ieronimus in prologo Ysaie hiis verbis, 'legant prius et intelligant et postea si voluerint despiciant ne videantur ex odii presumpcione igno-
125 rata dampnare,' cum multi ante iudicant quam intelligant et ante culpant quam iterando lecta perquirant: xxix d. Sciendum.

Tu ergo lector ora pro collectore et diligenter suscipe quesita cum alieno labore et gaude de inventis sine labore. Nomen autem collectoris exprimere nolo ne colleccio vilescerit cognito collectore.
130 Et ut noticia huius summe facilior habeatur et materie in ea contente cicius valeant reperiri, singulorum librorum plurimas premitto rubricas secundum ordinem rubricarum decretalium multas rubricas alias adiungendo, et super qualibet rubrica adiuncta ponitur in fine aliqua litera secundum ordinem alphabeti ut rubrice sic adiuncte a rubricis decretalium discerni
135 valeant evidenter, et ubi una litera alphabeti non sufficit tunc litere combinantur. Et hec patent plenius intuenti.

INCIPIT LIBER PRIMUS (*rubr.*)

Liber primus (*marg.*)

  i^{us}. De summa trinitate et fide catholica.   (x.1.1) (2rb)
  ii. De anima et genere humano.   a (4^r)

---

107 dictorum] doctorum PRLLu 118 ante] aut B 124-5 ignorata] ignorare B

---

115 D.9 cc.5, 9 123-5 *Ieronimus — dampnare*: PL 28.773 125-6 *ante iudicant — Sciendum*: D.29 c.1 128-9 *Nomen — collectore*: forsan ex Thomae de Hibernia prologo in *Manipulum florum* (ca. 1310; ed. Placentiae 1483): 'Nomen autem collectoris volui subticere ne colleccio vilesceret cognito collectore'

---

iii. ecclesiarum *om.* Kl   eorumdem Kl   xii. personis *om.* Tx   xiiii. *litt.* n] *potius*
x. 1.2 (de constit.)   xxiiii. et eciam electis *om.* Tx   xxv. *litt.* u *om.* Kl *praeter* Lu
xxviii. renunciacionibus Tx   xxxiiii. renunciavit] resignavit Tx   xxxvi. et virginum *add.* Tx   xxxix. de libertis] et non (?) de liberatis Kl

INCIPIT LIBER SECUNDUS (*rubr.*)

Liber ii^{us}. (*marg.*)

---

xl. vel non] ordinandis *add.* Tx.   xli. vel non ordinandis *om.* Tx   lxiii. tutore *om.* Tx
lxvi. mutandi *om.* Kl.

INCIPIT LIBER TERCIUS (*rubr.*)   (107^{r})

Lib iii^{us}. (*marg.*)

---

xxii. bonorum *add*. Tx   xxiii. et interrogacionibus *add*. Tx   xxvi. et eorum attestacionibus *add*. Tx   i. et habitu eorumdem *om*. Tx   ii. eorumdem *om*. Tx

iii. non *om*. Kl

---

v. beneficiis *om.* Tx   viii. et] vel Tx   x. ecclesie] prebende *praem.* Tx   xvi. alienandis vel *om.* Tx   xix. et compensacione *om.* Tx   xxvi. De stipulacionibus servorum *add.* Tx   xxxiii. et oblacionibus *om.* Tx   xli. eciam *om.* Tx   xlii. religiosis *om.* Tx   *litt.* as *om.* BKl

INCIPIT LIBER QUARTUS (*rubr.*)   (151v)

Liber iiiius.

---

xlv. procuracionibus] exaccionibus Tx   xlviii. et de divinis officiis *om.* Tx
xlix. Ihesu Christi Tx   *litt.* ax *ad tit.* xlviii. RLu   lviii. et] vel Tx   *ante tit.* x.
rubr. x.4.10 (de natis ex libero ventre) *deest* KlTx

xix. De donacionibus — uxorem et de dote — restituenda *tr.* Tx   iii. eciam *om.* Tx
iv. calumpniatoribus] et *add.* Tx   vi. vel ecclesias *om.* Tx   et de firmis *om.* Tx
viii. *litt.* bd *om.* BLKl   xi. *rubr. om.* Tx   xvii. et balistariis *add.* Tx   xviii. et
de incestuoso coitu *om.* Tx   xix. eciam aliis criminibus *om.* Tx   xxiiii. sortile-
giis] sorti egiis Tx   xxx. *litt. auctoris deest* Kl

---

xxxi. deposito excommunicato *tr*. Tx   ministrante *om*. Tx   xli. et detraccione *add*. Tx   xlii. *littera auctoris deest* Kl   xliiii. Casus] tocius *add*. Tx   xlv. Casus] tocius *add*. Tx   deiciunt iam promotos] impediunt promovendos Tx   xlvi. tocius *om*. Tx   lix. De questoribus ibidem *add*. BKl *marg*.

Volens igitur lector huius summe aliquam questionem seu materiam iuris canonici faciliter invenire bene debet rubricas premissas in memoria retinere et videre cui rubrice questio illa seu materia plus conveniat, et tunc contenta in illa rubrica debet respicere diligenter. Et quia una questio seu materia convenire potest quandoque duabus vel tribus seu pluribus rubricis, videat per ordinem ea que continentur in illis rubricis, et sic quamcumque questionem seu materiam iuris canonici et responsionem ad eandem faciliter poterit invenire.

---

lxv. De sententia interdicti Tx   lxix. *litt. auctoris deest* Kl *praeter* Lu

Appendix II

INCIPITS

Summa summarum

Prologue: Ad honorem et laudem nominis Ihesu Christi quod quando recolo debeo caput inclinare seu flectere genua saltim cordis, ut extra. de immunitate ecclesiarum, c. Decet, libro vi⁰.

Text (c.1): Quot modis dicitur fides et quid sit fides? Dic quod fides dicitur multis modis. Quandoque dicitur fides idem quod sacramentum, quandoque dicitur fides castitas thori et est unum de tribus bonis matrimonii. Item dicitur fides securitas sive pactum que eciam hosti servanda est.

Speculum praelatorum

Prologue: Ut summe Trinitati et toti curie celesti debitus honor deferatur, debent omnes Christiani, maxime clerici qui in sortem Domini sunt electi (xii q. i. Clericus; xxi d. Cleros) et potissime prelati, qui debent esse exemplar laicorum, cum magna diligencia laborare ut peccata abiciant.

Text (c.1): Fides catholica est substancia rerum sperandarum, argumentum non apparencium. Dicitur enim substancia rerum sperandarum quia sperare debemus quod dictum est a prophetis esse futurum.

Speculum religiosorum

Prologue: Accipite vos religiosi hoc speculum et comedite, quoniam sicut mel est bonum et sanum, dulcissimum gutturi, sic et doctrina sapiencie animabus vestris.

(c.7:) Abbas vel prior seu alius presidens desiderans se et conventum suum servire Deo, fideliter et devote debet scire canones et regulas sanctorum patrum et constituciones provinciales ad eas et eorum ordinem precipue pertinentes. (The incipit of the Durham treatise *Abbas vel prior* is that of c. 7 here, with some small changes: 'Abbas vel prior seu quicumque presidens. . . . . ').

Appendix III

(a) MANUSCRIPTS OF THE 'SUMMA SUMMARUM'

1. Cambridge, Christ's College 2.
14th century. English hand. 40.1 x 26.7 cm. Double columns [=Dc.] 269 folios.
Fire has damaged some twelve folios at the beginning, and many gatherings are misplaced because of careless re-binding. The text ends on fol. 267^r and is followed by an alphabetical index. On fol. 269^r there occurs a note in a hand contemporary with that of the writer of the text: *Hoc opus compositum fuit per dominum Willelmum de Pabula.*

2. Cambridge, Pembroke College 201.
Late 14th century. English hand. 38.2 x 23 cm. Dc. 331 folios.
This is perhaps the *Summa summarum* which was given to the College by Master Michael de Causton (ob. 1396). (G. E. Corrie, 'A list of books presented to Pembroke College, Cambridge, by different donors during the 14th and 15th centuries,' *Cambridge Antiquarian Soc. Communications* 2 [1864] 15. Gorrie, however, lists the *Summa summarum* as *Summa sententiarum*, a not infrequent mistake in published inventories). The long version of the note in which Pagula refers to the *Sinistra pars oculi* and the *Speculum praelatorum* (see above n. 29), occurs on fol. 189^r.

3. Durham, Cathedral Library C.II.13.
Late 14th century. English hand. 40.5 x 27.5 cm. Dc. 249 folios.
This MS belonged to the Cathedral Priory in the late fourteenth century. (*Catalogi veteres librorum ecclesiae cathedralis Dunelmensis*, ed. J. Raine [Surtees Soc. 1838] 47).

4. Edinburgh, University Library 145 (Laing 136).
14th century. Italian hand. 37.5 x 26 cm. Dc. 257 folios. Incomplete. The text ends in the second-last chapter (5.68: *De regulis iuris*), and is followed by a folio which has been torn or cut in such a manner that two possibly valuable notes have been damaged, thus: *Iste liber* / and *Quando fuit iste liber compositus vide supra de*/

5. London, British Museum, Harley 5014-5015.
Late 14th century. English hand. 39 x 26.5 cm. Dc. 254 folios..
The *Summa* has been split into two volumes and many chapters are now out of place.

6. London, British Museum, Royal 10 D. X.
Late 14th century. English hand. 45 x 30 cm. Dc. 301 folios.

The MS belonged to Reading Abbey in the 14th century (fol. 1^r); see J. B. Hurry, *Reading Abbey* (London 1901) 108, and J. R. L(iddell), 'Some notes on the library of Reading Abbey,' *Bodleian Quarterly Record* 8 (1935) 47-54.

7. Lucca, Library of Cathedral Chapter 303.
14th century. English hand. 37 x 24.5 cm. Dc. 299 folios.
Listed by F. Blume, *Bibliotheca librorum manuscriptorum Italica* (Göttingen 1837) 57, as *Speculum Iuris Canonici*. The text is incomplete. No trace of provenance. Professor Kuttner kindly drew my attention to this MS.

8. Oxford, Bodleian Library, Bodley 293.
Mid-14th century. English hand. 40 x 25cm. Dc. 250 folios.
One of two copies in 1506 inventory of Exeter cathedral library (G. Oliver, *Lives of the Bishops of Exeter* [Exeter 1861] 369). It was presented to the Bodleian Library in 1602 by the Dean and Chapter of Exeter.

9. Oxford, Bodleian Library, Laud Misc. 624.
14th century, second half. English hand. 39.7 x 26 cm. Dc. 186 folios (incomplete).
The text ends in the second-last chapter (5.68: *De regulis iuris*). On fol. 108^v there occurs the long version of the note in which Pagula refers to his *Sinistra pars oculi* and *Speculum praelatorum* (see Cambridge, Pembroke College 201).

10. Oxford, Exeter College 19.
Early 15th century. English hand. 40.5 x 25.4 cm. Dc. 323 folios.
The prologue is missing, the index (which is really part of the prologue) beginning in 2.16 (*De intrusis*).

11. Oxford, Magdalen College lat. 134.
14th century, second half. English hand. 39.3 x 25.4 cm. Dc. 302 folios.
The text ends on fol. 296^v and is followed by an Index. On the endleaf there is a note to the effect that the MS was bought from an Oxford stationer by a T. Wyche for 33*s*.4*d*. on 1 Oct. 1457.

12. San Marino, California, Huntingdon Library EL.9.H.3.
14th century. English hand (Ashridge). 37 x 25cm. Dc. 404 folios.
The manuscript belonged to the Bonhommes of Ashridge, Bucks. in the fourteenth century (cf. Oxford, Trinity College MS 18: *Oculus sacerdotis*), and was bought by the Huntingdon Library from the Earl of Ellesmere (Bridgewater Collection): see H. C. Schultz, 'The monastic library and scriptorium at Ashridge,' *Huntingdon Library Quarterly* 1 (1937-38) 307.

13. Worcester, Cathedral Library F. 131.
Early 14th century. English hand. 35.5 x 21.6 cm. Dc. 361 folios.
The volume was bought by Henry Fowke, probably before 1340: 'Liber sancte Marie Wygornie per fratrem Henricum ffouke monachum loci eiusdem precio l. solid'. (flyleaf). He was professed in 1302 and was still alive in 1338. The text ends on fol. 358^v and is followed by an alphabetical index *Abbas-Usufructus*.

Fragments

1. Pastedown. Magdalen College, Oxford, D.20.12 (a book printed at Paris 1542): 2 fols. Dc., covering bk. 5 cc. 31, 32 (14th century).

454

2. Pastedown. Merton College, Oxford, B.9.j.6 (a book printed at Basle 1546):
2 fols. from the same MS as (1), covering 5.67.
(For these pastedowns see N.R.Ker, *Pastedowns in Oxford Bindings* [Oxford
Bibliographical Society Publications, New Series 5; 1951-2] nn. 373, 398).

3. Leicester Museum and Art Gallery.
Four folios from a 14th-century MS used as folders for municipal accounts
of 1570, etc. The chapters covered are 3.20 and 33, and 5.42 and 48.

> *Note.* E. Pellegrin, 'Manuscrits d'auteurs latins de l'époque classique conservés
> dans les bibliothèques publiques de Suède' *Bulletin d'information de l'Institut de
> recherche et d'histoire des textes* 4 (1955) 24, has suggested that the *Quaestiones in
> Decretales* in Uppsala University Library, MS C. 90, fols. 1^r-70^v, are part of the *Summa
> summarum*. However, although the incipit is similar to that of the *Summa*, the
> contents are not those of Pagula's work. My best thanks to Professor Sten Gagnér
> for information about this MS.

(b) THE SPECULUM PRAELATORUM

Oxford, Merton College 217.
Early 15th century. English hand. 37.5 x 23.5. Dc. 484 folios.
This is the only known MS. The text is not complete since bk. 2 cc. 54-81 are
missing. They were also missing from the exemplar which the scribe had before
him: 'Hic deficit de exemplari Thome de Holme usque ad finem secundi libri'
(fol. 179^v). (A Thomas Holme was a Queen's College fellow in 1401-19; Emden, *Biographical Register* II 962.) The division of text is as follows:

I   fols.   1^r-81^r: *De fide et ecclesie sacramentis.*
II   81^r-179^v: *De ministris ecclesie et officiis eorumdem.*
III   180^r-449^r: *De predicacionibus verbi divini et auctoritatibus sanctorum
                patrum:*
        180^r-248^r: Sermon *Themata.*
        248^r-441^r: *Distinctiones (Aperire-Zelus)* for the use of preachers.
        441^v-449^r: Alphabetical Index (*Abbas - Zelus*)
        [449^r-450^v: A later index (*Abbas - Zona*).
        450^v-484^r: Another index (*Abbas - Zona*).]

Note. The manuscript is not foliated, but a recent hand has entered folio
references in pencil at the end of each book. By our count (which is that used
above) the recent foliation misses one folio in the first part, and thus arrives
at 483 folios for the whole volume.

(c) THE SPECULUM RELIGIOSORUM

1. Cambridge, Jesus College 24, fols. 13^r-50^v (imperfect at beginning and end).
14th century. Belonged in that century to Durham Cathedral library.

2. Cambridge, Jesus College 41, fols. 1^r-29^v. 15th century. From Durham.

3. Cambridge, St. John's College 136, fols. 163^r-184^v. 15th century.

4. London, British Museum, Egerton 746, fols. 54^r-97^v (imperfect). Late 14th century.

5. London, British Museum, Royal 8. C. ii, fols. 1^r-47^v. Late 14th century.

6. London, Gray's Inn Library 11, fols. 1^r-101^r. Mid-14th century.

(The rearrangement known as *Abbas vel prior*)

1. Cambridge, Jesus College 61, fols. 48^r-69^r (and Table: 69^v-75^r). 14th century. Durham.

2. Durham, Cathedral Library B. iv. 26, fols. 148^v-182^v. 14th century. Durham.

3. Durham, Cathedral Library B. iv. 41, fols. 83^r-100^v. 14th century. Durham

4. Durham, Cathedral Library B. iv. 45 fols., 125^r-162^v. Mid-14th century. Durham.

APPENDIX IV

SUMMARY TABLE OF CIRCULATION AND INFLUENCE
OF THE 'SUMMA SUMMARUM'

(Numbers following entries refer to footnotes above)

1319-22	*Summa summarum* written.
1330-50	Used by *Omne bonum* 78
	Worcester Cathedral MS F.131 bought by H. Fowke 38, 57
c.1332-35	Given to Ipswich Franciscans by Fr. L. Bretoun 55
1336-37	Used by Carmelite John Baconthorpe in Postill on St. Matthew 79
1338	Among books of Adam Boothby Prior of Peterborough 53
1341-74	Two copies at Glastonbury purchased by Abbot Monyton 59
a.1343	Copy in possession of Thomas Poucyn Abbot of St. Augustine's, Canterbury 56
1343	Used extensively in *Regimen animarum* 77
1344-52	Among books of Simon Bozoun Prior of Norwich 54
1346	Quoted by John Acton in his *Septuplum* 63
c.1350	MS Bodley 293 written 62; App. IIIa
	Used by W. Elveden of Cambridge to gloss a *Tabula iuris* 65
1363-66	Mentioned in charges against Abbot of Eynsham 58
1366-67	Copy written for The Queen's College, Oxford 38,70
a.1369	Copy costing £4 at Southwell Minster 38
a.1369	With *Oculus* among books of L. Charlton Bishop of Hereford 40
a.1372	In library of Austin Friars, York 60
c.1380	Used (by T. Walkyngton?) to gloss Decretals 66
c.1382	Donated to New College, Oxford, by the Founder, William of Wykeham 71
a.1383	Owned by Dean of Chichester 42
a.1386	Among law books of King's Hall, Cambridge 73
a.1389	One copy at Dover Priory 60

INDEX

of principal names, places and subjects